CLYMER®

HONDA

XR80R, CRF80F, XR100R & CRF100F • 1992-2009

The world's finest publisher of mechanical how-to manuals

CLYMER®

P.O. Box 12901, Overland Park, Kansas 66282-2901

Copyright ©2010 Penton Business Media, Inc.

FIRST EDITION
First Printing February, 2010

Printed in U.S.A.

CLYMER and colophon are registered trademarks of Penton Business Media, Inc.

ISBN-10: 1-59969-327-5

ISBN-13: 978-1-59969-327-9

Library of Congress: 2010920293

AUTHOR: Ron Wright.

TECHNICAL PHOTOGRAPHY: Ron Wright with assistance from Clawson Motorsports in Fresno, California and Brad Wright.

TECHNICAL ILLUSTRATIONS: Steve Amos.

WIRING DIAGRAMS: Bob Meyer.

EDITOR: Steve Thomas.

PRODUCTION: Kendra Lueckert.

TOOLS AND EQUIPMENT: K & L Supply Co. at www.klsupply.com.

COVER: Mark Clifford Photography at www.markclifford.com.

CLYMER®

Publisher Ron Rogers

EDITORIAL

Editorial Director
James Grooms

Editor
Steven Thomas

Associate Editor
Rick Arens

Authors
Michael Morlan
George Parise
Ed Scott
Ron Wright

Technical Illustrators
Steve Amos
Errol McCarthy
Mitzi McCarthy
Bob Meyer

SALES

Sales Manager
Matt Tusken

CUSTOMER SERVICE

Customer Service Manager
Terri Cannon

Customer Service Account Specialist
Courtney Hollars

Customer Service Representatives
Dinah Bunnell
April LeBlond
Suzanne Myers
Sherry Rudkin

PRODUCTION

Group Production Manager
Dylan Goodwin

Production Manager
Greg Araujo

Production Editors
Holly McComas
Adriane Roberts

Associate Production Editor
Kendra Lueckert

Graphic Designer
Jason Hale

P.O. Box 12901, Overland Park, KS 66282-2901 • 800-262-1954 • 913-967-1719

More information available at *clymer.com*

CONTENTS

QUICK REFERENCE DATA

MOTORCYCLE INFORMATION

MODEL: _____ YEAR: _____

VIN NUMBER: _____

ENGINE SERIAL NUMBER: _____

CARBURETOR SERIAL NUMBER OR I.D. MARK: _____

TIRE INFLATION PRESSURE

	kPa	psi
Front	100	15
Rear		
XR80R and XR100R	125	18
CRF80F and CRF100F	100	15

RECOMMENDED LUBRICANTS AND FUEL

Air filter	Foam air filter oil
Engine oil	
Classification	
JASCO T 903 standard rating	MA
API rating	SG or higher*
Viscosity rating	SAE 10W-30
Fork oil	Pro Honda Suspension Fluid SS-8 or equivalent 10 wt fork oil
Fuel	Unleaded gasoline; 86 pump octane/91 RON or higher
Grease	Multipurpose waterproof grease

*API "SG" or higher classified oils not specified as "ENERGY CONSERVING" can be used. See Chapter One for additional information.

ENGINE OIL CAPACITY

	ml	oz.
XR80R		
1993-1997 models		
Oil change	700	23.7
After engine disassembly	900	30.4
1998-2003 models		
Oil change	800	27.1
After engine disassembly	900	30.4
XR100R		
Oil change	900	30.4
After engine disassembly	1000	33.8
CRF80F and CRF100F		
Oil change	900	30.4
After engine disassembly	1100	37.2

FRONT FORK OIL CAPACITY

	ml	oz.
XR80R		
1993-1997 models	83.0	2.8
1998-2003 models	80.5-85.5	2.72-2.90
CRF80F	82.5-87.5	2.80-2.96
XR100R		
1992-1997 models	88.0	3.0
1998-2000 models	85.5-90.5	2.90-3.06
2001-2003 models	83.5-88.5	2.82-3.00
CRF100F	81.5-86.5	2.76-2.92

FRONT FORK OIL LEVEL

	mm	in.
XR80R	184	7.24
CRF80F	177	6.97
XR100R		
1992-2000 models	205	8.07
2001-2003 models	200	7.87
CRF100F	207	8.15

MAINTENANCE SPECIFICATIONS

Clutch lever free play	10-20 mm (3/8-3/4 in.)
Drive chain 41 pin service limit	511 mm (20.1 in.)
Drive chain free play	25-35 mm (1.0-1.4 in.)
Drive chain slider wear depth	6 mm (1/4 in.) or more
Engine compression	
XR80R	
1993-1997 models	98.1-1373 kPa (143-199 psi)
1998-2003 models	1176 kPa (171 psi) at 1000 rpm
CRF80F	1176 kPa (171 psi) at 1000 rpm
XR100R	
1992-1997 models	98.1-1275 kPa (143-105 psi)
1998-2003 models	1127 kPa (164 psi) at 800 rpm
CRF100F	1176 kPa (171 psi) at 1000 rpm
Engine idle speed	
80 cc models	1400-1600 rpm
100 cc models	1300-1500 rpm
Front brake lever free play	20-30 mm (3/4-1 1/4 in.)
Ignition timing	15.5° BTDC at idle speed
Idle drop adjustment[1]	Refer to *Carburetor Adjustments* in Chapter Eight
Rear brake pedal free play	20-30 mm (3/4-1 1/4 in.)
Spark plug gap	0.6-0.7 mm (0.024-0.028 in.)
Spark plug type	
Standard	NGK CR7HSA or DENSO U22FSR-U
Cold weather operation[2]	NGK CR6HSA or DENSO U20FSR-U
Extended high speed riding	NGK CR8HSA or DENSO U24FSR-U
Tire tread depth limit	3.0 mm (0.12 in.)
Throttle cable free play	2-6 mm (1/16-1/4 in.)
Valve clearance	
Intake and exhaust	0.05 mm (0.002 in.)

1. This is often referred to as the air screw (80 cc models) or pilot screw (100 cc models) adjustment.
2. Below 5° C (41° F).

MAINTENANCE TORQUE SPECIFICATIONS

	N•m	in.-lb.	ft.-lb.
Axle nut	62	–	46
Cam chain tensioner adjuster locknut	12	106	–
Cylinder head cover bolt	12	106	–
Engine oil drain bolt	24	–	18
Fork cap	23	–	17
Rim lock nut	12	106	–
Sidestand pivot nut*	39	–	29
Spark plug	14	–	10
Upper fork tube pinch bolt			
1992-2003 models	11	97	–
2004-on models	18	–	13
Valve adjuster locknut	10	88	–

*Refer to text.

CHAPTER ONE

GENERAL INFORMATION

This detailed and comprehensive manual covers the 1992-2009 Honda XR/CRF 80-100 series. The text provides complete information on maintenance, tune-up, repair and overhaul. Hundreds of photos and drawings guide the reader through every job. All procedures are in step-by-step format and designed for the reader who may be working on the motorcycle for the first time.

MANUAL ORGANIZATION

A shop manual is a reference tool and, as in all Clymer manuals, the chapters are thumb-tabbed for easy reference. Important items are indexed at the end of the manual. Frequently used specifications and capacities from individual chapters are summarized in the *Quick Reference Data* at the front of the manual.

During some of the procedures there will be references to headings in other chapters or sections of the manual. When a specific heading is called out in a step it is *italicized* as it appears in the manual. If a sub-heading is indicated as being "in this section" it is located within the same main heading. For example, the sub-heading *Handling Gasoline Safely* is located within the main heading *SAFETY*.

This chapter provides general information on shop safety, tool use, service fundamentals and shop supplies. **Tables 1-7** at the end of the chapter provide general motorcycle, mechanical and shop information.

Chapter Two provides methods for quick and accurate diagnoses of problems. Troubleshooting procedures present typical symptoms and logical methods to pinpoint and repair a problem.

Chapter Three explains all routine maintenance.

Subsequent chapters describe specific systems, such as engine, clutch, transmission shafts, fuel system, drive system, suspension, brakes and body components.

Specification tables, when applicable, are located at the end of each chapter.

WARNINGS, CAUTIONS AND NOTES

The terms WARNING, CAUTION and NOTE have specific meanings in this manual.

A WARNING emphasizes areas where injury or even death could result from negligence. Mechanical damage may also occur. WARNINGS are to be taken seriously.

A CAUTION emphasizes areas where equipment damage could result. Disregarding a CAUTION could cause permanent mechanical damage, though injury is unlikely.

A NOTE provides additional information to make a step or procedure easier or clearer. Disregarding a NOTE could cause inconvenience, but would not cause equipment damage or injury.

SAFETY

Professional mechanics can work for years and never sustain a serious injury or mishap. Follow these guidelines and practice common sense to safely service the motorcycle:

1. Do not operate the motorcycle in an enclosed area. The exhaust gasses contain carbon monoxide, an odorless, colorless and tasteless poisonous gas. Carbon monoxide levels build quickly in small enclosed areas and can cause unconsciousness and death in a short time. Make sure the work area is properly ventilated, or operate the motorcycle outside.

2. *Never* use gasoline or any flammable liquid to clean parts. Refer to *Handling Gasoline Safely and Cleaning Parts* in this section.

3. *Never* smoke or use a torch in the vicinity of flammable liquids, such as gasoline or cleaning solvent.

4. Avoid contact with engine oil and other chemicals. Most are known carcinogens. Wash your hands thoroughly after coming in contact with engine oil. If possible, wear a pair of disposable gloves.

5. If welding or brazing on the motorcycle, remove the fuel tank and shock to a safe distance at least 50 ft. (15 m) away.

6. Use the correct types and sizes of tools to avoid damaging fasteners.

7. Keep tools clean and in good condition. Replace or repair worn or damaged equipment.

8. When loosening a tight fastener, be guided by what would happen if the tool slips.

9. When replacing fasteners, make sure the new fasteners are the same size and strength as the originals.

10. Keep the work area clean and organized.

11. Wear eye protection *any time* the safety of your eyes is in question. This includes procedures involving drilling, grinding, hammering, compressed air and chemicals.

12. Wear the correct clothing for the job. Tie up or cover long hair so it can not catch in moving equipment.

13. Do not carry sharp tools in clothing pockets.

14. Always have an approved fire extinguisher available. Make sure it is rated for gasoline (Class B) and electrical (Class C) fires.

15. Do not use compressed air to clean clothes, the motorcycle or the work area. Debris may be blown into the eyes or skin. *Never* direct compressed air at anyone. Do not allow children to use or play with any compressed air equipment.

16. When using compressed air to dry rotating parts, hold the part so it cannot rotate. Do not allow the force of the air to spin the part. The air jet is capable of rotating parts at extreme speeds. The part may be damaged or disintegrate, causing serious injury.

17. Do not inhale the dust created by brake pad and clutch wear. These particles may contain asbestos. In addition, some types of insulating materials and gaskets may contain asbestos. Inhaling asbestos particles is hazardous to health.

18. Never work on the motorcycle while someone is working under it.

19. When placing the motorcycle on a stand, make sure it is secure before walking away.

Handling Gasoline Safely

Gasoline is a volatile flammable liquid and is one of the most dangerous items in the shop. Because gasoline is used so often, many people forget that it is hazardous. Only use gasoline as fuel for gasoline internal combustion engines. Keep in mind when working on a motorcycle, gasoline is always present in the fuel tank, fuel line and carburetor. To avoid an accident when working around the fuel system, carefully observe the following precautions:

1. *Never* use gasoline to clean parts. Refer to *Cleaning Parts* in this section.

2. When working on the fuel system, work outside or in a well-ventilated area.

3. Do not add fuel to the fuel tank or service the fuel system while the motorcycle is near open flames, sparks or where someone is smoking. Gasoline vapor is heavier than air, collects in low areas and is more easily ignited than liquid gasoline.

4. Allow the engine to cool completely before working on any fuel system component.

5. Do not store gasoline in glass containers. If the glass breaks, an explosion or fire may occur.

6. Immediately wipe up spilled gasoline with rags. Store the rags in a metal container with a lid until they can be properly disposed, or place them outside in a safe place for the fuel to evaporate.

7. Do not pour water onto a gasoline fire. Water spreads the fire and makes it more difficult to put out. Use a class B, BC or ABC fire extinguisher to extinguish the fire.

8. Always turn off the engine before refueling. Do not spill fuel onto the engine or exhaust system. Do not overfill the fuel tank. Leave an air space at the top

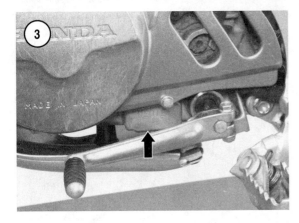

8. Keep chemicals away from children and pets, especially coolant.

9. Thoroughly clean all oil, grease and cleaner residue from any part that must be heated.

10. Use a nylon brush when cleaning parts. Metal brushes may cause a spark.

11. When using a parts washer, only use the solvent recommended by the manufacturer. Make sure the parts washer is equipped with a metal lid that will lower in case of fire.

Warning Labels

Most manufacturers attach information and warning labels to the motorcycle. These labels contain instructions that are important to safety when operating, servicing, transporting and storing the motorcycle. Refer to the owner's manual for the description and location of labels. Order replacement labels from the manufacturer if they are missing or damaged.

SERIAL NUMBERS AND INFORMATION LABELS

Serial numbers are located on the frame, engine and carburetor. Record these numbers in the *Quick Reference Data* section in the front of the manual. Have these numbers available when ordering parts.

The vehicle identification number (VIN) is stamped on the front, left frame tube (**Figure 1**). This number is also used as the frame identification number.

The Model Identification Label (U.S.) or Safety Certification Label (Canada) is located on the front, right frame tube (**Figure 2**).

The engine serial number is stamped on the left side of the left crankcase (**Figure 3**).

The carburetor identification number is stamped on the right side of the carburetor body (**Figure 4**).

Labels for tire pressure, emission control, paint code, and other miscellaneous data are located on various other places on the motorcycle.

of the tank to allow room for the fuel to expand due to temperature fluctuations.

Cleaning Parts

Cleaning parts is one of the more tedious and difficult service jobs performed in the home garage. Many types of chemical cleaners and solvents are available for shop use. Most are poisonous and extremely flammable. To prevent chemical exposure, vapor buildup, fire and injury, observe each product's warning label and note the following:

1. Read and observe the entire product label before using any chemical. Always know what type of chemical is being used and whether it is poisonous and/or flammable.

2. Do not use more than one type of cleaning solvent at a time. If mixing chemicals is required, measure the proper amounts according to the manufacturer.

3. Work in a well-ventilated area.

4. Wear chemical-resistant gloves that are appropriate the chemical being used.

5. Wear safety glasses.

6. Wear a vapor respirator if the instructions call for it.

7. Wash hands and arms thoroughly after cleaning parts.

FASTENERS

WARNING
Do not install fasteners with a strength classification lower than what was originally installed by the manufacturer. Doing so may cause equipment failure and/or damage.

Proper fastener selection and installation is important to ensure the motorcycle operates as designed and can be serviced efficiently. The choice of original equipment fasteners is not arrived at by chance.

Make sure replacement fasteners meet the requirements.

Threaded Fasteners

Threaded fasteners secure most of the components on the motorcycle. Most are tightened by turning them clockwise (right-hand threads). If the normal rotation of the component being tightened would loosen the fastener, it may have left-hand threads. If a left-hand threaded fastener is used, it is noted in the text.

Two dimensions are required to match the thread size of the fastener: the number of threads in a given distance and the outside diameter of the threads.

Two systems are currently used to specify threaded fastener dimensions: the U.S. Standard system and the metric system (**Figure 5**). Pay particular attention when working with unidentified fasteners; mismatching thread types can damage threads.

To ensure the fastener threads are not mismatched or cross-threaded, start all fasteners by hand. If a fastener is difficult to start or turn, determine the cause before tightening with a wrench.

Match fasteners by their length (L, **Figure 6**), diameter (D) and distance between thread crests (pitch, T). A typical metric bolt may be identified by the numbers, 8–1.25 × 130. This indicates the bolt has a diameter of 8 mm, the distance between thread crests is 1.25 mm and the length is 130 mm. Always measure bolt length as shown in L, **Figure 6** to avoid installing replacements of the wrong lengths.

If a number is located on the top of a metric fastener (**Figure 6**), this indicates the strength. The higher the number, the stronger the fastener. Typically, unnumbered fasteners are the weakest.

Many screws, bolts and studs are combined with nuts to secure particular components. To indicate the size of a nut, manufacturers specify the internal diameter and thread pitch.

The measurement across two flats on a nut or bolt indicates the wrench size.

Torque Specifications

The materials used in the manufacture of the motorcycle may be subjected to uneven stresses if fasteners are not installed and tightened correctly. Improperly installed fasteners or ones that worked loose can cause extensive damage. It is essential to use an accurate torque wrench, as described in this chapter, with the torque specifications in this manual.

Specifications for torque are provided in Newton-meters (N•m), foot-pounds (ft.-lb.) and inch-pounds

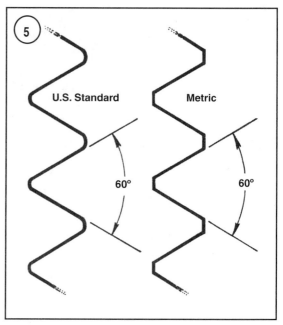

(in.-lb.). Refer to **Table 7** for general torque recommendations. To use **Table 7**, first determine the size of the fastener as described in *Threaded Fasteners* in this section. Torque specifications for specific components are at the end of the appropriate chapters. Torque wrenches are covered in *Tools* in this chapter.

Self-Locking Fasteners

Several types of bolts, screws and nuts incorporate a system that creates interference between the two fasteners. Interference is achieved in various ways. The most common type used is the nylon insert nut and a dry adhesive coating on the threads of a bolt.

Self-locking fasteners offer greater holding strength than standard fasteners, which improves their resistance to vibration. Self-locking fasteners cannot be reused. The materials used to form the lock become distorted after the initial installation and removal.

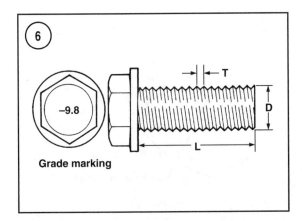

Grade marking

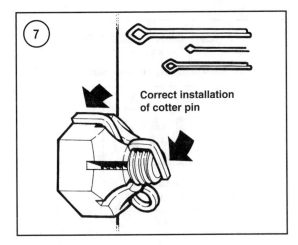

Correct installation of cotter pin

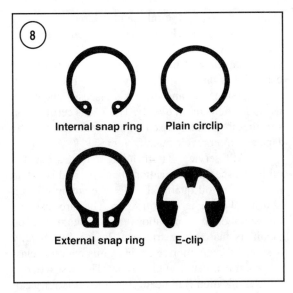

Internal snap ring   Plain circlip

External snap ring   E-clip

Do not replace self-locking fasteners with standard fasteners.

Some original equipment replacement fasteners are equipped with a threadlock preapplied to the fastener threads. When replacing these fasteners, do not apply a separate threadlock. When it is necessary to reuse one of these fasteners, remove the threadlock residue from the threads. Then apply the threadlock specified in the text.

Washers

The two basic types of washers are flat washers and lockwashers. Flat washers are simple discs with a hole to fit a screw or bolt. Lockwashers are used to prevent a fastener from working loose. Washers can be used as spacers and seals or to help distribute fastener load and prevent the fastener from damaging the component.

As with fasteners, when replacing washers make sure the replacements meet the original specifications.

Cotter Pins

A cotter pin is a split metal pin inserted into a hole or slot to prevent a fastener from loosening. In certain applications, such as the rear axle, the fastener must be secured in this way. For these applications, a cotter pin and castellated (slotted) nut is used.

To use a cotter pin, first make sure the diameter is correct for the hole in the fastener. After correctly tightening the fastener and aligning the holes, insert the cotter pin through the hole and bend the ends over the fastener (**Figure 7**). Unless instructed to do so, never loosen a tightened fastener to align the holes. If the holes do not align, tighten the fastener just enough to achieve alignment.

Cotter pins are available in various diameters and lengths. Measure length from the bottom of the head to the tip of the shortest pin.

Snap Rings and E-clips

Snap rings (**Figure 8**) are circular-shaped metal retaining clips. They are required to secure parts and gears in place on parts such as shafts, pins or rods. External type snap rings are used to retain items on shafts. Internal type snap rings secure parts within housing bores. In some applications, in addition to securing the component(s), snap rings of varying thicknesses also determine endplay. These are usually called selective snap rings.

The two basic types of snap rings are machined and stamped snap rings. Machined snap rings (**Figure 9**) can be installed in either direction because both faces have sharp edges. Stamped snap rings (**Figure 10**) are manufactured with a sharp edge and round edge. When installing a stamped snap ring in a thrust application, install the sharp edge facing away from the part producing the thrust.

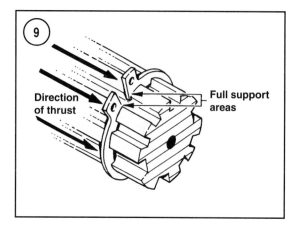

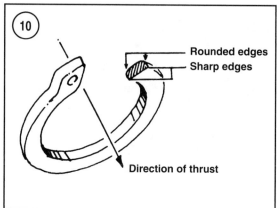

E-clips are used when it is not practical to use a snap ring. Remove E-clips with a flat blade screwdriver by prying between the shaft and E-clip. To install an E-clip, center it over the shaft groove and push or tap it into place.

Observe the following when installing snap rings:
1. Remove and install snap rings with snap ring pliers. Refer to *Tools* in this chapter.
2. In some applications, it may be necessary to replace snap rings after removing them.
3. Compress or expand snap rings only enough to install them. If overly expanded, they lose their retaining ability.
4. After installing a snap ring, make sure it seats completely.
5. Wear eye protection when removing and installing snap rings.

SHOP SUPPLIES

Lubricants and Fluids

Periodic lubrication helps ensure a long service life for any type of equipment. Using the correct type of lubricant is as important as performing the lubrication service, although in an emergency the wrong type is better than not using one. The following section describes the types of lubricants most often required. Make sure to follow the manufacturer's recommendations.

Engine oils

Engine oil for a four-stroke motorcycle engine use is classified by three standards: the American Petroleum Institute (API) service classification, the Society of Automotive Engineers (SAE) viscosity rating and the Japanese Automobile Standards Organization (JASO) T 903 certification standard.

The API and SAE information is on all oil container labels. The JASO information is found on oil

containers sold by the oil manufacturer specifically for motorcycle use (**Figure 11**). Two letters indicate the API service classification (**Figure 12**). The number or sequence of numbers and letter (10W-40 for example) is the oil's viscosity rating. The API service classification and the SAE viscosity index are not indications of oil quality. The JASO certification specifies the oil has passed requirements specified by Japanese motorcycle manufacturers.

The API service classification indicates that the oil meets specific lubrication standards and is not an indication of oil quality. Do not use automotive oil with an SJ or higher classification. They are designed for automotive applications and contain friction modifiers that reduce frictional losses. Specifically designed for automotive engines, oils with this classification can cause engine wear. The first letter in the classification S indicates that the oil is for gasoline engines. The second letter indicates the standard the oil satisfies.

The JASO certification label (**Figure 11**) identifies two separate oil classifications and a registration number to ensure the oil has passed all JASO certification standards for use in four-stroke motorcycle engines. The classifications are: MA (high friction applications) and MB (low friction applications).

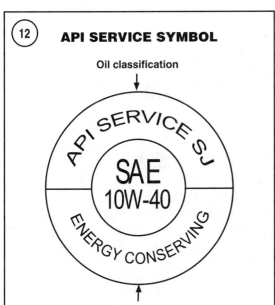

API SERVICE SYMBOL

Oil classification

SAE 10W-40

When ENERGY CONSERVING is listed in this part of the label, the oil has demonstrated energy conserving properties in standard tests. Do not use ENERGY CONSERVING classified oil in motorcycle engines. Instead, look for this API service symbol.

SAE 10W-40

Oil viscosity

Viscosity is an indication of the oil's thickness. Thin oils have a lower number while thick oils have a higher number. Engine oils fall into the 5- to 50-weight range for single-grade oils.

Most manufacturers recommend multi-grade oil. These oils perform efficiently across a wide range of operating conditions. Multi-grade oils are identified by a W after the first number, which indicates the low-temperature viscosity.

Engine oils are most commonly mineral (petroleum) based; however, synthetic and semi-synthetic types are used more frequently. Always use oil with a classification recommended by the manufacturer (Chapter Three). Using oil with a different classification can cause engine damage.

Consider the following when selecting engine oil for the engines covered in this manual:

1. Do not use oil with oil additives or oil with graphite or molybdenum additives. These may adversely affect clutch operation.

2. Do not use vegetable, non-detergent or castor based racing oils.

3. Use only a high-quality motorcycle oil with a JASCO rating of MA (**Figure 11**) or an API oil with an SG or higher rating that does not specify it as ENERY CONSERVING (**Figure 12**). Use SAE 10W-30 weight oil in all cold and normal climates. Use a heavier viscosity oil (10W-40) in hot climates. The classification is printed on the container.

Grease

Grease is lubricating oil with thickening agents added to it. The National Lubricating Grease Institute (NLGI) grades grease. Grades range from No. 000 to No. 6, with No. 6 being the thickest. Typical multipurpose grease is NLGI No. 2. For specific applications, manufacturers may recommend a water-resistant type grease or one with an additive, such as molybdenum disulfide (MoS_2).

Chain lubricant

There are many types of chain lubricants available. Which type of chain lubricant to use depends on the type of chain.

The 80 cc and 100 cc models covered in this manual are equipped with standard (non-O-ring) drive chains, which can be lubricated with most aerosol motorcycle chain lubricants. The manufacturer also specifies the use of an 80 or 90 weight gear oil as an acceptable chain lubricant.

On O-ring (sealed) drive chains, the actual chain lubricant is enclosed in the chain by the O-rings. O-ring chains are lubricated to keep the O-rings pliable and to prevent corrosion. Only lubricate an O-ring drive chain with an aerosol spray specifically designed for O-ring chains and conventional engine or gear oils.

Do not use high-pressure washers, solvents or gasoline to clean an O-ring chain. Only clean with kerosene.

Foam air filter oil

Filter oil is specifically designed to use on foam air filters. The oil is blended with additives making it easy to pour and apply evenly to the filter. Some filter oils include additives that evaporate quickly, making the filter oil very tacky. This allows the oil to remain suspended within the foam pores, trapping dirt and preventing it from being drawn into the engine.

Do not use engine oil as a substitute for foam filter oil. Engine oils do not remain in the filter. Instead, they are drawn into the engine, leaving the filter ineffective.

When oiling an aftermarket air filter, use the oil recommended by the manufacturer.

Cleaners, Degreasers and Solvents

Many chemicals are available to remove oil, grease and other residue from the motorcycle. Before using cleaning solvents, consider their uses and disposal methods, particularly if they are not water-soluble. Local ordinances may require special procedures for the disposal of many types of cleaning chemicals. Refer to *Safety* and *Cleaning Parts* in this chapter for more information on their uses.

Use brake parts cleaner to clean brake system components when contact with petroleum-based products will damage seals. Brake parts cleaner leaves no residue. Use electrical contact cleaner to clean electrical connections and components without leaving any residue. Carburetor cleaner is a powerful solvent used to remove fuel deposits and varnish from fuel system components. Use this cleaner carefully; it may damage finishes.

Generally, degreasers are strong cleaners used to remove heavy accumulations of grease from engine and frame components.

Most solvents are designed to be used with a parts washing cabinet for individual component cleaning. For safety, use only nonflammable or high flash point solvents.

Gasket Sealant

Sealants are used in combination with a gasket or seal or occasionally alone. Follow the manufacturer's recommendation when using sealants. Use extreme care when choosing a sealant different from the type originally recommended. Choose sealants based on their resistance to heat, various fluids and their sealing capabilities.

One of the most common sealants is RTV, or room temperature vulcanizing, sealant. This sealant cures at room temperature over a specific time period. This allows the repositioning of components without damaging gaskets.

Moisture in the air causes the RTV sealant to cure. Always install the tube cap as soon as possible after applying RTV sealant. RTV sealant has a limited shelf life and will not cure properly if the shelf life has expired. Keep partial tubes sealed and discard them

if they have surpassed the expiration date. If there is no expiration date on a sealant tube, use a permanent marker and write the date on the tube when it is first opened. Manufacturers usually specify a shelf life of one year after a container is opened, though it is recommended to contact the sealant manufacturer to confirm shelf life.

Removing RTV sealant

Silicone sealant is used on many engine gasket surfaces. When cleaning parts after disassembly, a razor blade or gasket scraper is required to remove the silicone residue that cannot be pulled off by hand from the gasket surfaces. To avoid damaging gasket surfaces, use Permatex Silicone Stripper (part No. 80647) to help soften the residue before scraping.

Applying RTV sealant

Clean all old sealer residue from the mating surfaces. Then inspect the mating surfaces for damage. Remove all sealer material from blind threaded holes; it can cause inaccurate bolt torque. Spray the mating surfaces with aerosol parts cleaner, and then wipe with a lint-free cloth. Because gasket surfaces must be dry and oil-free for the sealant to adhere, be thorough when cleaning and drying the parts.

Apply RTV sealant in a continuous bead 2-3 mm (0.08-0.12 in.) thick. Circle all the fastener holes unless otherwise specified. Do not allow any sealant to enter these holes. Assemble and tighten the fasteners to the specified torque within the time frame recommended by the RTV sealant manufacturer.

Gasket Remover

Aerosol gasket remover can help remove stubborn gaskets. This product can speed up the removal process and prevent damage to the mating surface when scraping gaskets. Most of these types of products are very caustic. Follow the gasket remover manufacturer's instructions for use, plus the following:

1. The paper gaskets used on the engines covered in this manual are difficult to remove. Do not attempt to remove them without the use of a gasket remover.

2. Depending on a gaskets thickness and other factors, the gasket remover will not always penetrate completely through the gasket with a single application. This becomes evident when attempting to remove the gasket as the gasket scraper may only remove an upper portion of the gasket. When this happens, reapply the gasket remover and repeat until the gasket can be easily removed. Do not try and

force the tool through the gasket as it may damage the gasket surface.

3. To apply an aerosol gasket remover to the gasket surface when the engine is assembled, spray a small amount of gasket remover into a small container and then apply with an acid brush to the engine gasket surfaces. Block off engine areas as necessary with a paper towel.

4. Make sure and remove all gasket material and gasket remover from the engine and cover surfaces.

Threadlocking Compound

> *CAUTION*
> *Threadlocking compounds are anaerobic and damage most plastic parts and surfaces. Use caution when using these products in areas where plastic components are located.*

A threadlocking compound is a fluid applied to the threads of fasteners. After tightening the fastener, the fluid dries and becomes a solid filler between the threads. This makes it difficult for the fastener to work loose from vibration or heat expansion and contraction. Some threadlocking compounds also provide a seal against fluid leaks.

Before applying threadlocking compound, remove any old compound from both thread areas and clean them with aerosol parts cleaner. Use the compound sparingly. Excess fluid can run into adjoining parts.

Threadlocking compounds are available in various strengths, temperatures and repair applications.

TOOLS

Most of the procedures in this manual can be carried out with hand tools and test equipment familiar to the home mechanic. Always use the correct tools for the job. Keep tools organized and clean and store them in a tool chest with related tools organized together.

Quality tools are essential. The best are constructed of high-strength alloy steel. These tools are light, easy-to-use and resistant to wear. Their working surfaces are devoid of sharp edges and the tools are carefully polished. They have an easy-to-clean finish and are comfortable to use. Quality tools are a good investment.

When purchasing tools to perform the procedures covered in this manual, consider the tool's potential frequency of use. If a tool kit is just now being started, consider purchasing a tool set from a quality tool supplier. These sets are available in many tool combinations and offer substantial savings when compared to individually purchased tools. As work experience grows and tasks become more complicated, specialized tools can be added.

Some of the procedures in this manual specify special tools. In most cases, the tool is illustrated in use. Well-equipped mechanics may be able to substitute similar tools or fabricate a suitable replacement. However, in some cases, the specialized equipment or expertise may make it impractical for the home mechanic to attempt the procedure. When necessary, such operations are identified in the text with the recommendation to have a dealership or specialist perform the task. It may be less expensive to have a professional perform these jobs, especially when considering the cost of the equipment.

The manufacturer's part number is provided for many of the tools mentioned in this manual. These part numbers are correct at the time of original publication. The publisher cannot guarantee the part number of the tools in this manual will be available in the future.

Screwdrivers

The two basic types of screwdrivers are the slotted tip (flat blade) and the Phillips tip. These are available in sets that often include an assortment of tip sizes and shaft lengths.

As with all tools, use the correct screwdriver. Make sure the size of the tip conforms to the size and shape of the fastener. Use them only for driving screws. Never use a screwdriver for prying or chiseling. Repair or replace worn or damaged screwdrivers. A worn tip may damage the fastener, making it difficult to remove.

Phillips-head screws are often damaged by incorrectly fitting screwdrivers. Quality Phillips screwdrivers are manufactured with their crosshead tip machined to Phillips Screw Company specifications. Poor quality or damaged Phillips screwdrivers can back out and round over the screw head (camout). Compounding the problem of using poor quality screwdrivers are Phillips-head screws made from weak or soft materials and screws initially installed with air tools.

An effective screwdriver to use on Phillips screws is the ACR Phillips II screwdriver. Anti-camout ribs found on the driving faces or flutes of the screwdriver's tip (**Figure 13**) improves the driver-to-fastener grip. While designed for ACR Phillips II screws, they work well on all common Phillips screws. ACR Phillips II screwdrivers are available in different tip sizes and as interchangeable bits to fit screwdriver bit holders.

Another way to prevent camout and increase the grip of a Phillips screwdriver is to apply valve grind-

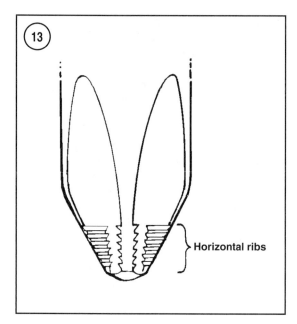

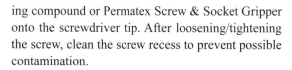

Horizontal ribs

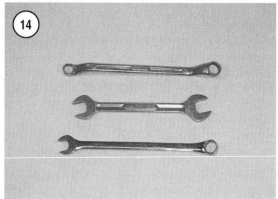

ing compound or Permatex Screw & Socket Gripper onto the screwdriver tip. After loosening/tightening the screw, clean the screw recess to prevent possible contamination.

Wrenches

Open-end, box-end and combination wrenches (**Figure 14**) are available in a variety of types and sizes.

The number stamped on the wrench refers to the distance between the work areas. This size must match the size of the fastener head.

The box-end wrench is an excellent tool because it grips the fastener on all sides. This reduces the chance of the tool slipping. The box-end wrench is designed with either a 6- or 12-point opening. For stubborn or damaged fasteners, the 6-point provides superior holding ability by contacting the fastener across a wider area at all six edges. For general use, the 12-point works well. It allows the wrench to be removed and reinstalled without moving the handle over such a wide arc.

An open-end wrench is fast and works best in areas with limited overhead access. It contacts the fastener at only two points, and is subject to slipping under heavy force or if the tool or fastener is worn. A box-end wrench is preferred in most instances, especially when breaking loose and applying the final tightness to a fastener.

The combination wrench has a box-end on one end, and an open-end on the other. This combination makes it a convenient tool.

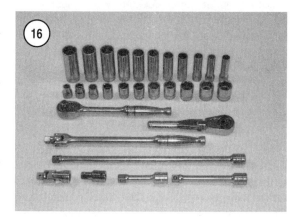

Adjustable Wrenches

An adjustable wrench (**Figure 15**) can fit nearly any nut or bolt head that has clear access around its entire perimeter.

However, adjustable wrenches contact the fastener at only two points, which makes them more subject to slipping off the fastener. One jaw is adjustable and may loosen, which increases this possibility. Make certain the solid jaw is the one transmitting the force.

However, adjustable wrenches are typically used to prevent a large nut or bolt from turning while the

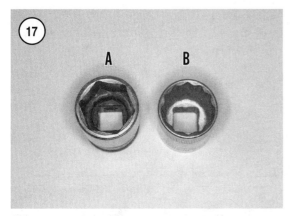

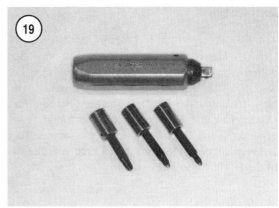

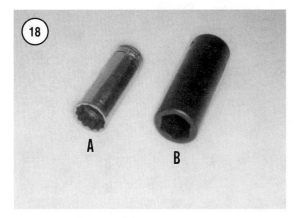

other end is being loosened or tightened with a box-end or socket wrench.

Socket Wrenches, Ratchets and Handles

WARNING
Do not use hand sockets with air or impact tools; they may shatter and cause injury. Always wear eye protection when using impact or air tools.

Sockets that attach to a ratchet handle (**Figure 16**) are available with 6-point (A, **Figure 17**) or 12-point (B) openings and different drive sizes. The drive size indicates the size of the square hole that accepts the ratchet handle. The number stamped on the socket is the size of the work area and must match the fastener head.

As with wrenches, a 6-point socket provides superior-holding ability, while a 12-point socket needs to be moved only half as far to reposition it on the fastener.

Sockets are designated for either hand or impact use. Impact sockets are made of a thicker material for more durability. Compare the size and wall thickness of a 19-mm hand socket (A, **Figure 18**) and the 19-mm impact socket (B). Use impact sockets when

using an impact driver or air tool. Use hand sockets with hand-driven attachments.

Various handles are available for sockets. The speed handle is used for fast operation. Flexible ratchet heads in varying lengths allow the socket to be turned with varying force and at odd angles. Extension bars allow the socket setup to reach difficult areas. The ratchet is the most versatile. It allows the user to install or remove the nut without removing the socket.

Sockets combined with any number of drivers make them undoubtedly the fastest, safest and most convenient tool for fastener removal and installation.

Impact Driver

WARNING
Do not use hand sockets with air or impact tools because they may shatter and cause injury. Always wear eye protection when using impact or air tools.

An impact driver provides extra force for removing fasteners by converting the impact of a hammer into a turning motion. This makes it possible to remove stubborn fasteners without damaging them. Impact drivers and interchangeable bits (**Figure 19**) are available from most tool suppliers. When using a socket with an impact driver, make sure the socket is designed for impact use. Refer to *Socket Wrenches, Ratchets and Handles* in this section.

Allen Wrenches

Allen, or setscrew wrenches (**Figure 20**), are used on fasteners with hexagonal recesses in the fastener head. These wrenches are available in a L-shaped bar, socket and T-handle types. Allen bolts are sometimes called socket bolts.

Torx Fasteners

A Torx fastener head is a 6-point star-shaped pattern (A, **Figure 21**). Torx fasteners are identified with a T and a number indicating their drive size. For example, T25. Torx drivers are available in L-shaped bars, sockets and T-handles. Tamper-resistant Torx fasteners are also used and have a round shaft in the center of the fastener head. Tamper-resistance Torx fasteners require a Torx bit with a hole in the center of the bit (B, **Figure 21**).

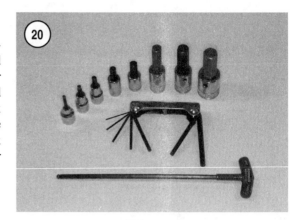

Torque Wrenches

A torque wrench (**Figure 22**) is used with a socket, torque adapter or similar extension to tighten a fastener to a measured torque. Torque wrenches come in several drive sizes (1/4, 3/8, 1/2 and 3/4) and have various methods of reading the torque value. The drive size indicates the size of the square drive that accepts the socket, adapter or extension. Common methods of reading the torque value are the reflecting beam, the dial indicator and the audible click. When choosing a torque wrench, consider the torque range, drive size and accuracy. The torque specifications in this manual provide an indication of the range required. A torque wrench is a precision tool that must be properly cared for to remain accurate. Store torque wrenches in cases or separate padded drawers within a toolbox. Follow the manufacturer's instructions for their care and calibration.

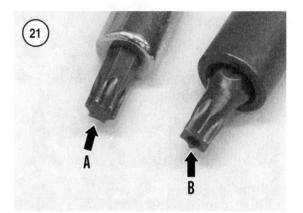

Torque Adapters

Torque adapters (**Figure 23**), or extensions, extend or reduce the reach of a torque wrench. Specific adapters are required to perform some of the procedures in this manual. These are available from the motorcycle manufacturer or fabricated to suit a specific purpose.

If a torque adapter changes the effective lever length, the torque reading on the wrench will not equal the actual torque applied to the fastener. It is necessary to recalibrate the torque setting on the wrench to compensate for the change of lever length. When a torque adapter is used at a right angle to the drive head, calibration is not required because the lever length has not changed.

To recalculate a torque reading when using a torque adapter, use the following formula, and refer to **Figure 24**.

$$TW = \frac{TA \times L}{L + A}$$

TW is the torque setting or dial reading on the wrench.

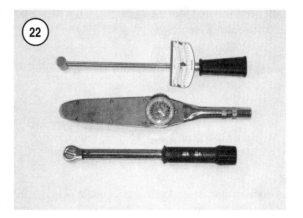

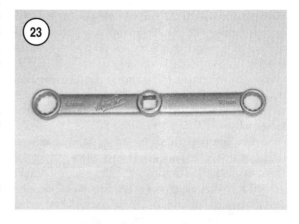

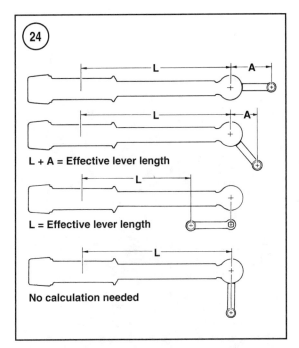

L + A = Effective lever length

L = Effective lever length

No calculation needed

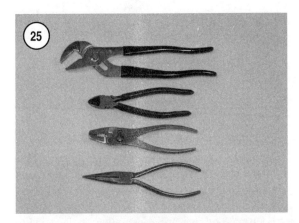

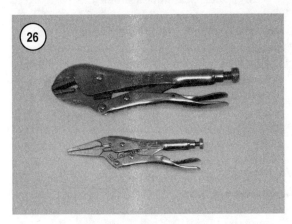

L is the lever length of the wrench as measured from the center of the drive to the center of the grip.

The effective lever length is the sum of L and A.

Example:

TA = 20 ft.-lb.

A = 3 in.

L = 14 in.

$$TW = \frac{20 \times 14}{14 + 3} = \frac{280}{17} = 16.5 \text{ ft.-lb.}$$

In this example, the torque wrench would be set to the recalculated torque value (TW = 16.5 ft.-lb.). When using a beam-type wrench, tighten the fastener until the pointer aligns with 16.5 ft.-lb. In this example, although the torque wrench is pre set to 16.5 ft.-lb., the actual torque is 20 ft.-lb.

Pliers

Pliers come in a wide range of types and sizes. Pliers are useful for holding, cutting, bending, and crimping. Do not use them to turn fasteners unless they are designed to do so. **Figure 25** and **Figure 26** show several types of pliers. Each design has a specialized function. Slip-joint pliers are general-purpose pliers used for gripping and bending. Diagonal cutting pliers are needed to cut wire and can be used to remove cotter pins. Needlenose pliers are used to hold or bend small objects. Locking pliers (**Figure 26**), sometimes called Vise Grips, hold objects tightly. They have many uses ranging from holding two parts together, to gripping the end of a broken stud. Use caution when using locking pliers; the sharp jaws will damage the objects they hold.

Snap Ring Pliers

> *WARNING*
> *Snap rings can slip and fly off when removing and installing them. In addition, the snap ring pliers tips may break. Always wear eye protection when using snap ring pliers.*

Snap ring pliers are specialized pliers with tips that fit into the ends of snap rings to remove and install them.

Snap ring pliers (**Figure 27**) are available with a fixed action (either internal or external) or are convertible (one tool works on both internal and external snap rings). They may have fixed tips or interchangeable ones of various sizes and angles. For general use, select convertible type pliers with interchangeable tips.

TA is the torque specification and the actual amount of torque that will be applied to the fastener.

A is the amount the adapter increases (or in some cases reduces) the effective lever length as measured along the centerline of the torque wrench.

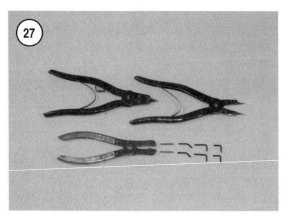

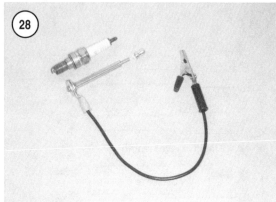

Hammers

WARNING
Always wear eye protection when using hammers. Make sure the hammer face is in good condition and the handle is not cracked. Select the correct hammer for the job and make sure to strike the object squarely. Do not use the handle or the side of the hammer to strike an object.

Various types of hammers are available to fit a number of applications. A ball-peen hammer is used to strike another tool, such as a punch or chisel. Soft-faced hammers are required when a metal object must be struck without damaging it. Never use a metal-faced hammer on engine and suspension components; damage will occur in most cases.

Ignition Grounding Tool

Some test procedures in this manual require kicking the engine over without starting it. Do not remove the spark plug cap and crank the engine without grounding the plug cap. Doing so will damage the ignition system.

An effective way to ground the system is to fabricate the tool shown in **Figure 28** from a No. 6 screw, two washers and a length of wire with an alligator clip soldered on one end. To use the tool, insert it into the spark plug cap and attach the alligator clip to a known engine ground.

This tool is safer than a spark plug or spark tester because there is no spark firing across the end of the plug/tester to potentially ignite fuel vapor spraying from an open spark plug hole or leaking fuel component.

MEASURING TOOLS

The ability to accurately measure components is essential to successfully service many components. Equipment is manufactured to close tolerances, and obtaining consistently accurate measurements is essential.

Each type of measuring instrument is designed to measure a dimension with a certain degree of accuracy and within a certain range. When selecting the measuring tool, make sure it is applicable to the task.

As with all tools, measuring tools provide the best results if cared for properly. Improper use can damage the tool and cause inaccurate results. If any measurement is questionable, verify the measurement using another tool. A standard gauge is usually provided with measuring tools to check accuracy and calibrate the tool if necessary.

Accurate measurements are only possible if the mechanic possesses a feel for using the tool. Heavy-handed use of measuring tools produces less accurate results. Hold the tool gently by the fingertips so the point at which the tool contacts the object is easily felt. This feel for the equipment will produce more accurate measurements and reduce the risk of damaging the tool or component. Refer to the following sections for specific measuring tools.

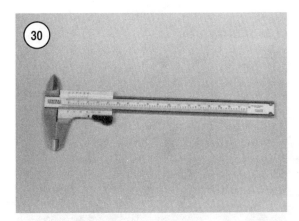

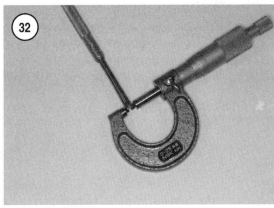

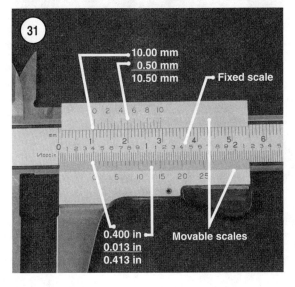

Feeler Gauge

The feeler, or thickness gauge (**Figure 29**), is used for measuring the distance between two surfaces.

A feeler gauge set consists of an assortment of steel strips of graduated thicknesses. Each blade is marked with its thickness. Blades can be of various lengths and angles for different procedures.

A common use for a feeler gauge is to measure valve clearance. Wire (round) type gauges are used to measure spark plug gap.

Calipers

Calipers (**Figure 30**) are excellent tools for obtaining inside, outside and depth measurements. Although not as precise as a micrometer, they allow reasonable precision, typically to within 0.05 mm (0.001 in.). Most calipers have a range up to 150 mm (6 in.).

Calipers are available in dial, vernier or digital versions. Dial calipers have a dial readout that provides convenient reading. Vernier calipers have marked scales that must be compared to determine the measurement. The digital caliper uses a LCD to show the measurement.

Properly maintain the measuring surfaces of the caliper. There must not be any dirt or burrs between the tool and the object being measured. Never force the caliper closed around an object; close the caliper around the highest point so it can be removed with a slight drag. Some calipers require calibration. Always refer to the manufacturer's instructions when using a new or unfamiliar caliper.

To read a vernier caliper refer to **Figure 31**. The fixed scale is marked in 1 mm increments. Ten individual lines on the fixed scale equal 1 cm. The moveable scale is marked in 0.05 mm (hundredth) increments. To obtain a reading, establish the first number by the location of the 0 line on the moveable scale in relation to the first line to the left on the fixed scale. In this example, the number is 10 mm. To determine the next number, note which of the lines on the movable scale align with a mark on the fixed scale. A number of lines will seem close, but only one will align exactly. In this case, 0.50 mm is the reading to add to the first number. The result of adding 10 mm and 0.50 mm is a measurement of 10.50 mm.

Micrometers

A micrometer (**Figure 32**) is an instrument designed for linear measurement using the decimal divisions of the inch or meter. While there are many types and styles of micrometers, most of the procedures in this manual call for an outside micrometer. The outside micrometer is used to measure the outside diameter of cylindrical forms and the thicknesses of materials.

A micrometer's size indicates the minimum and maximum size of a part that it can measure. The usual sizes are 0-25 mm (0-1 in.), 25-50 mm (1-2 in.), 50-75 mm (2-3 in.) and 75-100 mm (3-4 in.).

Micrometers that cover a wider range of measurements are available. These use a large frame with interchangeable anvils of various lengths. This type of micrometer offers a cost savings; however, its overall size may make it less convenient.

Adjustment

Before using a micrometer, check its adjustment as follows.

1. Clean the anvil and spindle faces.

2A. To check a 0-1 in. or 0-25 mm micrometer:

   a. Turn the thimble until the spindle contacts the anvil. If the micrometer has a ratchet stop, use it to ensure the proper amount of pressure is applied.

   b. If the adjustment is correct, the 0 mark on the thimble will align exactly with the 0 mark on the sleeve line. If the marks do not align, the micrometer is out of adjustment.

   c. Follow the manufacturer's instructions to adjust the micrometer.

2B. To check a micrometer larger than 1 in. or 25 mm, use the standard gauge supplied by the manufacturer. A standard gauge is a steel block, disc or rod that is machined to an exact size.

   a. Place the standard gauge between the spindle and anvil and measure its outside diameter or length. If the micrometer has a ratchet stop, use it to ensure the proper amount of pressure is applied.

   b. If the adjustment is correct, the 0 mark on the thimble will align exactly with the 0 mark on the sleeve line. If the marks do not align, the micrometer is out of adjustment.

   c. Follow the manufacturer's instructions to adjust the micrometer.

Care

Micrometers are precision instruments. They must be used and maintained with great care. Note the following:

1. Store micrometers in protective cases or separate padded drawers in a toolbox.

2. When in storage, make sure the spindle and anvil faces do not contact each other or another object. If they do, temperature changes and corrosion may damage the contact faces.

3. Do not clean a micrometer with compressed air. Dirt forced into the tool causes wear.

4. Lubricate micrometers to prevent corrosion.

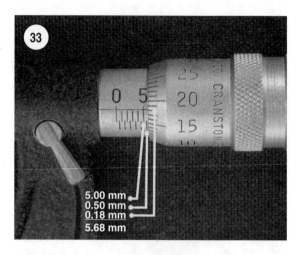

5.00 mm
0.50 mm
0.18 mm
5.68 mm

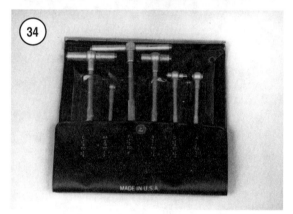

Reading

When reading a micrometer, numbers are taken from different scales and added together.

For accurate results, properly maintain the measuring surfaces of the micrometer. There cannot be any dirt or burrs between the tool and the measured object. Never force the micrometer closed around an object. Close the micrometer around the highest point so it can be removed with a slight drag.

The standard metric micrometer is accurate to one one-hundredth of a millimeter (0.01 mm). The sleeve line is graduated in millimeter and half millimeter increments. The marks on the upper half of the sleeve line equal 1.00 mm. Each fifth mark above the sleeve line is identified with a number. The number sequence depends on the size of the micrometer. A 0-25 mm micrometer, for example, will have sleeve marks numbered 0 through 25 in 5 mm increments. This numbering sequence continues with larger micrometers. On all metric micrometers, each mark on the lower half of the sleeve equals 0.50 mm.

The tapered end of the thimble has 50 lines marked around it. Each mark equals 0.01 mm. One complete turn of the thimble aligns its 0 mark with the first line on the lower half of the sleeve line, or 0.50 mm.

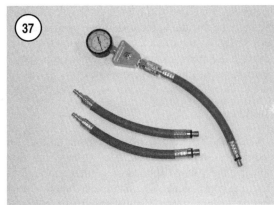

When reading a metric micrometer, add the number of millimeters and half-millimeters on the sleeve line to the number of one one-hundredth millimeters on the thimble. Perform the following steps while referring to **Figure 33**.

1. Read the upper half of the sleeve line and count the number of lines visible. Each upper line equals 1 mm.
2. See if the half-millimeter line is visible on the lower sleeve line. If so, add 0.50 mm to the reading in Step 1.
3. Read the thimble mark that aligns with the sleeve line. Each thimble mark equals 0.01 mm.
4. If a thimble mark does not align exactly with the sleeve line, estimate the amount between the lines. For accurate readings in two-thousandths of a millimeter (0.002 mm), use a metric vernier micrometer.
5. Add the readings from Steps 1-4.

Telescoping and Small Hole Gauges

Use telescoping gauges (**Figure 34**) and small hole gauges (**Figure 35**) to measure bores. Neither gauge has a scale for direct readings. An outside micrometer must be used to determine the reading.

To use a telescoping gauge, select the correct size gauge for the bore. Compress the moveable post and carefully insert the gauge into the bore. Carefully move the gauge in the bore to make sure it is centered. Tighten the knurled end of the gauge to hold the moveable post in position. Remove the gauge and measure the length of the posts. Telescoping gauges are typically used to measure cylinder bores.

To use a small hole gauge, select the correct size gauge for the bore. Carefully insert the gauge into the bore. Tighten the knurled end of the gauge to carefully expand the gauge fingers to the limit within the bore. Do not overtighten the gauge; there is no built-in release. Excessive tightening can damage the bore surface and tool. Remove the gauge and measure the outside dimension with a micrometer (**Figure 32**). Small hole gauges are typically used to measure valve guides.

Dial Indicator

A dial indicator (**Figure 36**) is a gauge with a dial face and needle used to measure variations in dimensions and movements. Measuring brake rotor runout is a typical use for a dial indicator.

Dial indicators are available in various ranges and graduations and with three types of mounting bases: magnetic, clamp or screw-in stud.

Cylinder Bore Gauge

A cylinder bore gauge is similar to a dial indicator. These typically consist of a dial indicator, handle and different length adapters (anvils) to fit the gauge to various bore sizes. The bore gauge is used to measure bore size, taper and out-of-round. When using a bore gauge, follow the manufacturer's instructions.

Compression Gauge

A compression gauge (**Figure 37**) measures combustion chamber (cylinder) pressure, usually in psi or kg/cm^2. The gauge adapter is either inserted and held in place or screwed into the spark plug hole to obtain the reading. Disable the engine so it will not start and hold the throttle in the wide-open position when performing a compression test. An engine that does not have adequate compression cannot be properly tuned. Refer to Chapter Three.

Multimeter

A multimeter (**Figure 38**) is an essential tool for electrical system diagnosis. The voltage function indicates the voltage applied or available to various electrical components. The ohmmeter function tests circuits for continuity, or lack of continuity, and measures the resistance of a circuit.

Some manufacturers' specifications for electrical components are based on results using a specific test meter. Results may vary if using a meter not recommend by the manufacturer. Such requirements are noted when applicable.

Ohmmeter (analog) calibration

Each time an analog ohmmeter is used or the scale is changed, the ohmmeter must be calibrated.

Digital ohmmeters do not require calibration.

1. Make sure the meter battery is in good condition.
2. Make sure the meter probes are in good condition.
3. Touch the two probes together and observe the needle location on the ohms scale. The needle must align with the 0 mark to obtain accurate measurements.
4. If necessary, rotate the meter ohms adjust knob until the needle and 0 mark align.

ELECTRICAL SYSTEM FUNDAMENTALS

A thorough study of the many types of electrical systems used in today's motorcycles is beyond the scope of this manual. However, a basic understanding of voltage, resistance and amperage is necessary to perform diagnostic tests.

Refer to Chapter Two for troubleshooting.

Voltage

Voltage is the electrical potential or pressure in an electrical circuit and is expressed in volts. The more pressure (voltage) in a circuit, the more work can be performed.

Direct current (DC) voltage means the electricity flows in one direction. All circuits powered by a battery are DC circuits.

Alternating current (AC) means the electricity flows in one direction momentarily and then switches to the opposite direction. Alternator output is an ex-

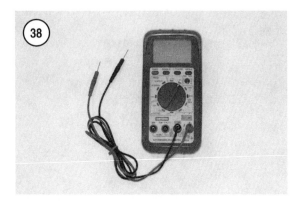

ample of AC voltage. This voltage must be changed or rectified to direct current to operate in a battery powered system.

Resistance

Resistance is the opposition to the flow of electricity within a circuit or component and is measured in ohms. Resistance causes a reduction in available current and voltage.

Resistance is measured in an inactive circuit with an ohmmeter. The ohmmeter sends a small amount of current into the circuit and measures how difficult it is to push the current through the circuit.

An ohmmeter, although useful, is not always a good indicator of a circuit's actual ability under operating conditions. This is due to the low voltage (6-9 volts) that the meter uses to test the circuit. The voltage in an ignition coil secondary winding can be several thousand volts. Such high voltage can cause the coil to malfunction, even though it tests acceptable during a resistance test.

Resistance generally increases with temperature. Perform all testing with the component or circuit at room temperature. Resistance tests performed at high temperatures may indicate false resistance readings and cause the unnecessary replacement of a component.

Amperage

Amperage is the unit of measure for the amount of current within a circuit. Current is the actual flow of electricity. The higher the current, the more work can be performed up to a given point. If the current flow exceeds the circuit or component capacity, the system will be damaged.

SERVICE METHODS

Many of the procedures in this manual are straightforward and can be performed by anyone reasonably competent with tools. However, consider previous experience carefully before performing any operation involving complicated procedures.

1. Front, in this manual, refers to the front of the motorcycle. The front of any component is the end closest to the front of the motorcycle. The left and right sides refer to the position of the parts as viewed by the rider sitting on the seat facing forward.

2. When servicing the motorcycle, secure it in a safe manner.

3. Label all similar parts for location and mark all mating parts for position. If possible, photograph or draw the number and thickness of any shim as it is removed. Identify parts by placing them in sealed and labeled plastic bags. It is possible for carefully laid out parts to become disturbed, making it difficult to reassemble the components correctly without a diagram.

4. Label disconnected wires and connectors with masking tape and a marking pen. Do not rely on memory alone.

5. Protect finished surfaces from physical damage or corrosion. Keep gasoline and other chemicals off painted surfaces.

6. Use penetrating oil on frozen or tight bolts. Avoid using heat where possible. Heat can warp, melt or affect the temper of parts. Heat also damages the finish of paint and plastics. Refer to *Heating Components* in this section.

7. When a part is a press fit or requires a special tool for removal, the information or type of tool is identified in the text. Otherwise, if a part is difficult to remove or install, determine the cause before proceeding.

8. To prevent objects or debris from falling into the engine, cover all openings.

9. Read each procedure thoroughly and compare the figures to the actual components before starting the procedure. Perform the procedure in sequence.

10. Recommendations are occasionally made to refer service to a dealership or specialist. In these cases, the work can be performed more economically by the specialist than by the home mechanic.

11. The term *replace* means to discard a defective part and replace it with a new part. *Overhaul* means to remove, disassemble, inspect, measure, repair and/or replace parts as required to recondition an assembly.

12. Some operations require the use of a hydraulic press. If a press is not available, have these operations performed by a shop equipped with the necessary equipment. Do not use makeshift equipment that may damage the motorcycle. Do not direct high-pressure water at steering bearings, fuel body hoses, wheel bearings, suspension and electrical compo-

nents. The water forces the grease out of the bearings and could damage the seals.

13. Repairs are much faster and easier if the motorcycle is clean before starting work. Degrease the motorcycle with a commercial degreaser; follow the directions on the container for the best results. Clean all parts with cleaning solvent.

14. If special tools are required, have them available before starting the procedure. When special tools are required, they will be described at the beginning of the procedure.

15. Make sure all shims and washers are reinstalled in the same location and position.

16. Whenever rotating parts contact a stationary part, look for a shim or washer.

17. Use new gaskets if there is any doubt about the condition of old ones.

18. If self-locking fasteners are used, replace them. Do not install standard fasteners in place of self-locking ones.

19. Use grease to hold small parts in place if they tend to fall out during assembly. Do not apply grease to electrical or brake components.

Heating Components

> *WARNING*
> *Wear protective gloves to prevent burns and injury when heating parts.*

> *CAUTION*
> *Do not use a welding torch when heating parts. A welding torch applies excessive heat to a small area very quickly, which can damage parts.*

A heat gun or propane torch is required to disassemble, assemble, remove and install many parts and components in this manual. Read the safety and operating information supplied by the manufacturer of the heat gun or propane torch while also noting the following:

1. The work area should be clean and dry. Remove all combustible components and materials from the work area. Wipe up all grease, oil and other fluids from parts. Check for leaking or damaged fuel system components. Repair or remove these parts before beginning work.

2. Never use a flame near the battery, fuel tank, fuel lines or other flammable materials.

3. When using a heat gun, remember that the temperature can be in excess of 540° C (1000° F).

4. Have a fire extinguisher near the job.

5. Always wear protective goggles and gloves when heating parts.

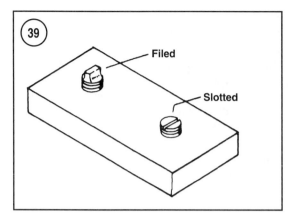

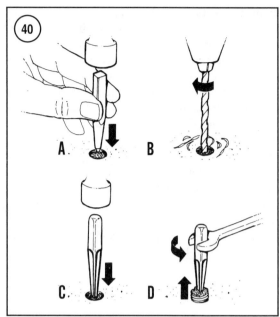

6. Before heating a part installed on the motorcycle, check areas around the part and those *hidden* that could be damaged or possibly ignite. Do not heat surfaces than can be damaged by heat. Shield materials near the part or area to be heated. For example, cables and wiring harnesses.

7. Before heating a part, read the entire procedure to make sure the required tools are available. This allows quick work while the part is at its optimum temperature.

8. The amount of heat recommended to remove or install a part is typically listed in the procedure. However, before heating parts without a specific recommendation, consider the possible effects. To avoid damaging a part, monitor the temperature with heat sticks or an infrared thermometer, if possible. Another way, though not as accurate, is to place tiny drops of water on the part. When the water starts to sizzle, the part is hot enough. Keep the heat in motion to prevent overheating.

Removing Frozen Fasteners

If a fastener cannot be removed, several methods may be used to loosen it. First, liberally apply penetrating oil, and let it penetrate for 10-15 minutes. Rap the fastener several times with a small hammer. Do not hit it hard enough to cause damage. Reapply the penetrating oil if necessary.

For frozen screws, apply penetrating oil as described, and then insert a screwdriver in the slot and rap the top of the screwdriver with a hammer. This loosens the rust so the screw can be removed in the normal way. If the screw head is too damaged to use this method, grip the head with locking pliers and twist it out.

If heat is required, refer to *Heating Components* in this section.

Removing Broken Fasteners

If the head breaks off a screw or bolt, several methods are available for removing the remaining portion. If a large portion of the remainder projects out, try gripping it with locking pliers. If the projecting portion is too small, file it to fit a wrench or cut a slot in it to fit a screwdriver (**Figure 39**).

If the head breaks off flush, use a screw extractor. To do this, center punch the exact center of the screw or bolt (A, **Figure 40**), and then drill a small hole in the screw (B) and tap the extractor into the hole (C). Back the screw out with a wrench on the extractor (D, **Figure 40**).

Repairing Damaged Threads

Occasionally, threads are stripped through carelessness or impact damage. Often the threads can be repaired by running a tap (for internal threads on nuts) or die (for external threads on bolts) through the threads (**Figure 41**). To clean or repair spark plug threads, use a spark plug tap.

If an internal thread is damaged, it may be necessary to install a Helicoil or some other type of thread insert. Follow the manufacturer's instructions when installing its insert.

If it is necessary to drill and tap a hole, refer to **Table 5** for metric tap and drill sizes.

Stud Removal/Installation

A stud removal tool (**Figure 42**) is available from most tool suppliers. This tool makes the removal and

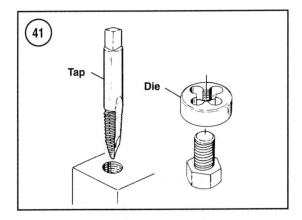

Tap

Die

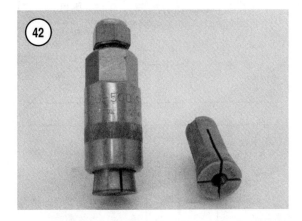

installation of studs easier. If one is not available and the threads on the stud are not damaged, thread two nuts onto the stud and tighten them against each other. Remove the stud by turning the lower nut.

1. Measure the height of the stud above the surface.

2. Thread the stud removal tool onto the stud and tighten it, or thread two nuts onto the stud.

3. Remove the stud by turning the stud remover or the lower nut.

4. Remove any threadlocking compound from the threaded hole. Clean the threads with an aerosol parts cleaner.

5. Install the stud removal tool onto the new stud, or thread two nuts onto the stud.

6. Apply threadlocking compound to the threads of the stud.

7. Install the stud and tighten with the stud removal tool or the top nut.

8. Install the stud to the height noted in Step 1 or its torque specification.

9. Remove the stud removal tool or the two nuts.

Bearings

Bearings are precision parts and must be maintained with proper lubrication and maintenance. If a bearing is damaged, replace it immediately. When

installing a new bearing, make sure to prevent damaging it. Bearing replacement procedures are included in the individual chapters where applicable; however, use the following sections as a guideline.

Unless otherwise specified, install bearings with the manufacturer's mark or number facing outward.

Removal

While bearings are normally removed only when damaged, there may be times when it is necessary to remove a bearing that is in good condition. However, improper bearing removal will damage the bearing and maybe the shaft or case half. Note the following when removing bearings:

1. Before removing the bearings, note the following:
   a. Refer to the bearing replacement procedure in the appropriate chapter for any special instructions.
   b. Remove any seals that interfere with bearing removal. Refer to *Seal Replacement* in this section.
   c. When removing more than one bearing, identify the bearings before removing them. Refer to the bearing manufacturer's numbers on the bearing.
   d. Note and record the direction in which the bearing numbers face for proper installation.
   e. Remove any set plates or bearing retainers before removing the bearings.

2. When using a puller to remove a bearing from a shaft, make sure the shaft is not damaged. Always place a piece of metal between the end of the shaft and the puller screw. In addition, place the puller arms next to the inner bearing race. Refer to **Figure 43**.

3. When using a hammer to remove a bearing from a shaft, do not strike the hammer directly against the shaft. Instead, use a brass or aluminum rod between the hammer and shaft (**Figure 44**) and make sure to support both bearing races with wooden blocks as shown.

4. The ideal method of bearing removal is with a hydraulic press. Note the following when using a press:
   a. Always support the inner and outer bearing races with a suitable size wooden or aluminum ring (**Figure 45**). If only the outer race is supported, pressure applied against the balls and/or the inner race will damage them.
   b. Always make sure the press arm (**Figure 45**) aligns with the center of the shaft. If the arm is not centered, it may damage the bearing and/or shaft.
   c. The moment the shaft is free of the bearing, it will drop to the floor. Secure or hold the shaft to prevent it from falling.

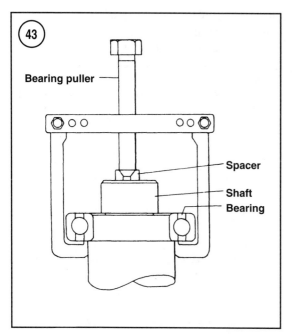

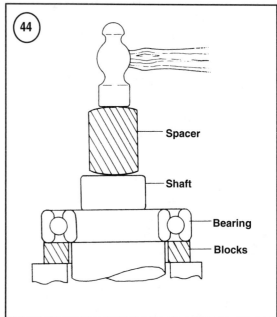

d. When removing bearings from a housing, support the housing with 4 × 4 in. wooden blocks to prevent damage to gasket surfaces.

5. Use a blind bearing puller to remove bearings installed in blind holes (**Figure 46**).

Installation

1. When installing a bearing in a housing, apply pressure to the *outer* bearing race (**Figure 47**). When installing a bearing on a shaft, apply pressure to the *inner* bearing race (**Figure 48**).

2. When installing a bearing as described in Step 1, a driver is required. Never strike the bearing directly with a hammer or the bearing will be damaged. When installing a bearing, use a piece of pipe or a driver with a diameter that matches the bearing race. **Figure 49** shows the correct way to use a driver and hammer to install a bearing on a shaft.

3. Step 1 describes how to install a bearing in a housing or over a shaft. However, when installing a bearing over a shaft and into the housing at the *same time*, a tight fit will be required for both outer and inner bearing races. In this situation, install a spacer underneath the driver tool so pressure is applied evenly across both races. Refer to **Figure 50**. If the outer race is not supported, the balls push against the outer bearing race and damage it.

Interference fit

1. Follow this procedure when installing a bearing over a shaft. When a tight fit is required, the bearing

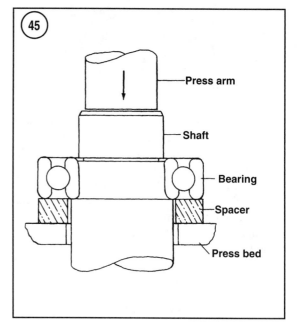

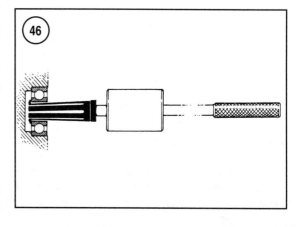

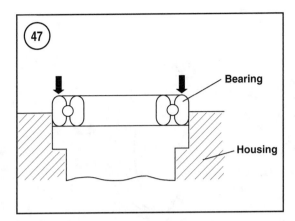

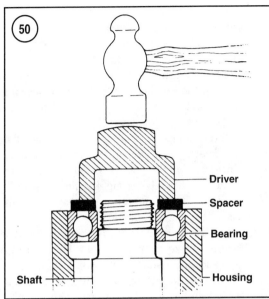

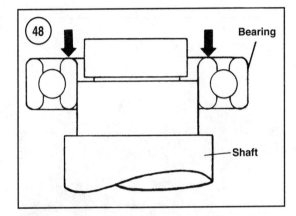

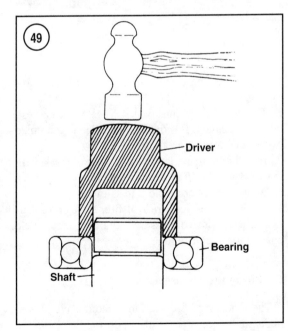

b. Clean all residues from the bearing surface of the shaft. Remove burrs with a file.

c. Fill a suitable pot or beaker with clean mineral oil. Place a thermometer rated above 120° C (248° F) in the oil. Support the thermometer so it does not rest on the bottom or side of the pot.

d. Remove the bearing from its wrapper and secure it with a piece of heavy wire bent to hold it in the pot. Hang the bearing in the pot so it does not touch the bottom or sides of the pot.

e. Turn the heat on and monitor the thermometer. When the oil temperature rises to approximately 120° C (248° F), remove the bearing from the pot and quickly install it. If necessary, place a socket on the inner bearing race and tap the bearing into place. As the bearing chills, it tightens on the shaft, so installation must be done quickly. Make sure the bearing is installed completely.

2. Follow this step when installing a bearing in a housing. Bearings are generally installed in a housing with a slight interference fit. Driving the bearing into the housing using normal methods may damage the housing or cause bearing damage. Instead, heat the housing before the bearing is installed. Note the following:

a. Before heating the housing in this procedure, wash the housing thoroughly with detergent and water. Rinse and rewash the housing as required to remove all oil and chemicals.

b. Heat the housing to approximately 100° C (212° F) with a heat gun or on a hot plate. Monitor temperature with an infrared thermometer, heat sticks or place tiny drops of water on the housing; if they sizzle and evaporate

inside diameter will be smaller than the shaft. In this case, driving the bearing on the shaft using normal methods may cause bearing damage. Instead, heat the bearing before installation. Note the following:

a. Secure the shaft so it is ready for bearing installation.

immediately, the temperature is correct. Heat
only one housing at a time.
c. If a hot plate is used, remove the housing and
place it on wooden blocks.
d. Hold the housing with the bearing side down
and tap the bearing out with a suitable size
socket and extension. Repeat for all bearings
in the housing.
e. Before heating the bearing housing, place the
new bearing in a freezer, if possible. Chilling
a bearing slightly reduces its outside diameter
while the heated bearing housing assembly
is slightly larger due to heat expansion. This
makes bearing installation easier.
f. While the housing is still hot, install the new
bearing(s) into the housing. Install the bearings
by hand, if possible. If necessary, lightly tap
the bearing(s) into the housing with a socket
placed on the outer bearing race (**Figure 47**).
Do not install bearings by driving on the inner-
bearing race. Install the bearing(s) until it seats
completely.

Seal Replacement

Seals (**Figure 51**) are used to contain oil, water,
grease or combustion gasses in a housing or shaft.
Improper removal of a seal can damage the housing
or shaft. Improper installation of the seal can damage
the seal.
1. Prying is generally the easiest and most effective method of removing a seal from the housing.
However, always place a rag under the pry tool
(**Figure 52**) to prevent damage to the housing.
2. Before installing a typical rubber seal, pack waterproof grease in the seal lips.
3. In most cases, install seals with the manufacturer's numbers or marks face out.
4. Install seals either by hand or with tools. Center
the seal in its bore and attempt to install it by hand.
If necessary, install the seal with a socket or bearing
driver placed on the outside of the seal. Drive the
seal squarely into the housing until it is flush with its
mounting bore or at a position described in the text.
Never install a seal by hitting against the top of the
seal with a hammer.

STORAGE

Several months of non-use can cause a general
deterioration of the motorcycle. This is especially
true in areas of extreme temperature variations. This
deterioration can be minimized with careful preparation for storage. A properly stored motorcycle is
much easier to return to service.

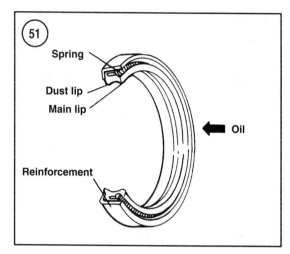

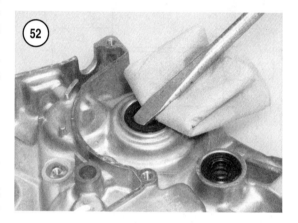

Storage Area Selection

When selecting a storage area, consider the following:
1. The storage area must be dry. A heated area is best,
but not necessary. It should be insulated to minimize
extreme temperature variations.
2. If the building has large window areas, mask them
to keep sunlight off the motorcycle.
3. Avoid storage areas close to saltwater.
4. Consider the area's risk of fire, theft or vandal-
ism. Check with your insurer regarding motorcycle
coverage while in storage.

Preparing the Motorcycle for Storage

The amount of preparation a motorcycle should
undergo before storage depends on the expected
length of non-use, storage area conditions and personal preference. Consider the following list the
minimum requirement:
1. Wash the motorcycle thoroughly. Make sure all
dirt, mud and road debris are removed.
2. Start the engine and allow it to reach operating
temperature. Drain the engine oil regardless of the

riding time since the last service. Fill the engine with the recommended type and quantity of oil.

3. Fill the fuel tank completely.

4. Remove the spark plug (Chapter Three). Turn the ignition switch off. Pour a teaspoon (15-20 ml) of engine oil into the cylinder. Place a rag over the opening and slowly turn the engine over to distribute the oil. Reinstall the spark plug.

5. Cover the exhaust and intake openings.

6. Lubricate the control cables as described in Chapter Three.

7. Apply a protective substance to the plastic and rubber components, including the tires. Make sure to follow the manufacturer's instructions for each type of product being used.

8. Rotate the tires periodically to prevent a flat spot from developing and damaging the tire.

9. Cover the motorcycle with old bed sheets or something similar. Do not cover it with any plastic material that will trap moisture.

Returning the Motorcycle to Service

The amount of service required when returning a motorcycle to service after storage depends on the length of non-use and storage conditions. In addition to performing the reverse of the above procedure, make sure the brakes, clutch, throttle and engine stop switch work properly before operating the motorcycle. Refer to Chapter Three and evaluate the service intervals to determine which areas require service.

Table 1 GENERAL MOTORCYCLE DIMENSIONS

	mm	in.
Footpeg height		
XR80R and CRF80F		
1993-1997 models	Not specified	
1998-2000 models	265	10.4
2001-2003 models	257	10.1
2004-on models	271	10.7
XR100R and CRF100F		
1992-1997 models	Not specified	
1998-2000 models	320	12.6
2001-2003 models	308	12.1
2004-on models	319	12.6
Ground clearance		
XR80R and CRF80F		
1993-1997 models	210	8.3
1998-2000 models	220	8.7
2001-2003 models	206	8.1
2004-on models	218	8.6
XR100R and CRF100F		
1992-2000 models	265	10.4
2001-2003 models	253	10.0
2004-on models	252	9.9
Overall height		
XR80R and CRF80F		
1993-1997 models	955	37.6
1998-2000 models	980	38.6
2001-2003 models	1030	40.6
2004-on models	995	39.2
XR100R and CRF100F		
1992-1997 models	1030	40.6
1998-2000 models	1050	41.3
2001-2003 models	1102	43.4
2004-on models	1046	41.2
Overall length		
XR80R and CRF100F		
1993-1997 models	1730	68.1
1998-2000 models	1740	68.5
2001-2003 models	1743	68.6
2004-on models	1749	68.9
(continued)		

Table 1 GENERAL MOTORCYCLE DIMENSIONS (continued)

	mm	in.
Overall length (continued)		
XR100R and CRF100F		
1992-2000 models	1855	73.0
2001-2003 models	1869	73.6
2004-on models	1853	73.0
Overall width		
XR80R and CRF80F		
1993-2000 models	755	29.7
2001-2003 models	778	30.6
2004-on models	727	28.6
XR100R and CRF100F		
1992-2000 models	800	31.5
2001-2003 models	816	32.1
2004-on models	786	30.9

Table 2 MOTORCYCLE WEIGHT SPECIFICATIONS

	kg	lb.
Curb weight		
XR80R and CRF80F		
1993-1997 models	Not specified	
1998-2000 models	69	152
2001-on models	74	163
XR100R and CRF100F		
1992-1997 models	Not specified	
1998-2000 models	75	165
2001-2007 models	79	174
2008-on models	77	170
Dry weight		
XR80R and CRF80F		
1993-2000 models	64	141
2001-on models	70	154
XR100R and CRF100F		
1992-2000 models	68	150
2001-on models	75	165

Table 3 CONVERSION FORMULAS

Multiply:	By:	To get the equivalent of:
Length		
Inches	25.4	Millimeter
Inches	2.54	Centimeter
Miles	1.609	Kilometer
Feet	0.3048	Meter
Millimeter	0.03937	Inches
Centimeter	0.3937	Inches
Kilometer	0.6214	Mile
Meter	3.281	Feet
Fluid volume		
U.S. quarts	0.9463	Liters
U.S. gallons	3.785	Liters
U.S. ounces	29.573529	Milliters
Imperial gallons	4.54609	Liters
Imperial quarts	1.1365	Liters
Liters	0.2641721	U.S. gallons
Liters	1.0566882	U.S. quarts
Liters	33.814023	U.S. ounces
Liters	0.22	Imperial gallons
Liters	0.8799	Imperial quarts

(continued)

Table 3 CONVERSION FORMULAS (continued)

Multiply:	By:	To get the equivalent of:
Fluid volume (continued)		
Milliters	0.033814	U.S. ounces
Milliters	1.0	Cubic centimeters
Milliters	0.001	Liters
Torque		
Foot-pounds	1.3558	Newton-meters
Foot-pounds	0.138255	Meters-kilograms
Inch-pounds	0.11299	Newton-meters
Newton-meters	0.7375622	Foot-pounds
Newton-meters	8.8507	Inch-pounds
Meters-kilograms	7.2330139	Foot-pounds
Volume		
Cubic inches	16.387064	Cubic centimeters
Cubic centimeters	0.0610237	Cubic inches
Temperature		
Fahrenheit	(°F − 32) × 0.556	Centigrade
Centigrade	(°C × 1.8) + 32	Fahrenheit
Weight		
Ounces	28.3495	Grams
Pounds	0.4535924	Kilograms
Grams	0.035274	Ounces
Kilograms	2.2046224	Pounds
Pressure		
Pounds per square inch	0.070307	Kilograms per square centimeter
Kilograms per square centimeter	14.223343	Pounds per square inch
Kilopascals	0.1450	Pounds per square inch
Pounds per square inch	6.895	Kilopascals
Speed		
Miles per hour	1.609344	Kilometers per hour
Kilometers per hour	0.6213712	Miles per hour

Table 4 TECHNICAL ABBREVIATIONS

ABDC	After bottom dead center
ATDC	After top dead center
BBDC	Before bottom dead center
BDC	Bottom dead center
BTDC	Before top dead center
C	Celsius (Centigrade)
cc	Cubic centimeters
cid	Cubic inch displacement
CDI	Capacitor discharge ignition
cu.in.	Cubic inches
F	Fahrenheit
ft.	Feet
ft.-lb.	Foot-pounds
gal.	Gallons
hp	Horsepower
ICM	Ignition control module
in.	inches
in.-lb.	Inch-pounds
I.D.	Inside diameter
Kg	Kilograms
Kgm	Kilogram meters
Km	Kilometer
KPa	Kilopascals
L	Liter
m	Meter
mA	Milliampere
MAG	Magneto
ml	Milliliter
mm	Millimeter
N•m	Newton-meters

(continued)

Table 4 TECHNICAL ABBREVIATIONS (continued)

O.D.	Outside diameter
OHC	Overhead cam
oz.	Ounces
PAIR	Pulse secondary air injection system
psi.	Pounds per square inch
PTO	Power take off
pt.	Pint
qt.	Quart
rpm	Revolutions per minute
RTV	Room temperature vulcanizing

Table 5 METRIC TAP AND DRILL SIZES

Metric size	Drill equivalent	Decimal fraction	Nearest fraction
3 × 0.50	No. 39	0.0995	3/32
3 × 0.60	3/32	0.0937	3/32
4 × 0.70	No. 30	0.1285	1/8
4 × 0.75	1/8	0.125	1/8
5 × 0.80	No. 19	0.166	11/64
5 × 0.90	No. 20	0.161	5/32
6 × 1.00	No. 9	0.196	15/64
7 × 1.00	16/64	0.234	15/64
8 × 1.00	J	0.277	9/32
8 × 1.25	17/64	0.265	17/64
9 × 1.00	5/16	0.3125	5/16
9 × 1.25	5/16	0.3125	5/16
10 × 1.25	11/32	0.3437	11/32
10 × 1.50	R	0.375	11/32
11 × 1.50	3/8	0.375	3/8
12 × 1.50	13/32	0.406	13/32
12 × 1.75	13/32	0.406	13/32

Table 6 METRIC, INCH AND FRACTIONAL EQUIVALENTS

mm	in.	Nearest fraction	mm	in.	Nearest fraction
1	0.0394	1/32	26	1.0236	1 1/32
2	0.0787	3/32	27	1.0630	1 1/16
3	0.1181	1/8	28	1.1024	1 3/32
4	0.1575	5/32	29	1.1417	1 5/32
5	0.1969	3/16	30	1.1811	1 3/16
6	0.2362	1/4	31	1.2205	1 7/32
7	0.2756	9/32	32	1.2598	1 1/4
8	0.3150	5/16	33	1.2992	1 5/16
9	0.3543	11/32	34	1.3386	1 11/32
10	0.3937	13/32	35	1.3780	1 3/8
11	0.4331	7/16	36	1.4173	1 13/32
12	0.4724	15/32	37	1.4567	1 15/32
13	0.5118	1/2	38	1.4961	1 1/2
14	0.5512	9/16	39	1.5354	1 17/32
15	0.5906	19/32	40	1.5748	1 9/16
16	0.6299	5/8	41	1.6142	1 5/8
17	0.6693	21/32	42	1.6535	1 21/32
18	0.7087	23/32	43	1.6929	1 11/16
19	0.7480	3/4	44	1.7323	1 23/32
20	0.7874	25/32	45	1.7717	1 25/32
21	0.8268	13/16	46	1.8110	1 13/16
22	0.8661	7/8	47	1.8504	1 27/32
23	0.9055	29/32	48	1.8898	1 7/8
24	0.9449	15/16	49	1.9291	1 15/16
25	0.9843	31/32	50	1.9685	1 31/32

Table 7 GENERAL TORQUE RECOMMENDATIONS

Fastener size or type	N·m	in.-lb.	ft.-lb.
5 mm screw	4	35	–
5 mm bolt and nut	5	44	–
6 mm screw	9	80	–
6 mm bolt and nut	10	88	–
6 mm flange bolt (8 mm head, small flange)	9	80	–
6 mm flange bolt (10 mm head) and nut	12	106	–
8 mm bolt and nut	22	–	16
8 mm flange bolt and nut	27	–	20
10 mm bolt and nut	35	–	25
10 mm flange bolt and nut	40	–	29
12 mm bolt and nut	55	–	40

1

CHAPTER TWO

TROUBLESHOOTING

The troubleshooting procedures described in this chapter provide typical symptoms and logical methods for isolating the cause(s). There may be several ways to solve a problem, but only a systematic approach will be successful in avoiding wasted time and possibly unnecessary parts replacement. Gather as much information as possible to aid in diagnosis. Never assume anything and do not overlook the obvious. On 2001-on models, make sure the ignition switch is on and there is fuel in the tank.

An engine needs three basics to run properly: correct air/fuel mixture, compression and a spark at the correct time. If one of these is missing, the engine will not run.

Learning to recognize symptoms makes troubleshooting easier. In most cases, expensive and complicated test equipment is not needed to determine whether repairs can be performed at home. On the other hand, be realistic and do not start procedures that are beyond your experience and equipment available. If the motorcycle requires the attention of a professional, describe symptoms and conditions accurately and fully. The more information a technician has available, the easier it is to diagnose the problem.

STARTING THE ENGINE

The following sections describe the recommended starting procedures. In all cases, make sure there is an adequate supply of fuel in the tank.

A rich air/fuel mixture is required when starting a cold engine. For this to work the carburetor is equipped with a choke plate. Use the choke plate when the ambient temperature is 35° C (95° F) or below.

The choke plate is controlled by the choke lever (A, **Figure 1**) mounted on the carburetor. To close the choke plate to start a cold engine, pull the choke lever up. After the engine starts and warms up, push the choke lever down all the way.

Engine is Cold

1. Shift the transmission into neutral.
2. On 2001-on models, turn the ignition switch (**Figure 2**) on.
3. Pull the choke lever (A, **Figure 1**) up.
4. Turn the fuel valve (A, **Figure 3**) on.
5. Hold the throttle slightly open and operate the kickstarter.
6. When the engine starts, turn the throttle slightly to keep it running.
7. After the engine idles approximately 30 seconds, push the choke lever down to the closed position. Warm the engine sufficiently until the engine accelerates cleanly when the throttle is opened.

Engine is Warm or Hot

1. Shift the transmission into neutral.
2. On 2001-on models, turn the ignition switch (**Figure 2**) on.

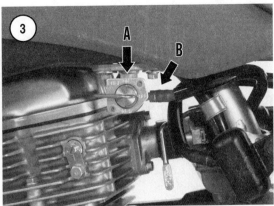

3. Make sure the choke lever (A, **Figure 1**) is fully down.
4. Turn the fuel valve (A, **Figure 3**) on.
5. Hold the throttle slightly open and operate the kickstarter.
6. When the engine starts, turn the throttle slightly to keep it running.

Engine is Flooded

Flooding occurs when too much fuel is drawn into the engine and the spark plug fails to ignite it. The smell of gasoline is often evident when the engine is flooded. Troubleshoot a flooded engine as follows:
1. Look for gasoline overflowing from the carburetor or overflow hose (B, **Figure 1**, typical). If gasoline is evident, the engine is flooded and/or the float in the carburetor bowl is stuck and allowing the carburetor to overfill. Tap the carburetor several times and recheck the overflow hose. If fuel continues to run out of the overflow hose, turn the fuel valve off and service the carburetor as described in Chapter Eight. If the carburetor is not overflowing, continue with Step 2.
2. Shift the transmission into neutral.
3. On 2001-on models, turn the ignition switch (**Figure 2**) off.

4. Make sure the choke lever (A, **Figure 1**) is fully down.
5. Open the throttle fully and hold in this position. Press the engine stop button and kick the kickstarter firmly through its entire stroke several times to clear the engine. Close the throttle.
6. On 2001-on models, turn the ignition switch (**Figure 2**) on.
7. Hold the throttle slightly open and operate the kickstarter.
8A. If the engine starts, turn the throttle slightly to keep it running.
8B. If the engine does not start, remove the spark plug as described in Chapter Three. Dry the insulator, or install a new plug. Reinstall the spark plug and repeat the starting procedure.
9. If the engine still will not start, refer to *Engine Will Not Start* in this chapter.

ENGINE WILL NOT START

Identifying the Problem

If the engine does not start, perform the following steps in order. Because there are so many things that can cause a starting problem, it is important to narrow the possibilities by following a specific troubleshooting procedure. If the engine fails to start after performing these checks, refer to the troubleshooting procedures indicated in the steps. If the engine starts, but idles or runs roughly, refer to *Poor Engine Performance* in this chapter.

NOTE
If the engine backfires during starting, the ignition timing may be incorrect. This can be caused by a loose flywheel nut, a sheared flywheel key, a defective ignition system component or from water that has contaminated one of the ICM connectors.

1. Refer to *Starting the Engine* in this chapter to make sure all starting procedures are correct.

2. If the engine seems flooded, refer to *Starting The Engine* in this chapter. If the engine is not flooded, continue with Step 3.

3. Remove the cap from the fuel tank and rock the bike from side to side. Listen for fuel sloshing around. Make sure the fuel tank vent tube (**Figure 4**) is not plugged. Remove the tube from the filler cap, wipe off one end and blow through it. Remove the filler cap and check that its hose nozzle is not plugged with debris.

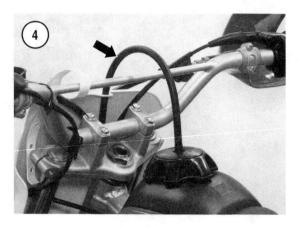

> *WARNING*
> *Do not use an open flame to look into the tank. The flame may ignite the fuel vapors.*

4. If there is sufficient fuel in the fuel tank, remove the spark plug immediately after attempting to start the engine. The plug's insulator should be wet, indicating that fuel is reaching the engine. If the plug tip is dry, fuel is not reaching the engine. A faulty fuel flow problem will cause this condition. Continue with Step 5 to check fuel flow. If there is fuel on the spark plug and the engine will not start, the engine may not have adequate spark. Go to Step 7.

5. Disconnect the fuel line (B, **Figure 3**) from the fuel tank. Connect a short length of hose onto the fuel valve and place the other end in a plastic cup. Turn the fuel valve (A, **Figure 3**) to the on position and see if fuel flows freely. If not, turn the fuel valve to the reserve position and check again. If fuel does not flow and there is fuel in the tank, the fuel strainer screen installed inside the fuel tank may be clogged or damaged or the fuel valve may be blocked by debris. Disconnect the accessory hose and reconnect the fuel line to the carburetor fitting. Refer to Chapter Eight to service the fuel valve assembly.

> *NOTE*
> *If fuel is reaching the carburetor, the fuel system could still be the problem. The jets (pilot and main) could be plugged or the air filter could be severely restricted. However, before removing the carburetor or air filter, continue with Step 7 to make sure the choke is working properly and the ignition provides an adequate spark.*

6. A damaged carburetor choke assembly can cause hard starting, especially in cold weather. This is more of a problem on 100 cc models because of its linkage and tension spring mechanism. Refer to Chapter Eight for additional information.

> *NOTE*
> *When examining the spark plug cap, check for the presence of water.*

> *NOTE*
> *A cracked or damaged spark plug cap and wire can cause intermittent problems that are difficult to diagnose. If the engine occasionally misfires or cuts out, use a spray bottle to wet the plug cap and plug wire while the engine is running. Water that enters one of these areas causes an arc through the insulating material, resulting in an engine misfire.*

> *NOTE*
> *Engine misfire can also be caused by water that enters through connectors. Check the connectors for loose wire ends. On waterproof connectors, check for damage where the wires enter the connector.*

7. Make sure the spark plug wire is secure. Push the spark plug cap and slightly rotate to clean the electrical connection between the plug and the connector. If the engine does not start, continue with Step 8.

8. Perform the *Spark Test* as described in this section. If there is a strong spark, perform Step 9. If there is no spark or if the spark is very weak, refer to *Ignition System Testing* in Chapter Nine.

> *NOTE*
> *Performing a spark test is the quickest way to isolate an ignition or fuel system problem. If a strong spark is recorded, the ignition system is working correctly. Refer to **Fuel System** in this chapter.*

9. Perform a basic cylinder compression test as follows:

a. On 2001-on models, turn the ignition switch off.
b. Turn off the fuel valve.
c. Remove the spark plug as described in Chapter Three.
d. Ground the spark plug shell against the cylinder head.
e. Place your finger over the spark plug hole.
f. Have an assistant operate the kickstarter. When the piston comes up on the compression stroke, pressure in the cylinder should force your finger from the spark plug hole. If so, the engine probably has sufficient compression to start the engine.

NOTE
*A compression problem may exist even though it seems good with the previous test. If the fuel and ignition systems are working correctly, perform the **Cylinder Leakdown Test** as described in this chapter. Also perform the **Cylinder Compression Test** as described in Chapter Three. If the leakdown test indicates a problem, or the compression is low, refer to **Engine Compression** in **Engine** in this chapter.*

Spark Test

Perform a spark test to determine if the ignition system is producing adequate spark. This test should be performed with a spark tester. A spark tester looks like a spark plug with an adjustable gap between the center electrode and grounded base. Because the voltage required to jump the spark tester gap is sufficiently larger than that of a normally gapped spark plug, the test results are more accurate than with a spark plug. Do not assume that because a spark jumped across a spark plug gap, the ignition system is working correctly.

Perform this test on the engine when it is both cold and hot, if possible. If the test results are positive for each test, the ignition system is considered to be working correctly.

CAUTION
After removing the spark plug cap and before removing the spark plug in Step 1, clean the area around the spark plug with compressed air. Dirt that falls into the cylinder causes rapid engine wear.

NOTE
The spark tester used in this procedure is available from Motion Pro (part No. 08-0122) and can be purchased through motorcycle dealerships.

1. Disconnect the spark plug cap. Check for the presence of water.
2. Inspect the spark plug for damage.
3. Connect a spark tester (**Figure 5**) or new spark plug to the spark plug cap and ground it against the engine. Position the spark tester or spark plug so the electrodes are visible. If the original spark plug was removed, position the spark tester or spark plug firing tip away from the open spark plug hole.

WARNING
If the original spark plug was removed, mount the spark tester or spark plug away from the spark plug hole in the cylinder head so the spark plug or tester cannot ignite gasoline vapors in the cylinder. If the engine is flooded, do not perform this test. The spark generated by the spark plug or spark tester can ignite fuel ejected through the spark plug hole.

4. Shift the transmission into neutral.
5. On 2001-on models, turn the ignition switch (**Figure 2**) on.

WARNING
Do not hold the spark tester, spark plug or connector or a serious electrical shock may result.

6. Turn the engine over with the kickstarter. A fat blue spark must be evident between the spark tester or spark plug terminals.
7. If there is a strong, blue spark, the ignition system is functioning properly. Check for one or more of the following possible malfunctions:
   a. Faulty fuel system component.
   b. Flooded engine.
   c. Engine damage (low compression).

8. If the spark was weak (white or yellow) or if there was no spark, check for one or more of the following conditions:

    a. Fouled or wet spark plug. If a spark jumps across a spark tester but not across the original spark plug, the plug is fouled. Repeat the spark test with a new spark plug.

    b. Loose or damaged spark plug cap connection. Hold the spark plug wire and turn the spark plug cap to tighten it. Then install the spark plug into the cap and repeat the spark test. If there is still no spark, bypass the plug cap as described in the next step.

    c. Check for a damaged spark plug cap. Hold the spark plug wire and unscrew the spark plug cap. Hold the end of the spark plug wire approximately 6 mm (1/4 in.) from the cylinder head as shown in **Figure 6**. Have an assistant turn the engine over and repeat the spark test. If there is a strong spark, the spark plug cap is faulty or its wire terminal was not contacting the terminal wire in the plug wire. Examine the end of the plug wire and the terminal in the plug cap for corrosion or damage. If necessary, repeat the test with a new plug cap.

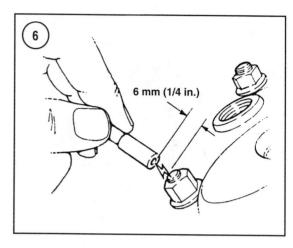

NOTE
Refer to Chapter Nine to test the problems identified in substeps d-j.

    d. Faulty engine stop switch.
    e. Faulty ignition switch (2001-on models).
    f. Loose or dirty electrical connections.
    g. Loose flywheel nut.
    h. Sheared flywheel key.
    i. Faulty ignition coil or faulty ignition coil ground wire connection.
    j. Faulty ICM unit or stator coil.

POOR ENGINE PERFORMANCE

If the engine runs, but performance is unsatisfactory, refer to the following procedure(s) that best describes the symptom(s).

Engine Starts but Stalls and is Hard to Restart

Check for the following:
1. Incorrect choke operation. This can be due to improper use or the choke valve is stuck in the carburetor.
2. Plugged fuel tank vent hose (**Figure 4**).
3. Plugged fuel hose, fuel shutoff valve or fuel strainer screen.
4. Clogged air filter.
5. Incorrect carburetor adjustment.

6. Incorrect float level adjustment.
7. Plugged carburetor jets.

NOTE
If a warm or hot engine will start with the choke on, or if a cold engine starts and runs until the choke is turned off, the pilot jet is probably plugged.

8. Contaminated or stale fuel.
9. Intake pipe air leak.
10. Plugged exhaust system. Check the muffler, especially if the motorcycle was just returned from storage.
11. Faulty ignition system component. Perform the spark test as described in this chapter when the engine is cold and then when the engine stalls and will not restart.

Engine Backfires, Cuts Out or Misfires During Acceleration

A backfire occurs when fuel is burned or ignited in the exhaust system.
1. A lean air/fuel mixture can cause these engine performance problems. Check for the following conditions:
    a. Incorrect float level adjustment.
    b. Plugged pilot jet or pilot system.
2. Loose exhaust pipe-to-cylinder head connection.
3. Intake air leak.
4. Remove the spark plug as described in Chapter Three. Check for carbon or other deposits stuck between the electrodes.
5. Make sure the spark plug gap is within specification. Refer to *Gap Bridging* in *Spark Plug* in Chapter Three for additional information.
6. Incorrect ignition timing or a damaged ignition system can cause these conditions. Note the following:
    a. Check for a loose flywheel nut or a sheared flywheel key.

b. Check the ICM connectors for water contamination.

c. If the previous steps did not determine the problem, perform the peak voltage tests in Chapter Nine to isolate the damaged ignition system component. Check the ignition timing as described in Chapter Nine.

NOTE
The ignition timing is controlled by the ICM and cannot be adjusted. Checking the ignition timing can be used to diagnose problems.

7. Check for the following engine component problems:
   a. Broken valve springs.
   b. Stuck or leaking valves.
   c. Worn or damaged camshaft lobes.
   d. Incorrect valve timing due to incorrect camshaft installation or a mechanical failure.

Engine Backfires on Deceleration

If the engine backfires when the throttle is released, check the following:
1. Lean carburetor pilot system.
2. Loose exhaust pipe-to-cylinder head connection.
3. Faulty ignition system component.
4. Check for the following engine component problems:
   a. Broken valve springs.
   b. Stuck or leaking valves.
   c. Worn or damaged camshaft lobes.
   d. Incorrect valve timing due to incorrect camshaft installation or a mechanical failure.

Poor Fuel Mileage

1. Clogged fuel system.
2. Dirty or clogged air filter.
3. Incorrect ignition timing.
4. Incorrect carburetor jetting.

Engine Will Not Idle or Idles Roughly

1. Clogged air filter element.
2. Poor fuel flow resulting from a partially clogged pilot jet, fuel valve, fuel strainer screen or fuel hose.
3. Contaminated or stale fuel.
4. Incorrect carburetor adjustment.
5. Leaking head gasket.
6. Intake air leak.
7. Incorrect ignition timing.
8. Low engine compression.

Low Engine Power

1. Support the motorcycle on a stand with the rear wheel off the ground and shift the transmission into neutral. Spin the rear wheel by hand. If the wheel spins freely, perform Step 2. If the wheel does not spin freely, check for the following conditions:
   a. Dragging brakes. If a wheel does not spin freely, refer to *Brakes* in this chapter.
   b. Damaged or binding drive chain. Refer to Chapter Ten and remove the drive chain and see if the condition improves.
   c. Damaged wheel bearings (Chapter Ten).
   d. Bent axle (Chapter Ten).
   e. Remove the rear axle. If the axle is tight, it may have seized to the wheel bearings. This will require new wheel bearings and possibly a new rear axle.
2. Test ride the motorcycle and accelerate quickly from first to second gear. If engine speed increased according to throttle position, perform Step 3. If the engine speed did not increase, check for one or more of the following problems:
   a. Slipping clutch.
   b. Warped clutch plates.
   c. Worn clutch plates.
   d. Weak or damaged clutch springs.
3. Test ride the motorcycle and accelerate lightly. If the engine speed increased according to throttle position, perform Step 4. If the engine speed did not increase, check for one or more of the following problems:
   a. Clogged air filter.
   b. Restricted fuel flow.
   c. Pinched fuel tank breather hose (**Figure 4**).
   d. Clogged or damaged muffler.

NOTE
A clogged exhaust system will prevent some of the burned exhaust gases from exiting the exhaust port at the end of the exhaust stroke. This condition effects the incoming air/fuel mixture on the intake stroke and reduces engine power.

4. Check for a retarded ignition timing as described in Chapter Nine. A decrease in power results when the plug fires later than normal.
5. Check for one or more of the following problems:
   a. Low engine compression.
   b. Worn spark plug.
   c. Fouled spark plug.
   d. Incorrect spark plug heat range.
   e. Weak ignition coil.
   f. Incorrect ignition timing caused by a defective ICM or ignition pulse generator.

g. Plugged carburetor passages.

h. Incorrect oil level.

i. Contaminated oil.

j. Worn or damaged valve train assembly.

k. Engine overheating. Refer to *Engine Overheating* in *Engine* in this chapter.

6. If the engine knocks when accelerating or when running at high speed, check for one or more of the following:

a. Incorrect type of fuel.

b. Lean fuel mixture.

c. Advanced ignition timing caused by a defective ICM.

NOTE
Other signs of advanced ignition timing are engine overheating and hard or uneven engine starting.

d. Excessive carbon buildup in combustion chamber.

e. Worn piston and/or cylinder bore. This condition will also occur at idle speed and is worse when the engine is cold.

Poor Idle or Low Speed Performance

1. Check for an incorrect idle drop adjustment. Refer to *Carburetor Adjustments* in Chapter Eight.

2. Check for air leaks caused by a damaged or loose intake tube and air filter housing hose clamps.

3. Perform the spark test as described in this chapter. Note the following:

a. If the spark is good, go to Step 4.

b. If the spark is weak, perform *Ignition System Testing* as described in Chapter Nine.

4. Check the ignition timing as described in Chapter Nine. If ignition timing is correct, perform Step 5. If the timing is incorrect, perform *Ignition System Testing* as described in Chapter Nine.

5. Check the fuel system as described in *Fuel System* in this chapter.

Poor High Speed Performance

1. Check ignition timing as described in Chapter Nine. If ignition timing is correct, perform Step 2. If the timing is incorrect, perform the peak voltage tests in Chapter Nine.

2. Check the fuel system as described in *Fuel System* in this chapter.

3. Check the valve clearance as described in Chapter Three. Note the following:

a. If the valve clearance is correct, perform Step 4.

b. If the clearance is incorrect, readjust the valves.

4. Incorrect valve timing and worn or damaged valve springs can cause poor high-speed performance. If the camshaft was timed just prior to the motorcycle experiencing this problem, the cam timing may be incorrect. If the cam timing was not set or changed, and all of the other inspection procedures in this section failed to locate the problem, inspect the camshaft and valve assembly as described in Chapter Four.

FUEL SYSTEM

The following section isolates common fuel system problems under specific complaints. If there is a good spark, poor fuel flow may be preventing the correct amount of fuel from being supplied to the spark plug. Troubleshoot the fuel system as follows:

1. Check that there is a sufficient amount of fuel in the tank.

2. Check for a clogged fuel tank breather hose (**Figure 4**).

3. After attempting to start the engine, remove the spark plug (Chapter Three) and check for the presence of fuel on the plug tip. Note the following:

a. If there is no fuel visible on the plug, check for a clogged fuel shutoff valve, fuel strainer screen or fuel line.

b. If there is fuel present on the plug tip, and the engine has spark, check for an excessive intake air leak or the possibility of contaminated or stale fuel.

NOTE
If the motorcycle was not used for some time, and was not properly stored, the gasoline may have gone stale, where lighter parts of the gasoline have evaporated. Depending on the condition of the fuel, a no-start condition can result. Stale gasoline has a strong smell that is noticeably different from fresh gasoline.

c. If there is an excessive amount of fuel on the plug, check for a clogged air filter or flooded carburetor.

Rich Mixture

The following conditions can cause a rich air/fuel mixture:

1. Clogged air filter.

2. Choke lever in closed position.

3. Float level too high.

4. Contaminated float valve seat.

5. Worn or damaged float valve and seat.

6. Worn needle jet or jet needle.
7. Leaking or damaged float.
8. Loose or damaged carburetor jets.
9. Incorrect carburetor jetting.
10. Flooded carburetor.

Lean Mixture

The following conditions can cause a lean air/fuel mixture:
1. Intake air leak.
2. Float level too low.
3. Clogged fuel line, fuel strainer screen or fuel shutoff valve.
4. Partially restricted fuel tank breather hose.
5. Plugged carburetor air vent hose.
6. Damaged float.
7. Damaged float valve.
8. Incorrect carburetor jetting.
9. Damaged throttle valve.
10. Clogged fuel jets.

ENGINE

Engine Smoke

The color of engine smoke can help diagnosis engine problems or operating conditions.

Black smoke

Black smoke is an indication of a rich air/fuel mixture where an excessive amount of fuel is being burned in the combustion chamber.

Blue smoke

Blue smoke indicates that the engine is burning oil in the combustion chamber as it leaks past worn valve stem seals and piston rings. Excessive oil consumption is another indicator of an engine that is burning oil. Perform the *Engine Compression Check* as described in Chapter Three to isolate the problem.

White smoke or steam

It is normal to see white smoke or steam from the exhaust after first starting the engine in cold weather. This is actually condensed steam formed by the engine during combustion. If the motorcycle is ridden far enough, the water cannot collect in the crankcase and should not become a problem. Once the engine heats up to normal operating temperature, the water evaporates and exits the engine through the crankcase vent system. However, if the motorcycle is ridden for short rides or repeatedly started and stopped and allowed to cool off without the engine getting warm enough, water will start to collect in the crankcase. With each short run of the engine, more water collects. As this water mixes with the oil in the crankcase, sludge is produced. Water sludge can eventually cause engine damage as it circulates through the lubrication system and blocks off oil passages.

Engine Compression

Problems with the engine top end will affect engine performance and drivability. When the engine is suspect, perform the cylinder leakdown test as described in this chapter and perform the engine compression test as described in Chapter Three. Interpret the results as described in each procedure to troubleshoot the suspect area.

Low

An engine can loose compression through the following areas:
1. Valves:
   a. Incorrect valve adjustment.
   b. Incorrect valve timing.
   c. Worn or damaged valve seats (valve and/or cylinder head).
   d. Bent valves.
   e. Weak or broken valve springs.
   f. Poor valve seating.
2. Cylinder head:
   a. Loose spark plug or damaged spark plug hole.
   b. Damaged cylinder head gasket.
   c. Warped or cracked cylinder head.

High

Excessive carbon build-up in the combustion chamber causes high engine compression.

Engine Overheating

1. Improper spark plug heat range.
2. Low oil level.
3. Oil not circulating properly.
4. Valves leaking.
5. Heavy engine carbon deposits on the piston crown or combustion chamber.
6. Dragging brake(s).
7. Slipping clutch.

Preignition

Preignition is the premature burning of fuel and is caused by hot spots in the combustion chamber. Glowing deposits in the combustion chamber, inadequate cooling or an overheated spark plug can all cause preignition. This is first noticed as a power loss but eventually results in damage to the internal parts of the engine because of higher combustion chamber temperatures.

Detonation

Commonly called spark knock or fuel knock, detonation is the explosion of fuel in the combustion chamber before the proper time of ignition. Severe damage can result. Use of low octane gasoline is a common cause of detonation.

Even when using a high octane gasoline, detonation can still occur. Other causes are over-advanced ignition timing, lean air/fuel mixture at or near full throttle, inadequate engine cooling, or the excessive accumulation of carbon deposits in the combustion chamber.

Power Loss

Refer to *Poor Engine Performance* in this chapter.

Engine Noises

Unusual noises are often the first indication of a developing problem. Investigate any new noises as soon as possible. Something that may be a minor problem, if corrected, could prevent the possibility of more extensive damage.

Use a mechanic's stethoscope or a small section of hose held near your ear (not directly on your ear) with the other end close to the source of the noise to isolate the location. Determining the exact cause of a noise can be difficult. If this is the case, consult with a professional mechanic to determine the cause. Do not disassemble major components until all other possibilities have been eliminated.

Consider the following when troubleshooting engine noises:

1. A knocking or pinging during acceleration is typically caused by using a lower octane fuel than recommended. May also be caused by poor fuel. Pinging can also be caused by an incorrect spark plug heat range or carbon build-up in the combustion chamber.

2. Slapping or rattling noises at low speed or during acceleration may be caused by excessive piston-to-cylinder wall clearance (piston slap).

> *NOTE*
> *Piston slap is easier to detect when the engine is cold and before the piston has expanded. Once the engine has warmed up, piston expansion reduces piston-to-cylinder clearance.*

3. A knocking or rapping while decelerating is usually caused by excessive rod bearing clearance.

4. A persistent knocking and vibration occurring every crankshaft rotation is usually caused by worn rod or main bearing(s). It can also be caused by broken piston rings or a damaged piston pin.

5. A rapid on-off squeal indicates a compression leak around the cylinder head gasket or spark plug.

6. If the valve train is noisy, check for the following:
   a. Excessive valve clearance.
   b. Worn or damaged camshaft.
   c. Loose or worn cam chain.
   d. Worn or damaged cam chain tensioner.
   e. Worn or damaged valve train components.
   f. Valve sticking in guide.
   g. Broken valve spring.
   h. Low oil pressure.
   i. Clogged cylinder oil hole or oil passage.

ENGINE LUBRICATION

An improperly operating engine lubrication system will quickly lead to engine seizure. Check the engine oil level as described in Chapter Three. Oil pump service is described in Chapter Six.

Cylinder Head Oil Check

The cylinder head is equipped with a check bolt that can be removed when the engine is run at idle

speed to check oil flow to the camshaft and valve train components. Refer to *Oil Flow Check* in *Engine Oil* in Chapter Three.

High Oil Consumption or Excessive Exhaust Smoke

1. Worn valve guides.
2. Worn valve guide seals.
3. Worn or damaged piston rings.
4. Improperly installed piston rings.
5. Worn cylinder bore.
6. Damaged cylinder head gasket.
7. External oil leak.

Low Oil Pressure

1. Low oil level.
2. Worn or damaged oil pump.
3. Clogged oil strainer screen.
4. Damaged oil pump drive gear.
5. Contaminated engine oil.
6. Infrequent engine oil changes.

High Oil Pressure

1. Clogged oil strainer.
2. Incorrect type engine oil.

No Oil Pressure

1. Low oil level.
2. Damaged oil pump.
3. Damaged oil pump drive gear.
4. Incorrect oil pump installation.
5. Internal oil leak.
6. Clogged internal oil passages.

Oil Level Too Low

1. Incorrect oil level.

2. Worn piston rings.
3. Worn cylinder.
4. Worn valve guides.
5. Worn valve guide seals.
6. Piston rings incorrectly installed during engine overhaul.
7. External oil leak.

Oil Contamination

1. Oil and filter not changed at specified intervals or when operating conditions demand more frequent changes.
2. Damaged head gasket.

CYLINDER LEAKDOWN TEST

A cylinder leakdown test can accurately pinpoint an engine compression loss from the head gasket, cylinder, valves and valve seats, and piston rings. This test is performed by applying compressed air to the cylinder through a tester and then measuring the leak rate percentage. A cylinder leakdown tester (**Figure 7**) and an air compressor are needed to perform this test.

When performing a leakdown test, set the engine at TDC on its compression stroke (valves closed). When the combustion chamber is pressurized, very little air should escape. However, the difficulty in performing a leakdown test on a single cylinder engine is in preventing the piston from moving as the combustion chamber starts to pressurize. Any piston movement will force the crankshaft to turn away from TDC and allow air to escape past an open valve.

Follow the tester manufacturer's directions along with the following information when performing a cylinder leakdown test.

1. Support the motorcycle on a work stand with the rear wheel off the ground.
2. Remove the air filter assembly (Chapter Three). Open and secure the throttle so that it is at its wide-open position.
3. Remove the fuel tank (Chapter Eight).
4. Remove the left crankcase cover (Chapter Nine).
5. Remove the spark plug (Chapter Three).
6. Connect the leakdown tester (**Figure 7**) into the spark plug hole following the manufacturer's instructions.
7. Turn the crankshaft *counterclockwise* and align the T mark (A, **Figure 8**) on the flywheel with the index mark on the left crankcase (B).
8. Disconnect the crankcase breather hose (**Figure 9**) from the crankcase breather separator.
9. Perform a cylinder leakdown test by applying air pressure to the combustion chamber. Follow the manufacturer's instructions while reading the leak

rate on the gauge. Listen for air leaking while noting the following:

> *NOTE*
> *If a large amount of air escapes from the exhaust pipe or through the carburetor, air is leaking through an open valve. Check the flywheel T mark (A, Figure 8) to make sure the engine is at TDC. If the T mark is properly aligned but there is still a large amount of air escaping from the engine, the crankshaft is off one revolution. Turn the engine 360° and realign the flywheel T mark as described in Step 7.*

a. Air leaking through the exhaust pipe indicates a leaking exhaust valve.

b. Air leaking through the carburetor indicates a leaking intake valve.

c. Air leaking through both the intake and exhaust valves indicates the engine is not set at TDC on its compression stroke or if it is on its compression stroke, the engine has suffered major damage.

d. Air leaking through the crankcase breather hose (**Figure 9**) indicates the rings are not sealing properly in the bore.

10. If the cylinder leakdown is 10 percent or higher, further service is required.

11. Disconnect the test equipment and install all of the parts previously removed.

CLUTCH

Basic clutch troubleshooting is listed in this section. Clutch service is covered in Chapter Six.

No Pressure at Clutch Lever

1. Incorrect clutch adjustment.
2. Broken clutch cable.
3. Damaged clutch lifter mechanism.

Clutch Lever Hard to Pull In

1. Dry or damaged clutch cable.
2. Kinked or stuck clutch cable.
3. Incorrect clutch cable routing.
4. Damaged clutch lifter mechanism.
5. Damaged clutch lifter plate bearing.

Rough Clutch Operation

Worn, grooved or damaged clutch hub and clutch housing slots.

Clutch Slip

If the engine speed increases without an increase in motorcycle speed, the clutch is probably slipping. The main causes of clutch slippage are:
1. No clutch lever free play.
2. Worn clutch plates.
3. Weak clutch springs.
4. Sticking or damaged clutch lifter.
5. Clutch plates contaminated by engine oil additive.

Clutch Drag

If the clutch will not disengage or if the motorcycle creeps with the transmission in gear and the clutch disengaged, the clutch is dragging. Some main causes of clutch drag are:
1. Excessive clutch lever free play.
2. Warped clutch plates.
3. Damaged clutch lifter assembly.
4. Damaged clutch housing snap ring or mainshaft groove.
5. High oil level.
6. Incorrect oil viscosity.
7. Engine oil additive being used.
8. Damaged clutch hub and clutch housing splines.

GEARSHIFT LINKAGE

The gearshift linkage assembly connects the shift pedal (external shift mechanism) to the shift drum (internal shift mechanism). Refer to Chapter Six and Chapter Seven to identify the components called out in this section.

Transmission Jumps Out of Gear

1. Damaged stopper arm.
2. Damaged stopper arm spring.
3. Loose stopper arm mounting bolt.
4. Worn shift drum cam.
5. Worn or damaged shift shaft return spring.

6. Worn or damaged shift drum grooves.
7. Worn or damaged gear dogs and slots.

Difficult Shifting

1. Incorrect clutch operation.
2. Incorrect oil viscosity.
3. Loose or damaged stopper arm assembly.
4. Bent shift fork shaft(s).
5. Bent or damaged shift fork(s).
6. Worn gear dogs or slots.
7. Damaged shift drum grooves.
8. Damaged shift shaft spindle.
9. Incorrect gearshift linkage installation.
10. Damaged shift lever assembly.

Shift Pedal Does Not Return

1. Bent shift shaft spindle.
2. Bent shift shaft engagement arm.
3. Damaged shift lever assembly.
4. Weak or damaged shift shaft arm return spring.
5. Shift shaft incorrectly installed (return spring incorrectly indexed around pin). Refer to A, **Figure 10**.

Excessive Engine/Transmission Noise

1. Loose or broken frame/engine mounts.
2. Damaged primary drive and driven gears or bearing.
3. Damaged transmission bearings or gears.

TRANSMISSION

Transmission symptoms are sometimes hard to distinguish from clutch symptoms. Refer to Chapter Seven for transmission service procedures. Prior to working on the transmission, make sure the clutch and gearshift linkage assembly are not causing the problem.

Difficult Shifting

1. Incorrect clutch operation.
2. Bent shift fork(s).
3. Damaged shift fork guide pin(s).
4. Bent shift fork shaft(s).
5. Damaged shift drum grooves.
6. Damaged gears.

Jumps Out of Gear

1. Loose or damaged shift drum cam mounting bolt.
2. Bent or damaged shift fork(s).
3. Bent shift fork shaft(s).
4. Damaged shift drum grooves.
5. Worn gear dogs or slots.

Incorrect Shift Lever Operation

1. Bent shift pedal or linkage.
2. Stripped shift pedal splines.
3. Damaged shift linkage.
4. Damaged shift shaft spindle.

Excessive Gear Noise

1. Worn or damaged transmission bearings.
2. Worn or damaged gears and bushings.
3. Excessive gear backlash.

Engine Vibration

1. Excessive crankshaft runout.
2. Damaged crankshaft bearings.
3. Bent connecting rod.
4. Twisted crankshaft.
5. Loose or damaged frame/engine mounts.

KICKSTARTER

The kickstarter mechanism is mounted inside the engine. The kick idle gear is mounted on the countershaft and the primary kick gear is mounted on the mainshaft. If the kickstarter fails to operate, first make sure the kick pedal is not slipping on the kick shaft splines. If the kick pedal is tight, remove the right crankcase cover (Chapter Six) and check the return spring and collar assembly (B, **Figure 10**) on the end of the kick shaft. If these parts are in good condition and assembled correctly, the problem is inside the engine and the crankcase will have to be disassembled. Refer to *Kickstarter* in Chapter Five.

DRIVE TRAIN NOISE

This section covers noises from the drive chain, clutch and transmission. While some drive train noises are normal, other noises may be a good indicator of a developing problem. The problem is recognizing the difference between a normal and abnormal noise. A new noise, no matter how minor, should be investigated.

1. Normal drive chain noise can be considered a low-pitched, continuous whining sound. The noise will vary, depending on the speed of the motorcycle and the terrain you are riding on, as well as proper lubrication, wear (both chain and sprocket) and alignment. When checking abnormal drive chain noise, consider the following:

    a. A dry chain will give off a loud whining sound. Clean and lubricate the drive chain at regular intervals as specified in Chapter Three.

    b. Check and adjust the drive chain as described in Chapter Three.

    c. Check chain wear at regular intervals, and replace it when it's overall length exceeds the wear limit specified in Chapter Three.

    d. Worn or damaged sprockets accelerate chain wear. Inspect the sprockets as described in Chapter Three.

    e. The chain sliders are in constant contact with the chain. Check each slider often for excessive wear and damage. A damaged chain slider will increase chain slack and can cause rapid wear against the frame or swing arm.

2. Investigate any noise that develops in the clutch. First, drain the engine oil (Chapter Three), checking for bits of metal or clutch plate material. If the oil is not contaminated or smells burnt, remove the clutch (Chapter Six) and inspect it for damage.

3. The transmission will exhibit more normal noises than the clutch, but like the clutch, a new noise in the transmission should be investigated. Drain the engine oil (Chapter Three) into a clean container. After the oil cools, wipe a small amount of oil on a finger and rub the finger and thumb together. Check for the presence of metallic particles. Inspect the oil in the drain pan for metal deposits. Wash hands after inspection.

NOTE
If metallic particles are found in Step 2 or Step 3, remove and inspect the clutch, then, if necessary, disassemble the engine and inspect the transmission.

ELECTRICAL TESTING

This section describes electrical troubleshooting and the use of test equipment.

Never assume anything and do not overlook the obvious, such as an electrical connector that has separated. Test the simplest and most obvious items first and try to make tests at easily accessible points on the motorcycle. Make sure to troubleshoot systematically.

Refer to the wiring diagrams at the end of the manual for component and connector identification.

Preliminary Checks and Precautions

Before starting any electrical troubleshooting, perform the following:

1. Disconnect each electrical connector in the suspect circuit and make sure there are no bent terminals in the electrical connector. A bent terminal will not connect to its mate, causing an open circuit.

2. Make sure the terminals are pushed all the way into the connector. If not, carefully push them in with a narrow blade screwdriver or a terminal tool.

3. Check the wires where they attach to the terminals for damage.

4. Make sure each terminal is clean and free of corrosion. Clean them, if necessary, and pack the connectors with dielectric grease.

5. Push the connector halves together. Make sure the connectors are fully engaged and locked together.

6. Never pull the wires when disconnecting a connector. Pull only on the connector housing.

Intermittent Problems

Problems that do not occur all the time can be difficult to isolate during testing. For example, when a problem only occurs when the motorcycle is ridden over rough roads (vibration) or in wet conditions (water penetration). Note the following:

1. Vibration. This is a common problem with loose or damaged electrical connectors.

    a. Perform a continuity test as described in the appropriate service procedure or under *Continuity Test* in this section.

    b. Lightly pull or wiggle the connectors while repeating the test. Do the same when checking the wiring harness and individual components, especially where the wires enter a housing or connector.

    c. A change in meter readings indicates a poor connection. Find and repair the problem or replace the part. Check for wires with cracked or broken insulation.

NOTE
An analog ohmmeter is useful when making this type of test. Slight needle movements are visibly apparent, which indicate a loose connection.

2. Heat. This is a common problem with connectors or joints that have loose or poor connections. As these connections heat up, the connection or joint expands and separates, causing an open circuit. Other heat related problems occur when a component starts to fail as it heats up.

    a. Troubleshoot the problem to isolate the circuit.

CAUTION
A heat gun will quickly raise the temperature of the component being tested. Do not apply heat directly to the ICM or use heat in excess of 60° C (140° F) on any electrical component.

    b. To check a connector, perform a continuity test as described in the appropriate service procedure or under *Continuity Test* in this section. Then repeat the test while heating the connector with a heat gun. If the meter reading was normal (continuity) when the connector was cold, and then fluctuated or read infinity when heat was applied, the connection is bad.

    c. To check a component, allow the engine to cool, and then start and run the engine. Note operational differences when the engine is cold and hot.

    d. If the engine will not start, isolate and remove the suspect component. Test it at room temperature and again after heating it with a heat gun. A change in meter readings indicates a temperature problem.

3. Water. When the problem occurs when riding in wet conditions or in areas with high humidity, start and run the engine in a dry area. Then, with the engine running, spray water onto the suspected component/circuit. Water-related problems often stop after the component heats up and dries.

Peak Voltage Testing

Peak voltage tests check the voltage output of the ignition coil, ignition pulse generator and exciter coil at normal cranking speed. These tests make it possible to identify ignition system problems quickly and accurately.

Peak voltage tests require a peak voltage adapter or tester. Refer to *Ignition System Testing* in Chapter Nine.

Ohmmeter

Use an ohmmeter to measure the resistance (in ohms) to current flow in a circuit or component.

Ohmmeters may be analog type (needle scale) or digital type (LCD or LED readout). Both types of ohmmeters have a switch that allows the user to select different ranges of resistance for accurate readings. The analog ohmmeter also has a set-adjust control which is used to zero or calibrate the meter (digital ohmmeters do not require calibration). Refer to the ohmmeter's instructions to determine the correct scale setting.

Use an ohmmeter by connecting its test leads to the circuit or component to be tested. If an analog meter is used, it must be calibrated by touching the test leads together and turning the set-adjust knob until the meter needle reads zero. When the leads are uncrossed, the needle should move to the other end of the scale, indicating infinite resistance.

During a continuity test, a reading of infinite resistance indicates there is an open in the circuit or component. A reading of zero indicates continuity, that is, there is no measurable resistance in the circuit or component. A measured reading indicates the actual resistance to current flow that is present in that circuit. Even though resistance is present, the circuit has continuity.

Continuity test

Perform a continuity test to determine the integrity of a circuit, wire or component. A circuit has continuity if it forms a complete circuit; that is, if there are no opens in either the electrical wires or components within the circuit. A circuit with an open, on the other hand, has no continuity.

This type of test can be performed with a self-powered test light or an ohmmeter. An ohmmeter gives the best results.

1. Attach one test lead (test light or ohmmeter) to one end of the part of the circuit to be tested.

2. Attach the other test lead to the other end of the part or the circuit to be tested.

3. The self-powered test light comes on if there is continuity. An ohmmeter reads 0 or low resistance if there is continuity. A reading of infinite resistance indicates no continuity; the circuit is open.

4. If testing a component, note the resistance and compare this to the specification if available.

HANDLING

When experiencing handling problems, check the following items:

1. Handlebars:
   a. Loose or damaged handlebar clamps.
   b. Incorrect handlebar clamp installation.
   c. Bent or cracked handlebar.
2. Tires:
   a. Incorrect tire pressure.
   b. Worn or damaged tires.
3. Wheels:
   a. Loose or damaged hub bearings.
   b. Loose or bent wheel axle.
   c. Damaged wheel.
   d. Loose axle nut.
   e. Excessive wheel run out.
   f. Damaged spokes.
4. Steering:
   a. Incorrect steering adjustment.
   b. Dry or damaged steering shaft bearings.
   c. Bent steering shaft or frame neck.
   d. Loose steering, fork tube and front wheel fasteners.
5. Front fork:
   a. Contaminated fork oil.
   b. Low fork oil level.
   c. Bent fork tubes.
   d. Plugged damper rod oil passage.
   e. Weak or damaged fork springs.
6. Swing arm:
   a. Damaged swing arm.
   b. Severely worn or damaged swing arm bushings.
   c. Improperly tightened swing arm pivot shaft.
   d. Bent or seized swing arm pivot shaft.
7. Shock absorber:
   a. Damaged damper rod.
   b. Leaking damper housing.
   c. Sagged or broken shock spring or spring seat.
   d. Loose or damaged shock mount bolts.
8. Shock linkage:
   a. Damaged linkage bushings.
   b. Seized or damaged linkage pivot bolts.
9. Frame:
   a. Damaged frame.
   b. Cracked or broken engine mount brackets.

BRAKES

The front and rear drum brakes are critical to riding performance and safety. Inspect the brakes frequently and repair or replace damaged parts immediately. Adjust the front and rear brakes as described in Chapter Three. Service the brake system as described in Chapter Thirteen.

Brake Squeal

1. Glazed or contaminated brake linings.
2. Glazed or contaminated brake drum.
3. Worn brake linings.
4. Worn brake drum.
5. Loose or damaged brake components.
6. Damaged brake panel.

Poor Brake Performance

1. Glazed brake linings.
2. Glazed brake drum.
3. Worn brake linings or drum.
4. Incorrect brake adjustment.
5. Worn or damaged brake cable or bent brake rod.
6. Severely worn or damaged brake return springs.
7. Incorrect brake arm and brake cam engagement angle.
8. Damaged brake arm and brake cam splines.
9. Incorrectly installed brake shoes.

Brakes Grab or Drag

1. Incorrect brake adjustment.
2. Severely worn or damaged brake return springs.
3. Brake drum out-of-round.
4. Warped or damaged brake shoe.
5. Cracked brake drum.
6. Damaged wheel hub.
7. Loose or severely worn wheel bearings.
8. Contaminated brake drum.
9. Damaged brake cable or bent brake rod.

Incorrect Brake Lever or Pedal Operation

1. Incorrect brake adjustment.
2. Bent brake lever or damage lever perch.
3. Bent or damaged brake pedal or pivot shaft bolt.
4. Severely worn or damaged brake lever mounting bolt.
5. Damaged brake cable or brake rod.
6. Missing or damaged brake cable or brake rod spring.
7. Dry, rusted or kinked brake cable.
8. Severely worn or damaged brake return springs.
9. Contaminated brake drum.
10. Incorrect brake arm and brake cam engagement angle.
11. Stripped brake arm and brake cam splines.

CHAPTER THREE

LUBRICATION, MAINTENANCE AND TUNE-UP

This chapter covers all of the required periodic service procedures that do not require major disassembly. Regular, careful maintenance is the best guarantee for a trouble-free, long-lasting motorcycle. All motorcycles, especially those designed for competition and off-road use require proper lubrication, maintenance and tune-up to maintain a high level of performance and to extend engine, suspension and chassis life.

Perform lubrication, maintenance and tune-ups following the correct procedures and exercising common sense. Always remember that damage can result from improper tuning and adjustment. In addition, if special tools or testers are required to perform a particular maintenance or adjustment procedure, use the correct tool or refer service to a dealership.

Tables 1-9 are at the end of this chapter.

PRE-RIDE INSPECTION

Perform the following inspections before the first ride of the day. All of these checks, unless noted otherwise, are described in this chapter. If a component requires service, refer to the appropriate section or chapter.

1. Make sure the fuel tank is full.
2. Check the fuel tank, fuel hose and fuel valve for leaks.
3. Check the engine oil level.
4. Check that the brakes work correctly.
5. Check the throttle for proper operation. Open the throttle all of the way and release it. The throttle must close fully and quickly with no binding or roughness. Repeat this step with the handlebar facing straight ahead and at both full lock positions. Then start the engine and open and release the throttle. It must open and close smoothly.
6. Check the front forks and rear shock absorber for oil leaks.
7. Place the motorcycle on a stand with the front wheel off the ground and check steering play (Chapter Eleven).
8. With the front wheel off the ground, turn the handlebar from side to side. Check that the control cables are routed properly and do not interfere with the handlebar or the handlebar controls.
9. Check the spark plug cap and high-tension lead for tightness.
10. Make sure all accessible fasteners are tightened correctly.
11. Make sure the air filter is clean.
12. Check each wheel for loose or damaged spokes. Check that the rear wheel rim lock is tight (Chapter Ten).
13. Check for excessively worn or damaged tires.
14. Check tire pressure.
15. Check for missing or damaged drive chain sliders. Check the slider mounted on and below the swing arm for excessive wear.
16. Lubricate the drive chain.

17. Check the drive chain alignment and adjustment.

18. Start the engine and then operate the engine stop switch. The engine should turn off.

19. Before trail riding, check to be sure needed tools and spare parts are packed.

MAINTENANCE AND SERVICE INTERVALS

The maintenance and service intervals in **Table 1** and **Table 2** are recommended by the manufacturer to help maintain motorcycle performance and ensure reliability.

Recording Maintenance and Engine Operating Times

Perform maintenance services at the intervals in this chapter. It is important to keep records on engine operating time, number of races completed and when and what services are performed. A small logbook is easy to use and can be kept handy in a toolbox for quick reference and note taking. The maintenance log section at the end of this manual can also be used to record service information.

Keep track of engine operating time by dividing the engine operating time into hours and tenths of an hour, where each five minutes represents 1/10 of an hour. For example, if the engine is run for approximately 45 minutes, 0.8 tenths would be recorded in a logbook. When the engine is run for approximately one hour and 25 minutes, 1.4 hours would be recorded. **Figure 1** shows how to divide one hour into tenths of an hour.

Record the date, the motorcycle operating time interval or number of races completed, and the type of service performed in the maintenance log section at the back of this manual. This information will provide an accurate record of the type of service performed. This record can also be used to schedule future service procedures at the correct time.

FUEL REQUIREMENTS

The engine is designed to operate on unleaded gasoline that is 86 pump octane/91 RON or higher. Unleaded fuel (automotive grade) is recommended. This fuel produces fewer engine emissions and spark plug deposits. Using a gasoline with a lower octane number can cause pinging or spark knock and lead to engine damage.

When choosing gasoline and filling the fuel tank, note the following:

1. In some areas of the United States and Canada, oxygenated fuels are used to reduce exhaust emis-

Engine operating time in minutes	Time recorded in tenths of an hour
5	0.1
10	0.2
15	0.3
20	0.3
25	0.4
30	0.5
35	0.6
40	0.7
45	0.8
50	0.8
55	0.9
60	1.0

sions. If using oxygenated fuel, make sure it meets the minimum octane requirements. Oxygenated fuels can damage plastic and paint. Do not spill fuel onto the fuel tank during filling. Wipe up spills with a soft cloth.

2. An ethanol (ethyl or grain alcohol) gasoline that contains more than 10 percent ethanol by volume may cause engine starting and performance related problems. Gasoline containing ethanol may be sold under the name Gasohol.

3. A methanol (methyl or wood alcohol) gasoline that contains more than 5 percent methanol by volume may cause engine starting and performance related problems. Gasoline that contains methanol must have corrosion inhibitors to protect the metal, plastic and rubber parts in the fuel system from damage.

4. Gasoline that contains more than 15 percent MTBE (Methyl Tertiary Butyl Ether) should not be used.

TUNE-UP

Perform tune-up procedures in a logical order. For example, some procedures must be done with the engine cold and others with the engine at operating temperature. Check the valve clearance when the engine is cold; adjust the carburetor and drain the engine oil when the engine is hot. Also, because the engine needs to run as well as possible when adjusting the carburetor, service the air filter and spark plug first. If the carburetor is adjusted and then the air filter is found to need service, the carburetor will require readjustment.

On models sold in California, an emission control label (**Figure 2**) is attached either to the rear fender (2003 models) or on the inside of the left fuel tank shroud (2004-on models). This label lists tune-up, fuel and engine oil information.

TEST RIDE

The test ride is an important part of the tune-up and service procedures because it helps determine

whether the motorcycle is ready to ride or if it needs additional work. When test riding a motorcycle, always start slowly and ride it in a safe place away from people and other vehicles. Concentrate on areas that were serviced and notice how these components affect other systems. If the brakes were serviced, check their operation at slower speeds and with moderate pressure before testing at higher speeds. Do not continue to ride the motorcycle if the engine, brakes or any suspension or steering component is not working correctly.

AIR FILTER

Never run the engine without a properly oiled and installed air filter. Likewise, running the engine with a dry or damaged air filter allows unfiltered air to enter the engine. A well-oiled but dirty or clogged air filter reduces the amount of air that enters the engine and causes a rich air/fuel mixture, resulting in poor engine starting, spark plug fouling and reduced engine performance. Frequent air filter inspection and cleaning is a critical part of minimizing engine wear and maintaining engine performance. **Figure 3** shows dirt that passed through an improperly serviced air filter.

Table 1 and **Table 2** list intervals for cleaning the air filter. These intervals are only guidelines, however. Clean the air filter more often when riding in wet, sandy or dusty conditions or under severe operating conditions.

NOTE
For competition riders, it is a good idea to have one or more pre-oiled air filters stored in plastic bags that can be installed between motos when conditions require filter replacement. Do not attempt to clean an air filter and reuse it between motos because there may not be enough time to properly dry the filter. An air filter that was damp when oiled will not trap fine dust. Make sure the air filter is dry before oiling it.

Removal/Installation

1. Remove the left side cover (Chapter Fourteen).
2. Pull the cover strap (A, **Figure 4**) and disconnect it from the bottom of the air box.
3. Remove the air box cover (B, **Figure 4**).
4. Push and release the air filter strap (A, **Figure 5**) and remove the air filter (B).
5. Pinch the air filter in several places and replace it if any foam breaks off, indicating the air filter has deteriorated. Replace the air filter if it is torn or damaged. If the air filter is okay, clean and oil the filter as

described in this section. Make sure both ends of the air filter (**Figure 6**) seat flush against the holder.

6. Check inside the air box for dirt and other debris that may have passed through or around the air filter. Wipe the inside of the air box with a clean rag.

7. Check the O-ring installed inside the cover and replace if damaged.

8. Make sure the filter strap cotter pin (C, **Figure 5**) is properly locked at its upper pivot point.

9. Check the air filter cover rubber strap and replace if damaged.

10. Install the air filter (B, **Figure 5**) by aligning its holder with the connecting tube inside the air box. Hold the air filter in place and secure with the air filter strap (A, **Figure 5**). Make sure the strap is securely locked over the tab inside the air box.

11. Install the air filter cover (B, **Figure 4**) and then pull and lock the cover strap (A, **Figure 4**). Make sure the strap is securely locked over the tab on the outside of the air box.

12. Install the left side cover (Chapter Fourteen).

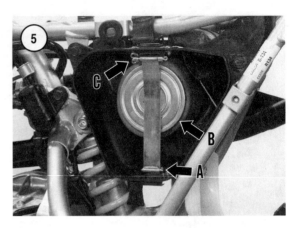

Cleaning and Reoiling

1. Remove the air filter as described in this section.

2. Remove the air filter (**Figure 6**) from the holder.

3. Before cleaning the air filter (A, **Figure 7**), check it for brittleness, separation or other damage. Replace the air filter if it is damaged or if parts of the filter flake off when pinched. If there is no damage, clean the air filter as follows.

WARNING
Do not clean the air filter or its holder with gasoline.

4. Soak the air filter in a container filled with a high flash point solvent, kerosene or an air filter cleaning solution. Gently squeeze the filter to dislodge and remove the oil and dirt from the filter pores. Swish the filter around in the cleaner while repeating this step a few times, then remove the filter and set it aside to dry.

5. Fill a clean pan with warm soapy water.

6. Submerge the air filter into the cleaning solution and gently work the soap solution into the filter pores. Soak and squeeze the air filter gently to clean it.

CAUTION
Do not wring or twist the air filter when cleaning it. This could damage the filter pores or tear the filter loose at a seam and allow unfiltered air to enter the engine.

7. Rinse the air filter under water while gently squeezing it.

8. Repeat these steps until there are no signs of dirt being rinsed from the air filter.

9. After cleaning the air filter, inspect it and replace it if it is torn or damaged. Do not run the engine with a damaged air filter, as it will allow dirt to enter and damage the engine.

10. Set the air filter aside and allow it to dry.

CAUTION
An air filter that was damp when oiled will not trap fine dust. Make sure the air filter is dry before oiling it.

11. Clean the holder (B, **Figure 7**) in solvent and dry with compressed air. Replace the holder if damaged.

12. Wear a pair of disposable rubber gloves when oiling the filter. Oil the air filter as follows:

   a. Place the air filter into a suitable size plastic storage bag.

CAUTION
Do not use engine oils to lubricate foam air filters. Foam air filter oil is specifically formulated for easy and thorough application into the filter pores and provides a tacky viscous medium to trap air borne contaminants. Oils are too thin to remain suspended in the filter; the oil

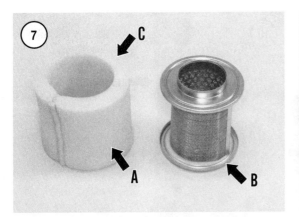

3

will be drawn into the engine and allow dirt to pass through the filter.

b. Pour foam air filter oil into the bag and onto the air filter to soak it.

c. Gently squeeze and release the air filter, from the outside of the bag, to soak the filter oil into the air filter pores. Repeat until all of the filter pores are saturated.

d. Remove the air filter from the bag and check the pores for uneven oiling. Light or dark areas on the filter indicate this. If necessary, work more oil into the filter and repeat substep c.

e. When the filter is oiled evenly, squeeze the filter a final time to remove excess oil.

f. Remove the air filter from the bag.

13. Apply a light coat of grease onto both ends of the air filter's sealing surface (C, **Figure 7**).

> *CAUTION*
> *Dirt will bypass the air filter if it's not properly installed on the holder.*

14. Slide the air filter over the holder and seat both ends flush against the holder shoulders.

15. Install the air filter as described in this section.

16. Pour the left over air filter oil from the bag back into the bottle for future use.

CRANKCASE BREATHER
(1992-2000 MODELS)

Inspection

Remove the drain plug from the crankcase breather hose and drain out all residue from the hose at the interval indicated in **Table 1** or **Table 2**. Perform this operation more often if a considerable amount of riding is done at full throttle or in the rain. Install the drain plug, making sure the clamp is tight.

AIR BOX DRAIN

Inspection

Periodically, or after riding in wet conditions, squeeze the plug in the bottom of the air box (**Figure 8**) to drain water and other contaminants. Make sure the drain is clamped tightly to the air box.

ENGINE OIL

If the motorcycle is operated under normal or moderate off-road and trail conditions, change the oil at the intervals specified in **Table 1** or **Table 2**. If the motorcycle is used in competition or under other severe conditions, the oil breaks down and gets dirty quicker and should be changed more frequently than recommended.

Refer to *Engine Oils* in *Shop Supplies* in Chapter One for information on engine oil selection.

Level Check

Check the engine oil level using the dipstick cap (**Figure 9**) mounted on the right crankcase cover.

1. If the engine is cold, start and run the engine for 3-5 minutes. Turn the engine off and support the motorcycle so the seat is level. Wait 2-3 minutes for the oil to drain back into the crankcase before checking the oil level.

CAUTION
Do not check the oil level with the motorcycle on its sidestand; the oil will flow away from the dipstick and result in a false reading.

2. Clean the area around the dipstick cap to prevent debris from falling into the engine. Remove the dipstick cap (**Figure 9**) and wipe the dipstick clean.

3. Reinsert the dipstick cap into the threads but do not screw it in.

4. Remove the dipstick cap and check the oil level. The oil level should be between the upper and lower level marks (**Figure 10**).

5. If the oil level is near or below the lower level mark (**Figure 10**) add the recommended oil (**Table 4**) to correct the level. Add oil while checking the level to avoid overfilling.

6. Replace the O-ring on the dipstick cap if it is cracked or damaged.

7. Install the dipstick cap (**Figure 9**) and tighten securely.

8. If the oil level is too high, do the following:
   a. Remove the dipstick cap (**Figure 9**) and draw out the excess oil using a syringe or suitable pump.
   b. Recheck the oil level and adjust if necessary.
   c. Install the dipstick cap and tighten securely.

Change

WARNING
Prolonged contact with oil may cause skin cancer. Wash hands thoroughly with soap and water after contacting engine oil.

NOTE
Never dispose of engine oil in the trash, on the ground or down a storm drain. Many service stations and oil retailers accept used oil for recycling. Do not combine other fluids with engine oil for recycling.

NOTE
Running the engine heats the oil, which allows the oil flow more freely and carry contamination and sludge with it when drained.

1. Start the engine and let it warm to normal operating temperature, then shut if off.

2. Support the motorcycle upright when draining the engine oil to ensure complete draining. Clean the area around the drain bolt (**Figure 11**).

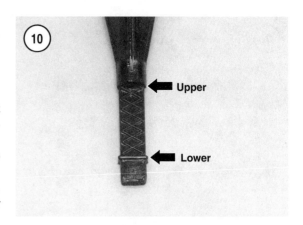
Upper
Lower

CAUTION
The engine and exhaust system are hot. Work carefully when removing the oil drain bolt to avoid contacting the oil or hot engine parts.

3. Place a clean drip pan under the crankcase and remove the oil drain bolt and washer (**Figure 11**).

4. Remove the dipstick cap (**Figure 9**) to help speed up the flow of oil. Allow the oil to drain completely.

5. Replace the drain bolt gasket if leaking or damaged.

6. Install the oil drain bolt and gasket and tighten to 24 N•m (18 ft.-lb.). Wipe up oil spilled on the skid plate.

NOTE
*Before filling the engine with oil, check the engine oil strainer screen cleaning intervals in **Table 1** or **Table 2**. If it is time to clean the screen, do so before filling the engine with oil. Refer to **Engine Oil Strainer Screen** in this chapter.*

7. Support the motorcycle on a stand with the seat in a level position.

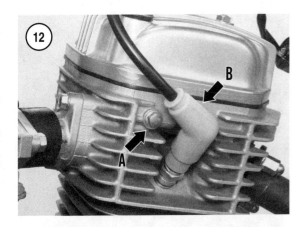

CAUTION
Do not run the engine above idle speed. If the oil passage is clogged, engine damage could result.

4. Loosen, but do *not* remove, the oil check bolt (A, **Figure 12**). Oil should immediately flow out of the bolt hole. Note the following:

  a. If oil does not flow out, turn the engine off. Remove the check bolt and check for any sign of contamination. If the bolt hole opening is clear, oil is not flowing to the engine top end. Inspect the oil pump as described in Chapter Six and the engine oil strainer screen as described in this chapter.

  b. If oil flows out, tighten the bolt securely and allow the engine to run while checking the bolt for leaks. Turn the engine off. If oil leaked past the bolt after the bolt was tightened, remove the bolt and install a new washer. Reinstall the bolt and run the engine again to check for leaks. Wipe up any oil from the cylinder head.

5. Tighten the cylinder head oil check bolt (A, **Figure 12**) securely.

ENGINE OIL STRAINER SCREEN

Removal/Cleaning

An engine oil strainer screen (**Figure 13**) is mounted behind the right crankcase cover and filters engine oil before it enters the oil pump. **Table 1** and **Table 2** list service intervals for removing and cleaning the oil strainer screen. Also, clean the oil strainer screen whenever the right crankcase cover is removed from the engine or whenever the engine has experienced a lubricating or overheating problem.

1. Remove the right crankcase cover (Chapter Six).
2. Remove the oil strainer screen (**Figure 13**).
3. Clean and inspect the oil strainer screen. Replace the screen if damaged.
4. Installation is the reverse of these steps. The sides of oil strainer screen are tapered (**Figure 14**). Install the oil strainer screen by inserting its narrow end into the engine first.

8. Insert a funnel into the oil filler hole and fill the engine with the correct weight (**Table 4**) and quantity of oil (**Table 5**).
9. Remove the funnel. Make sure the dipstick cap O-ring is in place and install the dipstick cap (**Figure 9**).
10. Start the engine and let it idle. Check the drain bolt for leaks.
11. If servicing a rebuilt engine, check the oil flow to the engine top end as described in *Oil Flow Check* in this section.
12. Turn the engine off after 2-3 minutes and check the oil level as described in this chapter. Adjust the oil level if necessary.

Oil Flow Check

The cylinder head oil check bolt (A, **Figure 12**) is located on the right side of the cylinder head and is used to check oil flow to the cylinder head and camshaft. Perform this check after reassembling the engine or when troubleshooting the lubrication system.

1. Start the engine and support it on its sidestand.
2. Place a shop cloth under the oil check bolt to catch the oil that should flow out.
3. Start the engine and run at idle speed.

ENGINE COMPRESSION CHECK

A cranking compression test checks the internal condition of the engine (piston rings, piston, head gasket, valves and cylinder). It is a good idea to check compression at each tune-up, record it and compare it with the reading obtained at the next tune-up.

Use a screw-in type compression gauge with a flexible adapter (**Figure 15**). Before using the gauge, check that the rubber gasket on the end of the adapter is not cracked or damaged; this gasket seals the cylinder to ensure accurate compression readings.

1. Run the engine until it reaches normal operating temperature, then turn it off.

2. On 2001-on models, turn the ignition switch off.

3. Remove the spark plug as described in this chapter.

4. Lubricate the threads of the compression gauge adapter with a small amount of antiseize compound and thread the gauge into the spark plug hole. Tighten the hose by hand to form a good seal.

> *CAUTION*
> *When the spark plug lead is disconnected, the electronic ignition will produce the highest voltage possible. This can damage the CDI or other ignition component. To protect the ignition system, make sure the ignition switch is turned off.*

5. Open the throttle completely, press the engine stop switch and kick the engine over while reading the compression gauge until there is no further increase in compression shown on the tester gauge. The compression reading should increase on each stroke. Record the reading and relieve the tester pressure valve.

6. Refer to **Table 8** for the standard compression pressure reading. If the compression reading is low, go to Step 7. If the compression reading is high, go to Step 8.

7. A low compression reading can be caused by the following:
   a. Incorrect valve adjustment.
   b. Worn piston rings, piston or cylinder bore.
   c. Leaking valve seat.
   d. Damaged cylinder head gasket.
   e. Combination of two or more listed conditions.

To isolate the problem to a valve or ring problem, perform a wet compression test. Pour about a teaspoon of engine oil into the spark plug hole. Repeat the compression test and record the reading. If the compression increases significantly, the valves are good but the rings are probably worn or defective. If there is little difference between the wet and dry readings, the problem is probably due to leaking or damaged valves and valve seats.

> *NOTE*
> *An engine with low compression cannot be tuned to maximum performance.*

8. A high compression reading can be caused by excessive carbon deposits on the piston crown or combustion chamber.

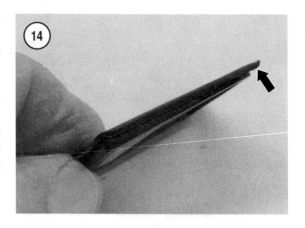

9. Remove the compression gauge. Reinstall the spark plug as described in this chapter.

IGNITION TIMING

Refer to Chapter Nine.

SPARK PLUG

Removal

Careful removal of the spark plug is important in preventing dirt from entering the combustion chamber. It is also important to know how to remove a plug that is seized, or is resistant to removal. Forcing a seized plug can destroy the threads in the cylinder head.

1. Blow any dirt that has accumulated around the spark plug.

> *CAUTION*
> *Dirt that falls through the spark plug hole will cause engine wear and damage.*

2. Twist the spark plug cap (B, **Figure 12**) back and forth while pulling it upward. Pulling on the wire instead of the cap may damage the wire or loosen the wire-to-cap connection. When the cap is free, hold

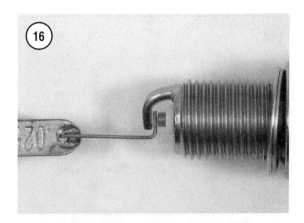

the wire and try to twist the cap lightly to make sure the connection is tight.

CAUTION
The spark plug porcelain can be easily damaged from mishandling. Make sure the spark plug socket fits the plug fully before removing the plug.

3. Remove the spark plug with the correct size spark plug socket. If the plug is seized or drags excessively during removal, stop and perform the following:
   a. Apply penetrating lubricant, such as Liquid Wrench or WD-40 and allow it to stand for about 15 minutes.
   b. If the plug is completely seized, apply moderate pressure in both directions with the wrench. Only attempt to break the seal so lubricant can penetrate under the spark plug and into the threads. If this does not work, and the engine can still be started, install the spark plug cap and start the engine. Allow to completely warm up. The heat of the engine may be enough to expand the parts and allow the plug to be removed.
   c. When a spark plug is loose, but drags excessively during removal, apply penetrating lubricant around the spark plug threads. Turn

the plug in (clockwise) to help distribute the lubricant onto the threads. Slowly remove the plug, working it in and out of the cylinder head while continuing to add lubricant. Do no reuse the spark plug.
   d. Inspect the threads in the cylinder head for damage. Clean and true the threads with a spark plug thread-chaser. Apply a thick grease onto the thread-chaser threads before using it. The grease will help trap some of the debris cut from the threads to prevent it from falling into the engine. Severely damaged spark plug threads will require removal of the cylinder head (Chapter Four) and repair.
4. Inspect the plug carefully as described in *Reading/ Inspection* in this section.

Gap Measurement

Use only a wire feeler gauge when measuring spark plug gap.
1. If installing a new spark plug, remove the small terminal adapter installed on the end of the plug.
2. Refer to the spark plug gap listed in **Table 8**. Select the correct size wire feeler gauge and try to slide it past the gap between both electrodes (**Figure 16**). If there is a slight drag as the wire gauge passes through the gap, the setting is correct. If there is no drag or if the wire will not pull through, bend the side electrode with the gapping tool (**Figure 17**) to change the gap, then remeasure with the wire gauge.

CAUTION
Never try to close the electrode gap by tapping the spark plug on a solid surface. This can damage the plug internally. Always use the gapping/adjusting tool to open or close the gap.

Installation

1. Wipe a small amount of antiseize compound to the plug threads before installing the spark plug. Do not allow the compound to get on the electrodes.
2. Screw the spark plug in by hand until it seats. Very little effort should be required; if force is necessary, the plug may be cross-threaded. Unscrew it and try again.
3. Tighten the spark plug to 14 N•m (10 ft.-lb.) or turn it 1/4 turn after it seats with the plug wrench.

NOTE
Do not overtighten the spark plug. This may crush the gasket and cause a compression leak or damage the cylinder head threads.

4. Press the plug cap (B, **Figure 12**) onto the spark plug.

Selection

The proper spark plug is very important in obtaining maximum performance and reliability. The condition of a used spark plug can tell a trained mechanic or experienced rider a lot about engine condition and carburetion. **Table 8** lists standard and both hot and cold spark plugs.

> *NOTE*
> *A hotter or cooler spark plug does not make a hotter or cooler spark. Heat range numbers determine how quickly a plug resists the transfer of heat into the cylinder head.*

If the engine is run in hot climates, at high speed or under heavy loads for prolonged periods, a spark plug with a colder heat range may be required. A colder plug quickly transfers heat away from its firing tip and to the cylinder head. This is accomplished by a short path up the ceramic insulator and into the body of the spark plug (**Figure 18**). By transferring heat quickly, the plug remains cool enough to avoid overheating and preignition problems. If the engine is run slowly for prolonged periods, this type of plug will foul and result in poor performance. A colder plug will not cool down a hot engine.

If the engine is run in cold climates or at a slow speed for prolonged periods, a spark plug with a hotter heat range may be required. A hotter plug slowly transfers heat away from its firing tip and to the cylinder head. This is accomplished by a long path up the ceramic insulator and into the body of the plug (**Figure 18**). By transferring heat slowly, the plug remains hot enough to avoid fouling and buildup. If the engine is run in hot climates for fast or prolonged periods, this type of plug will overheat, cause preignition problems and possible melt the electrode. Damage to the piston and cylinder assembly is possible.

When running a stock engine, changing to a different heat range plug is normally not required. Changing to a different heat range plug may be necessary when operating a motorcycle with a modified engine. This type of change is usually based on a recommendation made by the engine builder. Experience in reading spark plugs is also required when trying to determine if a different heat range plug is required. When installing a different heat range plug, go one step hotter or colder from the recommended plug. Do not try to correct poor carburetor or ignition problems by using different spark plugs. This will only compound

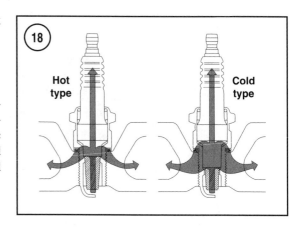

the existing problem(s) and possibly lead to severe engine damage.

The reach (length) of a plug is also important (**Figure 19**). A shorter than normal plug causes hard starting, reduce engine performance and carbon buildup on the exposed cylinder head threads. A longer than normal plug can hit and damage the top of the piston. These same conditions can occur if the correct length plug is used without a gasket. Trying to thread a spark plug into threads with carbon buildup may damage the threads in the cylinder head.

Reading/Inspection

The spark plug is an excellent indicator of how the engine is operating. By correctly evaluating the condition of the plug, engine problems can be diagnosed. To correctly read a spark plug, perform the following:

1. If using a new spark plug, remove it from the box and inspect it. Measure the gap as described in this section. If necessary, set the gap as described in this section.

2. Refer to *Removal* and *Installation* in this section when removing and installing the spark plug during this procedure.

3. If a new plug was installed, ride the motorcycle for approximately 15 to 20 minutes so that it will begin to color. Then continue with Step 4.

4. Accelerate on a straight road at full throttle. Then push the engine stop switch, pull the clutch lever in and coast to a stop. Do not stop by downshifting the transmission.

5. Remove the spark plug and examine its firing tip while noting the following:

   a. Inspect the spark plug with a magnifying glass or spark plug reader.

   b. **Figure 20** and the following paragraphs provide a description, as well as common causes for each of the conditions.

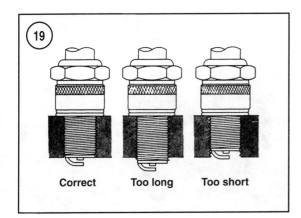

Correct   Too long   Too short

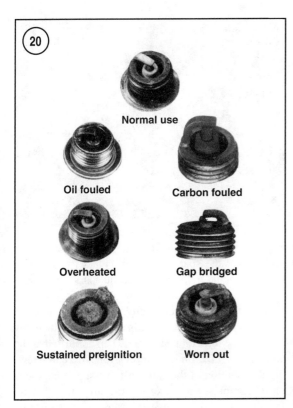

Normal use

Oil fouled   Carbon fouled

Overheated   Gap bridged

Sustained preignition   Worn out

CAUTION
In all cases, when a spark plug is abnormal, find the cause of the problem before continuing engine operation. Severe engine damage is possible when abnormal plug readings are ignored.

Normal condition

The porcelain insulator around the center electrode is clean and colorless. There should be a gray ring around the center electrode where it separates from the porcelain. No erosion or rounding of the electrodes or abnormal gap is evident. This indicates an engine that has properly adjusted carburetion, ignition timing and proper fuel mixture. This heat range

of plug is appropriate for the conditions in which the engine has been operated. The plug can be reused.

Oil fouled

The plug is wet with black, oily deposits on the electrodes and insulator. The electrodes do not show wear. Replace the spark plug.
Possible causes include:
1. Incorrect carburetor jetting.
2. Float level set too high.
3. Clogged air filter.
4. Faulty ignition component.
5. Spark plug heat range too cold.
6. Low engine compression.
7. Engine not properly broken in.

Carbon fouled

The plug is black with a dry, sooty deposit on the entire plug surface. This dry sooty deposit is conductive and can create electrical paths that bypass the electrode gap. This often results in misfiring of the plug. Replace the spark plug.
Possible causes include:
1. Rich fuel mixture.
2. Spark plug heat range too cold.
3. Clogged air filter.
4. Too much oil applied to air filter during service.
5. Faulty ignition component.
6. Low engine compression.
7. Prolonged idling.

Overheating

The plug is dry and the insulator has a white or light gray cast. The insulator may also appear blistered. The electrodes may have a burnt appearance and there may be metallic specks on the center electrode and porcelain. This material is being removed from the piston crown. Replace the spark plug.
Possible causes include:
1. Lean fuel mixture.
2. Spark plug heat range too hot.
3. Faulty ignition component.
4. Air leak at the exhaust port or in the intake boot.
5. Overtightened spark plug.
6. No crush washer on spark plug.
7. Spark plug heat range too hot.
8. Modified air box (holes drilled in sides of air box).
9. Less-restrictive exhaust system.

3

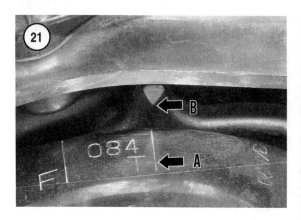

Gap bridging

The plug is clogged with deposits between the electrodes. The engine may run with a bridged spark plug, but it will misfire. Clean the spark plug gap or replace the spark plug if damaged.

Possible causes include:

1. Excessive carbon deposits in the combustion chamber.
2. Incorrect oil type.
3. Incorrect fuel or fuel contamination.

Preignition

The plug electrodes are severely eroded or melted. This condition can lead to severe engine damage. Replace the spark plug.

Possible causes include:

1. Faulty ignition system component.
2. Spark plug heat range too hot.
3. Air leaks.
4. Excessive carbon deposits in the combustion chamber.

Worn out

The center electrode is rounded from normal combustion. There is no indication of abnormal combustion or engine conditions.

VALVE CLEARANCE

Measurement/Adjustment

> *NOTE*
> *Do not check or adjust the valve clearance when the air or engine temperature is above 35° C (95° F).*

1. Support the motorcycle on a stand so the seat is level.
2. Remove the cylinder head cover (Chapter Four).

3. Remove the left crankcase cover (Chapter Nine).
4. Remove the spark plug. This makes it easier to turn the engine by hand. Cover the spark plug opening to prevent items from falling into the engine.
5. Turn the flywheel counterclockwise and align the T mark on the flywheel (A, **Figure 21**) with the index mark on the left crankcase (B). Then confirm that the engine is at TDC on its compression stroke by viewing the position of the camshaft lobes. The engine is on its compression stroke when both cam lobes are facing down and the valve adjusters can be moved by hand. If not, turn the crankshaft one full revolution (360°) counterclockwise and realign the T mark.
6. Check the clearance of both the intake and exhaust valves by inserting a flat feeler gauge between the valve adjuster and the valve stem (**Figure 22**). Refer to **Table 8** for the valve clearance. When the clearance is correct, there will be a slight drag or resistance on the feeler gauge when it is inserted and withdrawn.
7. To correct the clearance, loosen the locknut (A, **Figure 23**) and turn the valve adjuster (B) until the valve clearance is correct. Hold the valve adjuster to prevent it from turning and tighten the locknut to 10 N•m (88 in.-lb.).
8. Recheck the valve clearance. If the clearance changed when the locknut was tightened, loosen the locknut and readjust the valve clearance. Repeat un-

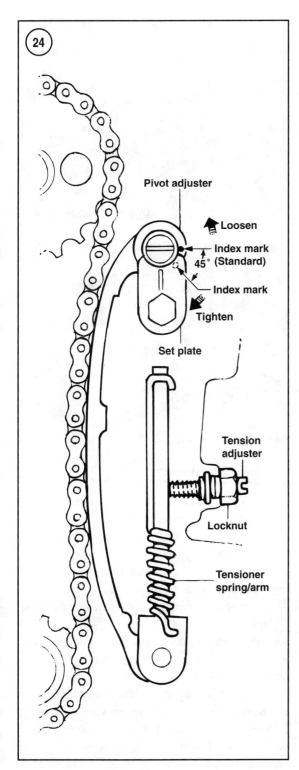

Pivot adjuster

Loosen

**Index mark
(Standard)**

45°

Index mark

Tighten

Set plate

**Tension
adjuster**

Locknut

**Tensioner
spring/arm**

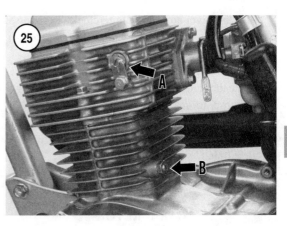

11. Install the cylinder head cover (Chapter Four).

CAM CHAIN TENSION

Inspection/Adjustment

In time, cam chain stretch and chain guide wear will increase chain play or slack. This will cause engine noise and if neglected too long can cause engine damage. Adjust the cam chain tension at the intervals specified in **Table 1** or **Table 2** or whenever chain noise seems excessive.

Refer to **Figure 24** to identify the cam chain tensioner assembly. Note that there are two adjusters: pivot adjuster (A, **Figure 25**) and tensioner adjuster (B).

1. Start the engine and let it reach normal operating temperature. Then turn the engine off.

2. Loosen the pivot adjuster set plate bolt (**Figure 24**).

3. Refer to **Figure 24** and note the index mark on the pivot adjuster and its standard position. Turn the pivot adjuster clockwise so its index mark is 45° below the standard position.

> *NOTE*
> *Do not turn the pivot adjuster more than 45° as specified in Step 3 or the tensioner will be too tight.*

4. Tighten the pivot adjuster set plate bolt (**Figure 24**).

5. Loosen the locknut (**Figure 24**) and turn the tensioner adjuster (B, **Figure 25**) counterclockwise to loosen it. This will automatically tighten the tensioner arm.

6. Tighten the tensioner adjuster (B, **Figure 25**) and then tighten its locknut to 12 N•m (106 in.-lb.).

7. Loosen the pivot adjuster set plate bolt (**Figure 24**).

til the valve clearance is correct after the locknut is tightened.

9. Rotate the crankshaft two complete revolutions and repeat Step 6 to make sure the adjustment is correct. If the clearance is incorrect, readjust the valve(s) until the clearance is correct.

10. Install the left crankcase cover (Chapter Nine).

8. Turn the pivot adjuster counterclockwise and set its index mark at its standard position (**Figure 24**). Tighten the set plate bolt.

9. Start the engine and run at idle speed.

10. Note the cam chain noise. If the chain is too tight or too loose, loosen the pivot adjuster set plate bolt and turn the pivot adjuster as required to fine tune the cam chain. Tighten the pivot adjuster (A, **Figure 25**) set plate bolt.

11. Turn the engine off.

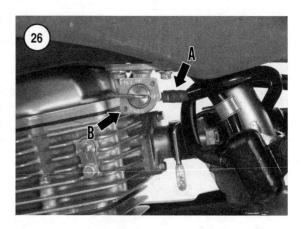

CARBURETOR

Fuel Hose and Shutoff Valve Inspection

> *WARNING*
> *A leaking fuel hose may cause a fire; do not start the engine with a leaking or damaged fuel hose or fuel shutoff valve.*

Inspect the fuel hose and shutoff valve at the intervals specified in **Table 1** or **Table 2**.

Inspect the fuel hose (A, **Figure 26**) for cracks, leaks, soft spots and deterioration. Make sure each end of the hose is installed to the proper depth on the fuel shutoff valve (B, **Figure 26**) and carburetor fittings. Secure each end of the hose with a clamp. Replace the fuel hose and hose clamps if damaged.

Inspect the fuel shutoff valve (B, **Figure 26**) for any leaks or damage. O-rings in the valve can deteriorate and cause the valve to leak fuel. If there is insufficient fuel flow, the fuel strainer screen mounted inside the fuel valve may be partially clogged. To service the fuel filter, refer to *Fuel Valve* in Chapter Eight.

> *CAUTION*
> *Do not try to stop the fuel shutoff valve from leaking by overtightening its mounting bolts. These bolts thread into square brass inserts installed in the bottom of the fuel tank. Overtightening the bolts will cause the brass inserts to spin and damage their mounting holes. It is difficult to remove the mounting bolts once this happens.*

Fuel Filter Screen

At the intervals specified in **Table 1** or **Table 2**, remove and clean the fuel filter screen. Refer to *Fuel Valve* in Chapter Eight for service procedures.

Idle Speed Adjustment

1. Check the air filter for cleanliness. Clean if necessary as described in this chapter.

2. Make sure the throttle cable free play is correct. Check and adjust as described in this chapter.

3. Connect a shop tachometer to the engine following the manufacturer's instructions.

4. Start and allow the engine to reach operating temperature.

5A. With a tachometer, adjust the engine idle speed with the throttle stop screw (**Figure 27**) to the specification in **Table 8**.

5B. Without a tachometer, set the idle speed until the engine runs smoothly and does not seem excessively high or too low (engine stalls).

6. Open and close the throttle a few times to make sure the idle speed returns to the rpm set in Step 5.

7. Turn off the engine and disconnect the shop tachometer.

8. Test ride the motorcycle. If throttle response is poor from an idle, the air screw (80 cc) or pilot screw (100 cc) may need adjustment. Refer to *Idle Drop Adjustment* in *Carburetor Adjustments* in Chapter Eight.

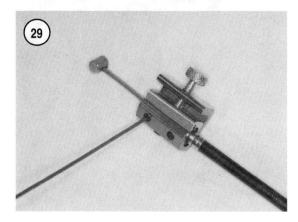

Crankcase Breather Separator Inspection

Periodically inspect the crankcase breather separator (**Figure 28**) and connecting hoses for loose, missing or damaged parts. Refer to Chapter Eight for service.

EXHAUST SYSTEM

Refer to Chapter Four for service and repair procedures.

Inspection

1. Inspect the exhaust system for cracks or dents that could alter performance. Refer all repairs to a qualified dealership or welding shop.
2. Check all of the exhaust pipe fasteners and mounting points for loose or damaged parts.

Spark Arrestor Cleaning

Remove and clean the spark arrestor at the intervals specified in **Table 1** or **Table 2**. Refer to Chapter Four for service procedures.

CONTROL CABLES

Inspection and Lubrication

This section describes complete lubrication procedures for the original equipment control cables. Clean and lubricate the throttle, clutch and front brake cables whenever the cable operation becomes sluggish or stiffens. At the same time, check the cables for signs of wear and damage or fraying that could cause the cables to bind or break. The most positive method of cable lubrication involves using a cable lubricator like the one shown in **Figure 29** and a can of cable lubricant.

> **CAUTION**
> *Do not use chain lubricant to flush and lubricate the control cables.*

1. Disconnect both clutch cable ends as described in *Clutch Cable* in Chapter Six.
2. Disconnect both throttle cable ends as described under in *Throttle Cable* in Chapter Eight.
3. Disconnect both front brake cable ends as described in *Front Brake Cable* in Chapter Thirteen.

> **WARNING**
> *Do not lubricate the throttle cable with its lower cable end mounted at the carburetor. Debris that flushes out of the end of the cable will contaminate the carburetor.*

4. Attach a cable lubricator (**Figure 29**) to one end of the cable, following the manufacturer's instructions.
5. Tie a plastic bag around the opposite cable end to catch the lubricant.
6. Fit the nozzle of the cable lubricant into the hole in the lubricator.
7. Hold a rag over the lubricator, then press and hold the button on the lubricant can. Continue until lubricant drips from the opposite end of the cable.
8. Disconnect the cable lubricator, then pull the inner cable back and forth to help distribute the lubricant.
9. Allow time for excess lubricant to drain from the cable before reconnecting it.
10. Apply a light coat of grease to the upper throttle cable ball before reconnecting it.
11. Lubricate the brake and clutch cable pivot bolts with grease, if necessary.
12. Reverse Steps 1-3 to reconnect the cables.
13. Adjust the cables as described in this chapter.

THROTTLE CABLE

Operation

Cable wear and stretch affect the operation of the carburetor. Normal amounts of cable wear and stretch can be controlled by the free play adjustment described in this section. If the cable cannot be adjusted within its adjustment limits, the cable is excessively worn or damaged and requires replacement. Replace the cable as described in Chapter Eight.

Free play is the distance the throttle grip can be rotated, measured at the throttle grip flange, until resistance from the throttle valve can be felt.

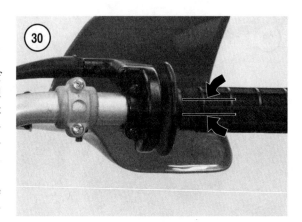

Inspection/Adjustment

Throttle cable free play is necessary to prevent variation in the idle speed when turning the handlebars. In time, the throttle cable free play increases as the cable stretches. This delays throttle response and affects low speed operation. On the other hand, if there is no throttle cable free play, an excessively high idle speed can result.

1. Rotate the throttle grip from low idle position as if accelerating, with the handlebar pointed in different steering positions. In each position, the throttle must open and close smoothly and completely. If the throttle cable binds or moves roughly, inspect the cable for kinks, bends or other damage. Replace the cable if damaged as described in Chapter Eight. If the cable moves smoothly and is not damaged, continue with Step 2.

2. Determine the throttle grip free play as shown in **Figure 30**. The specified free play is 2-6 mm (1/16-1/4 in.). If out of adjustment, continue with Step 3.

3. Slide the rubber cover (A, **Figure 31**) away from the throttle housing.

4. Loosen the cable adjuster locknut (B, **Figure 31**) and turn the cable adjuster (C) in or out to achieve the correct free play. Tighten the locknut.

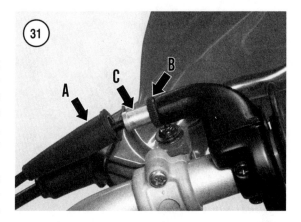

NOTE
There is no cable adjuster at the carburetor.

5. Recheck the free play.

6. Slide the rubber cover over the throttle housing.

7. Make sure the throttle grip rotates freely from a fully closed to fully open position.

8. Start the engine and run at idle speed in neutral. Turn the handlebar from side to side. If the idle increases, the throttle cable is routed incorrectly or there is not enough throttle cable free play. Repair this condition before riding the motorcycle.

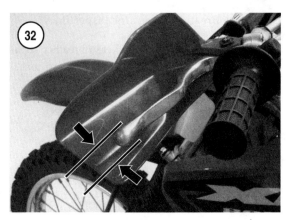

CLUTCH LEVER

Inspection/Adjustment

The clutch lever free play is continually changing due to the clutch cable wear and stretch, as well as clutch plate wear. Maintain the clutch lever free play within the specification listed in **Table 8**. Free play is the lever movement required to actuate the clutch. Insufficient free play causes the clutch to slip and premature clutch plate wear. Excessive free play causes clutch drag and rough shift pedal operation.

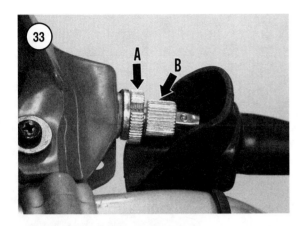

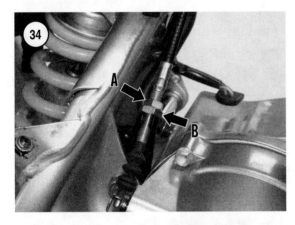

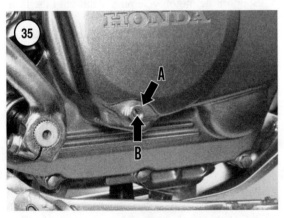

1. Determine the clutch lever free play at the end of the clutch lever as shown in **Figure 32**. The correct clutch lever free play is 10-20 mm (3/8-3/4 in.). If out of adjustment, continue with Step 2.

2. Loosen the clutch cable adjuster locknut (A, **Figure 33**) and turn the upper cable end adjuster (B) in or out to change free play to the amount specified in Step 1. Tighten the locknut.

3. If the proper amount of free play cannot be achieved at the upper cable end adjuster, perform the following:

    a. Loosen the clutch cable adjuster locknut (A, **Figure 33**) and turn the upper cable end adjuster (B) in all the way and then back out two turns.

    b. Loosen the lower cable end adjuster locknut (A, **Figure 34**) and turn the adjuster (B) all the way in so there are no cable threads visible above the locknut.

    c. At the right crankcase cover, loosen the locknut (A, **Figure 35**) and turn the adjuster (B) counterclockwise until resistance is felt and stop. Then turn the adjuster (B, **Figure 35**) 1/8-1/4 turn clockwise. Hold the adjuster and tighten the locknut.

    d. Turn the lower cable end adjuster (B, **Figure 34**) until there is 25 mm (1.0 in.) of free play at the end of the clutch lever (**Figure 32**). Hold the adjuster and tighten the locknut (A, **Figure 34**).

    e. Turn the upper cable end adjuster (B, **Figure 33**) until the free play at the clutch lever is 10-20 mm (3/8-1/4 in.). Tighten the locknut (A, **Figure 33**) and recheck the free play.

4. If the correct free play cannot be achieved, either the cable has stretched to the point it needs to be replaced or the friction discs inside the clutch assembly are worn and need replacing. Refer to Chapter Six to service the clutch cable and clutch plates.

BRAKES

This section describes routine maintenance procedures for the front and rear drum brakes. Refer to **Table 1** or **Table 2** for service intervals. Refer to Chapter Thirteen for service procedures.

Brake Lining Inspection

1. Fully apply either the front or rear brake.

2. Replace the brake shoes if the arrow mark on the indicator plate aligns with the wear indicator triangle on the brake panel. Refer to **Figure 36** (front) or **Figure 37** (rear brake).

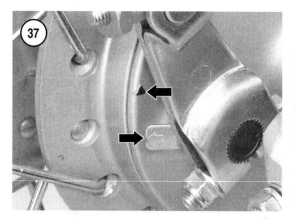

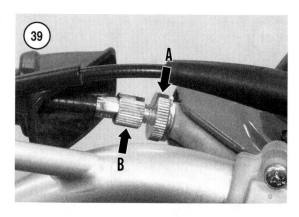

3. If necessary, service the brake shoes as described in Chapter Thirteen.

Front Brake Lever Adjustment

The brake lever free play is continually changing due to the brake cable wearing and stretching over time, as well as brake shoe wear. Maintain the brake lever free play within the specifications listed in **Table 8**. Free play is the lever movement required to actuate the front brake. Too much free play causes inadequate brake stopping force. Slight or no free play causes the brake shoes to drag against the brake drum.

1. Determine the brake lever free play at the end of the brake lever as shown in **Figure 38**. The correct brake lever free play is 20-30 mm (3/4-1 1/4 in.). If out of adjustment, continue with Step 2.

2. Loosen the brake cable adjuster locknut (A, **Figure 39**) and turn the upper cable end adjuster (B) in or out to change free play to the amount specified in Step 1. Tighten the locknut.

3. If the proper amount of free play cannot be achieved at the upper cable end adjuster, perform the following:

   a. Loosen the brake cable adjuster locknut (A, **Figure 39**) and turn the upper cable end adjuster (B) in all the way and then back out two turns.

   b. Loosen the locknut (A, **Figure 40**) on the lower end of the brake cable. Turn the adjuster (B, **Figure 40**) as needed to obtain the free play to the amount specified in Step 1. Tighten the locknut (A, **Figure 40**).

   c. Readjust the upper adjuster as needed to fine tune the brake adjustment.

4. If brake lever free play cannot be adjusted to meet specification and the brake linings are not excessively worn, replace the front brake cable as described in Chapter Thirteen.

5. Support the motorcycle on a stand with the front wheel off the ground.

6. Spin the front wheel and check for brake drag. If there is brake drag and the brake is adjusted properly, refer to Chapter Thirteen for further brake inspection.

Rear Brake Pedal Adjustment

Brake pedal height

1. Loosen the locknut (A, **Figure 41**) and turn the adjust bolt (B) to adjust the brake pedal height position. Tighten the locknut and recheck the adjustment.

2. Adjust the rear brake pedal free play as described in this section.

Rear brake pedal free play

Maintain the brake pedal free play within the specifications listed in **Table 8**. Brake pedal free play is the pedal movement required to actuate the rear brake. Too much free play causes inadequate brake stopping force. Slight or no free play causes the brake shoes to drag against the brake.

1. Determine the brake pedal free play at the end of the brake pedal as shown in **Figure 42** using light hand pressure. The correct brake pedal free play is

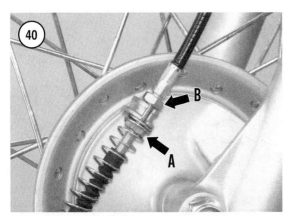

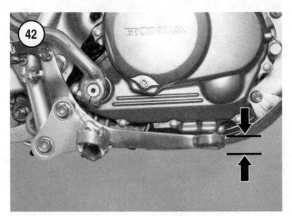

DRIVE CHAIN AND SPROCKETS

All models were originally equipped with standard (non-O-ring) drive chains.

Refer to **Table 1** and **Table 2** for drive chain and sprocket service intervals. Perform the maintenance procedures more often when riding in mud and sand.

Drive Chain Cleaning

1. Remove the drive chain (Chapter Ten).
2. Immerse the chain in a plastic pan containing kerosene and flex the links to loosen the dirt. Allow the chain to soak for approximately one half-hour. If necessary, remove dirt from the outside of the chain with a stiff brush.
3. Rinse the chain with clean kerosene. Hang the chain up to allow the cleaning solution to drain. Place a drain pan under the chain to collect the runoff.
4. Lay the chain on a workbench and check for binding or kinked links and damaged pins. If the chain is not damaged, hang it back up and lubricate it with SAE 80 or 90-weight gear lube or a chain lubricant.
5. Before installing the drive chain, clean the driven sprocket of all dirt and chain residue.
6. Install the drive chain (Chapter Ten).
7. Lubricate and adjust the drive chain as described in this section.

20-30 mm (3/4-1 1/4 in.). If out of adjustment, continue with Step 2.

2. Turn the adjustment nut (**Figure 43**) on the end of the brake rod in or out until the desired pedal free play is obtained. Make sure the curved part of the adjustment nut aligns with the collar. Operate the pedal several times to make sure it returns to the at-rest position.
3. Support the motorcycle on a stand with the rear wheel off the ground.
4. Spin the rear wheel and check for brake drag. If there is brake drag and the brake is adjusted properly, refer to Chapter Thirteen for further brake inspection.

Drive Chain and Sprocket Wear Inspection

A worn drive chain and sprockets are both unreliable and potentially dangerous. Inspect the chain and both sprockets for wear and replace if necessary. If wear is detected, replace both sprockets and the chain at the same time. Mixing old and new parts will prematurely wear the new parts.

1. Perform a quick inspection of the chain by pulling one link away from the rear sprocket. If more than 1/2 the height of the tooth is visible (**Figure 44**), the

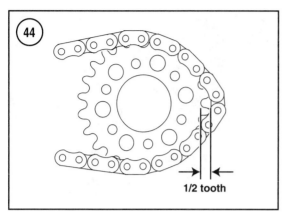

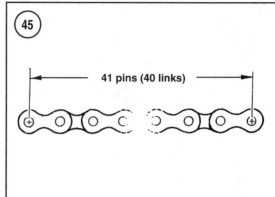

chain is worn out. Confirm by measuring the chain as described in Step 2.

> *NOTE*
> *Clean the chain before measuring chain wear in the following steps.*

> *NOTE*
> *Step 2 measures chain wear with the chain installed on the motorcycle. The same measurement can be performed with the chain stretched tightly on a workbench*

2. Measure drive chain wear as follows:

> *NOTE*
> *There must be no kinks in the part of the chain being measured.*

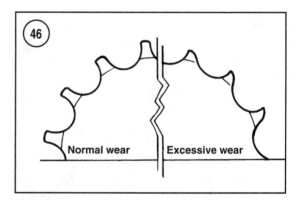

a. Remove the upper chain guide as described in this section.

b. Loosen the axle nut and turn the chain adjusters until the chain is tight.

c. Measure the length of any 41-pin (40 links) span along the top chain run (**Figure 45**).

d. Replace the drive chain if the length measurement exceeds 511 mm (20.1 in.).

e. Turn the rear wheel and repeat the measurement at different points around the chain. If any measured distance exceeds the service limit, replace the chain and both sprockets as described in Chapter Ten.

f. Reinstall the upper chain guide as described in this chapter.

3. If the chain is not worn, inspect the inside surfaces on both sides of the chain. The plates should be shiny at both ends of the chain roller. If one side of the chain is worn, the chain has been running out of alignment. This also causes premature wear of the rollers and pins. Replace the chain and both sprockets as described in Chapter Ten if uneven wear is detected. Also check

for a damaged chain guide and worn bushings and bearings in the swing arm and drive system.

4. Inspect the teeth on each sprocket. The teeth should be symmetrical and uniform. Look for hooked and broken teeth (**Figure 46**). Check the rear sprocket for cracks and damaged Allen bolt recesses.

5. Adjust the drive chain and tighten the rear axle nut as described in this section.

Drive Chain Slider Inspection

The sliders mounted on the swing arm (A, **Figure 47**) and frame (B, **Figure 47** and **Figure 48**) protect the swing arm, frame and upper engine mount spacer from chain damage. Inspect the sliders at the

than 6 mm (1/4 in.) deep. The lower slider will wear faster than the upper slider.

Chain Guide Inspection

Inspect the upper (A, **Figure 50**) and lower (B) chain guides for loose mounting bolts or damage. Check the lower chain guide for excessive wear. Because the small sheet metal screws used to secure the upper chain guide to the swing arm strip easily, apply a medium strength threadlock onto the screw threads to help secure them in place without over-tightening.

Drive Chain Lubrication

Lubricate the drive chain throughout the day as required. A properly maintained chain provides maximum service life and reliability.
1. Ride the motorcycle a short distance (5 minutes) to heat the chain.
2. Support the motorcycle with the rear wheel off the ground.
3. Shift the transmission into neutral.
4. Turn the rear wheel and lubricate the chain with SAE 80 or 90-weight gear oil or a chain lubricant. Do not over-lubricate, as this causes dirt to collect on the chain and sprockets.
5. Wipe off all excess oil from the rear hub, wheel and tire.
6. Check that the master link is properly installed and secured with the spring clip's closed end facing toward the direction of chain travel (**Figure 51**).

Drive Chain Adjustment

The drive chain must have adequate play to accommodate swing arm movement. A tight chain will cause unnecessary wear to the drive line components, while a loose chain may jump off the sprockets, possibly causing damage and personal injury.

intervals specified in **Table 1** or **Table 2** or whenever replacing the drive chain.

Swing arm slider

1. Remove the left crankcase cover.
2. Lift the drive chain and clean the top of the slider with a rag.
3. Inspect the chain slider for excessive wear or damage.
4. Lift the drive chain and measure the chain slider wear groove (**Figure 49**). When the chain slider is new, there is no wear groove. Replace the slider when the wear groove is more than 6 mm (1/4 in.) deep.
5. If there is extensive damage or wear, inspect the swing arm. To replace the slider and inspect the swing arm, remove the swing arm as described in Chapter Twelve.
6. Install the left crankcase cover.

Frame sliders

Inspect the upper (**Figure 48**) and lower (B, **Figure 47**) frame sliders for excessive wear, damage or loose mounting bolts. Replace the slider(s) when damage is noted or when the wear groove is more

Consider weather and riding conditions when checking and adjusting chain free play. Mud and sand will build up on a chain, reducing free play. Check and loosen the chain if necessary.

Check chain free play before riding the motorcycle. **Table 8** lists drive chain free play.

1. Support the motorcycle with the rear wheel off the ground.

2. Slowly turn the rear wheel and check the chain for binding and tight spots by moving the links up and down by hand. If a group of links does not move freely, remove and clean the chain as described in this section.

3. Refer to **Figure 52**. Check the amount of free play by measuring midway between the two sprockets at the lower chain run. Since chains do not wear evenly, check several sections of the chain to find the tightest section (least amount of play) and measure free play at this point. The correct amount of chain free play is 25-35 mm (1.0-1.4 in.). If the free play is out of specification, continue with Step 4.

CAUTION
Chain slack in excess of 50 mm (2.0 in.) or more may damage the frame.

4. Mark the chain's tight spot with chalk. After adjusting and spinning the chain, recheck free play at the same spot. Because drive chains do not wear evenly, always measure and adjust the chain at its tightest spot.

NOTE
When adjusting the drive chain, maintain rear wheel alignment. A misaligned rear wheel can cause poor handling and pulling to one side or the other, as well as increased chain and sprocket wear. All models have wheel alignment marks on the swing arm and chain adjuster plates.

5. Loosen the rear axle nut (A, **Figure 53**).

6. Turn the adjuster nuts (B, **Figure 53**) equally so the chain adjuster plate index marks (C) align with the same index marks on each side of the swing arm. Remeasure chain free play at the original spot (chalk mark).

7. When the chain slack is correct, verify proper wheel alignment by sighting along the chain from the rear sprocket. The chain must leave the sprocket in a straight line (A, **Figure 54**). If it is turned to one side or the other (B and C, **Figure 54**), perform the following:

   a. Adjust wheel alignment by turning one adjuster or the other. Recheck chain free play.

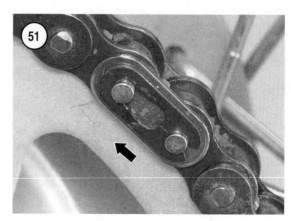

   b. Confirm swing arm index mark accuracy, if necessary, by measuring from the center of the swing arm pivot shaft to the center of the rear axle.

8. Tighten the rear axle nut (A, **Figure 53**) to 62 N•m (46 ft.-lb.).

9. Securely tighten the adjuster nuts (B, **Figure 53**) against the swing arm.

10. Spin the wheel several times and note the following:

   a. Recheck the free play at its tightest point. Make sure the free play is within specification.

   b. Check the chain alignment as it runs through the swing arm slider.

   c. Check the rear brake pedal free play as described in this chapter.

TIRES AND WHEELS

Tire Pressure

Check and set the tire pressure to maintain good traction and handling and to prevent rim damage. Keep an accurate tire gauge in the toolbox. **Table 3** lists the standard tire pressure for the front and rear wheels. Check the tire pressure when the tires are cold.

Tire Inspection

Off-road tires take a lot of punishment and should be inspected often for damage. To check for internal sidewall damage, remove the tire from the rim as described in Chapter Ten. Inspect the inner tire casing for tears or sharp objects embedded in the tire.

Check the valve stem. If a valve stem is turned sideways (**Figure 55**), the tire and tube have slipped on the rim. The valve will eventually pull out of the tube, causing a flat. Straighten the tube as described in *Tube Alignment* in this section.

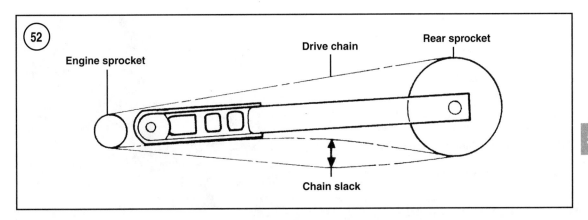

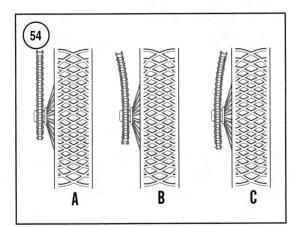

Measure the tread depth in the center of the tire. Replace the tire when the minimum tread depth is 3.0 mm (0.12 in.) or less.

Tube Alignment

Check the valve stem alignment. **Figure 55** shows a valve stem that has slipped with the tire. If the tube is not repositioned, the valve stem will eventually pull out of the tube, causing a flat. To realign the tube and tire:

1. Wash the tire and rim.

2. Remove the valve stem core to deflate the tire.

3. Loosen the rim lock nut (rear tire).

4. With an assistant steadying the motorcycle, break the tire-to-rim seal all the way around the wheel on both sides.

5. Put the motorcycle on a stand with the wheel off the ground.

6. Spray soapy water along both tire beads.

7. Have an assistant apply the brake.

8. Grasp the tire at two opposite places and turn it and the tube until the valve stem is straight up (90°).

9. Install the valve stem core and inflate the tire. If necessary, reapply the soap and water to help the tire seat on the rim. Check the tire to make sure it seats evenly around the rim.

WARNING
Do not over-inflate the tire and tube. If the tire does not seat properly, remove the valve stem core and re-lubricate the tire with soap and water again.

10. Tighten the rim lock nut to 12 N•m (106 in.-lb.).

11. Adjust the tire pressure (**Table 3**) and install the valve stem nut (if used) and cap.

Some riders choose to leave the valve stem nut off so that if the tire does slip, the nut does not catch against the rim and cause the valve stem to pull out of the tube.

Wheel Spoke Tension and Wheel Inspection

Refer to *Wheel Service* in Chapter Ten.

WHEEL BEARINGS

Inspection

Check the wheel bearings when checking the tires and wheels at the intervals specified in **Table 1** or **Table 2**. Refer to *Inspection* in *Front and Rear Hubs* in Chapter Ten.

STEERING

Check all steering components at the intervals specified in **Table 1** and **Table 2**.

Steering Head Bearings

Lubricate the bearings when necessary. Remove the steering head as described in Chapter Eleven to clean and lubricate the bearings.

Steering Head Adjustment Check

The steering head assembly consists of upper and lower roller bearings, the steering stem and the steering head. Because the motorcycle is subjected to rough terrain and conditions, check the bearing play at the specified intervals or whenever it feels loose. A loose bearing adjustment hampers steering and causes premature bearing and race wear. In extreme conditions, a loose bearing adjustment can cause loss of control. Refer to *Steering Play Check and Adjustment* in Chapter Eleven.

Front Suspension Check

1. With the front wheel touching the ground, apply the front brake and pump the fork up and down vigorously. Check fork movement, paying attention to any abnormal noises or oil leaks.
2. Check that the upper and lower fork tube pinch bolts are tightened to specification (Chapter Eleven).
3. Check that the handlebar holder bolts are tightened to specification (Chapter Eleven).

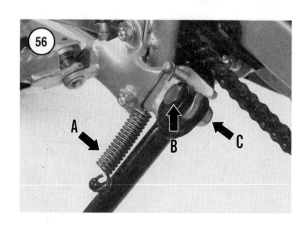

4. Check that the front axle nut is tightened to specification (Chapter Ten).

REAR SHOCK ABSORBER

Inspection

1. Check that the damper rod is not bent and that there is no oil leaking from the damper rod seal.
2. Check that the shock mounting nuts and bolts are tightened to specification (Chapter Twelve).

SWING ARM AND LINKAGE

Rear Suspension Check

1. Support the motorcycle on a stand with the rear wheel off the ground.
2. Check swing arm bearing play as described in Chapter Twelve.
3. Check the tightness of all rear suspension mounting bolts (Chapter Twelve).
4. Check that the rear axle nut is tightened to 62 N•m (46 ft.-lb.).

Swing Arm and Shock Linkage Bushing Lubrication

The manufacturer does not specify a recommended bushing lubrication interval. A good practice is to remove and lubricate the swing arm and linkage bushings several times a year, especially after riding the motorcycle in mud and sandy conditions. Refer to Chapter Twelve for complete service and lubrication procedures.

SIDESTAND

WARNING
A sidestand that will not stay in its retracted position when the motorcycle

is being ridden is hazardous and can cause an accident. Do not ride the motorcycle until the sidestand assembly is working correctly.

Check sidestand operation and pivot bolt tightness at the intervals specified in **Table 1** or **Table 2** or whenever the sidestand is damaged or fails to operate properly.

Inspection

1. Support the motorcycle on a workstand.
2. Raise and lower the sidestand by hand. Make sure the return spring has sufficient tension to lock the sidestand in its upper and lower positions.
3. Check the return spring (A, **Figure 56**) for cracks, damaged spring ends and stretched coils. Check that both spring ends are hooked securely around their respective posts. Then check the posts for damage. If necessary, replace the return spring (Chapter Fourteen).
4. Remove and lubricate the sidestand pivot bolt if it appears the bolt is in need of lubrication (Chapter Fourteen).
5. When operating the sidestand by hand, check the sidestand for bending or other damage that could prevent it from locking in its upper or lower positions. Replace the sidestand if necessary (Chapter Fourteen).
6. If the return spring, pivot bolt and sidestand are in good condition and working correctly, check the sidestand pivot bolt torque as follows:
   a. Tighten the pivot bolt (B, **Figure 56**) to 10 N•m (88 in.-lb.).
   b. Loosen the pivot bolt 1/8 to 1/4 turn. Then hold the pivot bolt and tighten the locknut (C, **Figure 56**) to 39 N•m (29 ft.-lb.).
   c. Operate the sidestand by hand to make sure it pivots and locks in its upper and lower positions correctly.

FRONT FORK OIL CHANGE

The manufacturer does not specify a recommended oil change interval. A good practice is to establish a change interval after draining and inspecting the fork oil after one year of normal usage, then adjusting the oil change interval accordingly.

1992-1997 models

The sliders on these models are equipped with drain bolts. Refer to *Front Fork* and *Fork Service* in Chapter Eleven for additional information.

NOTE
One or more assistants will be required for this procedure. Read the procedure through before starting.

1. Place a drain pan underneath one of the fork tube drain bolts (**Figure 57**), then sit on the motorcycle so it is sitting straight up. Have an assistant remove the drain bolt while catching the oil in the drain pan.
2. When the oil flow starts to slow down, apply the front brake and pump the front fork up and down by applying pressure against the handlebars. Continue until the oil stops draining out of the drain hole.
3. Replace the drain bolt gasket if leaking or damaged. Clean and dry the drain bolt and gasket.
4. Reinstall the drain bolt (**Figure 57**) and gasket and tighten securely.
5. Repeat Steps 1-4 for the other fork tube.

WARNING
Remove any oil that has spilled onto the front tire, brake drum or floor.

6. Support the motorcycle on a workstand with the front wheel off the ground.
7. Remove the handlebar (Chapter Eleven) and number plate (Chapter Fourteen).
8. Loosen the upper fork tube pinch bolt.

WARNING
The fork cap is under spring tension. After loosening the fork cap, use a speed handle and socket to help control the fork cap during its removal and installation. Wear safety goggles when removing and installing the fork cap.

9. Have an assistant steady the motorcycle and remove the fork cap.
10. Place a plastic tie on top of the fork spring to identify its upper end.
11. Wrap a shop cloth around the top of the fork tube to catch oil and remove the fork spring. Clean the fork spring in solvent and dry with compressed air.

12. Repeat Steps 8-11 for the other fork tube.

13. Pour the specified type (**Table 4**) and quantity (**Table 6**) of fork oil into the fork tube. Repeat for the other fork tube.

14. After filling each fork tube, have an assistant steady the motorcycle and then slowly lift and lower the front wheel to pump the forks several times to expel air from the fork oil.

15. With an assistant's help, raise the front wheel until the front forks are bottomed out and then support the wheel in this position with wooden blocks. If this is difficult to do, remove the fork tubes as described in Chapter Eleven. The fork tubes must be bottomed out when setting the oil level.

16. Use an oil level gauge to set the oil level in each fork tube as described in *Fork Oil Adjustment* in *Fork Service* in Chapter Eleven. If the fork tubes are mounted on the motorcycle, refer to the oil level position in **Figure 58**.

17. After the oil level is set in both fork tubes, remove the blocks from underneath the front wheel and slowly lower the front wheel until the fork tubes are completely extended.

18. Slowly install the fork spring with its tapered spring end facing down. If an aftermarket spring is used, install it facing in its original position. If a plastic tie was used to identify the spring, install the spring with the plastic tie end facing up. Cut and remove the plastic tie from the fork spring.

19. Install a new O-ring onto the fork cap, if needed.

20. Lubricate the fork cap O-ring with fork oil. Install the fork cap with a speed handle and socket. Tighten hand-tight.

21. Tighten the fork cap to 23 N•m (17 ft.-lb.).

22. Tighten the upper fork tube pinch bolt to 11 N•m (97 in.-lb.).

23. Repeat Steps 18-22 for the other fork tube.

24. Install the handlebar (Chapter Eleven) and number plate (Chapter Fourteen).

25. Check the fork drain bolts for leaks.

1998-on Models

Because there are no oil drain bolts on the sliders installed on these models, the fork tubes must be removed and partially disassembled to change the fork oil and set the oil level. Refer to *Fork Service* in Chapter Eleven.

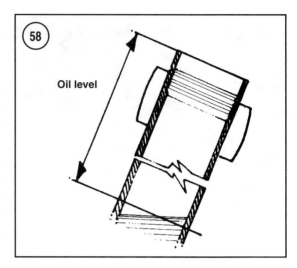

FASTENERS

Inspection

Vibration can loosen many of the fasteners on the motorcycle. Make sure the following fasteners are tightened to specification at the intervals noted in **Table 1** and **Table 2**:

1. Engine mounting hardware.
2. Engine crankcase covers.
3. Handlebar and front fork.
4. Shift pedal.
5. Kick pedal.
6. Clutch lever.
7. Brake pedal and lever.
8. Exhaust system.
9. Fuel tank.
10. Seat and side covers.
11. Check all hose and cable guides and clamps.

ENGINE BREAK-IN

If the engine bearings, crankshaft, piston, piston rings or cylinder have been serviced, perform the following break-in procedure.

NOTE
During engine break-in, oil consumption may be higher than normal. It is important to frequently check and correct the oil level. At no time during the break-in or later should the oil level be allowed to drop below the bottom line on the dipstick cap; if the oil level is low, the oil will overheat and result in insufficient lubrication and increased wear.

1. Observe the following conditions when breaking in the engine:

a. Operate the motorcycle on flat ground. Do not perform the break-in while riding in sand, mud or up hills. This will overload and possibly overheat the engine.

b. Vary the throttle position. Do not keep the throttle in the same position for more than a few seconds.

c. Check the spark plug frequently. Refer to *Spark Plug* in this chapter to identify spark plug condition.

2. Perform the *Pre-Ride Inspection* in this chapter.

3. Service the air filter as described in this chapter.

4. Check the engine oil level as described in this chapter.

5. Make sure there is no mud or other debris clogging the cylinder head cooling fins.

6. Start the engine and allow it to warm up. During this time, check for proper idle speed and leaks.

7. Break-in time consists of the motorcycle's first 15 miles (25 km).

Table 1 MAINTENANCE AND SERVICE INTERVALS (1992-1997 MODELS)

Initial maintenance: First week of operation or 200 miles (350 km)
Check valve clearance; adjust if necessary
Change engine oil
Check cam chain tension; adjust if necessary
Check engine idle speed; adjust if necessary
Lubricate and adjust drive chain*
Lubricate drive chain
Check brake system
Check clutch adjustment; adjust if necessary
Check for loose or missing fasteners
Check wheels and tires
Check front steering for looseness
Every 300 miles (500 km)
Lubricate and adjust drive chain*
Every 30 operating days or 1000 miles (1600 km)
Clean and check air filter element*
Check spark plug; regap if necessary
Check valve clearance; adjust if necessary
Change engine oil
Clean engine oil strainer screen
Check cam chain tension; adjust if necessary
Clean spark arrestor
Drain crankcase breather
Check engine idle speed; adjust if necessary
Check drive chain sliders
Check brake shoe wear
Check brake system
Check clutch adjustment; adjust if necessary
Check wheels and tires
Inspect fuel line and fuel tank vent
Clean fuel filter screen
Check and adjust throttle operation and free play
Check sidestand operation and fastener tightness
Check all suspension components
Check front suspension for looseness
Check for loose or missing fasteners
*Service more frequently if operated in wet or dusty environment.

Table 2 MAINTENANCE AND SERVICE INTERVALS (1998-ON MODELS)

Initial maintenance: 100 miles (150 km) or 20 hours, whichever comes first
Check valve clearance; adjust if necessary
Change engine oil
Check cam chain tension; adjust if necessary
Check engine idle speed; adjust if necessary
Lubricate and adjust drive chain*

(continued)

Table 2 MAINTENANCE AND SERVICE INTERVALS (1998-ON MODELS) (continued)

Initial maintenance: 100 miles (150 km) or 20 hours, whichever comes first (continued)
  Lubricate drive chain
  Check brake system
  Check clutch adjustment; adjust if necessary
  Check for loose or missing fasteners
  Check wheels and tires
  Check front steering for looseness

Every 3 months or 300 miles (500 km)
  Lubricate and adjust drive chain*

Every 6 months or 600 miles (1000 km)
  Clean and check air filter element*
  Check spark plug; regap if necessary
  Check valve clearance; adjust if necessary
  Change engine oil
  Check cam chain tension; adjust if necessary
  Clean spark arrestor on 1998-2000 models
  Drain crankcase breather on 1998-2000 models
  Check engine idle speed; adjust if necessary
  Check drive chain sliders
  Check brake shoe wear
  Check brake system
  Check clutch adjustment; adjust if necessary
  Check wheels and tires

Every 100 operating hours or 1000 miles (1600 km)
  Clean spark arrestor on 2001-on models

Every 12 months or 1200 miles (2000 km)
  Inspect fuel line and fuel tank vent
  Clean fuel filter screen
  Check and adjust throttle operation and free play
  Clean and inspect air filter*
  Inspect spark plug; regap if necessary
  Check valve adjustment; adjust if necessary
  Change engine oil
  Clean engine oil strainer screen
  Check cam chain tension; adjust if necessary
  Check engine idle speed; adjust if necessary
  Check drive chain sliders
  Check brake shoe wear
  Check brake system
  Check clutch adjustment; adjust if necessary
  Check sidestand operation and fastener tightness
  Check all suspension components
  Check front suspension for looseness
  Check for loose or missing fasteners

Every 18 months or 1800 miles (3000 km)
  Clean and inspect air filter*
  Inspect spark plug gap; regap if necessary
  Change engine oil
  Check cam chain tension; adjust if necessary
  Check engine idle speed; adjust if necessary
  Check drive chain sliders
  Check brake shoe wear
  Check brake system
  Check clutch adjustment; adjust if necessary
  Check tires and wheels

*Service more frequently if operated in wet, dusty or sandy environments.

Table 3 TIRE INFLATION PRESSURE

	kPa	psi
Front	100	15
Rear		
XR80R and XR100R	125	18
CRF80F and CRF100F	100	15

3

Table 4 RECOMMENDED LUBRICANTS AND FUEL

Air filter	Foam air filter oil
Engine oil	
Classification	
JASCO T 903 standard rating	MA
API rating	SG or higher*
Viscosity rating	SAE 10W-30
Fork oil	Pro Honda Suspension Fluid SS-8 or equivalent 10 wt fork oil
Fuel	Unleaded gasoline; 86 pump octane/91 RON or higher
Grease	Multipurpose waterproof grease

*API "SG" or higher classified oils not specified as "ENERGY CONSERVING" can be used. See Chapter One for additional information.

Table 5 ENGINE OIL CAPACITY

	ml	oz.
XR80R		
1993-1997 models		
Oil change	700	23.7
After engine disassembly	900	30.4
1998-2003 models		
Oil change	800	27.1
After engine disassembly	900	30.4
XR100R		
Oil change	900	30.4
After engine disassembly	1000	33.8
CRF80F and CRF100F		
Oil change	900	30.4
After engine disassembly	1100	37.2

Table 6 FRONT FORK OIL CAPACITY

	ml	oz.
XR80R		
1993-1997 models	83.0	2.8
1998-2003 models	80.5-85.5	2.72-2.90
CRF80F	82.5-87.5	2.80-2.96
XR100R		
1992-1997 models	88.0	3.0
1998-2000 models	85.5-90.5	2.90-3.06
2001-2003 models	83.5-88.5	2.82-3.00
CRF100F	81.5-86.5	2.76-2.92

Table 7 FRONT FORK OIL LEVEL

	mm	in.
XR80R	184	7.24
CRF80F	177	6.97

(continued)

Table 7 FRONT FORK OIL LEVEL (continued)

	mm	in.
XR100R		
1992-2000 models	205	8.07
2001-2003 models	200	7.87
CRF100F	207	8.15

Table 8 MAINTENANCE SPECIFICATIONS

Clutch lever free play	10-20 mm (3/8-3/4 in.)
Drive chain 41 pin service limit	511 mm (20.1 in.)
Drive chain free play	25-35 mm (1.0-1.4 in.)
Drive chain slider wear depth	6 mm (1/4 in.) or more
Engine compression	
XR80R	
1993-1997 models	98.1-1373 kPa (143-199 psi)
1998-2003 models	1176 kPa (171 psi) at 1000 rpm
CRF80F	1176 kPa (171 psi) at 1000 rpm
XR100R	
1992-1997 models	98.1-1275 kPa (143-105 psi)
1998-2003 models	1127 kPa (164 psi) at 800 rpm
CRF100F	1176 kPa (171 psi) at 1000 rpm
Engine idle speed	
80 cc models	1400-1600 rpm
100 cc models	1300-1500 rpm
Front brake lever free play	20-30 mm (3/4-1 1/4 in.)
Ignition timing	15.5° BTDC at idle speed
Idle drop adjustment[1]	Refer to *Carburetor Adjustments* in Chapter Eight
Rear brake pedal free play	20-30 mm (3/4-1 1/4 in.)
Spark plug gap	0.6-0.7 mm (0.024-0.028 in.)
Spark plug type	
Standard	NGK CR7HSA or DENSO U22FSR-U
Cold weather operation[2]	NGK CR6HSA or DENSO U20FSR-U
Extended high speed riding	NGK CR8HSA or DENSO U24FSR-U
Tire tread depth limit	3.0 mm (0.12 in.)
Throttle cable free play	2-6 mm (1/16-1/4 in.)
Valve clearance	
Intake and exhaust	0.05 mm (0.002 in.)

1. This is often referred to as the air screw (80 cc models) or pilot screw (100 cc models) adjustment.
2. Below 5° C (41° F).

Table 9 MAINTENANCE TORQUE SPECIFICATIONS

	N•m	in.-lb.	ft.-lb.
Axle nut	62	–	46
Cam chain tensioner adjuster locknut	12	106	–
Cylinder head cover bolt	12	106	–
Engine oil drain bolt	24	–	18
Fork cap	23	–	17
Rim lock nut	12	106	–
Sidestand pivot nut*	39	–	29
Spark plug	14	–	10
Upper fork tube pinch bolt			
1992-2003 models	11	97	–
2004-on models	18	–	13
Valve adjuster locknut	10	88	–

*Refer to text.

ENGINE TOP END

Refer to Chapter Three for valve adjustment. **Tables 1-4** are at the end of the chapter.

EXHAUST SYSTEM

WARNING
The exhaust system must be cool to prevent burns.

Removal/Installation

1. Remove the right side cover and seat (Chapter Fourteen).
2. Remove the exhaust pipe joint nuts at the cylinder head (A, **Figure 1**). Slide the pipe flange (B, **Figure 1**) away from the cylinder head.
3. Remove the bolts (A, **Figure 2**) securing the exhaust pipe/muffler to the frame and remove the exhaust pipe assembly (B). On 1993-2000 models, one bolt secures the muffler to the frame. 2001-on models use two muffler mounting bolts.
4. Remove the exhaust pipe gasket from the exhaust port (**Figure 3**). Discard the gasket.
5. Inspect the exhaust pipe for damage. Refer damage to a qualified welding shop. Service the heat shield and spark arrestor as described in this chapter.

6. Apply a few dabs of grease onto a new exhaust pipe gasket to help hold it in place and install it into the exhaust port. The grease will burn off soon after the engine is first started.
7. Install the exhaust pipe, making sure the exhaust pipe enters the cylinder head fully. Install the exhaust pipe mounting bolts (A, **Figure 2**) finger-tight.

NOTE
*If the exhaust pipe will not line up so all of the exhaust pipe bolts (A, **Figure 2**) can be installed, the exhaust pipe is probably not centered inside the cylinder head or the exhaust pipe is damaged.*

8. Slide the flange (B, **Figure 1**) over the cylinder head studs and install the two nuts (A) finger-tight.
9. Tighten the exhaust pipe joint nuts (A, **Figure 1**) in several steps and in a crossing pattern to 12 N•m (106 in.-lb.). Tightening these nuts also compresses the exhaust pipe gasket.
10. Tighten the exhaust pipe mounting bolts (A, **Figure 2**) to 26 N•m (20 ft.-lb.).
11. Start the engine and run at idle speed to burn off the grease installed on the gasket. Then check for exhaust leaks.

12. Install the seat and right side cover (Chapter Fourteen).

Heat Shield Removal/Installation

The heat shield can be serviced with the exhaust pipe installed on the motorcycle. Each mounting bolt is equipped with two fiber type heat resistant washers. These must be placed so they seat against both sides of the heat shield. Tighten the heat shield mounting bolts to 14 N•m (10 ft.-lb.).

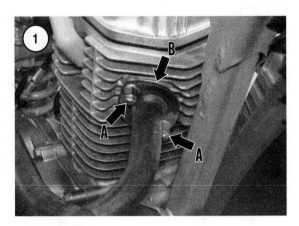

Spark Arrestor Removal/Cleaning/Installation

Clean the spark arrestor at the service intervals specified in Chapter Three or anytime it is suspected that the spark arrestor may be clogged.

1993-2000 models

> **WARNING**
> *To avoid burning hands, do not perform the cleaning operation with the exhaust system hot. Work in a well-ventilated area (outside of garage) and where the area is free of any fire hazards. Make sure to wear thick glove when blocking the muffler opening and to wear safety glasses or goggles.*

1. Remove the bolts securing the spark arrestor lid to the bottom of the muffler.
2. Remove the spark arrestor lid and gasket.
3. Start the engine and while blocking the end of the muffler with a gloved hand, rev the engine approximately 20 times to blow accumulated carbon out of the lid opening on the bottom of the muffler.
4. Turn the engine off and allow the exhaust system to cool.
5. Reinstall the spark arrestor lid and a new gasket and tighten the mounting bolts securely.

2001-on models

> **NOTE**
> *It is easier to remove the spark arrestor when the exhaust pipe is mounted on the engine.*

1. Support and block the motorcycle so it cannot move.
2. Remove the spark arrestor mounting bolts (**Figure 4**), spark arrestor (A, **Figure 5**) and its gasket (B). Note the following:

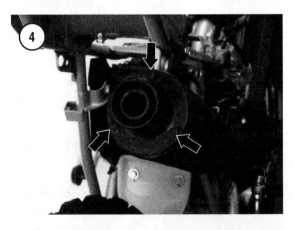

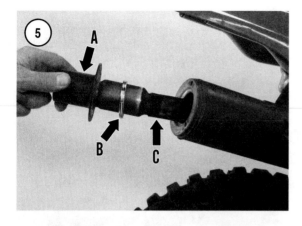

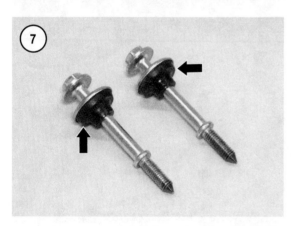

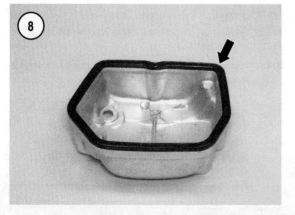

a. The bolts rust easily and may be difficult to remove.

b. Twist the spark arrestor to break it loose. If
necessary, mount a strap wrench on the end of
the spark arrestor and twist to break loose.

3. Clean the spark arrestor screen (C, **Figure 5**) with
a brush. Replace the spark arrestor if the screen is
damaged.

4. Replace the bolts if damaged.

5. Installation is the reverse of removal. Note the
following:

a. Install a new gasket (B, **Figure 5**).

b. Apply anti-seize to the bolt threads and tighten
the bolts securely.

CYLINDER HEAD COVER

Removal/Installation

1. Remove the fuel tank (Chapter Eight).

2. Clean the area on the frame above the cylinder
head of all dirt and debris. If necessary, wrap this
area with a towel to prevent dirt from falling into the
engine.

3. Remove the two bolts (A, **Figure 6**), cylinder
head cover (B) and gasket.

4. Clean and dry the cylinder head cover, mounting
bolts and gasket.

5. Check the mounting bolt rubber washers (**Figure
7**) and cylinder head cover gasket (**Figure 8**) for
damage.

6. Clean and dry the cylinder head mating surface.

7. Place the cover gasket into the groove in the cylinder head cover (**Figure 8**) and install the cylinder
head cover (B, **Figure 6**).

8. Thread the cylinder head mounting bolts into the
cylinder head and tighten finger tight. Check the cover gasket to make sure it is setting flush against the
cylinder head cover and cylinder head. Tighten the
cylinder head cover bolts to 12 N•m (106 in.-lb.).

9. Install the fuel tank (Chapter Eight).

10. Start the engine and check for leaks.

CAMSHAFT

The camshaft can be removed with the engine
mounted in the frame.

Camshaft Removal

1. Remove the cylinder head cover as described in
this chapter.

2. Remove the left crankcase cover (Chapter Nine).

3. Turn the flywheel counterclockwise and align the
T mark on the flywheel (A, **Figure 9**) with the index

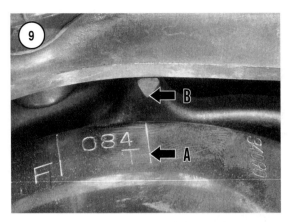

mark on the left crankcase (B). Check that the 0 mark on the cam sprocket is facing up (A, **Figure 10**). Then confirm that the engine is at TDC on its compression stroke by viewing the position of the camshaft lobes. The engine is on its compression stroke when both cam lobes are facing down and the valve adjusters can be moved by hand. If not, turn the crankshaft one full revolution (360°) counterclockwise and realign the T mark.

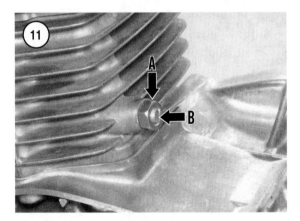

NOTE
Rotate the engine and check the camshaft timing marks a few times before removing the camshaft. Confirm that the timing mark and camshaft position are correct and note how the camshaft lobes are positioned when the engine is at TDC on its compression stroke.

4. Loosen the cam chain as follows:
   a. Try to turn the camshaft sprocket/camshaft by hand. Note how tight it feels.
   b. Loosen the cam chain tensioner adjust bolt locknut (A, **Figure 11**) and bolt (B).
   c. Insert a screwdriver between the cam chain and tensioner rail (**Figure 12**) and pry the tensioner rail rearward. Hold the tensioner rail in this position and tighten the adjust bolt (B, **Figure 11**) and locknut (A). Remove the screwdriver.
   d. Move the camshaft sprocket/camshaft by hand. It should move easily when compared to its movement in substep a, indicating the cam chain is loose. If not, repeat these steps until the cam chain is loose.

5. If the cylinder head will be removed, remove the cam chain tensioner adjuster set plate bolt, plate and adjuster (B, **Figure 10**).

6. Turn the flywheel counterclockwise until one of the camshaft sprocket mounting bolts (**Figure 13**) is accessible. Hold the flywheel with a rotor holding tool (**Figure 14**) and loosen the camshaft sprocket bolt (**Figure 13**).

7. Turn the flywheel counterclockwise one turn and repeat Step 6 to loosen the other camshaft sprocket bolt.

8. Set the engine at TDC on its compression stroke as described in Step 3.

NOTE
In Step 9, maintain the engine position at TDC on its compression stroke. It should only be necessary to turn the flywheel a few degrees either way in order to remove the camshaft sprocket bolts.

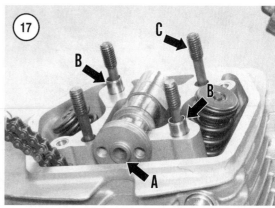

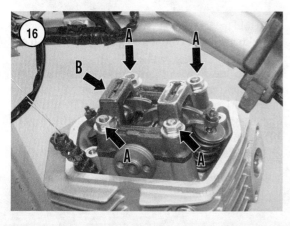

9. Remove the camshaft sprocket mounting bolts (C, **Figure 10**). If necessary, turn the flywheel slightly as required to access the bolts.

10. Slide the camshaft sprocket (A, **Figure 15**) off the camshaft and then slip the cam chain off the sprocket. Secure the cam chain with a piece of wire and remove the camshaft sprocket.

11. Loosen the camshaft holder nuts (A, **Figure 16**) in 2-3 steps and in a crossing pattern. Then remove the nuts and washers.

12. Remove the camshaft holder (B, **Figure 16**). Do not drop the dowel pins into the engine when the camshaft holder is lifted off the camshaft.

13. Remove the camshaft (A, **Figure 17**).

14. Remove the dowel pins (B, **Figure 17**).

15. Service the camshaft, camshaft holder and rocker arms as described in this section.

Camshaft Installation

1. Assemble the camshaft holder, rocker arms and shafts as described in this section.

2. Lubricate the camshaft journals with engine assembly lube or molybdenum disulfide grease.

3. Install the camshaft (A, **Figure 17**) into the cylinder head journals with its lobes facing down.

4. Install the dowel pins (B, **Figure 17**).

5. Spray some electrical contact cleaner on a clean lint-free cloth and wipe the cylinder stud threads (C, **Figure 17**) to remove all oil residue.

6. Clean and dry the cylinder head holder nuts and washers.

7. Install the camshaft holder (B, **Figure 16**) over the studs and dowel pins and seat against the camshaft. Check that the camshaft holder seats flush against the cylinder head.

8. Install the camshaft holder washers and nuts (A, **Figure 16**) and tighten in 2 steps and in a crossing pattern to 20 N•m (15 ft.-lb.).

9. If the cylinder head was previously installed, tighten the cylinder head mounting bolt (**Figure 18**) securely.

10. Lift the cam chain and turn the flywheel counterclockwise and align the T mark on the flywheel (A, **Figure 9**) with the index mark on the left crankcase (B).

11. Lift the cam chain and install the camshaft sprocket with its 0 mark (B, **Figure 15**) facing up and with both bolt holes aligned with the cylinder head surface. A small square can be used to check the alignment as shown in **Figure 19**.

12. With the camshaft sprocket and camshaft bolt holes aligned, insert a small awl through one of the bolt holes and into the camshaft. Then turn the camshaft sprocket and camshaft counterclockwise at the same time (**Figure 20**) until the front bolt hole is accessible.

> *NOTE*
> *Two different type camshaft sprocket bolts are used. When the engine is positioned at TDC on its compression stroke, the silver bolt (A, Figure 21) is installed on the exhaust side and the black bolt (B) is installed on the intake side.*

13. Install the silver bolt (**Figure 22**) and tighten finger-tight.

14. Turn the flywheel counterclockwise and install the black bolt (**Figure 21**) and tighten finger-tight.

15. Hold the flywheel with the rotor holder (**Figure 14**) and tighten the camshaft sprocket bolts (A and B, **Figure 21**) to 12 N•m (106 in.-lb.). Turn the flywheel counterclockwise as necessary to access the bolts.

16. Hold the camshaft sprocket with one hand, then loosen the cam chain tensioner adjust bolt locknut (A, **Figure 11**) and adjust bolt (B). The chain tensioner will move and tighten the cam chain, which will pull and tighten the camshaft sprocket.

17. Hold the adjust bolt (B, **Figure 11**) with a screwdriver to prevent it from turning and tighten the locknut (A) to 12 N•m (106 in.-lb.).

18. Turn the flywheel counterclockwise and align the T mark on the flywheel (A, **Figure 9**) with the index mark on the left crankcase (B). Check that the 0 mark on the cam sprocket is facing up (A, **Figure 10**).

> *CAUTION*
> *The timing marks must align correctly at this time; otherwise, camshaft timing is incorrect. Do not proceed if the*

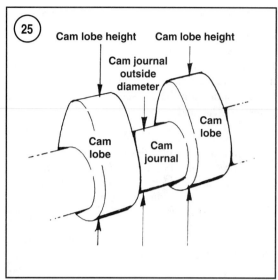

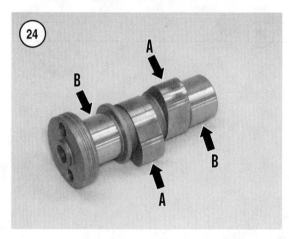

camshaft sprocket timing marks are positioned incorrectly.

19. Check and adjust the valve clearance (Chapter Three).

20. Fill the cylinder head pocket underneath the camshaft (**Figure 23**) with new engine oil.

21. Install the cylinder head cover (this chapter).

22. Install the left crankcase cover (Chapter Nine).

23. Start the engine and adjust the cam chain tension as described in Chapter Three.

Camshaft Inspection

Refer to the specifications in **Table 2**. Replace the camshaft if worn or damaged as described in this section.

1. Clean the camshaft in solvent and dry thoroughly. Flush the camshaft oil passages with solvent and compressed air.

2. Check the cam lobes (A, **Figure 24**) for wear. The lobes should not be scored and the edges should be square. Replace the camshaft if the lobes are damaged.

3. Check the camshaft bearing journals (B, **Figure 24**) for wear or scoring. Replace the camshaft if the journals are damaged.

4. If the camshaft lobes or journals are excessively worn or damaged, check the journal surfaces in the cylinder head and in the camshaft holder as described in this section.

5. Measure each cam lobe height (**Figure 25**).

6. Measure each cam journal outside diameter (**Figure 25**).

Camshaft Sprocket Inspection

1. Inspect the camshaft sprocket for broken or chipped teeth (A, **Figure 26**). If damage is noted, inspect the cam chain and timing sprocket mounted on the crankshaft (Chapter Five).

2. Inspect the camshaft sprocket mounting bolts and replace if damaged. Note the silver (B, **Figure 26**) and black (C) bolts. Replace with manufacturer replacement bolts only.

Camshaft Holder, Rocker Arms and Shafts

Disassembly

1. Before cleaning and disassembling the camshaft holder (**Figure 27**), inspect the oil lubrication holes for contamination. Make sure these passages and holes are clean and open.

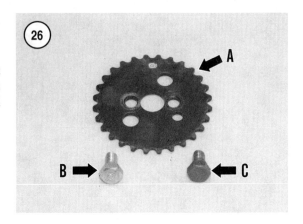

> *NOTE*
> *Infrequent oil changes and filter screen cleaning are indicated if the camshaft holder passages are dirty. Contaminated oil passages can result in camshaft and journal failure.*

2. Clean the assembled camshaft holder assembly. Then dry with compressed air.

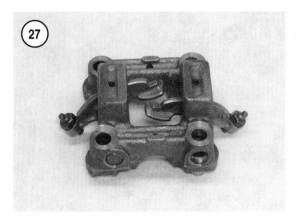

> *NOTE*
> *The intake and exhaust rocker arms are identical. During removal, identify the rocker arms so they can be reinstalled in their original mounting positions.*

3. Insert an 8 mm bolt into the exhaust rocker arm shaft and remove the shaft (A, **Figure 28**) and rocker arm. Leave the bolt in place until assembly so the rocker arm shaft is not installed backward.

4. Remove the intake rocker arm shaft (B, **Figure 28**) with a magnet. Then remove the rocker arm.

Camshaft holder inspection

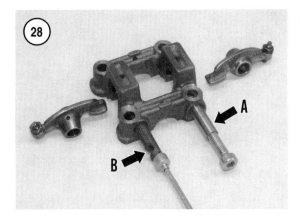

1. Clean and dry the camshaft holder.
2. Check the camshaft holder for stress cracks and other damage.
3. Check the camshaft bearing journals in the camshaft holder (**Figure 29**) and cylinder head for wear and scoring. If damaged, replace the cylinder head and camshaft holder as a set. To determine operational clearance perform the *Camshaft Oil Clearance Measurement* procedure in this section.
4. To measure the camshaft holder inside diameter, mount the camshaft holder onto the cylinder head (without the camshaft). Install the washers and nuts and tighten as described in *Camshaft Installation* in this section. Measure the bore with a bore gauge or telescoping gauge and compare to the specification in **Table 2**. If the bore is too large, repeat the measurement with a new camshaft holder. If the measurement is still too large, replace the cylinder head.

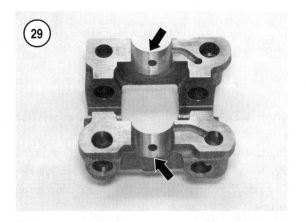

Rocker arms and shafts inspection

Refer to the specifications in **Table 2**. Replace parts that are out of specification or are damaged.
1. Clean and dry the parts.

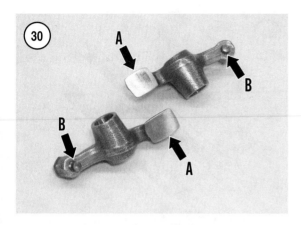

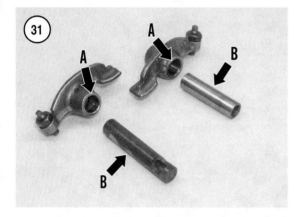

2. Inspect the rocker arm pad (A, **Figure 30**) where it rides on the cam lobe and where the adjuster (B) rides on the valve stem. Check the contact surfaces for flat spots, scoring and damage.

3. Inspect the valve adjuster locknuts for rounding and other damage.

4. Inspect the rocker arm shafts for scoring, cracks or other damage.

5. Measure the rocker arm bore (A, **Figure 31**) inside diameter.

6. Measure the rocker arm shaft (B, **Figure 31**) outside diameter.

7. Calculate the rocker arm-to-rocker arm shaft clearance as follows:

a. Subtract the rocker arm shaft outside diameter (Step 6) from the rocker arm bore inside diameter (Step 5).

b. Replace the rocker arm and/or the rocker arm shaft if the clearance is out of specification (**Table 2**).

Reassembly

1. Make sure the oil passages through the camshaft holder and rocker arms are clear.

2. Lubricate the valve adjuster threads and seating surfaces with engine oil.

3. Lubricate the rocker arm shafts with assembly lube or molybdenum oil solution.

NOTE
The rocker arm shafts are different. The intake shaft (B, Figure 28) is longer and has a notch on one end to provide clearance for the crankcase stud.

4. Position the exhaust rocker arm into the camshaft holder and install the exhaust rocker arm shaft (A, **Figure 28**) with its threaded side facing out.

5. Position the intake rocker arm into the camshaft holder and install the intake rocker arm shaft (B, **Figure 28**) with its notch facing out. Turn the rocker arm shaft so a bolt can pass through the stud hole as shown in **Figure 32**.

6. Compare the assembled camshaft holder assembly with **Figure 27**.

Camshaft Oil Clearance Measurement

Use Plastigage to measure the clearance between the camshaft and the camshaft holder and cylinder head journals. The camshaft and camshaft holder must be installed on the cylinder head when performing this procedure.

1. Wipe all oil residue from each cam bearing journal (camshaft, camshaft holder and cylinder head). These surfaces must be clean and dry.

2. Install the camshaft into the cylinder head. Position the cam lobes so they are facing down (the valves will not be pressed open when the cam is installed). Refer to *Camshaft Installation* in this section.

3. Place a strip of Plastigage material on the top of each camshaft bearing journal (**Figure 33**), parallel to the cam.

4. Install and tighten the camshaft holder as described in *Camshaft Installation* in this section.

CAUTION
Do not rotate the camshaft with the Plastigage in place.

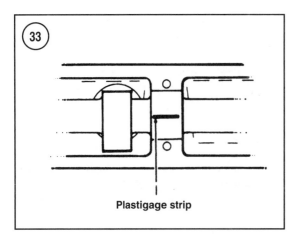

Plastigage strip

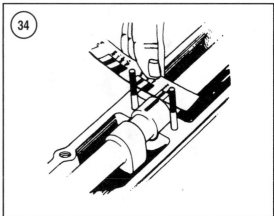

CAUTION
Loosen the camshaft holder nuts as de-
scribed or the camshaft holder may be
damaged.

5. Loosen and remove the camshaft holder nuts and washers as described in *Camshaft Removal* in this section.

6. Remove the camshaft holder, making sure the camshaft does not rotate. Do not drop the dowel pins into the engine when the camshaft holder is lifted off the camshaft.

7. Measure the widest portion of the flattened Plastigage according to the manufacturer's instructions (**Figure 34**) and compare to the camshaft oil clearance specification in **Table 2**. Note the following:

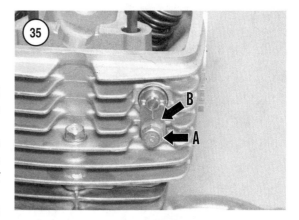

   a. If all the measurements are within specification, the cylinder head, camshaft and camshaft holder can be reused.

   b. If any measurement exceeds the service limit, replace the camshaft and recheck the oil clearance.

   c. If the new measurement exceeds the service limit with the new camshaft, measure the camshaft holder inside diameter to isolate the worn part(s). Refer to *Camshaft Holder Inspection* in this section.

8. Remove all Plastigage material from the camshaft, camshaft holder and cylinder head.

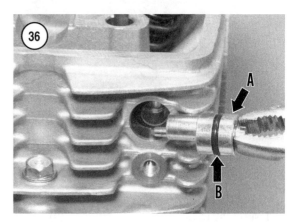

CYLINDER HEAD

Removal

1. Remove the camshaft as described in this chapter.

2. Remove the intake tube as described in *Carburetor and Intake Tub*e in Chapter Eight.

3. Remove the engine from the frame as described in *Engine* in Chapter Five.

4. Remove the cam chain tensioner set plate bolt (A, **Figure 35**), set plate (B, **Figure 35**) and adjuster (A,

CAM CHAIN

A continuous cam chain is used. Do not cut the chain; replacement link components are not available.

The engine lower end must be disassembled to replace the cam chain. Refer to Chapter Five.

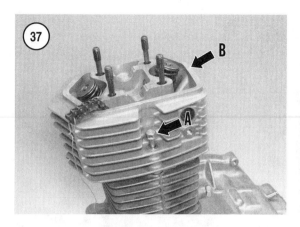

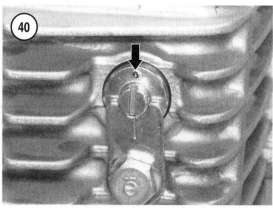

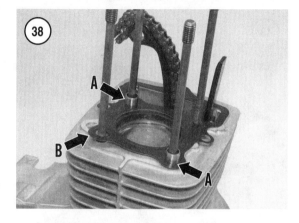

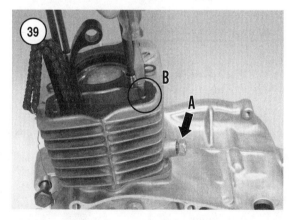

possible cylinder head and cylinder warp or other damage.

7. Cover the cylinder and chain tunnel with a clean shop cloth.

8. Inspect the cylinder head as described in this section.

9. Refer to *Valves and Valve Components* in this chapter to service the valve assembly.

Installation

1. Clean the cylinder head and cylinder block gasket surfaces.

2. Position the cam chain inside the chain tunnel so it does not interfere with the cylinder head.

3. Install the dowel pins (A, **Figure 38**).

4. Install a *new* cylinder head gasket (B, **Figure 38**).

5. Loosen the cam chain tensioner adjust bolt locknut and bolt (A, **Figure 39**).

6. Push the tensioner rod down with a screwdriver (B, **Figure 39**) until it is below the cylinder head surface, then tighten the cam chain tensioner adjust bolt and locknut (A).

7. Install the cylinder head (B, **Figure 37**) over the studs and dowel pins.

8. Install the cylinder head mounting bolt (A, **Figure 37**) and tighten finger-tight.

9. Lubricate a new O-ring (B, **Figure 36**) with engine oil and install it on the cam chain tensioner (A).

10. Install the cam chain tensioner (A, **Figure 36**) through the cylinder head and the top of the rear cam chain guide. Then install the set plate (B, **Figure 35**) and bolt (A). Turn the cam chain adjuster until its index mark faces up (**Figure 40**).

11. Install the engine in the frame (Chapter Five).

12. Install the intake tube (Chapter Eight).

13. Install the camshaft as described in this chapter.

Figure 36) if they were not removed previously during camshaft removal.

5. Remove the bolt (A, **Figure 37**) and cylinder head (B).

6. Remove the dowel pins (A, **Figure 38**) and head gasket (B).

NOTE
After removing the cylinder head, check the top and bottom gasket surfaces for any indications of leaks. Also, check the head and base gaskets for signs of leaks. A blown gasket could indicate

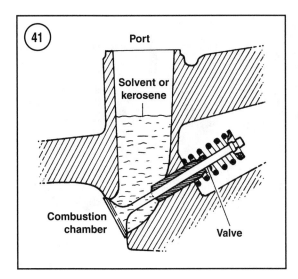

Inspection

1. Before removing the valves from the cylinder head, perform a solvent test to check the valve face-to-valve seat seal.

   a. Support the cylinder head with the exhaust port facing up (**Figure 41**). Pour solvent or kerosene into the port. Check the combustion chamber for fluid leaking past the exhaust valve. There should be no leaks past the seat in the combustion chamber.

   b. Repeat Step 2 for the intake valve.

   c. If there is fluid leaking, the combustion chamber will appear wet, indicating that the valve is not seating correctly. Check for a damaged valve stem, valve seat and/or face, or possibly a cracked combustion chamber.

2. Remove the spark plug (Chapter Three).

3. Clean the cylinder head and cylinder gasket surfaces. Do not scratch the gasket surface. If the gasket residue is hard to remove, place a solvent soaked rag across the cylinder head gasket surface to soften the deposits.

4. Before removing the valves, remove all carbon deposits from the combustion chamber (**Figure 42**) with a wire brush. Do not damage the head, valves or spark plug threads.

> *CAUTION*
> *Cleaning the combustion chamber with the valves removed can damage the valve seat surfaces. A damaged or slightly scratched valve seat will cause poor valve seating.*

5. Examine the spark plug threads in the cylinder head for damage. If damage is minor or if the threads are contaminated with carbon, use a spark plug thread tap to clean the threads following the manufacturer's instructions. If thread damage is severe, repair the head by installing a steel thread insert.

> *CAUTION*
> *When using a tap to clean spark plug threads, lubricate the tap with an aluminum tap cutting fluid or kerosene.*

6. Clean the head in solvent. Make sure the oil passageway is clear.

> *CAUTION*
> *If the cylinder head was bead blasted, cleaning grit must be removed from all head areas.*

7. Check for cracks in the combustion chamber (**Figure 42**) and exhaust. A cracked head must be replaced.

8. Examine the piston crown. The crown should show no signs of wear or damage. If the crown appears pecked or spongy-looking, check the spark plug, valves and combustion chamber for aluminum deposits. If these deposits are found, the cylinder is overheating.

> *CAUTION*
> *Do not clean the piston crown while the piston is installed in the cylinder.*

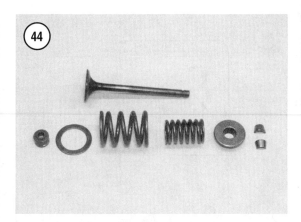

Carbon scraped from the top of the piston may fall between the cylinder wall and piston and onto the piston rings. Because carbon grit is very abrasive, premature cylinder, piston and ring wear will occur. If the piston crown has heavy carbon deposits, remove the piston as described in this chapter to clean properly. Excessive carbon buildup on the piston crown reduces piston cooling, raises engine compression and causes overheating.

9. Measure cylinder head warp with a feeler gauge and a straightedge (**Figure 43**). Check at several locations. Maximum allowable warp is listed in **Table 2**. If the warp exceeds this limit, the cylinder head must be resurfaced or replaced.

10. Check the exhaust pipe studs for looseness or thread damage. Slight thread damage can be repaired with a thread file or die. If thread damage is severe, replace the damaged stud(s) as described in *Service Methods* in Chapter One.

11. Check the valves and valve guides as described under *Valves and Valve Components* in this chapter.

VALVES AND VALVE COMPONENTS

Due to the number of special tools and the skills required to use them, it is general practice by those who do their own service to remove the cylinder head and entrust valve service to a dealership or machine shop.

Valve Removal

Refer to **Figure 44**.

1. Remove the cylinder head as described in this chapter.

2. Identify the parts as they are removed so they can be reinstalled in their original position.

> *CAUTION*
> *To avoid loss of spring tension, do not compress the springs any more than necessary when removing the valve keepers.*

3. Install a valve spring compressor (**Figure 45**) squarely over the upper retainer with the other end of the tool placed against the valve head.

4. Tighten the valve spring compressor until the valve keepers (**Figure 46**) separate and remove them.

5. Remove the valve spring compressor. Remove the upper retainer (A, **Figure 47**) and the outer (B) and inner (C) valve springs.

> *CAUTION*
> *Remove any burrs from the valve stem groove (**Figure 48**) before removing the valve; otherwise, the valve guide will be damaged as the valve stem passes through it.*

6. Remove the valve from its guide while rotating it slightly.

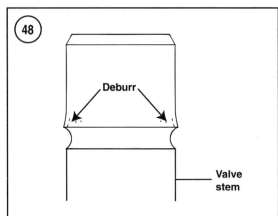

NOTE
If a valve is difficult to remove, it may be bent, causing it to stick in its valve guide. This condition will require valve and valve guide replacement.

7. Remove the spring seat (**Figure 49**).

NOTE
1992-2000 XR100R models do not use an oil seal on the intake valve guide.

8. Pull the oil seal (**Figure 50**) off the valve guide and discard it.
9. Repeat for the other valve.
10. Clean and inspect the valves, valve seats and valve guides as described in this section.

NOTE
Do not remove the valve guides unless they require replacement.

Valve Installation

Install the valves and their components in their original locations as recorded during removal.

NOTE
1992-2000 XR100R models do not use an oil seal on the intake valve guide.

1. Lubricate the inside of a *new* oil seal with engine oil. Then align and push the seal straight down the valve guide until it snaps into the groove in the top of the guide (**Figure 51**). Check that the oil seal is centered and seats squarely on top of the guide. If the seal is cocked to one side, oil will leak past the seal during engine operation.

NOTE
Replace the oil seals whenever the valves are removed. Also, if a new seal was installed and then removed, do not reuse it.

2. Install the spring seat (**Figure 49**).
3. Install the valve as follows:
   a. Coat the valve stem with molybdenum oil solution.
   b. Install the valve partway into its guide and slowly turn the valve as it enters the valve stem seal and continue turning it until the valve is installed all the way.
   c. Make sure the valve moves up and down smoothly.
4. Install the inner (C, **Figure 47**) and outer (B) valve springs.

5. Install the retainer (A, **Figure 47**).

> *CAUTION*
> *To avoid loss of spring tension, do not compress the springs any more than necessary when installing the valve keepers.*

6. Compress the valve springs with a valve spring compressor tool (**Figure 45**) and install the valve keepers (**Figure 46**). Make sure the keepers fit into the rounded groove in the valve stem.
7. Gently tap the upper retainer with a plastic hammer, to ensure that the keepers (**Figure 52**) are properly seated.

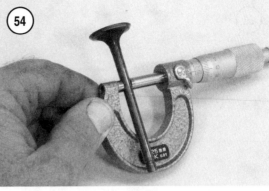

8. Repeat for the other valve.
9. After installing the cylinder head, camshaft and camshaft holder, check and adjust the valve clearance as described in Chapter Three.

Valve Inspection

Valve components

Refer to the specifications in **Table 2**. Replace parts that are damaged or out of specification as described in this section.
1. Clean the valve components (**Figure 44**) in solvent. Do not damage the valve seating surface.
2. Inspect the valve face (A, **Figure 53**) for burning, pitting or other signs of wear. Unevenness of the valve face is an indication that the valve is not serviceable. If the wear on a valve is too extensive to be corrected by hand-lapping the valve into its seat, replace the valve. The face on the valve cannot be ground. Replace the valve if damaged.
3. Inspect the valve stems for wear and roughness. Check the valve keeper grooves for damage.
4. Measure each valve stem outside diameter (**Figure 54**). Note the following:
   a. If a valve stem is out of specification, discard the valve.
   b. If a valve stem is within specification, record the measurement so it can be used to determine the valve stem-to-guide clearance in Step 7.

> *NOTE*
> *The manufacturer recommends reaming the valve guides to remove any carbon buildup before checking and measuring the guides. Remove carbon and varnish from the valve guides with a stiff spiral wire brush. Then clean the valve guides with solvent to wash out all particles and dry with compressed air.*

5. Insert each valve into its respective valve guide and move it up and down by hand. The valve should move smoothly.

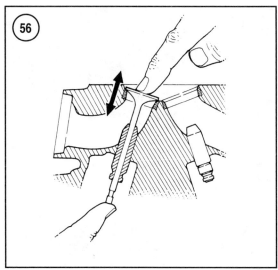

6. Measure each valve guide inside diameter with a small hole gauge and record the measurements. Note the following:

NOTE
Because valve guides wear unevenly (oval shape), measure each guide at different positions. Use the largest bore diameter measurement when determining its size.

   a. If a valve guide is out of specification, replace it as described in this section.
   b. If a valve guide is within specification, record the measurement so it can be used to determine the valve stem-to-guide clearance in Step 7.

7. Subtract the measurement made in Step 4 from the measurement made in Step 6 to determine the valve stem-to-guide clearance. Note the following:
   a. If the clearance is out of specification, determine if a new guide would bring the clearance within specification.
   b. If the clearance would be out of specification with a new guide, replace the valve and guide as a set.

8. Inspect the valve springs as follows:
   a. Inspect each spring for any cracks or other visual damage.
   b. Measure the free length of each valve spring (**Figure 55**).
   c. Replace damaged springs or springs outside of the free length specification.

9. Check the valve keepers. Replace in pairs as necessary.

10. Inspect the spring retainer and spring seat for damage.

11. Inspect the valve seats as described in this section.

Valve seat

The most accurate method for checking the valve seal is to use a marking compound (machinist's dye),

available from auto parts and tool stores. Marking compound is used to locate high or irregular spots when checking or making close fits. Follow the manufacturer's directions.

NOTE
Because of the close operating tolerances within the valve assembly, the valve stem and guide must be within tolerance; otherwise the inspection results will be inaccurate.

1. Remove the valves as described in this chapter.
2. Clean the valve seat in the cylinder head and valve mating areas with contact cleaner.
3. Clean all carbon deposits from the valve face with solvent and dry.
4. Spread a thin layer of marking compound evenly on the valve face.
5. Slowly insert the valve into its guide and tap the valve against its seat several times (**Figure 56**) without spinning it.
6. Remove the valve and examine the impression left by the marking compound. If the impression (on the valve or in the cylinder head) is not even and continuous, and the valve seat width (**Figure 57**) is not within the specified tolerance listed in **Table 2**, the valve seat in the cylinder head must be reconditioned.
7. Closely examine the valve seat in the cylinder head (B, **Figure 53**). It should be smooth and even with a polished seating surface.
8. If the valve seat is not in good condition, recondition the valve seat as described in this chapter.
9. Repeat for the other valve and valve seat.

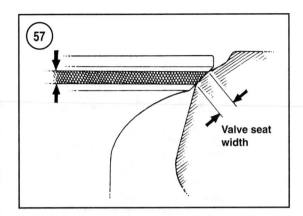

Valve seat width

Valve Guide Removal/Installation

Tools

The following tools (or equivalents) are required to remove and install the valve guides. Confirm part numbers with a dealership before ordering them.

1. 5.5 mm valve guide driver: Honda part No.07942-3290100 (U.S. only) or 07942-0010100.
2. 5.5 mm valve guide reamer: Honda part No. 07984-090001 or 07984-098000D.

Procedure

Read the entire procedure before beginning and have the required tools. It is necessary to work quickly with hot components.

1. Remove all of the valves and valve guide seals from the cylinder head.
2. Place the new valve guides in the freezer for approximately one hour prior to heating the cylinder head. Chilling them will slightly reduce the outside diameter, while the cylinder is lightly larger due to heat expansion. This makes valve guide installation much easier.
3. Place the cylinder head on a hot plate and heat to a temperature of 130-140° C (275-290° F). Do not ex-

ceed 150° C (300° F). Monitor the temperature with an infrared thermometer or heat sticks.

> *WARNING*
> *Wear protective gloves as the cylinder head is very hot.*

> *CAUTION*
> *Do not heat the cylinder head with a torch. The direct heat will damage the case hardening of the valve guide and may warp the cylinder head.*

4. Remove the head from the hot plate. Place the head on wooden blocks with the combustion chamber facing up.
5. From the combustion chamber side of the head, drive out the valve guide with the valve guide driver. Quickly repeat this step for the other guide if it is to be replaced. Reheat the cylinder head as required. Discard the valve guides after removing them. Make sure the O-ring originally installed on the valve guide is also removed.

> *CAUTION*
> *Do not attempt to remove the valve guides if the head is not hot enough. Doing so may damage the valve guide bore in the cylinder head and require replacement of the head.*

6. Allow the head to cool.
7. Inspect and clean the valve guide bores. Check for cracks or any scoring along the bore wall.
8. Reheat the cylinder head as described in Step 3. Then remove it from the hot plate and install it onto the wooden blocks with the valve spring side facing up.
9. Remove one new valve guide, either intake or exhaust, from the freezer.
10. Install a new O-ring below the shoulder on the valve guide.
11. Align the valve guide in the bore. Use the valve guide driver tool and hammer and drive in the valve guide until its shoulder seats against the cylinder head (**Figure 58**).
12. Repeat to install the other valve guide, if necessary.
13. Allow the head to cool to room temperature.
14. Ream each valve guide as follows:
   a. Place the head on wooden blocks with the combustion chamber facing *up*. The guides are reamed from this side.
   b. Coat the valve guide and valve guide reamer with cutting oil.
   c. Rotate the reamer clockwise into the valve guide.

CAUTION
*Always rotate the reamer **clockwise** through the entire length of the guide, both when reaming the guide and when removing the reamer. Rotating the reamer counterclockwise will reverse cut and damage (enlarge) the valve guide bore.*

CAUTION
Do not allow the reamer to tilt. Keep the tool square to the hole and apply even pressure and twisting motion during the entire operation.

d. Slowly rotate the reamer through the guide, while periodically adding cutting oil.

e. As the end of the reamer passes through the valve guide, maintain the clockwise motion and work the reamer back out of the guide while continuing to add cutting oil.

f. Clean the reamer of all chips and relubricate with cutting oil before starting on the next guide. Repeat for the other valve guide if necessary.

15. Thoroughly clean the cylinder head and all valve components in solvent, then with detergent and hot water to remove all cutting residue. Rinse in cold water. Dry with compressed air.

16. Measure the valve guide inside diameter with a small hole gauge. The measurement must be within the specification listed in **Table 2**.

17. Apply engine oil to the valve guides to prevent rust.

18. Lubricate a valve stem with engine oil and pass it through each valve guide, verifying that it moves without any roughness or binding.

19. Reface the valve seats as described under *Valve Seat Reconditioning* in this section.

Valve Seat Reconditioning

Tools

Before reconditioning the valve seats, inspect and measure them as described in *Valve Inspection* in this section.

To cut the cylinder head valve seats the following tools are required:

1. Valve seat cutters (**Figure 59**). See a dealership for current part numbers.

2. Vernier caliper.

3. Gear-marking compound.

4. Valve lapping tool.

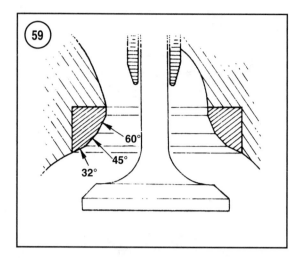

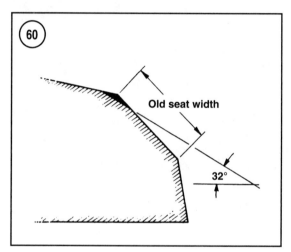

Procedure

NOTE
Follow the manufacturer's instructions when using valve facing equipment.

1. Carefully rotate and insert the solid pilot into the valve guide. Be sure the pilot is correctly seated.

2. Install the 45° cutter and cutter holder onto the solid pilot.

CAUTION
Work slowly and make light cuts. Overcutting the valve seats will recede the valves into the cylinder head, reducing the valve adjustment range. If cutting is excessive, the ability to set the valve adjustment may be lost. This condition requires cylinder head replacement.

3. Using the 45° cutter, de-scale and clean the valve seat with one or two turns.

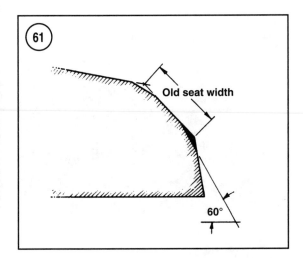

Old seat width

60°

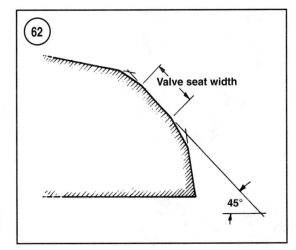

Valve seat width

45°

a. Clean the valve seat with contact cleaner.
b. Spread a thin layer of marking compound evenly on the valve face.
c. Slowly insert the valve into its guide.
d. Support the valve with two fingers (**Figure 56**) and tap the valve up and down in the cylinder head several times. Do not rotate the valve or a false reading will result.
e. Remove the valve and examine the impression left by the marking compound.
f. Measure the valve seat width as shown in **Figure 57**. Refer to **Figure 2** for specified valve width.
g. The valve contact should be approximately in the center of the valve seat area.

10. If the contact area is too high on the valve, or if it is too wide, use the 32° cutter and remove a portion of the top area of the valve seat material to lower and narrow the contact area on the valve (**Figure 60**).

11. If the contact are is too low on the valve, or too wide, use the 60° cutter and remove a portion of the lower area of the valve seat material to raise and narrow the contact area on the valve (**Figure 61**).

12. After the desired valve seat position and width is obtained, use the 45° cutter to lightly clean off any burrs that may have been caused by previous cuts.

13. When the contact area is correct, lap the valve as described in this chapter.

14. Repeat Steps 1-13 for the other valve seat.

15. Thoroughly clean the cylinder head and all valve components in solvent, then with detergent and hot water. Rinse in cold water and dry with compressed air. Lubricate the valve guides to prevent rust.

Valve Lapping

Valve lapping can restore the valve seat without machining if the amount of wear or distortion is not too great.

Perform this procedure after determining that the valve seat width and outside diameter are within specifications (**Table 2**). A valve lapping tool and compound are required.

1. Apply a light coating of fine grade valve lapping compound on the valve face seating surface.

2. Insert the valve into the head.

3. Wet the suction cup of the lapping stick and stick it onto the head of the valve. Spin the tool in both directions, while pressing it against the valve seat and lap the valve to the seat. Every 5 to 10 seconds, lift and rotate the valve 180° in the valve seat. Continue until the gasket surfaces on the valve and seat are smooth and equal in size.

4. Examine the valve seat in the cylinder head (**Figure 57**). It should be smooth and even with a smooth, polished seating ring.

4. If the seat is still pitted or burned, turn the 45° cutter additional turns until the surface is clean.

5. Measure the valve seat with a vernier caliper (**Figure 57**). Record the measurement to use as a reference point when performing the following.

CAUTION
The 32° cutter removes material quickly. Work carefully and check the progress often.

6. Install the 32° cutter onto the solid pilot and lightly cut the seat to remove 1/4 of the existing valve seat (**Figure 60**).

7. Install the 60° cutter onto the solid pilot and lightly cut the seat to remove 1/4 of the existing valve seat (**Figure 61**).

8. Measure the valve seat with a vernier caliper (**Figure 57**). Then fit the 45° cutter onto the solid pilot and cut the valve seat to the specified width (**Figure 62**) listed in **Table 2**.

9. When the valve seat width is correct, check valve seating as follows:

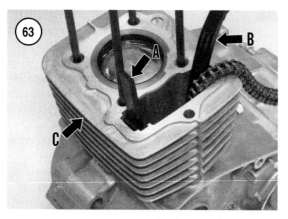

5. Repeat for the other valve seat.

6. Thoroughly clean the cylinder head and all valve components in solvent, then with detergent and hot water. Rinse in cold water and dry with compressed air. Lubricate the valve guides to prevent rust.

> *CAUTION*
> *Any compound left on the valves or in the cylinder head causes excessive wear to the engine components.*

7. Install the valve assemblies as described in this chapter.

8. Perform a solvent test as described in *Inspection* in *Cylinder Head* in this chapter. There should be no leaks past the seat. If fluid leaks past any of the seats, disassemble that valve assembly and repeat the lapping procedure until there are no leaks.

9. After cleaning the cylinder head and valve components in detergent and hot water, apply a light coat of engine oil to all bare metal surfaces to prevent rust.

CYLINDER AND CHAIN TENSIONER

This section services the cylinder and chain tensioner assembly. The chain tensioner is mounted onto and removed with the cylinder.

Removal

> *CAUTION*
> *When rotating the crankshaft, pull up the cam chain so it cannot bind internally.*

1. Remove the engine from the frame (Chapter Five).

2. Remove the cylinder head and camshaft as described in this chapter.

3. Remove the front cam chain guide (A, **Figure 63**). The rear cam chain guide (B, **Figure 63**) will remove with the cylinder.

> *NOTE*
> *If broken piston rings are suspected, turn the crankshaft to raise the piston and the cylinder to TDC. Then place clean shop rags underneath the cylinder to prevent broken parts from falling into the crankcase.*

4. Remove the cylinder (C, **Figure 63**).

5. Remove and discard the base gasket (A, **Figure 64**).

6. Remove the dowel pins (B, **Figure 64**).

7. Cover the crankcase opening.

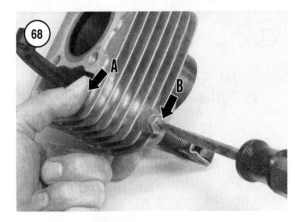

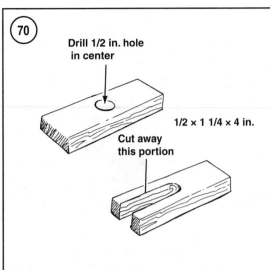

Drill 1/2 in. hole
in center

1/2 × 1 1/4 × 4 in.

Cut away
this portion

1. Install and lock the cam chain tensioner as follows:
   a. Lubricate and install a new O-ring on the cam
      chain tensioner adjust bolt. Loosely install the
      adjust bolt and locknut (**Figure 65**) so it will
      not interfere with cam chain tensioner instal-
      lation.
   b. Install the cam chain tensioner (**Figure 66**)
      through the guide hole in the cylinder.
   c. Hook the end of the spring into the cylinder
      spring hole (A, **Figure 67**).
   d. Push the tensioner rod (B, **Figure 67**) down
      until it is below the cylinder surface (A, **Figure
      68**) and tighten the adjust bolt and locknut (B,
      Figure 68) securely.
   e. Set the cylinder aside until installation.
2. Install the piston and rings as described in this
chapter.

> *CAUTION*
> *Make sure the piston pin circlips have*
> *been properly installed.*

3. Install the dowel pins (B, **Figure 64**) and a new
gasket (A).
4. Install a piston holding fixture (A, **Figure 69**) under the piston (B).

> *NOTE*
> *To fabricate a wooden piston holding*
> *fixture, refer to the example in **Figure**
> **70***.

5. Lubricate the cylinder wall, piston and rings with
engine oil. Liberally lubricate the oil control rings to
fill them with oil.
6. Stagger the piston ring end gaps 120° apart
around the piston circumference. This includes the
oil ring rails.

8. Remove the cam chain tensioner adjust bolt locknut and adjust bolt (**Figure 65**).
9. Slide the cam chain tensioner (**Figure 66**) from
the cylinder.
10. Clean and inspect the cylinder as described in
this section.
11. Clean and inspect the cam chain tensioner as described in this section.

Installation

> *CAUTION*
> *When rotating the crankshaft, pull up the*
> *cam chain so it cannot bind internally.*

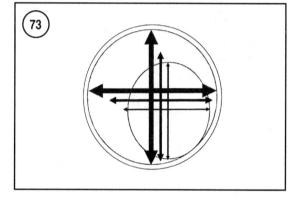

7. Align the cylinder with the cylinder studs and lower it onto the piston. Compress each piston ring by hand as it enters the cylinder. Push the cylinder down until it bottoms on the piston holding fixture.

8. Remove the piston holding fixture and push the cylinder down into place over the dowel pins and against the base gasket.

9. Install a length of hose over the 6 mm cylinder head mounting bolt (**Figure 71**) and secure it with a nut. The hose will hold the cylinder in place when the crankshaft is turned over in the following step.

10. Pull the cam chain up and rotate the crankshaft counterclockwise. The piston must move up and down in the bore with no binding or roughness. If there is any interference, a piston ring may have broken during cylinder installation.

11. Install the front cam chain guide (A, **Figure 63**).

12. Install the cylinder head and camshaft as described in this chapter.

13. Install the engine into the frame (Chapter Five).

Inspection

Cylinder

Refer to the specifications in **Table 3**.

1. The paper base gasket sets up hard and is difficult to remove. Use an aerosol gasket remover to soften the gasket before removal. Refer to *Gasket Remover* in *Shop Supplies* in Chapter One for additional information. Do not nick or gouge the gasket surfaces or leaks will result.

2. Wash the cylinder block in solvent. Dry with compressed air.

3. Check the dowel pin holes for cracks or other damage.

4. Use a straight edge and feeler to check for upper cylinder warp (**Figure 72**). Check at different locations.

5. Measure the cylinder bore with a bore gauge or inside micrometer at the points shown in **Figure 73**. Measure in line with the piston pin and 90° to the

pin. Use the largest measurement to determine cylinder bore. If the taper or out-of-round is greater than specifications, bore the cylinder oversize and install a new piston and rings.

6. Determine piston-to-cylinder clearance as described under *Piston Clearance Inspection* in *Piston and Piston Rings* in this chapter.

7. If the cylinder is not worn past the service limit, check the bore for scratches or gouges. The bore still may require boring and reconditioning.

8. After the cylinder has been serviced, clean the cylinder as follows:

CAUTION
A combination of soap and hot water is the only solution that will completely clean the cylinder wall. Solvent and kerosene cannot wash fine grit out of cylinder crevices. Any grit left in the cylinder will act as a grinding compound and cause premature wear to the new rings.

a. Wash the cylinder bore in hot soapy water.

b. After washing the cylinder, wipe the cylinder wall with a clean white cloth. It should *not* show any traces of grit or debris. If the rag is the slightest bit dirty, the wall is not thoroughly cleaned and must be washed again.

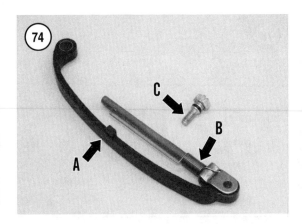

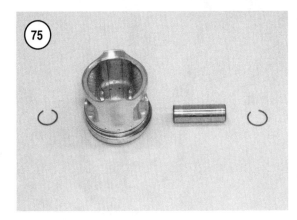

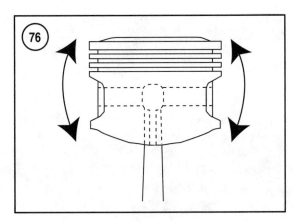

5. Remove the old adjust bolt O-ring and replace with new.

PISTON AND PISTON RINGS

The piston is made of an aluminum alloy. The piston pin is made of steel and is a slip fit in the piston. The piston pin is held in place by a clip at each end.

Replacement piston and rings are available in standard size and four oversizes: 0.25, 0.50, 0.75 and 1.00 mm.

Refer to **Figure 75** when servicing the piston and rings in the following section.

Piston Removal

> *CAUTION*
> *When rotating the crankshaft, pull up the cam chain so it cannot bind internally. Guide the piston so it is not damaged when retracted into the crankcase.*

1. Remove the cylinder head as described in this chapter.
2. Mark the top of the piston with a directional arrow pointing toward the front of the engine. OEM pistons are marked with either EX (exhaust side) or IN (intake side). Aftermarket pistons may be marked differently.
3. Block off the crankcase below the piston with a clean shop cloth to prevent the piston pin circlips from falling into the crankcase.
4. Before removing the piston, hold the rod and rock the piston (**Figure 76**). Any rocking motion (do not confuse with the normal sliding motion) indicates wear on the piston pin, rod bushing bore, or a combination of both.
5. Support the piston with a piston holder fixture (A, **Figure 69**).
6. Remove a piston circlip (**Figure 77**) from one side of the piston.

c. When the cylinder is clean, lubricate the liner with clean engine oil to prevent rust.

Cam chain tensioner

1. Clean and dry the cam chain tensioner assembly.
2. Inspect the front and rear chain tensioner rails (A, **Figure 74**) for cracks, abnormal wear or other damage.
3. Check the spring (B, **Figure 74**) for stretched coils or damage.
4. Check the adjust bolt and locknut (C, **Figure 74**) for damaged threads.

NOTE
The operating clearance between the piston pin and pin bore is such that the piston pin can be removed and installed by hand. However, problems such as varnish on the piston pin, a burred pin bore or circlip groove, or a damaged piston can make it difficult to remove the piston pin.

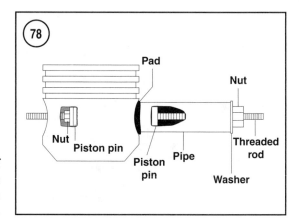

7. Push the piston pin out of the piston by hand. If the pin is tight, use a homemade tool (**Figure 78**) to remove it. Do not drive the piston pin out as this action may damage the piston pin, connecting rod or piston. Heat can also be used to ease removal. Heat the piston crown (and not the side of the piston) with a heat gun.

8. Lift the piston off the connecting rod.

9. Inspect the piston, piston pin and piston rings as described in this section.

Piston Installation

CAUTION
When rotating the crankshaft, pull up the cam chain so it cannot bind internally. Guide the piston so it is not damaged when retracted into the crankcase.

1. Make sure the crankcase gasket surface is clean.

2. Install the piston rings onto the piston as described in this section.

CAUTION
Do not align the piston pin circlip end gap with the cut out in the piston.

3. Install one *new* piston pin circlip (**Figure 77**) into the piston. Make sure it seats in the groove completely.

4. Coat the connecting rod small end, piston pin and piston with engine oil.

5. Slide the piston pin into the piston until its end is flush with the piston pin boss.

6. Place the piston over the connecting rod:
   a. If the piston has an EX on its crown (**Figure 79**), install the piston with the EX mark facing forward (exhaust side of engine).
   b. If the piston has an IN mark on its crown (**Figure 80**), install the piston with the IN mark facing rearward (intake side of engine).
   c. If installing an aftermarket piston, follow the manufacturer's instructions.

7. Line up the piston pin with the hole in the connecting rod. Push the piston pin through the connecting rod and into the other side of the piston. Center the piston pin in the piston.

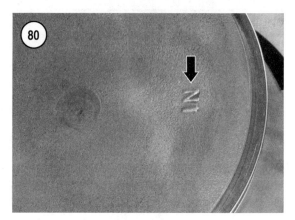

8. Block off the crankcase below the piston with a clean shop cloth to prevent the piston pin circlip from falling into the crankcase.

9. Install a *new* piston pin circlip (**Figure 77**) in the end of the piston pin boss. The first circlip was installed in Step 3. Make sure they seat in the piston grooves completely.

Piston Inspection

1. Remove the piston rings as described in this section.

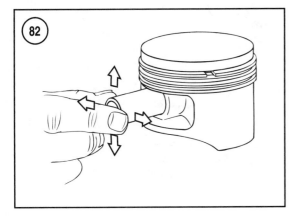

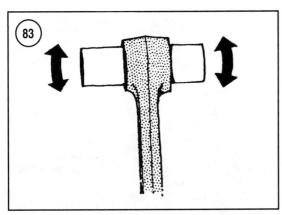

2. Soak the piston in solvent to soften the carbon deposits.

3. Clean the carbon from the piston crown with a soft scraper or wire wheel mounted in a drill. A thick carbon buildup reduces piston cooling and results in detonation and piston damage.

CAUTION
Do not wire brush the piston skirt.

4. After cleaning the piston, examine the crown. The crown must show no signs of wear or damage. If the crown appears pecked or spongy-looking, also check the spark plug, valves and combustion chamber for aluminum deposits. If these deposits are found, the engine is overheating.

5. Examine each ring groove (A, **Figure 81**) for burrs, dented edges or other damage. Pay particular attention to the top compression ring groove as it usually wears more than the others. Because the oil rings are bathed in oiled, these rings and grooves wear little compared to compression rings and their grooves. If there is evidence of oil ring groove wear or if the oil ring is tight and difficult to remove, the piston skirt may have collapsed due to excessive heat. Replace the piston.

6. Clean the oil control holes in the piston.

7. Check the piston skirt (B, **Figure 81**) for damage. If the piston shows signs of partial seizure (bits of aluminum built up on the piston skirt), replace the piston.

NOTE
If the piston skirt is worn or scuffed unevenly from side-to-side, the connecting rod may be bent or twisted.

8. Check the piston circlip grooves (C, **Figure 81**) for wear, cracks or other damage.

9. Measure piston-to-cylinder clearance as described in *Piston Clearance Inspection* in this section.

Piston Pin Inspection

Refer to the specifications in **Table 3**.

1. Clean and dry the piston pin.

2. Inspect the piston pin for chrome flaking or cracks.

3. Oil the piston pin and install it in the piston. Rotate the piston pin and check for tightness or excessive play (**Figure 82**).

4. Lubricate the piston pin and install it in the connecting rod. Rotate the piston pin and check for radial play (**Figure 83**).

5. Measure the piston pin bore (A, **Figure 84**) inside diameter.

6. Measure the piston pin (B, **Figure 84**) outside diameter.

7. Subtract the measurement made in Step 6 from the measurement made in Step 5. The difference is the piston-to-piston pin clearance.

Connecting Rod Small End Inspection

1. Inspect the connecting rod small end (**Figure 85**) for cracks or heat damage.

2. Measure the connecting rod small end inside diameter check against the dimension in **Table 3**. If out

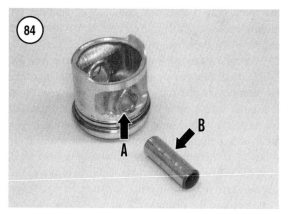

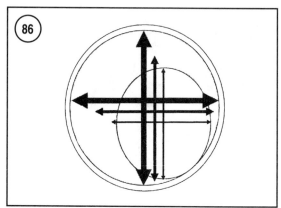

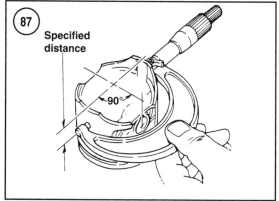

of specification, replace the crankshaft as described in Chapter Five.

Piston Clearance Inspection

1. Make sure the piston skirt and cylinder walls are clean and dry.

2. Measure the cylinder bore with a bore gauge or inside micrometer at the points shown in **Figure 86**. Measure in line with the piston pin and 90° to the pin. Use the largest measurement to determine cylinder bore diameter. If the cylinder bore is out of specification, replace the piston and bore the cylinder oversize. If the cylinder bore is within specification, continue with Step 3.

3. Measure the piston diameter at a right angle to the piston pin bore. Measure up 7 mm (0.3 in. [80 cc]) or 10 mm (0.4 in. [100 cc]) from the bottom edge of the piston skirt (**Figure 87**).

4. Subtract the piston diameter from the largest bore diameter. The difference is piston-to-cylinder clearance. If clearance exceeds the service limit in **Table 3**, determine if the piston, cylinder or both are worn. If necessary, take the cylinder to a dealership to re-bore the cylinder to accept an oversize piston.

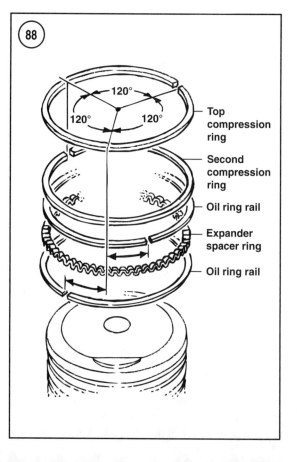

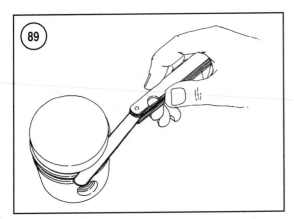

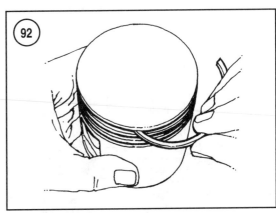

4

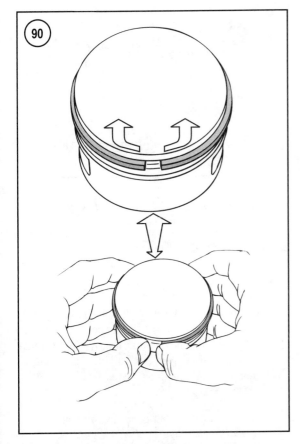

Piston Ring Inspection and Removal

A 3-ring type piston and ring assembly is used (**Figure 88**). The top and second rings are compression rings. The lower ring is an oil control ring assembly consisting of two ring rails and a spacer.

Refer to the specifications in **Table 3**. Replace the piston rings as a set if out of specification or if they show damage as described in this section.

1. Measure the side clearance of each ring in its groove with a flat feeler gauge (**Figure 89**):
    a. If the clearance is greater than specified, replace the rings. If the clearance is still excessive with new rings, replace the piston.
    b. If the clearance is too small, check the ring and ring groove for carbon and oil residue. Clean the ring without removing any metal from its surface. Clean the piston ring groove as described in *Piston Ring Installation* in this section.

WARNING
The edges of all piston rings are very sharp. Be careful when handling them to avoid cut fingers.

NOTE
Store the rings in order of removal. Identify the top of each ring.

2. Remove the compression rings by spreading the ring ends by hand (**Figure 90**).
3. Remove the oil ring assembly (**Figure 91**) by first removing the upper and then the lower ring rails. Then remove the spacer.
4. Remove carbon and oil residues from the piston ring grooves (**Figure 92**) with a broken piston ring. Do not remove aluminum material from the ring grooves as this will increase the side clearance.
5. Inspect the ring grooves for burrs, nicks or broken or cracked lands. Replace the piston if necessary.
6. Check the end gap of each ring. Insert the ring into the bottom of the cylinder bore and square it

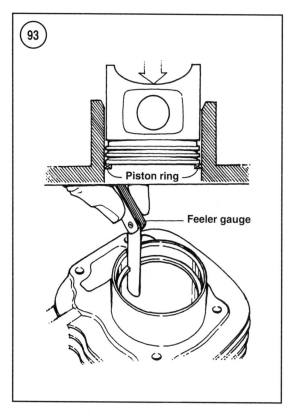

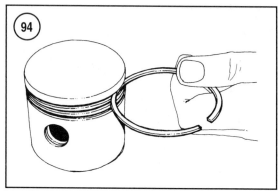

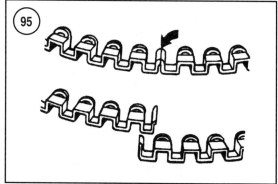

with the cylinder wall by tapping it with the piston (**Figure 93**). Measure the end gap with a feeler gauge (**Figure 93**). Replace the rings if the gap is too large. If the gap on the new ring is smaller than specified, hold a small file in a vise. Then grip the ends of the ring with your fingers and slowly enlarge the gap.

NOTE
When measuring the oil control ring end gap, measure the upper and lower ring rail end gaps only. Do not measure the spacer.

7. Roll each compression ring around its piston groove (**Figure 94**) to check for binding. If binding is noted, inspect the piston for damage. Repair minor binding with a fine-cut file.

Piston Ring Installation

1. When installing new piston rings, hone or deglaze the cylinder wall. This will help the new rings to seat in the cylinder. If necessary, refer this service to a dealership. After honing, measure the end gap of each ring and compare to the dimensions in **Table 3**.

NOTE
If the cylinder was honed or deglazed, clean the cylinder as described in

Inspection in *Cylinder and Chain Tensioner* in this chapter.

2. Clean and dry the piston and rings.
3. Install the piston rings as follows:
   a. Install the oil ring assembly into the bottom ring groove. Install the spacer first, and then the bottom and top ring rails (**Figure 88**). Make sure the ends of the spacer butt together (**Figure 95**). They should not overlap. If reassembling used parts, install the ring rails in their original positions.

NOTE
*The top and second compression rings are different. Refer to **Figure 96** (2003 models) or **Figure 97** (2004-on models) to identify the rings.*

   b. Install the compression rings by spreading the ring ends by hand (**Figure 90**).
   c. Install the compression rings with their marks facing up.
4. Make sure the rings are seated completely in their grooves all the way around the piston and that the end gaps are distributed around the piston as shown in **Figure 88**. To prevent combustion from escaping past them, the ring gaps must not align.
5. If new parts were installed, follow the *Engine Break-In* procedure in Chapter Three.

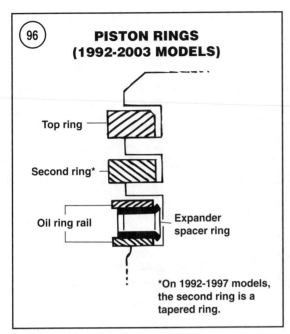

PISTON RINGS (1992-2003 MODELS)

Top ring

Second ring*

Oil ring rail

Expander spacer ring

*On 1992-1997 models, the second ring is a tapered ring.

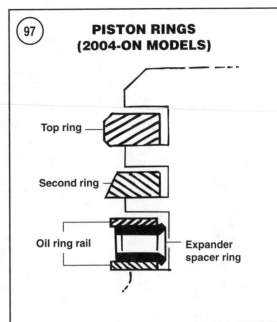

PISTON RINGS (2004-ON MODELS)

Top ring

Second ring

Oil ring rail

Expander spacer ring

CYLINDER STUD

Removal/Installation

The cylinder studs can be replaced without splitting the crankcase.

1. Check for loose, bent or damaged studs. Retighten or replace damaged studs as described in the following steps.

2. The left and right side crankcase studs are different.

3. Measure the studs installed height before removal.

4. Remove the stud as described in *Basic Service Methods* in Chapter One.

5. Clean the threaded hole in the crankcase. Check for any debris or damaged threads.

6. Install the stud to the dimensions recorded in Step 3.

Table 1 GENERAL ENGINE SPECIFICATIONS

Bore and stroke	
80 cc models	47.5 × 45.0 mm (1.87 × 1.77 in.)
100 cc models	53.0 × 45.0 mm (2.09 × 1.77 in.)
Compression ratio	
80 cc models	9.7:1
100 cc models	9.4:1
Cooling system	Air cooled
Displacement	
80 cc models	79.7 cc (4.86 cu.-in.)
100 cc models	99.2 cc (6.1 cu.-in.)
Engine	Four-stroke, overhead camshaft engine
Engine dry weight	
80 cc models	18.9 kg (41.7 lbs.)
100 cc models	21.4 kg (47.2 lbs)
Valve timing (at 1 mm [0.04 in.] lift)	
80 cc models	
Intake valve opens	8° BTDC
Intake valve closes	40° ABDC
Exhaust valve opens	40° BBDC
Exhaust valve closes	8° ATDC
100 cc models	
Intake valve opens	10° BTDC
Intake valve closes	35° ABDC
Exhaust valve opens	40° BBDC
Exhaust valve closes	5° ATDC

Table 2 CYLINDER HEAD AND VALVE SERVICE SPECIFICATIONS

	New mm (in.)	Service limit mm (in.)
Camshaft holder inside diameter	20.008-20.063 (0.7877-0.7899)	20.15 (0.793)
Camshaft journal outside diameter		
Left and right side	19.950-19.968 (0.7854-0.7861)	19.90 (0.783)
Camshaft lobe height		
80 cc models		
Intake	28.017-28.197 (1.1030-1.1101)	27.95 (1.003)
Exhaust	27.835-28.015 (1.0959-1.1030)	27.75 (1.093)
100 cc models		
Intake		
1992-1997 models	27.840-28.020 (1.0961-1.1031)	27.80 (1.094)
1998-on models	27.860-28.040 (1.0968-1.1039)	27.80 (1.094)
Exhaust	27.776-27.950 (1.0935-1.1004)	27.70 (1.091)
Camshaft oil clearance	0.040-0.113 (0.0016-0.0044)	0.20 (0.008)
Cylinder head warp	–	0.10 (0.004)
Rocker arm bore inside diameter	10.000-10.015 (0.3937-0.3943)	10.1 (0.40)
Rocker arm shaft outside diameter	9.978-9.987 (0.3928-0.3932)	9.91 (0.39)
Rocker arm-to-shaft clearance	0.013-0.037 (0.0005-0.0015)	0.08 (0.003)
Valve clearance	0.05 (0.002)	–
Valve guide inside diameter	5.475-5.485 (0.2156-0.2159)	5.50 (0.2165)
Valve seat width		
1992-1997 models	1.0 (0.04)	1.5 (0.06)
1998-on models	1.70 (0.07)	2.1 (0.08)
Valve spring free length		
Inner	28.05 (1.104)	27.6 (1.087)
Outer	34.80 (1.370)	33.7 (1.327)
Valve stem outside diameter		
Intake	5.450-5.465 (0.2146-0.2152)	5.420 (0.2134)
Exhaust	5.430-5.445 (0.2138-0.2144)	5.400 (0.2126)
Valve stem-to-guide clearance		
Intake	0.010-0.035 (0.0004-0.0014)	0.08 (0.003)
Exhaust	0.030-0.055 (0.0012-0.0022)	0.10 (0.004)

Table 3 PISTON, RINGS AND BORE SPECIFICATIONS

	New mm (in.)	Service limit mm (in.)
Connecting rod small end inside diameter		
80 cc models	13.016-13.034 (0.5124-0.5131)	13.04 (0.513)
100 cc models	14.012-14.030 (0.5517-0.5524)	14.05 (0.553)
Connecting rod-to-piston pin clearance		
XR80R and XR100R	0.016-0.040 (0.0006-0.0016)	0.03 (0.001)
CRF80 and CRF100F	0.016-0.040 (0.0006-0.0016)	0.09 (0.003)
Cylinder bore diameter (standard bore)		
80 cc models	47.500-47.510 (1.8701-1.8705)	47.6 (1.87)
100 cc models	53.000-53.010 (2.0866-2.087)	53.1 (2.09)
Cylinder out of round	–	0.10 (0.004)
Cylinder taper	–	0.10 (0.004)
Cylinder warp	–	0.10 (0.004)
Piston diameter (standard diameter)		
80 cc models	47.465-47.490 (1.8686-1.8697)	47.40 (1.866)
100 cc models	52.960-52.990 (2.0850-2.0862)	52.90 (2.083)
Piston measuring point	Refer to text	–
Piston-to-cylinder clearance	0.010-0.040 (0.0004-0.0016)	0.10 (0.004)
Piston ring side clearance		
Compression rings		
1993-1999 XR80R		
Top	0.015-0.050 (0.0006-0.0020)	0.10 (0.004)
Second	0.015-0.045 (0.0006-0.0018)	0.10 (0.004)
All other models		
Top and second	0.015-0.045 (0.0006-0.0018)	0.10 (0.004)
Oil ring	No specification provided by manufacturer	
Piston ring end gap		
80 cc models		
Compression rings		
1993-1999 models	0.15-0.35 (0.006-0.014)	0.5 (0.02)
2000-on models	0.10-0.25 (0.004-0.010)	0.4 (0.02)
Oil ring (side rails)		
1993-1999 models	0.3-0.9 (0.01-0.04)	1.1 (0.04)
2000-on models	0.20-0.70 (0.01-0.03)	0.9 (0.04)
100 cc models		
Compression rings		
1992-1999 models	0.15-0.35 (0.006-0.014)	0.5 (0.02)
2000-on models	0.05-0.20 (0.002-0.008)	0.4 (0.02)
Oil ring (side rails)		
1992-1999 models	0.3-0.9 (0.01-0.04)	1.1 (0.04)

4

(continued)

Table 3 PISTON, RINGS AND BORE SPECIFICATIONS (continued)

	New mm (in.)	Service limit mm (in.)
Piston ring end gap (continued)		
100 cc models		
Oil ring (side rails)		
2000-on models	0.20-0.70	0.9
	(0.01-0.03)	(0.04)
Piston pin bore inside diameter		
80 cc models	13.002-13.008	13.04
	(0.5119-0.5121)	(0.513)
100 cc models	14.002-14.008	14.04
	(0.5513-0.5515)	(0.553)
Piston pin outside diameter		
80 cc models	12.994-13.000	12.96
	(0.5116-0.5118)	(0.5102)
100 cc models	13.994-14.000	13.96
	(0.5509-0.5512)	(0.550)
Piston-to-piston pin clearance	0.002-0.14	0.02
	(0.0001-0.0006)	(0.0008)

Table 4 ENGINE TOP END TORQUE SPECIFICATIONS

	N•m	in.-lb.	ft.-lb.
Cam chain tensioner adjuster locknut	12	106	–
Camshaft holder nut	20	–	15
Camshaft sprocket bolt	12	106	–
Cylinder head cover bolt	12	106	–
Engine oil drain bolt	24	–	18
Exhaust pipe joint nut	12	106	–
Exhaust pipe heat shield bolt	14	–	10
Exhaust pipe mounting bolt	26	–	20
Spark plug	14	–	10

CHAPTER FIVE

ENGINE LOWER END

This chapter describes service procedures for the following:
1. Engine removal and installation.
2. Crankcase.
3. Crankshaft.
4. Transmission and internal shift mechanism removal and installation.
5. Kickstarter.

Throughout the text there is frequent mention of the right and left sides of the engine. This refers to the engine as it sits in the frame, not how it may be positioned on the workbench.

Tables 1-3 are at the end of this chapter.

GENERAL INFORMATION

1. The following components can be serviced with the engine installed in the frame:
   a. Cylinder head cover and camshaft (Chapter Four).
   b. Flywheel (Chapter Nine).
   c. Clutch, primary drive gear, external shift linkage and oil pump (Chapter Six).
2. The following components are serviced after removing the engine from the frame:
   a. Cylinder head (Chapter Four).
   b. Cylinder, piston and rings (Chapter Four).
   c. Crankcase.
   d. Crankshaft.
   e. Kickstarter.
   f. Transmission and internal shift mechanism (Chapter Seven).

ENGINE

Removal/Installation

This procedure describes the steps to remove the complete engine assembly. If desired, remove the sub-assemblies attached to the crankcase while the engine is still in the frame.

1. If the engine will be disassembled, perform an engine compression test (Chapter Three) and cylinder leakdown test (Chapter Two).
2. Remove the side covers and seat (Chapter Fourteen).
3. Remove the fuel tank (Chapter Eight).
4. Remove the exhaust system (Chapter Four).
5. Remove the carburetor and intake tube (Chapter Eight).
6. Remove the left crankcase cover (Chapter Nine).
7. Remove the drive sprocket and drive chain (Chapter Ten).

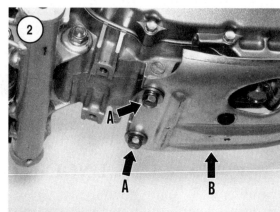

8. Remove the right footpeg assembly (Chapter Fourteen).

9. Remove the front lower engine mount nut and bolt (A, **Figure 1**).

10. Remove the skid plate mounting bolts (A, **Figure 2**) and skid plate (B).

11. Drain the engine oil (Chapter Three).

12. Support the motorcycle on a workstand or jack.

13. Remove the left footpeg and sidestand assembly (Chapter Fourteen).

14. Disconnect the spark plug cap at the spark plug.

15. Remove the fuel tank damper (A, **Figure 3**).

16. Disconnect the two stator plate electrical connectors (B, **Figure 3**).

17. Disconnect the clutch cable at the engine (**Figure 4**). If necessary, loosen the clutch cable adjuster at the handlebar to provide additional cable slack. Refer to Chapter Six.

18. Disconnect the breather hose (A, **Figure 5**) at the crankcase.

19. Remove the pinch bolt and the kick pedal.

20. Remove the front engine hanger plate nuts (B, **Figure 1**) and bolts and the hanger plate (C).

21. Remove the rear engine mounting nuts (**Figure 6**) and bolts. Remove the upper spacer (B, **Figure 5**) from the left side.

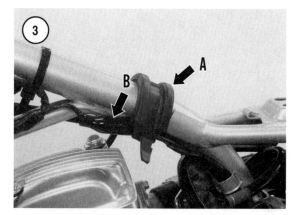

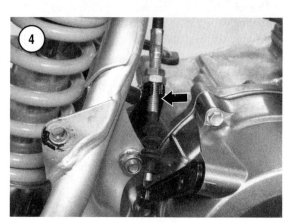

WARNING
An assembled dry engine weighs approximately 18.9 kg (41.7 lbs. [80 cc]) or 21.4 kg (47.18 lbs. [100 cc]). If necessary, have an assistant help remove and install the engine.

22. Pull the engine forward to release it from the frame and remove it.

23. Clean and inspect the frame and all exposed hardware, hoses and wiring. Check for cracks and damage, particularly at welded joints.

24. Refer to the procedures in this chapter for servicing the crankcase assembly.

25. Installation is the reverse of removal. Note the following:

    a. Install the engine mounting bolts from the left side.

    b. Install the engine in the frame and tighten the mounting nuts finger-tight. Install the front lower engine mount bolt (A, **Figure 1**) to maintain its mounting hole alignment, then remove before installing the skid plate.

    c. Tighten the front engine hanger plate nuts (B, **Figure 1**) to 34 N•m (25 ft.-lb.).

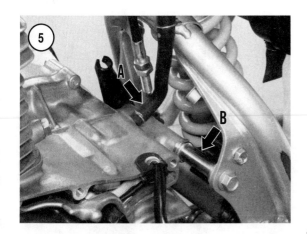

h. Fill the engine with the recommended type and quantity of oil (Chapter Three).

i. Adjust the clutch, drive chain and rear brake pedal (Chapter Three).

j. Start the engine and check for leaks.

k. If the engine top-end was rebuilt, perform a compression check. Record the results for future reference.

l. Review *Engine Break-In* in Chapter Three.

CRANKCASE

The following procedures detail the disassembly and reassembly of the crankcase. When the two halves of the crankcase are disassembled or split, the crankshaft, kickstarter and transmission assemblies can be removed.

The crankcase halves are made of cast aluminum alloy. Do not hammer or excessively pry on the cases. The cases will fracture or break. The cases are aligned and sealed at the joint by dowels and a gasket.

The crankshaft consists of two full-circle flywheels pressed onto the crankpin. The assembly is supported at each end by a ball bearing.

Disassembly

Identify parts or make written notes as required to help with reassembly. Note any damaged or worn parts.

1. Remove all exterior engine assemblies as follows:

a. Cylinder head, cylinder, and piston (Chapter Four).

b. Flywheel and stator plate (Chapter Nine).

c. Clutch (Chapter Six).

d. Primary drive assembly (Chapter Six).

e. Oil pump (Chapter Six).

f. External shift mechanism (Chapter Six).

2. Disconnect the kickstarter return spring (A, **Figure 7**) and allow it to unwind while maintaining pressure against the spring. Then remove the return spring (A, **Figure 7**) and spacer (B).

3. Place the engine on wooden blocks with the right side facing up.

4. Remove the two crankcase mounting bolts (A, **Figure 8**).

5A. Lightly tap the right crankcase half (B, **Figure 8**) to break the gasket seal and remove it. All of the internal crankcase components will remain in the left case half. If necessary, alternately tap on the ends of the transmission shafts to prevent them from binding the right crankcase half. There are no press-fits to interfere with removal.

d. On 1992-1997 and 2001-on models, tighten the rear engine mount nuts (**Figure 6**) to 44 N•m (32.5 ft.-lb.).

e. On 1998-2000 models, tighten the rear engine mount nuts (**Figure 6**) to 34 N•m (25 ft.-lb.).

f. Install the skid plate (B, **Figure 2**). Tighten the front lower engine mount nut (A, **Figure 1**) to 34 N•m (25 ft.-lb.). Tighten the rear skid plate mounting bolts (A, **Figure 2**) securely.

g. Tighten the kick pedal pinch bolt to 12 N•m (106 in.-lb.).

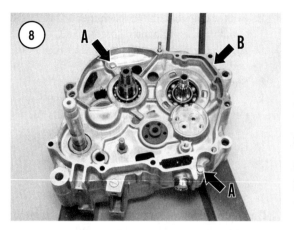

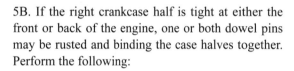

5B. If the right crankcase half is tight at either the front or back of the engine, one or both dowel pins may be rusted and binding the case halves together. Perform the following:

CAUTION
Do not hammer or pry on areas of the engine cases that are not reinforced. Do not pry on gasket surfaces.

a. Set the crankcase upright and thread a 6 mm knock puller (A, **Figure 9**) into one of the threaded holes in the left crankcase that is adjacent to the dowel pin. For the front dowel pin, there are no suitable threaded holes available to use in the right crankcase.

b. If there is a gap between the case halves that partially exposes the dowel pin, spray penetrating fluid between the case halves and allow it to soak down to the dowel pin (B, **Figure 9**).

c. Tilt the engine slightly toward its left side then operate the knock puller. When doing so, tap the exposed shafts on the right side of the engine to keep these components in the left crankcase. At the same time, make sure the case halves are splitting evenly along their perimeter (C, **Figure 9**).

d. When the dowel pin is free (**Figure 10**), lift the crankcase assembly and place it on wooden blocks with the right side facing up. Then remove the right crankcase half (B, **Figure 8**).

6. Immediately check for outer washers installed on the countershaft (A, **Figure 11**) and kickstarter (B). If a washer is missing, remove it from the right case half and reinstall it. The countershaft washer (12 mm) is smaller than the kickstarter washer (18 mm).

7. Remove the dowels pins (C, **Figure 11**) if they are not stuck.

8. Lift and remove the kickstarter (D, **Figure 11**) from the left crankcase.

NOTE
If the engine was experiencing shifting problems, examine the transmission assembly before removing it. Look for severe wear or damaged parts. Spin the countershaft and turn the shift drum by hand to shift the transmission. Check the movement and operation of each shift fork and sliding gear. Look for hard shifting and incomplete gear dog engagement. Check also for seized gears.

under and hold the lower end of each shaft during removal.

13. Position the left crankcase so the transmission shafts are parallel with the workbench. With the mainshaft and countershaft meshed together, tap the countershaft and remove both shafts as an assembly (**Figure 13**). If the shafts are difficult to remove, the countershaft may be seized against its crankcase bearing's inner race.

14. Clean and inspect the case halves and bearings as described in this chapter.

15. Inspect and service the crankshaft assembly as described in this chapter.

16. Inspect and service the kickstarter as described in this chapter.

17. Inspect and service the transmission assembly as described in Chapter Seven.

Assembly

1. Prior to assembly:
   a. Make sure a new center case gasket is on hand. Do not reuse an old gasket.
   b. Lubricate the seal lips with grease before installing the shafts.
   c. Confirm that the transmission shafts are properly assembled (Chapter Seven). Then apply grease to the outer thrust washer on each transmission shaft to help hold them in place.
   d. Lubricate the crankshaft, bearings and transmission sliding surfaces with engine oil.

2. Support the left crankcase on wooden blocks. Make sure the bearing holes are open so as not to interfere with shaft installation.

3. Install the cam chain (**Figure 14**) into the left crankcase and position it so it will not interfere with crankshaft installation.

4. Install the crankshaft (**Figure 15**) so the tapered end and cam chain sprocket are toward the left side

9. Remove the shift fork shaft (A, **Figure 12**).

10. Move the shift forks away from the shift drum (B, **Figure 12**) and remove them.

11. Remove the shift drum.

12. Remove the crankshaft and cam chain. The main bearings are pressed onto the crankshaft and should remain in place. Block the crankshaft so it cannot roll off the workbench.

NOTE
Parts can slide off both transmission shafts when removing them. Reach

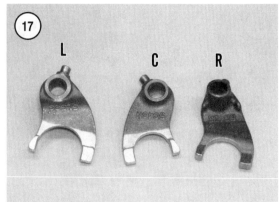

(facing down). Pull the cam chain to make sure it can mesh with the cam chain sprocket.

5. Mesh the transmission shaft assembly (**Figure 13**) and install them into the right crankcase at the same time (**Figure 16**). Make sure the left side thrust washer did not fall from the end of the countershaft when the shafts were installed.

6. Identify the shift forks (**Figure 17**) by the letter cast on each fork. The L (left) and R (right) shift forks engage with the countershaft, while the C (center) shift fork engages with the mainshaft.

NOTE
Install the shift forks with their identification marks facing up.

7. Install the left shift fork (A, **Figure 18**) into the countershaft fifth gear groove.

8. Install the center shift fork (B, **Figure 18**) into the mainshaft third gear groove.

9. Install the shift drum (A, **Figure 19**) while at the same inserting the center shift fork pin into the center shift drum groove (B, **Figure 19**).

10. Install the left shift fork pin (**Figure 20**) into the left shift drum groove.

11. Install the right shift fork (**Figure 21**) into the countershaft fourth gear groove and insert its pin into the right shift drum groove.

12. Lubricate the shift fork shaft (**Figure 22**) with engine oil and install it through the shift forks. Make sure the shaft bottoms in the left case half.

13. Spin the transmission shafts and turn the shift drum by hand to check transmission operation. Check that each shift fork travels through its operating groove in the shift drum and bottoms against both groove ends (**Figure 23**).

NOTE
It is difficult to identify the different gear positions when turning the shift drum without the stopper lever installed on the engine. Step 13 only determines if the shift forks can move through their

complete operational range. If not, the transmission is assembled incorrectly.

14. Install the kickstarter (A, **Figure 24**) into the left crankcase. Position the ratchet (A, **Figure 25**) next to the ratchet guide stop (B). Make sure the washer (C, **Figure 25**) is installed on the right side of the kickstarter.

15. Lubricate the shafts and bearings with engine oil.

16. Install the dowel pins (B, **Figure 24**) and a new gasket (C) onto the left crankcase. Trim the gasket where it interferes with the connecting rod.

17. Install the right crankcase (B, **Figure 8**) over the shafts and dowel pins and seat it against the gasket. Install the two crankcase mounting bolts (A, **Figure 8**) and tighten securely.

CAUTION
Crankcase halves should fit together without force as there are no press-fits between the crankshaft main bearings and the bearing bores in the crankcase. If the crankcase halves do not fit together completely, do not pull them together with the crankcase bolts. Separate the crankcase halves and investigate the cause of the interference. If the transmission shafts were disassembled, recheck to make sure that a gear was not installed backwards. If the interference is in the area of a dowel pin, check for a damaged dowel pin. Do not risk damage by trying to force the cases together.

18. Turn the crankshaft and both transmission shafts. Separate and inspect the cases if there is any binding.

19. Cover the crankcase opening and trim the center case gasket (**Figure 26**) at the cylinder base surface. Do not allow any of the gasket material to fall into the crankcase.

20. Check the transmission for proper shifting as follows:

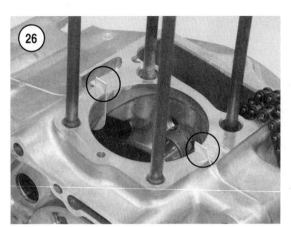

a. Install the shift drum cam (A, **Figure 27**), locating pins and mounting bolt (B). Then install the stopper lever (C, **Figure 27**) and its mounting bolt. The spring and washer used with the stopper lever is not required. Use your fingers to engage the stopper lever with the shift drum cam when checking shifting.

NOTE
*If necessary, refer to **External Shift Mechanism** in Chapter Six for steps on how to install the shift drum cam and stopper lever assembly.*

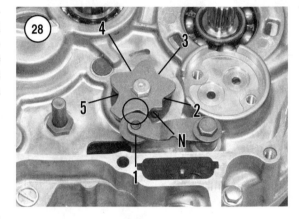

b. Turn the mainshaft while turning the shift drum cam and align its raised ramp with the stopper lever (D, **Figure 27**). This is the transmission's neutral position. The mainshaft and countershaft should turn independently of one another.

c. Turn the mainshaft while turning the shift drum cam *counterclockwise*. Stop when the stopper lever seats between the ramps of the shift drum cam as shown in **Figure 28**. This is the first gear position. The mainshaft and countershaft should be meshed together.

d. Turn the shift drum cam *clockwise* past neutral, then place the stopper lever between the ramps to check the remaining gears (2nd-4th, **Figure 28**) for proper engagement. The mainshaft and countershaft should mesh whenever the transmission is in gear.

e. Remove the shift drum cam and stopper lever when the check is completed. If the transmission did not engage properly, disassemble the crankcase and inspect the transmission for proper assembly or damaged parts.

21. Complete kickstarter assembly as follows:
    a. Install the spring by inserting the inner spring end (A, **Figure 29**) into the hole (B) in the kick shaft.
    b. Install the spacer by aligning the notch (**Figure 30**) with the inner spring end. Push the spacer

all the way down. Make sure the spring end did not slip out of the kick shaft hole (B, **Figure 29**).

c. Rotate the spring counterclockwise and hook the outer spring end onto the crankcase boss (**Figure 31**).

d. Set the crankcase upright and install the kick pedal and secure with its pinch bolt. Hold the crankcase with one hand (for support) and operate the kick pedal. Make sure the kick shaft engages the transmission and then returns under spring tension.

22. Install all exterior engine assemblies as follows:

NOTE
Because only two crankcase mounting bolts are used, the engine will leak some of the preassembly oil between the crankcase halves when the engine is sitting is upright. This is normal.

a. External shift mechanism (Chapter Six).
b. Oil pump (Chapter Six).
c. Primary drive assembly (Chapter Six).
d. Clutch (Chapter Six).
e. Flywheel and stator plate (Chapter Nine).

6. Blow through each oil passage with compressed air.
7. Lightly oil the engine bearings before inspecting their condition. A dry bearing will exhibit more sound and looseness than a properly lubricated bearing.
8. Inspect the bearings for roughness, pitting, galling and play. Replace any bearing that is not in good condition. Always replace the opposite bearing at the same time.
9. Inspect the cases for fractures around all mounting and bearing bosses, stiffening ribs and threaded holes. If necessary, refer repair to a dealership or machine shop.
10. Check all threaded holes for damage or buildup. Clean threads with the correct size metric tap. Lubricate the tap with kerosene or aluminum tap fluid.
11. Inspect the dowel pin holes in both case halves for damage and repair with a rotary file or sandpaper. Replace damaged dowel pins.

f. Cylinder head, cylinder, and piston (Chapter Four).

Inspection

1. Remove and discard the crankcase seals as described in this chapter.
2. The paper crankcase gasket sets up hard and is difficult to remove. Use an aerosol gasket remover to soften the gasket before attempting to scrape it from the crankcase surfaces. Refer to *Gasket Remover* in *Shop Supplies* in Chapter One for additional information. Do not nick or gouge the gasket surfaces or leaks will result.
3. After all of the gasket residue has been removed, clean the crankcase halves in solvent.
4. Using clean solvent, flush each bearing. Make sure all gasket residue is removed from the bearings, oil passages and bolt holes.
5. Dry the cases with compressed air.

> *WARNING*
> *When drying a bearing with compressed air, do not allow the inner bearing race to rotate. The air can spin the bearing at excessive speed, possibly causing bearing damage.*

CRANKCASE SEAL AND BEARING

Refer to *Service Methods* in Chapter One for bearing removal and installation techniques.

Seal Removal/Installation

Replace all of the crankcase seals (A, B and C, **Figure 32**) during an engine overhaul.

> *CAUTION*
> *Do not allow the pry tool to contact the seal bore when removing the seal. It may gouge the bore and cause an oil leak between the seal bore and the back of the seal.*

1A. On 80 cc models, measure the crankshaft seal (A, **Figure 32**) installed depth before removing it. This seal cannot be installed flush with the seal bore because it will interfere with an inner hub on the stator plate.

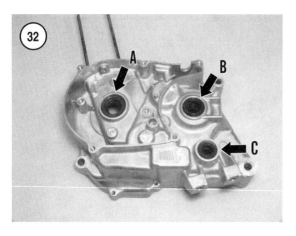

1B. On 100 cc models, the crankshaft seal is installed inside the stator plate. Refer to *Exciter Coil and Ignition Pulse Generator (Stator Plate Assembly)* in Chapter Nine to remove this seal.

2. Pry out the old seal with a seal puller or wide-blade screwdriver (**Figure 33**). Place a folded shop cloth under the tool to prevent bore damage.

NOTE
*The shift shaft seal (**Figure 34**) has a small outside diameter and a deep shoulder and can be difficult to remove if it has bonded to its bore surface. Remove this seal carefully to prevent bore damage.*

3. If a new left countershaft bearing will be installed, replace the bearing before installing the new seal.

4. Inspect the seal bore. Sand or file any raised grooves in the bore surface, then clean thoroughly.

5. Pack grease into the lip of the new seal.

6. Place the seal in the bore, with the closed side of the seal facing out. The seal must be square to the bore.

CAUTION
When driving seals, the driver must fit at the perimeter of the seal. If the driver presses toward the center of the seal, the seal can distort and the internal garter spring can become dislodged, causing the seal to leak.

7. Install the new seal with a socket or seal driver. Note the following:
  a. For 80 cc models, install the left crankshaft seal (A, **Figure 32**) to the dimensions recorded in Step 1A. Refer to *Exciter Coil and Ignition Pulse Generator (Stator Plate Assembly)* in Chapter Nine to install this seal.
  b. Install the countershaft (B, **Figure 32**) and shift shaft (C) seals so their upper edge is flush with the top of the seal bore.

Bearing Removal/Installation

1. Before replacing bearings, note the following:
  a. Identify and record the size code of each bearing before it is removed from the case. This will eliminate confusion when installing new bearings.
  b. Record the orientation of each bearing in its bore. Note if the size code faces toward the inside or outside of the case.
  c. Use a hydraulic press or a set of bearing drivers to remove and install bearings. Bearings can

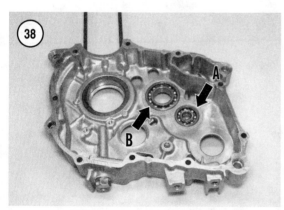

also be removed and installed using heat, as described in *Service Methods* in Chapter One. When using bearing drivers or properly-sized sockets (**Figure 35**) to replace bearings, the tool should fit on the outer edge of the bearing. Do not apply pressure to the inner race or the bearing will be damaged.

   d. Bearings that are only accessible from one side of the case are removed with a blind bearing puller (**Figure 36** [Motion Pro part No. 08-0292]). The puller is fitted through the bearing, then expanded to grip the back-side of the bearing.

2. The following identifies the left crankcase bearings:
   a. Countershaft bearing (A, **Figure 37**).
   b. Mainshaft bearing (B, **Figure 37**).
3. The following identifies the right crankcase bearings:
   a. Countershaft bearing (A, **Figure 38**).
   b. Mainshaft bearing (B, **Figure 38**).
4. Place the new bearing(s) in a freezer and chill for at least one hour.
5. Remove the crankcase seal, if applicable.
6. If using heat, heat the crankcase as described in *Interference Fit* in *Service Methods* in Chapter One. Observe all safety and handling procedures when the case is heated.

> *CAUTION*
> *Do not heat the housing or bearing with a propane or acetylene torch. The direct heat may destroy the case hardening of the bearing and warp the case.*

7. Support the crankcase on wooden blocks, allowing space for the bearing to fall from the bore.
8. Remove the bearing(s) from the bore, using a press, bearing-driver set or bearing puller. Discard the bearing(s).
9. Allow the case to cool.
10. Clean and inspect the bearing bore.
11. When the bearing(s) have chilled, reheat the crankcase.
12. Support the crankcase on wooden blocks, checking that the case is supported directly below the bearing bore.
13. Place the bearing squarely over the bore and check that it is properly oriented as noted prior to removal. Center the bearing into the bore. If the case was heated and the bearing drops into the bore, still apply pressure to the bearing as noted in Step 14 to make sure it bottoms correctly.
14. Drive or press the bearing into place using a driver that fits on the outer bearing race.
15. Install the seal (if applicable) as described in this section.

CRANKSHAFT

Connecting Rod Bearing Lubrication

Oil forced under pressure through a passageway in the right crankcase cover enters a hole in the right end of the crankshaft and lubricates the connecting rod big end bearing assembly. The side plate and O-ring installed on the crankshaft's right side wheel weight forms the outer part of the oil channel.

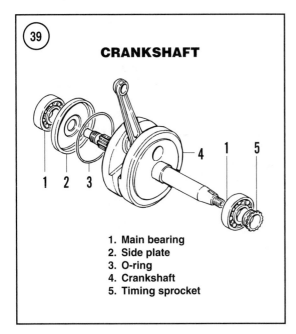

CRANKSHAFT

1. Main bearing
2. Side plate
3. O-ring
4. Crankshaft
5. Timing sprocket

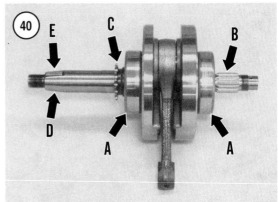

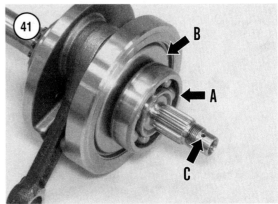

A seal installed in the left crankcase cover seals the end of the crankshaft and the oil passageway. Refer to *Right Crankcase Cover* in Chapter Six to service the oil seal and clean the cover oil passageway.

Inspection

Carefully handle the crankshaft assembly during inspection. Do not place the crankshaft where it could roll off the workbench.

The crankshaft is an assembly-type, with its two halves joined by the crankpin. The crankpin is pressed into the flywheels and aligned, both vertically and horizontally, with calibrated equipment. If the crankshaft assembly shows signs of wear, or is out of alignment, have a dealership inspect the crankshaft. The main bearings, side plate, O-ring and timing sprocket can be replaced separately (**Figure 39**). If the connecting rod big end or crankshaft is damaged, replace the crankshaft.

1. Clean the crankshaft with solvent.
2. Dry the crankshaft with compressed air.
3. Inspect the oil circulation hole located in the crankshaft's right side to make sure it is not plugged. Clean or unplug as required. Blow through all oil passages with compressed air.
4. Inspect the crankshaft bearing surfaces (A, **Figure 40**) for scoring, heat discoloration or other damage. Repair minor damage with 320 grit carborundum cloth.
5. Inspect the splines (B, **Figure 40**), timing sprocket (C), shaft taper (D) and keyway (E) for wear or damage. The timing sprocket can be replaced separately as described in this section.

NOTE
If the sprocket is damaged, check the cam chain, upper cam sprocket, chain guides and cam chain tensioner for damage as described in Chapter Four.

6. Hold the crankshaft and turn each main bearing (A, **Figure 41**) by hand. Check for any catching, binding or roughness. Then check that the inner race of both bearings fits tightly on the crankshaft. If damage or looseness is noted, replace both bearings at the same time as described in this section. If a bearing seizes and spins on the crankshaft, the crankshaft

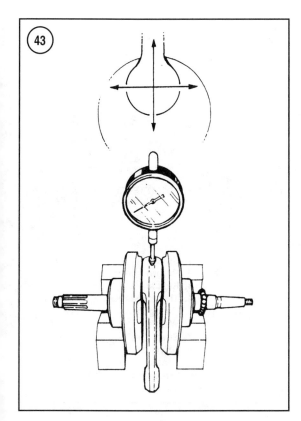

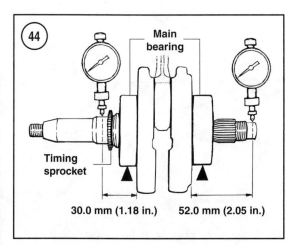

Main bearing

Timing sprocket

30.0 mm (1.18 in.)   52.0 mm (2.05 in.)

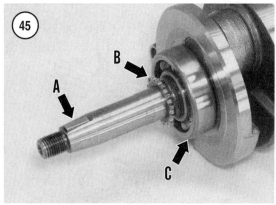

may have to be replaced if the bearing galled the shaft surface.

7. Check the side plate (B, **Figure 41**) for any dents or other signs of damage. Then check the side plate for any signs oil leaking, indicating damage to the side plate or O-ring (3, **Figure 39**). Any damage to the side plate or O-ring may cause the connecting big bearing to seize from a lack of lubrication. If necessary, replace the side plate and O-ring as described in this section.

8. Check the oil joint drive pin hole (C, **Figure 41**) on the end of the right shaft for cracks and other damage. Replace the crankshaft if the hole is damaged.

9. Inspect the connecting rod small end as described in *Piston and Piston Rings* in Chapter Four.

10. Inspect the connecting rod big end as follows:

   a. Turn the rod and inspect the bottom bearing and rod for scoring, galling or heat damage. Roughness indicates a damaged bearing and rod.

   b. Slide the connecting rod to one side and measure the connecting rod side clearance with a flat feeler gauge (**Figure 42**). Compare to dimensions listed in **Table 1**. If worn to service limit, replace the crankshaft.

   c. Support the crankshaft on a set of V-blocks and position the pointer of a dial indicator in the middle of the connecting rod big end (**Figure 43**). Hold the crankshaft and then move the connecting rod in the two directions shown in **Figure 43**. Replace the crankshaft if the clearance in either direction exceeds the connecting rod big end radial clearance service limit in **Table 1**.

11. Place the crankshaft on a set of V-blocks at the points indicated in **Figure 44**. Rotate the crankshaft two revolutions and measure crankshaft runout with a dial indicator at the two points indicated in **Figure 44**. If the runout exceeds the service limit in **Table 1**, take the crankshaft to a dealership for service or replacement.

Disassembly/Assembly

This section covers parts of the crankshaft (**Figure 39**) that can be replaced separately.

1. Remove the Woodruff key from the keyway (A, **Figure 45**).

2. Using a bearing splitter (**Figure 46**) and/or a press, press off the timing sprocket (B, **Figure 45**) and left main bearing (C) at the same time. Discard the bearing. Check the timing sprocket for damaged teeth or cracks along its bore surface and replace if necessary.

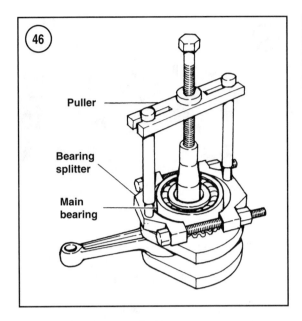

Puller

Bearing
splitter

Main
bearing

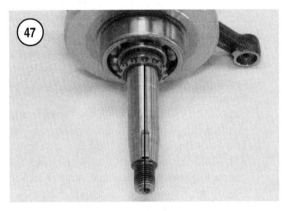

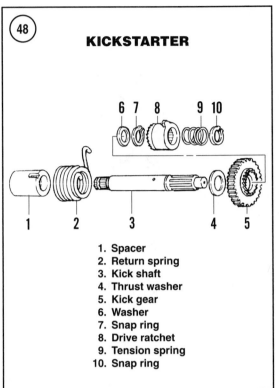

KICKSTARTER

6 7 8   9 10

1   2   3   4   5

1. Spacer
2. Return spring
3. Kick shaft
4. Thrust washer
5. Kick gear
6. Washer
7. Snap ring
8. Drive ratchet
9. Tension spring
10. Snap ring

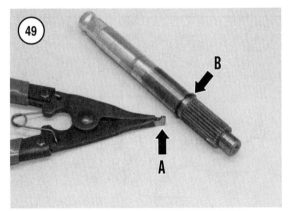

B

A

3. Repeat Step 2 to remove the right main bearing (A, **Figure 41**). Discard the bearing.

4. Remove the side plate (B, **Figure 41**) and O-ring. Discard the O-ring.

5. Check the bearing surfaces on both sides of the crankshaft for roughness, galling, cracks or other damage. Wear on a shaft indicates a spun or seized bearing.

6. Clean the crankshaft in solvent. Flush and dry the crankshaft and oil passage holes.

7. Check the side plate for any warp, dents, cracks or other damage. Replace if necessary.

8. Lubricate a new O-ring with engine oil and install it and the side plate.

9. Support the crankshaft in a press and press on the new right side main bearing until it bottoms. Check the side plate to make sure it was not damaged.

10. Repeat Step 9 to install a new left side main bearing.

11. Check the inner race on both bearings for tightness. Replace the crankshaft if there is any play between a bearings inner race and crankshaft.

12. Support the crankshaft in a press and press on the timing sprocket so the center point (valley) between two sprocket teeth is aligned with the keyway centerline (**Figure 47**). Because there are no timing marks on the timing sprocket, it does not matter which sprocket center point or valley is used for alignment. Bottom the sprocket against the bearing. Check the alignment carefully.

CAUTION
The position of the timing sprocket determines the accuracy of the camshaft timing.

13. Check the crankshaft runout as described in *Inspection* in this section.

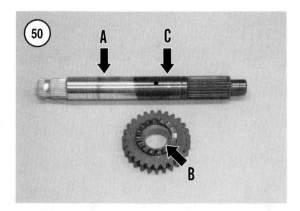

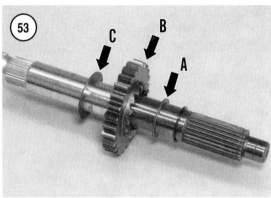

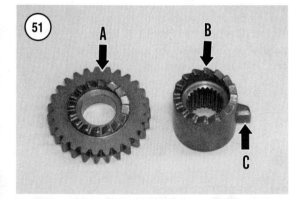

KICKSTARTER

Removal/Installation

Remove and install the kickstarter as described in *Crankcase* in this chapter.

Disassembly and Inspection

Refer to **Figure 48**.
1. Disassemble the kickstarter in the order shown in **Figure 48**. A pair of flat-tipped snap ring pliers (A, **Figure 49**) will be required to remove the inner snap

ring (B) as it is small and does not have holes drilled in its outer ears.
2. Check the kick shaft (A, **Figure 50**) for:
   a. Bending.
   b. Damaged splines.
   c. Elongation of the return spring hole.
   d. Damaged snap ring grooves.
3. Check the kick gear (A, **Figure 51**) for:
   a. Broken or chipped teeth.
   b. Worn, damaged or rounded-off ratchet teeth.
   c. Scored or damaged gear bore.
4. Check the drive ratchet (B, **Figure 51**) for:
   a. Damaged splines.
   b. Worn, damaged or rounded-off ratchet teeth.
   c. Worn or damaged drive lug (C, **Figure 51**)
5. Measure the kick gear inside diameter (B, **Figure 50**) and the kick shaft (C) outside diameter at the kick gear operating area. Compare to the dimensions in **Table 2**. Replace either part if worn to the service limit.
6. Check the spacer (1, **Figure 48**) for scoring or grooves caused by the return spring. Check the spring alignment groove for damage.
7. Check the return spring ends for damage. Check the spring coils for cracks and other damage.
8. Check the tension spring (9, **Figure 48**) if damaged.
9. Check the ratchet guide plate (**Figure 52**) mounted on the right crankcase for wear and damage. If the mounting bolts are loose, apply a medium strength threadlock and tighten securely.

Assembly

1. Install a new snap ring into the kick shaft groove identified in B, **Figure 49**. Make sure the snap ring seats in the groove completely.
2. Install the washer (A, **Figure 53**), kick gear (B) and thrust washer (C) on the shaft. The kick gear ratchet teeth must face toward the snap ring.
3. Install the drive ratchet by aligning its index mark (A, **Figure 54**) with the index mark on the kick shaft

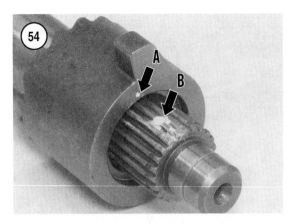

(B). This alignment times the kickstarter assembly to ensure a full kick. If the marks are not aligned, the kickstarter cannot work properly.

4. Install the tension spring (A, **Figure 55**) and seat

against the drive ratchet.

5. Install a new snap ring (B, **Figure 55**) into the groove on the end of the shaft. Make sure the snap ring seats in the groove completely.

Table 1 CRANKSHAFT SERVICE SPECIFICATIONS

	New mm (in.)	Service limit mm (in.)
Crankshaft runout		
Right side	0.035	0.085
	(0.0014)	(0.0033)
Left side	0.020	0.070
	(0.0008)	(0.0028)
Connecting rod big end radial clearance	0.0-0.008	0.010
	(0.0-0.0003)	(0.0004)
Connecting rod side clearance	0.10-0.35	0.60
	(0.0039-0.0138)	(0.024)
Connecting rod small end inside diameter		
80 cc models	13.016-13.034	13.04
	(0.5124-0.5131)	(0.513)
100 cc models	14.012-14.030	14.05
	(0.5517-0.5524)	(0.5531)

Table 2 KICKSTARTER SERVICE SPECIFICATIONS

	New mm (in.)	Service limit mm (in.)
Kick gear inside diameter	18.020-18.041	18.06
	(0.7094-0.7103)	(0.711)
Kick shaft outside diameter	17.959-17.980	17.88
	(0.7070-0.7079)	(0.704)

Table 3 ENGINE LOWER END TORQUE SPECIFICATIONS

	N•m	in.-lb.	ft.-lb.
Engine oil drain bolt	24	–	18
Front engine hanger plate nuts	34	–	25
Kick pedal pinch bolt	12	106	–
Rear engine mount nuts			
1992-1997 and 2001-on models	44	–	32.5
1998-2000 models	34	–	25

5

CHAPTER SIX

CLUTCH, OIL PUMP, PRIMARY DRIVE GEAR AND EXTERNAL SHIFT MECHANISM

This chapter describes service procedures for the clutch cable and components installed behind the right crankcase cover. Components covered include the following:

1. Clutch.
2. Clutch release lever.
3. Oil pump.
4. Primary drive gear.
5. External shift mechanism.

Tables 1-3 are at the end of this chapter.

RIGHT CRANKCASE COVER

Removal

1. Drain the engine oil (Chapter Three).

NOTE
Before removing the kick pedal, check the kick pedal and kick shaft index mark alignment.

2. Unbolt and remove the kick pedal (**Figure 1**).
3. Remove the right footpeg/brake pedal assembly (Chapter Fourteen).
4. Disconnect the clutch cable at the engine (**Figure 2**). If necessary, loosen the clutch cable adjuster at the handlebar to provide additional cable slack. Refer to *Clutch Cable* in this chapter.

CAUTION
If the kick pedal is stuck, spray penetrating oil around the kick shaft splines. Give the oil time to dissolve some of the rust, then tap the pedal and slide it off the shaft. If the kick pedal is tight from corrosion or damaged splines, mount a small two-jaw puller across the kick pedal boss, centering the pressure bolt against the kick shaft, then operate the puller to remove the kick pedal. Do not pry the kick pedal off as this may damage the right crankcase cover.

NOTE
Different length bolts secure the right crankcase cover to the engine. The longer bolts are also used to secure the crankcase halves. To ensure the bolts are correctly located during assembly, make an outline of the right crankcase cover on a piece of cardboard. Punch holes in the cardboard at the same locations as the bolts. As each bolt is removed from the cover, place the bolt in its respective hole in the template (Figure 3).

5. Remove the bolts securing the right crankcase cover (**Figure 4**) to the engine. If necessary, lightly tap the cover to loosen it from the engine.

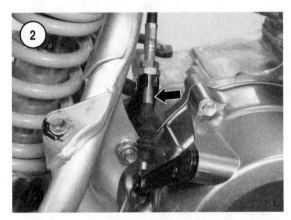

6. Remove the dowel pins (A, **Figure 5**).

7. Check for the oil joint and spring (**Figure 6**) in the end of the crankshaft as they may have fallen off when the cover was removed.

8. If necessary, service the clutch release mechanism as described in this chapter.

9. Perform the *Cleaning and Inspection* in this section.

Installation

1. Install the dowel pins (A, **Figure 5**) and a new gasket.

2. Make sure the oil joint and spring (**Figure 6**) assembly is properly installed. Refer to *Primary Drive Gear Assembly* in this chapter.

3. Install the right crankcase cover (**Figure 4**) and install the mounting bolts in their correct position as recorded during removal. Tighten the mounting bolts securely.

4. Install the right footpeg/rear brake pedal assembly (Chapter Fourteen).

5. Adjust the rear brake (Chapter Three).

6. Install the kick pedal (**Figure 1**) by aligning its index mark with the index mark on the kick shaft. Install the pinch bolt and tighten to 12 N•m (106 in.-lb.).

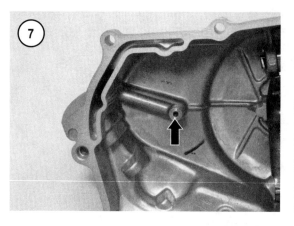

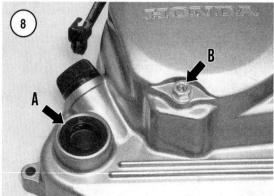

7. Reconnect the clutch cable (**Figure 2**). Refer to *Clutch Cable* in this chapter.

8. Fill the engine with the correct type and quantity engine oil (Chapter Three).

9. Adjust the clutch as described in *Clutch Lever* in Chapter Three.

10. Start the engine and check for leaks.

Cleaning and Inspection

1. The paper crankcase cover gasket sets up hard and is difficult to remove. Use an aerosol gasket remover to soften the gasket before attempting to scrape it from the cover and crankcase gasket surfaces. Refer to *Gasket Remover* in *Shop Supplies* in Chapter One for additional information. Do not nick or gouge the gasket surfaces or leaks will result.

2. The oil strainer screen (B, **Figure 5**) is located behind the clutch cover gasket at the bottom of the engine. Use a gasket scraper carefully in this area to avoid damaging the oil strainer screen's outer edge.

3. After all of the gasket residue has been removed, clean the cover in solvent.

4. The right crankcase cover is equipped with an oil passage and oil circulation hole (**Figure 7**) that provides lubrication for the crankshaft big end bearing. Clean the oil passage and dry with compressed air, making sure the oil circulation hole is not plugged. Then check and clean the mating oil passage area on the right crankcase. Make sure both areas are free of any gasket residue.

5. Inspect the cover for cracks and other damage.

6. Inspect the kickstarter seal (A, **Figure 8**) and replace if leaking or damaged. Install the new seal with the flat side facing out and lubricate the seal lip with grease.

> *NOTE*
> *If a new seal leaks after installing it, the kick shaft is probably pitted or worn in the area where the seal operates. Check the shaft's seal operating surface for damage.*

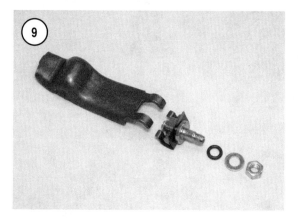

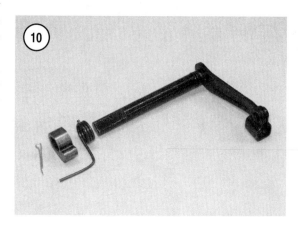

CLUTCH RELEASE MECHANISM

The clutch release mechanism is mounted inside the right crankcase cover and consists of the clutch adjusting screw assembly (**Figure 9**) and the clutch release lever assembly (**Figure 10**).

Removal

1. Remove the right crankcase cover as described in this chapter.

2. Remove the clutch adjusting screw locknut (B, **Figure 8**) and washer.

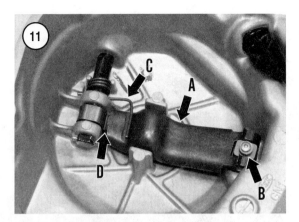

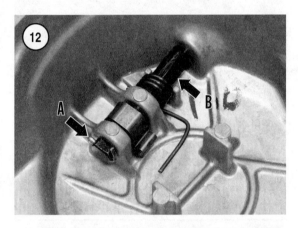

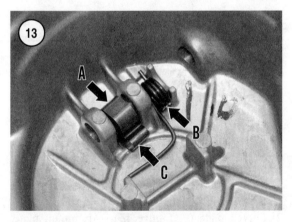

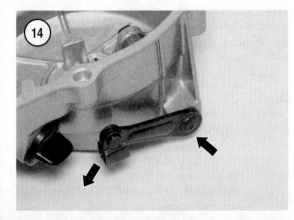

3. Lift the clutch adjust lever (A, **Figure 11**) to release the clutch adjust screw (B) and remove the screw assembly. Then slide the lever down to release it from the clutch lever spring and remove it.

4. Remove the O-ring from the clutch adjusting screw bore.

5. Remove the cotter pin (A, **Figure 12**) and remove the clutch release lever (B).

6. Remove the lifter cam (A, **Figure 13**) and tension spring (B).

7. Inspect the mechanism as described in this section.

Installation

1. Center the lifter cam (A, **Figure 13**) between the two bosses inside the cover with its ramp facing toward the inside of the cover as shown in C, **Figure 13**.

2. Position the spring between the boss and spring guide as shown in B, **Figure 13**.

3. Lubricate the clutch release lever and its O-ring with engine oil. Install the lever through the cover, spring and lifter cam as shown in B, **Figure 12**. Make sure the clutch cable end is facing down as shown in **Figure 14**.

4. Install a new cotter pin (A, **Figure 12**) through the hole in the end of the clutch release lever and bend the ends over to lock it.

5. Lubricate a new clutch release screw O-ring with engine oil and install it in the screw bore in the housing.

6. Install the two arms on the bottom of the clutch adjust lever under the two tension spring arms on the clutch release screw assembly while installing the screw (B, **Figure 11**) through the hole in the crankcase cover.

7. Lift the clutch release lever tension spring and install it over the top of the clutch adjust lever (C, **Figure 11**). Make sure the ramp on the lifter cam is positioned under the clutch adjust lever (D, **Figure 11**).

8. Install the clutch adjust screw washer and locknut (B, **Figure 8**).

9. Operate the clutch release lever by hand while checking that the lifter cam raises and lowers the clutch adjust lever.

10. Install the right crankcase cover as described in this chapter.

11. Adjust the clutch as described in *Clutch Lever* in Chapter Three.

Inspection

1. Clean and dry all parts.

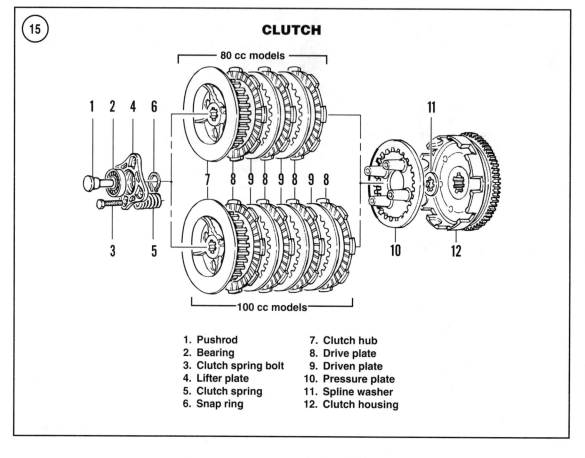

CLUTCH

─ 80 cc models ─

1 2 4 6

3   5

7   8 9 8 9 8 9 8

11

10   12

─100 cc models─

1. Pushrod
2. Bearing
3. Clutch spring bolt
4. Lifter plate
5. Clutch spring
6. Snap ring
7. Clutch hub
8. Drive plate
9. Driven plate
10. Pressure plate
11. Spline washer
12. Clutch housing

2. Replace the clutch adjust screw (B, **Figure 8**) if the threads are stripped or if the adjust screw head is damaged.

3. Install a new O-ring in the clutch release shaft groove.

4. Check the clutch release shaft for pitting, wear and other damage.

5. Check the lifter cam ramp for excessive wear.

6. Check the clutch release shaft tension spring for cracks or other damage.

7. Check the clutch release lever cover bosses for worn or damaged shaft bores or cracks where the bosses are cast into the crankcase cover.

CLUTCH

The clutch is a multi-plate type that operates immersed in the engine oil supply. The clutch assembly consists of a clutch hub and clutch housing. Clutch plates are alternately locked to the two parts. The gear-driven clutch housing is mounted on the transmission mainshaft. The housing receives power from the primary drive gear mounted on the crankshaft. The housing then transfers the power via its plates to the plates locked to the clutch hub. The clutch hub is splined to the mainshaft and powers the transmis-

sion. The clutch plates are engaged by springs and disengaged by a cable-actuated release lever assembly.

Part Identification

To prevent confusion, the following list gives part names used in this manual and common synonyms:

1. Drive plate (8, **Figure 15**)—Clutch disc, clutch plate, friction disc, outer plate and friction plate. The tabs on the drive plates engage with slots in the clutch housing (12, **Figure 15**).

2. Driven plate (9, **Figure 15**)—Aluminum plate, clutch disc, clutch plate, inner plate and steel plate. The inner teeth on the driven plates engage with the raised splines on the clutch hub (7, **Figure 15**).

NOTE
The terms drive and driven plates are given to these parts, depending on where they are installed in the clutch assembly. The drive plates operate in the clutch housing, which is driven by the engine. The drive plates are always spinning, no matter if the clutch is engaged or disengaged. The driven plates operate on the clutch hub, which

is connected to the transmission main-shaft. When the clutch is disengaged, the clutch hub and driven plates stop spinning.

3. Clutch plates—When clutch plates are used in the text, it refers to both the drive and driven plates as an assembly.

4. Clutch hub (7, **Figure 15**)—Clutch boss, clutch center and inner hub.

5. Clutch housing (12, **Figure 15**)—Clutch basket, clutch outer, outer clutch hub and primary driven gear basket.

Removal

Refer to **Figure 15**.

1. Remove the right crankcase cover as described in this chapter.

2. Remove the pushrod (A, **Figure 16**) from the bearing.

3. Loosen the clutch spring bolts (B, **Figure 16**) in a crisscross pattern and in several stages to relieve pressure on the bolts. Remove the bolts, lifter plate/bearing (C, **Figure 16**) and clutch springs.

NOTE
*If the clutch plates will be removed but not serviced, install one clutch spring (A, **Figure 17**), a 6 mm flat washer and one clutch spring bolt (B). Tighten the bolt to hold the clutch hub, clutch plates and pressure plate in alignment.*

4. Remove the snap ring (A, **Figure 18**).

5. Remove the clutch hub (B, **Figure 18**), clutch plates and pressure plate.

6. Remove the spline washer (A, **Figure 19**) and clutch housing (B).

7. Inspect as described in this section.

Installation

1. If other parts were removed, note the following:
   a. The spacer installed behind the primary drive gear must be installed before the clutch housing. Refer to *Primary Drive Gear Assembly* in this chapter.
   b. The external shift mechanism must be installed before the clutch housing.
   c. The oil pump can be installed either before or after the clutch housing.

2. Lubricate all sliding surfaces with engine oil.

3. Install the clutch housing (B, **Figure 19**) and mesh it with the primary drive gear (if installed).

4. Install the spline washer (A, **Figure 19**) and seat it against the clutch housing.

5. Assemble the clutch housing, clutch plates and pressure plate as follows:

    a. Refer to **Figure 15** to identify the alignment and number of clutch plates used in the engine being worked on.

    b. Lubricate all of the drive and driven plates with engine oil. Soak new drive plates in engine oil before installation.

> *NOTE*
> *The driven plates (9, **Figure 15**) are stamped during manufacturing and have one flat side and one chamfered side. Install all of the driven plates with their flat side facing in the same direction (either in or out).*

    c. Install the clutch plate assembly (A, **Figure 20**) onto the clutch hub (B, **Figure 20**) in the order shown in **Figure 15**. Mesh the driven plate (9, **Figure 15**) splines with the splines on the clutch hub (7). Align the drive plate (8, **Figure 15**) tabs.

    d. Install the pressure plate (C, **Figure 20**) through the clutch hub. Refer to **Figure 21**.

    e. Install a clutch spring, 6 mm flat washer and clutch spring bolt (A, **Figure 21**) to hold the assembly together. Maintain the drive plate tab alignment (B, **Figure 21**) when tightening the bolt.

6. Install the clutch plate assembly into the clutch housing by aligning the clutch hub and mainshaft splines and the drive plate tabs with the slots in the clutch housing (C, **Figure 17**).

7. Install a new snap ring (**Figure 22**) into the mainshaft groove with its flat side facing out. Make sure the snap ring seats in the groove completely.

8. Remove the bolt (B, **Figure 17**), washer and clutch spring (A).

9. Install a clutch spring over each pressure plate boss, then install the lifter plate/bearing (C, **Figure 16**) and the clutch spring bolts (B). Tighten the clutch spring bolts (B, **Figure 16**) securely in two or three steps and in a crossing pattern.

10. Install the pushrod (A, **Figure 16**) through the lifter plate bearing.

11. Install the right crankcase cover as described in this chapter.

12. Shift the transmission into neutral and start the engine. After the engine warms up, pull the clutch lever in and shift the transmission into first gear. Note the following:

    a. If the clutch makes a loud grinding and spinning noise immediately after the engine is

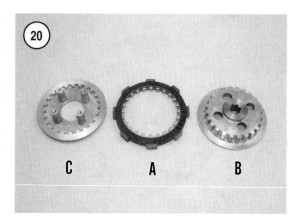

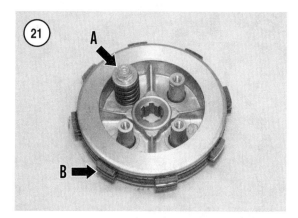

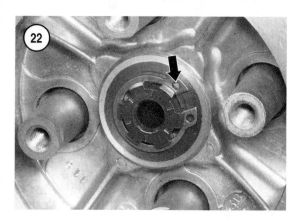

started, either the engine oil level is low or the new drive plates were not lubricated with oil.

    b. If the motorcycle jumps forwards and stalls, or creeps with the transmission in gear and the clutch lever pulled in, recheck the clutch adjustment as described in Chapter Three. If the clutch will not adjust properly, either the clutch cable or the drive plates are excessively worn. Replace them.

    c. If the clutch adjustment, clutch cable and clutch release lever seem to be working correctly, the clutch may have been assembled incorrectly or there is a broken part in the clutch.

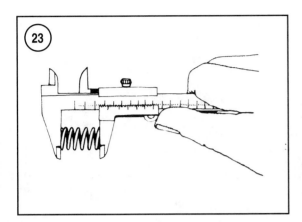

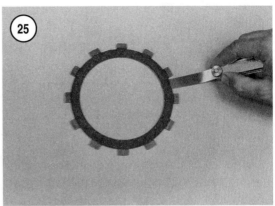

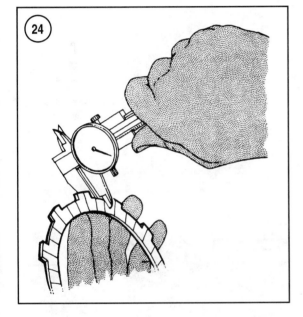

Disassemble the clutch and inspect the parts as described in this section.

Inspection

Always replace drive plates, driven plates and clutch springs as a set if individual components do not meet specifications (**Table 1**). If parts show other signs of wear or damage, replace them, regardless of their specifications.

1. Clean and dry all parts.

2. Inspect the clutch springs for cracks and blue discoloration (heat damage).

3. Measure the free length of each clutch spring (**Figure 23**). Replace the springs as a set if any one spring is not within specification (**Table 1**).

4. Inspect each drive plate (8, **Figure 15**) as follows:
   a. Inspect the friction material for excessive or uneven wear, cracks and other damage.

b. Inspect the tabs for cracks, grooves and wear. The tabs must be smooth to allow the drive plates to move when the clutch is released.

> *NOTE*
> *If the drive plate tabs are damaged, inspect the clutch housing grooves for damage as described in this section.*

c. Measure the thickness of each drive plate (**Figure 24**) at different locations around the plate.

5. Inspect each driven plate (9, **Figure 15**) as follows:
   a. Inspect the driven plates for cracks, damage or color change. Overheated driven plates will have a blue discoloration.
   b. After washing the driven plates in solvent, check them for an oil glaze buildup. Remove by lightly sanding both sides of each plate with 400-grit sandpaper placed on a surface plate or piece of glass.
   c. Inspect the inner teeth for wear, grooves and other damage. The plates must be able to move when the clutch is released.
   d. Check each driven plate for warp by placing it on a flat surface and measuring the gap around its perimeter with a feeler gauge (**Figure 25**).

6. Check the clutch housing as follows:
   a. Inspect the clutch housing slots (A, **Figure 26**) for notches, grooves or other damage. Repair minor damage with a file. If damage is excessive, replace the clutch housing. The slots must be smooth to allow the drive plates to move when the clutch is released.

> *NOTE*
> *Filing the clutch housing slots is only a temporary fix as removing metal from the sides of the slots provides more room for the plates to move around and start wearing new grooves.*

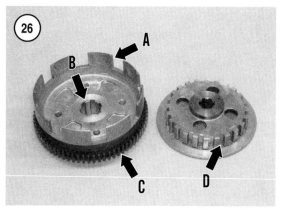

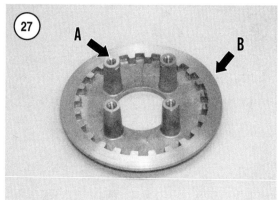

b. Check the clutch housing splines (B, **Figure 26**) for scoring, cracks or other damage. If damage is noted, inspect the mainshaft for similar damage.

c. Check the primary driven gear (C, **Figure 26**) for excessive wear, pitting, chipped gear teeth or other damage. If damaged is noted, check the primary drive gear and oil pump drive gear for the same damage.

7. Inspect the clutch hub outer splines (D, Figure 26) for rough spots, grooves or other damage. Repair minor damage with a file or oil stone. If the damage is excessive, replace the clutch hub. The splines must be smooth to allow the driven plates to move when the clutch is released.

8. Check the pressure plate as follows:

a. Inspect for damaged spring towers (A, **Figure 27**) and threads.

b. Inspect the plate surface area (B, **Figure 27**) for cracks, pitting and other damage.

9. Inspect the lifter plate and bearing assembly as follows:

a. Turn the bearing inner race (A, **Figure 28**) and check for roughness, pitting, galling and play. If necessary, replace the bearing. The bearing is a slip fit in the lifter plate and does not require force for replacement.

b. Inspect the lifter plate (B, **Figure 28**) for cracks and other damage.

10. Inspect the pushrod (C, **Figure 28**) for cracks and other damage.

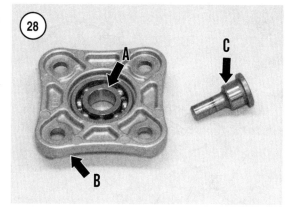

OIL PUMP

The oil pump is mounted on the right side of the engine and can be removed with the engine in the frame.

Removal/Installation

1. Remove the right crankcase cover as described in this chapter.

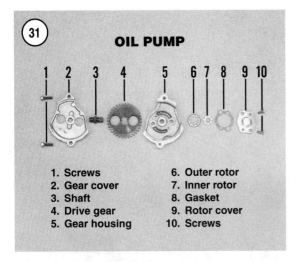

OIL PUMP

1. Screws
2. Gear cover
3. Shaft
4. Drive gear
5. Gear housing
6. Outer rotor
7. Inner rotor
8. Gasket
9. Rotor cover
10. Screws

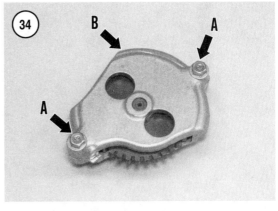

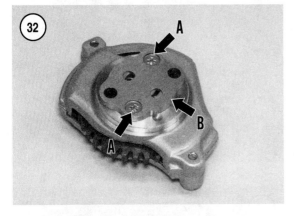

a. Lubricate new O-rings (**Figure 30**) and install them in the oil passage bores.

b. Tighten the oil pump bolts or screws (A, **Figure 29**) securely.

Disassembly/Assembly

Refer to **Figure 31**.

1. Remove the screws (A, **Figure 32**) securing the rotor cover (B) and its gasket.

NOTE
Identify the rotors so they can be rein-stalled facing in same direction.

2. Remove the outer (A, **Figure 33**) and inner (B) rotors.

3. Remove the bolts (A, **Figure 34**) and the gear cover (B).

4. Remove the drive gear (A, **Figure 35**) and the drive shaft (B).

5. Inspect as described in this section.

6. All threaded fasteners and threaded holes must be clean and dry before assembly.

7. Lubricate the drive shaft, both rotors and the housing rotor bore with engine oil.

8. Install the drive shaft (B, **Figure 35**) with its lon-ger shaft end facing toward the housing.

2. Turn the crankshaft and align the holes in the oil pump drive gear with the bolts (80 cc [A, **Figure 29**]) or screws (100 cc). Remove the bolts or screws and the oil pump (B, **Figure 29**). If the oil pump will not be serviced, store it in a plastic bag until instal-lation.

3. Remove the O-rings (**Figure 30**). Discard the O-rings.

4. Installation is the reverse of removal. Note the following:

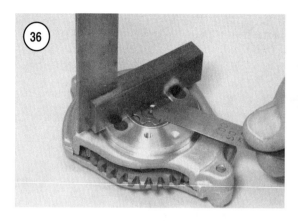

9. Install the drive gear (A, **Figure 35**) by aligning the flat sides in the gear bore with the flat sides on the rotor shaft.

10. Install the gear cover (B, **Figure 34**) and bolts (A). Tighten the bolts securely.

11. Align the inner rotor (B, **Figure 33**) by aligning the flat in the rotor bore with the flat on the shaft.

12. Install the outer rotor (A, **Figure 33**). If necessary, turn the drive gear until the teeth on the inner and outer rotors align.

13. Make sure the O-rings (**Figure 30**) are properly seated and then install a new rotor cover gasket (8, **Figure 31**). Make sure all screw and oil passage holes align. Install the rotor cover (B, **Figure 29**) and screws (A) and tighten to 3 N•m (27 in.-lb.).

14. Turn the drive gear by hand, making sure the rotors and drive shaft turn smoothly.

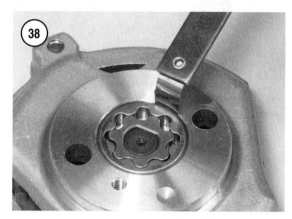

Inspection

Refer to **Table 2** for specifications. If any measurement is out of specification, or if any component shows damage, replace the part if available. If an individual part is not available separately, replace the oil pump assembly.

Refer to **Figure 31**.

1. Clean and dry all parts.

2. Inspect the gear cover and housing for cracks.

3. Check both rotors and the rotor bore for scoring and other damage.

4. Inspect both drive shafts ends for scoring and other damage.

5. Inspect the drive gear for:
    a. Broken or chipped teeth.
    b. Worn or damaged bore. The bore's flat sides must be straight.

6. Assemble the oil pump as described in this section.

7. Measure the side clearance between the rotors and pump housing with a straightedge and flat feeler gauge (**Figure 36**).

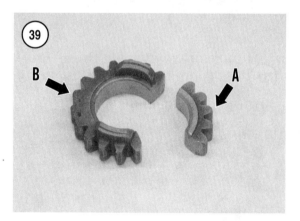

8. Where the tips of an inner and outer rotor align, measure the tip clearance with a flat feeler gauge (**Figure 37**).

9. Measure the body clearance between the outer rotor and housing bore with a flat feeler gauge (**Figure 38**).

PRIMARY DRIVE GEAR ASSEMBLY

Tool

Before servicing the primary drive gear, note that a gear holder is required to lock the primary drive and primary driven gears together when loosening and

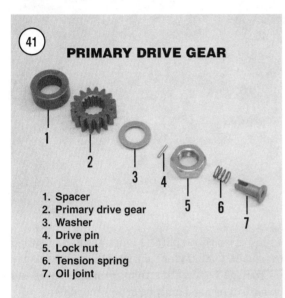

PRIMARY DRIVE GEAR

1. Spacer
2. Primary drive gear
3. Washer
4. Drive pin
5. Lock nut
6. Tension spring
7. Oil joint

2. Small cut-off wheels wear rapidly, especially when cutting gears and other hardened material. Purchase a sufficient amount of cut-off wheels for the job.

3. Mark the number of gear teeth to be removed, then mount the gear in a vise.

WARNING
Using a cut-off wheel and hand grinder as described in this procedure will cause flying particles. Do not operate a grinding tool without proper eye protection.

4. Cut through the gear with a hand grinder and cut-off wheel (**Figure 40**) at the marks made in step 3. If the gear holder is too long after cutting it, shorten it with a bench grinder.

WARNING
The gear holder and gear will be hot. Allow them to cool before handling them.

Removal

Refer to **Figure 41**.
1. Remove the right crankcase cover as described in this chapter.
2. Remove the oil pump as described in this chapter.
3. Remove the oil joint (A, **Figure 42**) and tension spring from the end of the crankshaft.
4. Mesh the gear holder between the primary drive and driven gears as shown in A, **Figure 43**.
5. Remove the primary drive gear locknut (B, **Figure 43**) and the drive pin (A, **Figure 44**).
6. Remove the washer (B, **Figure 44**) and the primary drive gear (C).
7. Remove the clutch as described in this chapter.
8. Remove the spacer (B, **Figure 42**).
9. Inspect as described in this section.

tightening the primary drive gear locknut. Use the gear holder (Honda part No. 07724-0010100), which is a small section of gear teeth, or make an equivalent tool by cutting a section of gear teeth (A, **Figure 39**) from a discarded gear as follows:
1. If possible, select a gear with a large inside diameter (B, **Figure 39**). This will reduce the amount of material that must be cut through the gear.

Installation

1. Lubricate the spacer (B, **Figure 42**) with engine oil and slide it on the crankshaft. Seat the spacer against the main bearing.

2. Install the clutch as described in this chapter.

3. Position the crankshaft so the drive pin hole in the end of the crankshaft is horizontal.

4. Install the primary drive gear (C, **Figure 44**), washer (B) and drive pin (A).

5. Install the primary drive gear locknut (A, **Figure 45**) and tighten finger-tight. Make sure the drive pin is positioned inside the crankshaft.

6. Mesh the gear holder between the primary drive and driven gears as shown in B, **Figure 45** and tighten the primary drive gear locknut (A) to 39 N•m (29 ft.-lb.).

7. Remove the gear holder (B, **Figure 45**) from the engine.

8. Install the spring (6, **Figure 41**) on the oil joint (7). Install the oil joint by aligning its slot with the drive pin (A, **Figure 44**).

9. Install the oil pump as described in this chapter.

10. Install the right crankcase cover as described in this chapter.

Inspection

Replace damaged parts as described in this section.

1. Clean and dry all parts.

2. Inspect the spacer (1, **Figure 41**) and washer (3) for cracks and other damage.

3. Inspect the primary drive gear (2, **Figure 41**) for:
   a. Broken or chipped teeth.
   b. Damaged splines.

NOTE
If damage is found in Step 3, also check the primary driven gear mounted on the clutch housing and the oil pump drive gear for the same defects. Refer to **Clutch** *and* **Oil Pump** *in this chapter.*

4. Inspect the drive pin (4, **Figure 41**), tension spring (6) and oil joint (7) for damage. These parts seal the oil passage between the right crankcase cover and crankshaft end and must be in good condition.

EXTERNAL SHIFT MECHANISM

The external shift mechanism consists of the shift shaft and pedal, stopper arm assembly and shift drum cam assembly. These parts can be removed with the engine mounted in the frame. Repair of the shift drum and forks requires engine removal and crankcase separation (Chapter Five).

NOTE
The shift pedal is subjected to a lot of abuse. If the bike has been in a hard spill, the shift pedal may have been hit and the shift shaft bent. It is very hard to straighten the shift shaft without subjecting the crankcase to abnormal stress where the shaft enters the case. If the shift shaft is bent enough to prevent it from being withdrawn from the crankcase, there is little recourse but to cut the shaft off with a hacksaw very close to the crankcase. It is less expensive in

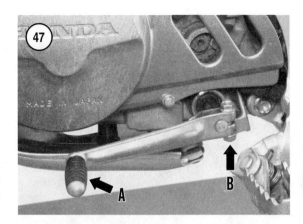

the long run to replace the shift shaft than risk damaging the crankcase.

Shift Shaft Seal Removal/Installation

The shift shaft seal (**Figure 46**) is mounted below the drive sprocket and drive chain and is subject to debris thrown off the chain. If the seal leaks oil, replace it as follows:

1. Clean the area around the shift shaft and seal to prevent dirt and other debris from entering the engine.
2. Remove the left crankcase cover (Chapter Nine).
3. Remove the shift shaft as described in this section.
4. Carefully pry the seal out of the crankcase. Do not gouge or damage the crankcase. If the seal is tight, work the pry tool around the seal to break it loose and remove it evenly. If the pry tool is inserted underneath the seal, do not allow it to contact and damage the seal bore as this would allow oil to leak between the bore and seal. This seal has a small diameter and deep shoulder and can be difficult to remove. Discard the seal.
5. Clean the seal bore in the crankcase. Check the bore for any nicks or gouges that would cause an oil leak.

6. Lubricate the lip of the new seal with grease.
7. Place the seal in the bore with its closed side facing out. Install the seal with a seal driver or socket until it bottoms in its bore.
8. Install the left crankcase cover (Chapter Nine).
9. Install the shift shaft as described in this section.
10. Fill the engine with oil (Chapter Three).
11. Start the engine and check the seal for leaks.

Removal

1. Remove the right crankcase cover, oil pump and clutch as described in this chapter.
2. Before removing the shift pedal (A, **Figure 47**), check for a punch mark on the end of the shift shaft that should align with the notch in the shift pedal. If there is no punch mark, make one with a drift and hammer. Then remove the pinch bolt (B, **Figure 47**) and shift pedal (A).

NOTE
If the shift pedal is tight, check the splines for bending or other damage. Insert a screwdriver into the slot in the pedal, then spread the slot and remove the pedal.

3. Remove the stopper lever bolt (A, **Figure 48**) and pull the stopper lever (B) out to release it from the shift drum cam. Then remove the stopper lever and its spring.

NOTE
Place a rag underneath the shift drum cam to prevent the dowel pins, which are installed behind the shift drum cam, from falling into the engine.

4. Turn the shift drum cam bolt and shift drum cam counterclockwise with a socket and ratchet until the shift drum cam stops, then loosen and remove the bolt (A, **Figure 49**), shift drum cam (B, **Figure 49**) and dowel pins (**Figure 50**).

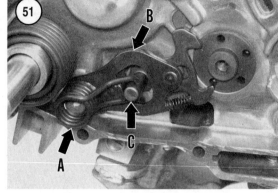

5. Remove the return spring (A, **Figure 51**) and the shift shaft (B).

6. If necessary, loosen and remove the shift shaft return spring pin (**Figure 52**).

7. Inspect as described in this section.

Installation

1. If removed, install the shift shaft return spring pin (**Figure 52**) and tighten to 30 N•m (22 ft.-lb.).

2. Install the shift shaft as follows:

   a. Clean the shift shaft oil seal (**Figure 46**) with a rag, then lubricate the seal lips with grease. If the seal is damaged, replace it as described in this section.

   b. Lubricate the shift shaft with transmission oil.

   c. Slide the shaft slowly through the engine and seal while centering the return spring with the spring pin (C, **Figure 51**).

NOTE
All four shift drum dowel pins are the same length. Two holes are drilled in the end of the shaft drum at a shallower depth to extend the reach of the pins that mate with the shift drum cam.

3. Install the dowel pins into the shift drum. Note that two of the pins extend farther from the end of the shift drum. Install the longer pins (A, **Figure 50**) and shorter pins (B) into the correct locations. Then install the shift drum cam by lining up the two extended pins (A, **Figure 50**) with the appropriate holes in the shift drum cam (**Figure 53**).

4. Hold the shift drum cam in place and install the shift drum cam bolt (A, **Figure 49**) finger-tight. Make sure the two pins are still installed into the shift drum cam holes. Then turn the shift drum cam bolt clockwise to lock the shift drum. Tighten the bolt (A, **Figure 49**) securely.

5. Install the stopper arm assembly as follows:

   a. Assemble the stopper arm as shown in **Figure 54**

   b. Install the stopper arm as shown in B, **Figure 48**. Finger-tighten the stopper arm mounting bolt. Make sure the spring is positioned against the stopper arm and crankcase.

   c. Using a screwdriver, push the stopper arm down and release it to make sure it moves under spring tension. If the stopper arm will not move it is pinched under the mounting bolt. Loosen the bolt and center the stopper arm on the bolt's shoulder, then retighten the bolt.

   d. When the stopper arm moves correctly, tighten the stopper arm pivot bolt (A, **Figure 48**) to 13 N•m (115 in.-lb.).

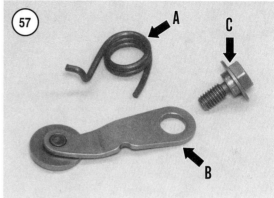

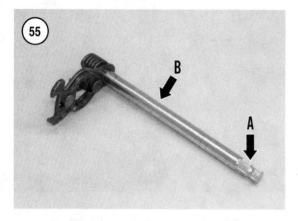

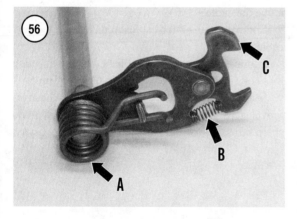

the shift drum cam. This is the shift drum's neutral position.

b. If the shift shaft moves and then locks in place, the return spring (A, **Figure 51**) may not be centered on the spring pin (C).

c. If the transmission over-shifts, check for an incorrectly assembled stopper arm assembly.

d. If the transmission does not shift properly, check for an incorrectly installed shift shaft return spring (A, **Figure 51**). Then check the shift lever assembly.

8. Install the oil pump, clutch and right crankcase cover as described in this chapter.

Inspection

Worn or damaged external shift linkage components will cause missed shifts and wear to the transmission gears, shift forks and shift drum. Replace parts that show excessive wear or damage.

1. Clean and dry the parts. Clean the shift drum cam and stopper arm bolt threads and their mating threads in the crankcase of all oil residue. These threads must be clean and dry.

2. Clean the shift shaft splines (A, **Figure 55**) with a brush. Replace the shift shaft (B, **Figure 55**) if the shaft is bent or the splines (A) are twisted or damaged. Check the shaft where it operates against the oil seal for pitting and other defects.

3. Inspect the return spring (A, **Figure 56**) for cracks and other damage. Check the tension spring (B, **Figure 56**) for stretched coils or damage. Pivot the pawl assembly (C, **Figure 56**) to make sure it returns and centers under spring tension. Check the pawl tips for rounding, cracks and other damage.

4. Check the stopper arm assembly for:

a. Weak or damaged spring (A, **Figure 57**). Check spring for cracks.

b. Bent, cracked or damaged stopper arm (B, **Figure 57**). Check roller for flat spots.

6. Install the shift pedal (B, **Figure 47**) by aligning the index mark on the shift shaft with the notch in the shift pedal. Install the bolt and nut and tighten securely.

7. Support the motorcycle with the rear wheel off the ground and check the shifting as follows:

a. Slowly turn the rear wheel and shift the transmission into first gear, then shift into neutral and the remaining forward gears.

NOTE

*Note in C, **Figure 48** the stopper arm's engagement with the raised ramp on*

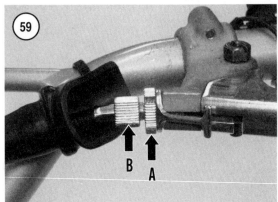

c. Damaged stopper arm mounting bolt (C,
   Figure 57).
5. Check the shift drum cam assembly (**Figure 58**)
for:
   a. Worn or damaged cam ramps.
   b. Cracked or damaged pin holes.
   c. Damaged pins.
   d. Damaged mounting bolt.

CLUTCH CABLE

Removal/Installation

1. Remove the fuel tank (Chapter Eight).
2. Before disconnecting or removing the clutch cable,
make a drawing of the cable routing from the handlebar to where it is attached at the engine. Replace the
cable exactly as it was, avoiding any sharp turns.
3. If used, remove the hand guard (Chapter
Fourteen).
4. Loosen the clutch cable adjuster locknut (A,
Figure 59) and adjuster (B) at the handlebar.
5. Loosen the clutch cable adjuster locknuts (**Figure
60**) at the engine.

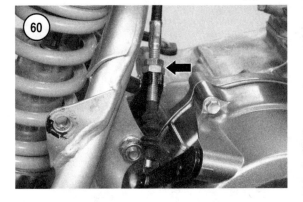

6. Disconnect both ends of the clutch cable and remove the cable.
7. Compare both clutch cables to make sure the new
cable is correct.
8. Lubricate the new clutch cable before reconnecting
it as described in *Control Cables* in Chapter Three.
9. Install the new clutch cable by reversing these removal steps. Make sure it is correctly routed with no
sharp turns. Adjust the clutch as described in *Clutch
Lever* in Chapter Three.

Table 1 CLUTCH SERVICE SPECIFICATIONS

	New mm (in.)	Service limit mm (in.)
Clutch spring free length		
1992-1997 models	26.1 (1.03)	24.1 (0.95)
1998-on models		
80 cc models	27.6 (1.09)	25.5 (1.00)
100 cc models	31.9 (1.25)	29.5 (1.16)
Drive plate thickness		
1992-1997 models	2.80-2.90 (0.110-0.114)	2.5 (0.10)
1998-on models		
XR80R	2.80-2.90 (0.110-0.114)	2.5 (0.10)
CRF80F	2.90-3.00 (0.114-0.118)	2.5 (0.10)
XR100R and CRF100F	2.92-3.08 (0.115-0.121)	2.7 (0.11)
Driven plate warp	–	0.20 (0.008)

Table 2 OIL PUMP SERVICE SPECIFICATIONS

	New mm (in.)	Service limit mm (in.)
Body clearance	0.15-0.21 (0.006-0.008)	0.40 (0.016)
Rotor tip clearance	0.15 (0.006)	0.20 (0.008)
Side clearance		
1992-1997 models	0.15-0.21 (0.006-0.008)	0.25 (0.010)
1998-on models	0.02-0.07 (0.001-0.003)	0.25 (0.010)

**Table 3 CLUTCH, OIL PUMP, PRIMARY DRIVE GEAR AND
EXTERNAL SHIFT MECHANISM TORQUE SPECIFICATIONS**

	N•m	in.-lb.	ft.-lb.
Kick pedal pinch bolt	12	106	–
Oil pump rotor cover screw	3	27	–
Primary drive gear locknut	39	–	29
Shift shaft return spring pin	30	–	22
Stopper arm pivot bolt	13	115	–

6

CHAPTER SEVEN

TRANSMISSION AND SHIFT MECHANISM

This chapter describes disassembly and reassembly of the transmission shafts and internal shift mechanism.

Tables 1-4 are located at the end of this chapter.

TRANSMISSION

Operation

The transmission is a five-speed constant-mesh. The gears on the mainshaft (A, **Figure 1**) mesh with the gears on the countershaft (B). Each pair of meshed gears represents one gear ratio. For each pair of gears, one of the gears is splined to its shaft, while the other gear freewheels on its shaft. Next to each freewheeling gear is another gear that is splined to the same shaft. This locked gear can move laterally on its splines and against the freewheeling gear. The splined gear and the freewheeling gear have mating dogs and slots that allow the two gears to lock together, thus locking the freewheeling gear to the shaft. Anytime the transmission is *in gear* a pair of meshed gears are locked to their shafts, and that gear ratio is selected. All other meshed gears have one freewheeling gear.

To engage and disengage the various gear ratios, the splined gears are moved by shift forks. Each fork fits in a groove at the side of one of the splined gears.

The guide pin, at the opposite end of each fork, fits in one of the shift drum grooves. As the transmission is shifted, the shift drum rotates and guides the forks to engage and disengage pairs of gears on the transmission shafts. The grooves are curved, to guide the forks to the selected gears by cam-action.

Service

1. Remove and install the transmission assembly as described in *Crankcase* in Chapter Five.
2. Clean and dry the transmission shafts before servicing them.
3. Before disassembling the transmission shafts, perform the following:
   a. Rotate each fixed gear and slide each grooved gear on its shaft. Any roughness or binding may indicate a problem with a gear bore, bushing (100 cc models) or shaft.
   b. Hold each transmission shaft, one at a time, and lock each sliding gear against its fixed gear. Check the engagement between the gear dogs on both gears. The dogs should be pointed.
   c. Gears should slide off and on both shafts easily. If force is required, the gear and/or shaft are damaged.

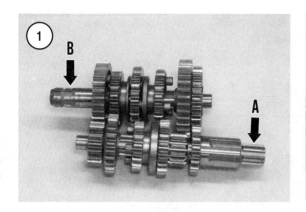

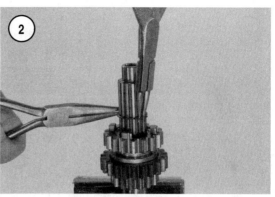

4. Parts with two different sides, such as gears, snap rings and shift forks can be installed backward. Maintain the correct alignment and position of the parts during disassembly by storing each part in order in a divided container.

5. Snap rings fatigue and distort when removed and must not be reused. Install *new* snap rings during reassembly.

6. To install new snap rings without distorting them, open the new snap ring with a pair of snap ring pliers while holding the back of the snap ring with a pair of pliers (**Figure 2**). Slide the snap ring down the shaft and seat it into its correct groove. This technique can also be used to remove snap rings from a shaft once they are free from their grooves. When securing a shaft in a vise, use soft jaws to prevent shaft damage.

7. The snap rings and washers used on the transmission shafts are stamped types. One edge is rounded, while the other is flat (sharp). Install snap rings so their flat side faces away from the part producing the thrust. The sharp edge prevents the snap ring from rolling out of its groove when thrust is applied. Drawings used in the text will show how to install the snap ring correctly. Refer to *Snap Rings and E-clips* in *Fasteners* in Chapter One for additional information.

MAINSHAFT

Use the following procedures to disassemble and assemble the mainshaft. Note that parts are removed from both sides of the shaft.

Refer to **Figure 3**.

Disassembly

1. Disassemble the mainshaft in the following order:
   a. Primary starter gear.

NOTE
*Second gear (1, **Figure 3**) is symmetrical with no identifying marks. Mark the*

outside of the gear so it can be reinstalled facing in its original direction.

   b. Second gear.
   c. Fifth gear.
   d. Spline washer.
   e. Snap ring.
   f. Third gear.
   g. Snap ring.
   h. Spline washer.
   i. Fourth gear.
   j. Thrust washer.

NOTE
First gear is an integral part of the mainshaft.

2. Inspect each part as described in this chapter.

Assembly

1. Before beginning assembly, note the following:
   a. Have two new snap rings on hand. Both snap rings have the same part number.
   b. Review the information in *Service* in *Transmission* in this chapter.
   c. Throughout the procedure, the orientation of many parts is made in relationship to first gear (A, **Figure 4**).

2. Lubricate all sliding surfaces with engine oil.

3. Install the thrust washer (B, **Figure 4**) with its flat side facing toward first gear.

4. Install fourth gear with its gear dogs facing away from first gear (**Figure 5**).

5. Install the spline washer (A, **Figure 6**) and seat it against fourth gear. The washer's flat side must face away from first gear.

6. Install a new snap ring (B, **Figure 6**) and seat it in the groove (C) next to fourth gear. The snap ring's flat side must face away from first gear. Make sure the snap ring seats in the groove completely.

7. Spin fourth gear to make sure it turns freely.

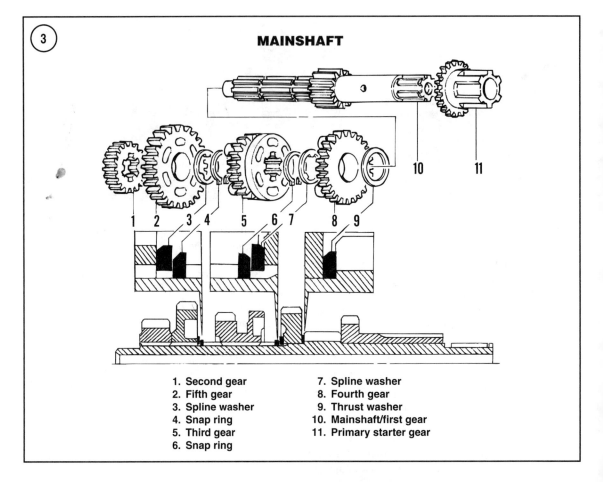

MAINSHAFT

1. Second gear
2. Fifth gear
3. Spline washer
4. Snap ring
5. Third gear
6. Snap ring
7. Spline washer
8. Fourth gear
9. Thrust washer
10. Mainshaft/first gear
11. Primary starter gear

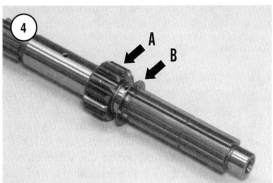

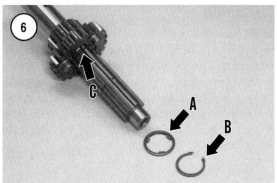

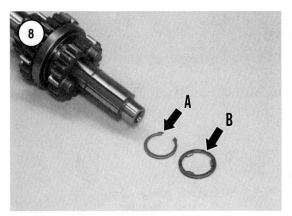

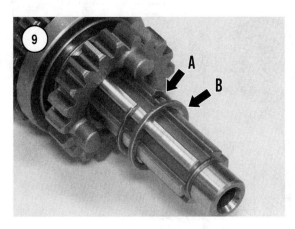

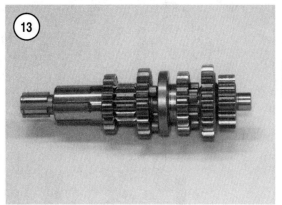

8. Install third gear with its shift fork groove (**Figure 7**) facing toward first gear.

9. Install a new snap ring (A, **Figure 8**) and seat it in the shaft groove (A, **Figure 9**). The snap ring's flat side must face toward first gear. Make sure the snap ring seats in the groove completely.

10. Install the spline washer (B, **Figure 8**) and seat it next to the snap ring (B, **Figure 9**). The washer's flat side must face toward first gear.

11. Install fifth gear (**Figure 10**) with its gear dogs facing toward first gear.

12. Install second gear (**Figure 11**) and seat it against fifth gear. If the original gear was marked, install it facing in its original direction. Spin the gear to make sure to turns freely.

13. Install the primary starter gear (**Figure 12**) with its gear facing toward first gear.

14. Compare the assembled mainshaft with **Figure 13**.

COUNTERSHAFT

Use the following procedures to disassemble and assemble the countershaft. Note that parts are removed from both sides of the shaft.

Refer to **Figure 14**.

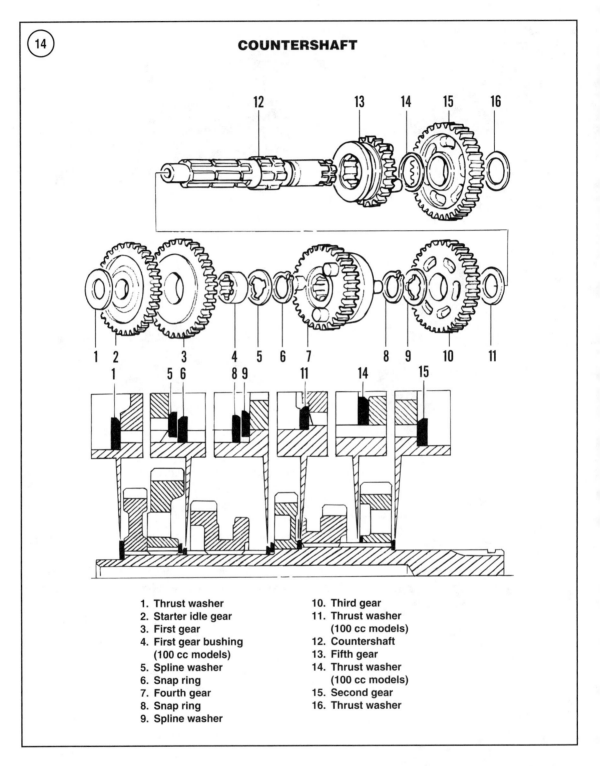

COUNTERSHAFT

1. Thrust washer
2. Starter idle gear
3. First gear
4. First gear bushing
   (100 cc models)
5. Spline washer
6. Snap ring
7. Fourth gear
8. Snap ring
9. Spline washer
10. Third gear
11. Thrust washer
    (100 cc models)
12. Countershaft
13. Fifth gear
14. Thrust washer
    (100 cc models)
15. Second gear
16. Thrust washer

Disassembly

1. Remove the following parts from the countershaft's splined end:
   a. Thrust washer.
   b. Second gear.
   c. Thrust washer (100 cc models).
   d. Fifth gear.

2. Remove the following parts from the countershaft's smooth end:
   a. Thrust washer.
   b. Starter idle gear.
   c. First gear.
   d. First gear bushing (100 cc models).
   e. Spline washer.
   f. Snap ring.

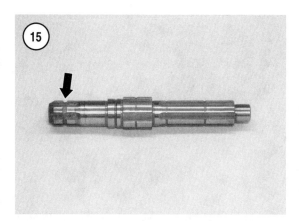

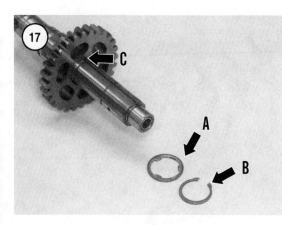

b. Review the information in *Service* in *Transmission* in this chapter.

c. Throughout the procedure, the orientation of many parts is made in relationship to the countershaft's splined end (**Figure 15**).

2. Lubricate all sliding surfaces with engine oil.

NOTE
*Parts 1-11 in **Figure 14** are installed from the countershaft's smooth end side.*

3. On 100 cc models, install the thrust washer (11, **Figure 14**) and seat it against the spline shoulder. The washer's flat side must face toward the shaft's splined end.

4. Install third gear (**Figure 16**) with its dog grooves facing away from the shaft's splined end.

5. Install the thrust washer (A, **Figure 17**) and seat it against third gear. The washer's flat side must face away from the shaft's splined end.

6. Install a new snap ring (B, **Figure 17**) and seat it in the groove (C) next to third gear. The snap ring's flat side must face away from the shaft's splined end. Make sure the snap ring seats in the groove completely.

7. Spin third gear to make sure it turns freely.

8. Install fourth gear with its shift fork groove (**Figure 18**) facing toward the shaft's splined end.

9. Install a new snap ring (A, **Figure 19**) and seat it in the countershaft groove (A, **Figure 20**). The snap ring's flat side must face toward the shaft's splined end.

10. Install the spline washer (B, **Figure 19**) and seat it against the snap ring (B, **Figure 20**). The washer's flat side must face toward the shaft's splined end.

11. On 100 cc models, install the first gear bushing (4, **Figure 14**) and seat it against the spline washer.

12. Install first gear with its inner shoulder recess (**Figure 21**) facing toward the shaft's splined end. **Figure 22** shows the opposite side of first gear used on 80 cc models. On 100 cc models, this side of first

g. Fourth gear.

h. Snap ring.

i. Spline washer.

j. Third gear.

k. Thrust washer (100 cc models).

3. Inspect each part as described in this chapter.

Assembly

1. Before beginning assembly, note the following:

a. Have two new snap rings on hand. Both snap rings have the same part number.

gear is solid. Spin the gear to make sure it turns freely.

13. Install the starter idle gear (A, **Figure 23**) and
seat it against first gear. Spin the gear to make sure
it turns freely.

14. Install the thrust washer (B, **Figure 23**) and seat
it against the starter idle gear. The washer's flat side
must face away from the shaft's splined end.

NOTE
Parts 13-16 in **Figure 14** *are installed*
from the countershaft's splined end
side.

15. Install fifth gear with its gear dogs (**Figure 24**)
facing toward the shaft's splined end.

16. On 100 cc models, install the thrust washer (14,
Figure 14) and seat it against fifth gear. The washer's flat side must face away from the shaft's splined
end.

17. Install second gear with its shoulder recess
(**Figure 25**) facing away from the shaft's splined end.
A, **Figure 26** shows the outer or flat side of second
gear. Spin the gear to make sure it turns freely.

18. Install the thrust washer (B, **Figure 26**) and seat
it against second gear. The washer's flat side must
face toward the shaft's splined end.

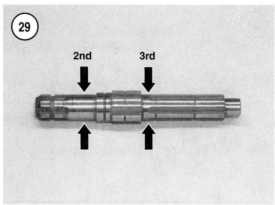

19. Compare the assembled countershaft with **Figure 27**.

TRANSMISSION INSPECTION

Refer to **Table 2** or **Table 3** when measuring the transmission components and calculating clearances in this section. Replace parts that are out of specification or show damage as described in this section.

NOTE
Maintain the alignment of the transmission components when cleaning and inspecting the parts in this section.

1. Inspect the mainshaft (**Figure 28**) and countershaft (**Figure 29**) for:
   a. Worn or damaged splines.
   b. Missing, broken or chipped first gear teeth (mainshaft).
   c. Worn or damaged bearing surfaces.
   d. Cracked or rounded snap ring grooves.
2. Measure the mainshaft outside diameter at its fourth and fifth gear operating positions (**Figure 28**).
3. Measure the countershaft outside diameter at its second and third gear operating positions (**Figure 29**).
4. Check each gear for excessive wear, burrs, pitting, or chipped or missing teeth. Check the splines on sliding gears and the bore on stationary gears for excessive wear or damage.
5. To check stationary gears for wear, install the gear and its bushing (if used) on their correct shaft and in their original operating position. If necessary, use the old snap rings to secure them in place. Then spin the gear by hand. The gear should turn smoothly. A rough turning gear indicates heat damage. Check for a dark blue color or galling on the operating surfaces. Rocking indicates excessive wear, either to the gear, bushing (100 cc models), shaft or washer(s).
6. To check the sliding gears, install them on their correct shaft and in their original operating position.

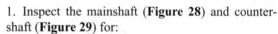

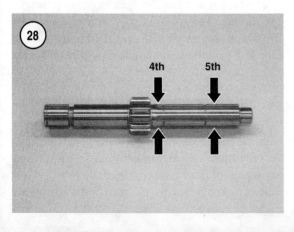

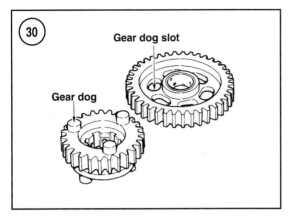

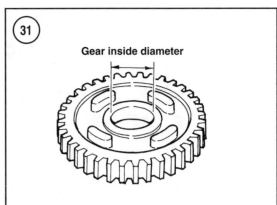

The gear should slide back and forth without any binding or excessive play.

7. Check the dogs and dog slots on the gears (**Figure 30**) for rounded or damaged engagement edges. Any wear on the dogs and mating recesses should be uniform. If the dogs are not worn evenly, the remaining dogs will be overstressed and possibly fail. Check the engagement of the dogs by placing the gears at their appropriate positions on each shaft, then twisting the gears together. Check for positive engagement in both directions. If damage is evident, inspect the condition of the shift forks as described in *Internal Shift Mechanism* in this chapter.

8. Check engaging gears by installing both gears on their respective shafts and in their original operating position, then twist the gears together to engage the dogs. Check for positive engagement in both directions. If damage is evident, inspect the condition of the shift forks, as described in *Internal Shift Mechanism* in this chapter.

> *NOTE*
> *The side of the gear dogs that carries the engine load will wear and eventually become rounded. The unloaded side of the dogs will remain unworn. Rounded dogs will cause the transmission to jump out of gear.*

9. Check for worn or damaged shift fork grooves. Check the gear groove and its mating shift fork.

10. Measure the mainshaft and countershaft gear inside diameters (**Figure 31**) specified in **Table 2** or **Table 3**.

11. On 100 cc models, check the first gear bushing (4, **Figure 14**) for worn or damaged bearing surface or damaged splines. Then measure the bushing outside diameter.

12. Using the measurements recorded in the previous steps, determine the gear-to-shaft and gear-to-bushing (100 cc models) clearances specified in **Table 2** or **Table 3**.

> *NOTE*
> *Replace defective gears and their mating gear at the same time, though they may not show equal wear or damage.*

13. Inspect the spline washers. The teeth in the washers should be uniform, and the washers should not be loose on the shaft.

14. Inspect the thrust washers for damage. While it is normal for the thrust washers to show wear, replace them when their thickness has been reduced.

15. Check the primary starter gear for:
  a. Damaged splines (A, **Figure 32**).
  b. Damaged gear teeth (B, **Figure 32**).
  c. Severely worn or damaged bushing surface (C, **Figure 32**).

16. Check the starter idle gear (2, **Figure 14**) for damaged gear teeth or a worn or damaged gear bore.

INTERNAL SHIFT MECHANISM

As the transmission is upshifted and downshifted, the shift drum and fork assembly engages and disengages pairs of gears on the transmission shafts. Gear shifting is controlled by the shift forks, which are guided by cam grooves in the shift drum.

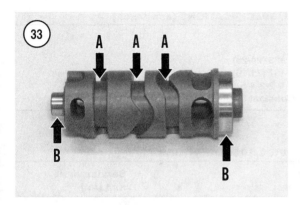

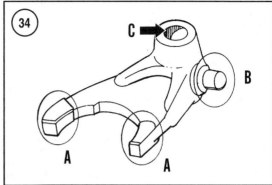

The shift drum grooves, shift forks and mating gear grooves must be in good condition. Too much wear between the parts will cause unreliable and poor engagement of the gears. This can lead to premature wear of the gear dogs and other parts.

Shift Drum Inspection

1. Clean and dry the shift drum.
2. Check the shift drum for wear and damage as follows:
   a. The shift drum grooves (A, **Figure 33**) should be a uniform width. Worn grooves can prevent complete gear engagement, which can cause rough shifting and allow the transmission to disengage.
   b. Check the shift drum bearing surfaces (B, **Figure 33**) for wear or overheating discoloration due to lack of lubrication.

Shift Fork and Shaft Inspection

Table 4 lists shift fork and shift fork shaft specifications. Replace the shift forks and shafts if out of specification or if they show damage as described in this section.

1. Inspect each shift fork for signs of wear or damage. Examine the shift fork pads where they contact the slider gear (A, **Figure 34**). These surfaces must be smooth with no signs of excessive wear, bending, cracks, heat discoloration or other damage.
2. Check each shift fork for arc-shaped wear or burn marks. These marks indicate a bent shift fork.
3. The guide pins (B, **Figure 34**) should be symmetrical and not flat on the sides.
4. Check the shift fork shafts for bending or other damage. Install each shift fork on its shaft and slide it back and forth. Each shift fork must slide smoothly with no binding or tight spots. If there is any noticeable binding, check for a bent shift fork shaft.
5. Measure the thickness of each shift fork pad (A, **Figure 34**).
6. Measure the inside diameter of each shift fork (C, **Figure 34**).
7. Inspect the shift fork shafts for wear and damage. Measure the shift fork shaft outside diameter at each shift fork operating position.

Table 1 TRANSMISSION GENERAL SPECIFICATIONS

Final reduction ratio	
80 cc models	3.285 (46/14)
100 cc models	3.571 (50/14)
Gear ratios	
80 cc models	
First gear	2.692 (35/13)
Second gear	1.823 (31/17)
Third gear	1.400 (28/20)
Fourth gear	1.130 (26/23)
Fifth gear	0.960 (24/25)
100 cc models	
First gear	3.083 (37/12)
Second gear	1.882 (32/17)
Third gear	1.400 (28/20)
Fourth gear	1.130 (26/23)

(continued)

Table 1 TRANSMISSION GENERAL SPECIFICATIONS (continued)

Gear ratios (continued)	
100 cc models	
Fifth gear	0.923 (24/26)
Primary reduction ratio	4.437 (71/16)
Shift pattern	1-N-2-3-4-5
Transmission	Constant mesh, 5-speeds

Table 2 MAINSHAFT SERVICE SPECIFICATIONS

	New mm (in.)	Service limit mm (in.)
Gear inside diameter		
Fourth and fifth gears	17.016-17.034 (0.6699-0.6706)	17.05 (0.671)
Gear-to-shaft clearance		
Fourth gear	0.032-0.068 (0.0013-0.0027)	0.10 (0.004)
Mainshaft outside diameter		
At fourth and fifth gear operating positions	16.966-16.984 (0.6680-0.6687)	16.95 (0.667)

Table 3 COUNTERSHAFT SERVICE SPECIFICATIONS

	New mm (in.)	Service limit mm (in.)
Bushing outside diameter		
First gear		
100 cc models	20.559-20.580 (0.8094-0.8102)	20.54 (0.809)
Countershaft outside diameter		
Second gear	19.450-19.480 (0.7657-0.7669)	19.44 (0.7654)
Third gear		
80 cc models	16.966-16.984 (0.6680-0.6687)	16.95 (0.667)
100 cc models	17.966-17.984 (0.7073-0.7080)	17.95 (0.707)
Gear inside diameter		
First gear		
80 cc models	17.022-17.043 (0.6702-0.6710)	17.06 (0.672)
100 cc models	20.662-20.643 (0.8135-0.8127)	20.66 (0.8134)
Second gear	19.520-19.541 (0.7685-0.7693)	19.56 (0.770)
Third gear		
80 cc models	17.016-17.034 (0.6699-0.6706)	17.05 (0.671)
100 cc models	18.016-18.034 (0.7093-0.7100)	18.05 (0.711)
Gear-to-bushing clearance		
100 cc models		
First gear	0.042-0.084 (0.0017-0.0034)	0.12 (0.005)
Gear-to-shaft clearance		
Second gear	0.040-0.082 (0.0016-0.0032)	0.12 (0.005)
Third gear	0.032-0.068 (0.0013-0.0027)	0.10 (0.004)

Table 4 SHIFT FORK SERVICE SPECIFICATIONS

	New mm (in.)	Service limit mm (in.)
Shift fork inside diameter	12.000-12.018 (0.4724-0.4731)	12.05 (0.474)
Shift fork pad thickness	4.93-5.00 (0.194-0.197)	4.7 (0.19)
Shift fork shaft outside diameter	11.976-11.994 (0.4715-0.4722)	11.96 (0.471)

CHAPTER EIGHT

FUEL SYSTEM

This chapter includes service procedures for all parts of the fuel system, crankcase breather system and throttle cable. Air filter service is covered in Chapter Three.

Tables 1-4 are at the end of this chapter.

FUEL SYSTEM SAFETY

When working on the fuel system, observe the following:

> *WARNING*
> *Fuel may spill from the fuel tank and carburetor when performing procedures in this chapter. Because gasoline is an extremely flammable and explosive petroleum, perform the service away from all open flames (including pilot lights) and sparks. Do not smoke or allow someone who is smoking in the work area. Always work in a well-ventilated area. Wipe up any spills immediately.*

1. Turn the fuel valve off.
2. Work very carefully when the engine is hot.
3. Wear eye protection when using compressed air and when using solvents and degreasers.
4. Keep a fire extinguisher in the work area, rated for class B (fuel) and class C (electrical) fires.

FUEL TANK

Refer to **Table 1** for fuel tank capacity.

Removal/Installation

1. Read *Fuel System Safety* in this chapter.
2. Support the motorcycle on its sidestand.
3. Remove the seat (Chapter Fourteen).
4. Remove the tank shrouds, if necessary as described in Chapter Fourteen. The fuel tank can be removed with the shrouds installed.
5. Turn the fuel valve off and disconnect the fuel line (A, **Figure 1**) at the fuel valve.
6. Remove the rubber retaining strap (B, **Figure 1**) securing the rear of the tank to the frame.
7. Remove the breather hose (A, **Figure 2**) from the number plate.
8. Remove the bolts and washers (B, **Figure 2**) and the fuel tank. Note the collars installed in the grommets at the front of the fuel tank. These may fall out.
9. Check the fuel tank damper mounted on the frame and the dampers mounted on the fuel tank for damage.
10. Install the fuel tank by reversing these removal steps. Note the following.
   a. Service the fuel valve as described in this chapter.

b. Replace the fuel hose if it has hardened, leaking or damaged.

c. Replace weak or damaged fuel hose clamps.

d. Secure the fuel hose to the fuel tank with its hose clamp.

e. Tighten the fuel tank mounting bolts to 12 N•m (106 in.-lb.).

f. After reconnecting the fuel hose, turn the fuel valve on and check the hose and valve for leaks. Repair leaks or other damage before riding the motorcycle.

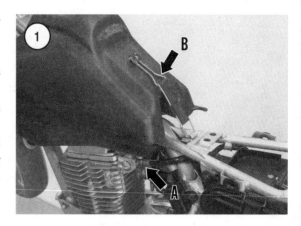

FUEL VALVE

The fuel valve is an assembled unit and cannot be rebuilt. Only the outer O-ring installed on the fuel valve can be replaced separately. If the fuel valve is damaged or if the fuel strainer screen is plugged and cannot be fully cleaned, replace the fuel valve assembly.

Removal/Cleaning/Installation

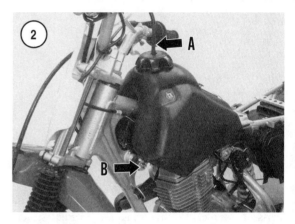

1. Read *Fuel System Safety* in this chapter.

2. Remove the fuel tank as described in this chapter.

3. Drain the fuel tank of all gas. Store the gas in a can approved for gasoline storage.

4. Remove the screws (A, **Figure 3**) securing the fuel valve (B) to the bottom of the fuel tank and remove the fuel valve.

5. Remove the O-ring (A, **Figure 4**).

6. Clean the fuel strainer screen (B, **Figure 4**) with a high-flash point solvent and a soft brush and allow to dry. If the screen is contaminated and cannot be cleaned or is damaged, replace the fuel valve assembly.

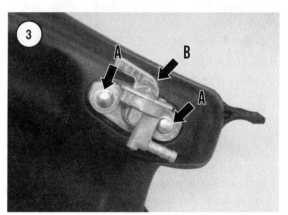

7. Clean the O-ring seat on the bottom of the fuel tank.

8. Inspect the square brass threaded inserts in the bottom of the fuel tank. The inserts should be a tight fit. If they have started to loosen, the fuel valve mounting screws have been overtightened.

9. Install a new O-ring (A, **Figure 4**) and seat it next to the fuel valve.

10. Install the fuel valve and secure with the mounting screws. Do not overtighten the screws.

11. After installing the fuel tank, pour a small amount of gas into the tank and check the fuel valve for leaks.

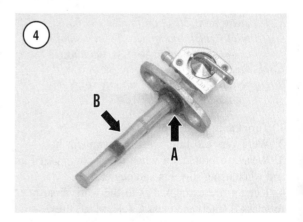

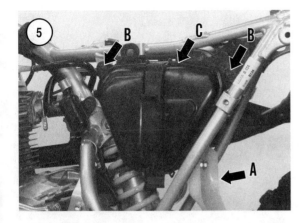

AIR BOX

Removal/Installation

1. Remove the seat and side covers (Chapter Fourteen).
2. Remove the mud guard (A, **Figure 5**).
3. Disconnect the crankcase breather hose (A, **Figure 6**) from the intake tube.
4. On 2004-on models, remove the air vent hose from the groove on the air box.
5. Loosen the hose clamp (B, **Figure 6**) securing the intake tube to the air box.
6. Remove the air box mounting bolt at the rear of the air box (C, **Figure 6**).
7. Remove the two air box mounting bolts (B, **Figure 5**) at the front of the air box and remove the air box (C).
8. Cover the intake tube opening with a plastic bag.
9. Installation is the reverse of removal.

CARBURETOR AND INTAKE TUBE

Refer to **Table 2** and **Table 3** for carburetor specifications.

Carburetor Removal

1. Support the motorcycle on its sidestand.
2. Turn the fuel valve off and disconnect the fuel hose (A, **Figure 1**) at the fuel tank.
3. Place a container under the carburetor drain hose (A, **Figure 7**, typical). Then open the drain screw and allow the fuel to drain out of the float bowl. Close and tighten the drain screw. Refer to B, **Figure 7** (80 cc models) or **Figure 8** (100 cc models). Discard the fuel.

> *CAUTION*
> *Before removing the top cap, thoroughly clean the area around it so no dirt falls into the carburetor.*

4. Loosen the top cap (C, **Figure 7**) and remove the throttle valve assembly (**Figure 9**).

> *NOTE*
> *If the throttle valve is not going to be removed from the throttle cable, wrap it in a clean shop cloth and place in a plastic bag to keep it clean. Protect the jet needle by sliding a hose over it.*

5. If throttle valve and jet needle removal is required, perform the following:

a. Hold the throttle valve and pull the spring toward the cap (A, **Figure 10**). Hold the spring in place.

b. Disengage the throttle cable end from the throttle valve by moving the cable end out of the retaining hole, then route the cable through the slot (B, **Figure 10**) in the side of the throttle valve.

c. Remove the retainer (A, **Figure 11**), jet needle and E-clip (B) from the throttle valve.

NOTE
The carburetor top cap (A, Figure 12) is permanently mounted onto the throttle cable (B). Do not attempt to separate these parts.

6. On 2004-on models, remove the air vent hose from the groove in the air box.

7. Loosen the hose clamp screw on the air intake tube (A, **Figure 13**). Slide the clamp away from the carburetor.

8. Remove the mounting nuts (B, **Figure 13** [80 cc models] or **Figure 14** [100 cc models]) and the carburetor.

9. Examine the intake tube. If there is dirt in the tube, dirt is bypassing the air filter. Service the air filter as described in Chapter Three.

10. Plug the intake boot and intake tube to prevent dust and other debris from entering the air box and engine.

11. Service the carburetor as described in *Carburetor Service* in this chapter.

12. Service the intake tube as described in this section.

Carburetor Installation

1. Install a new O-ring (**Figure 15**) in the carburetor groove.

2. Remove the plugs from the intake boot and intake tube and install the carburetor.

3. Install the mounting nuts (B, **Figure 13** [80 cc models] or **Figure 14** [100 cc models]) and tighten securely.

4. Position the clamp (A, **Figure 13**) into the groove on the end of the intake boot and tighten securely.

5. On 2004-on models, install the air vent hose into the groove in the air box.

6. If the throttle valve and jet needle were removed, perform the following:

a. Make sure the E-clip is positioned on the jet needle. On 1992-2005 models, refer to **Table 2** or **Table 3** for standard jet needle clip position. On 2006-on models, the jet needle is not adjustable.

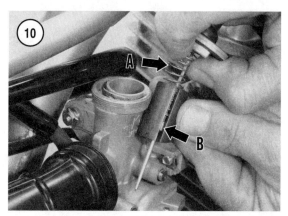
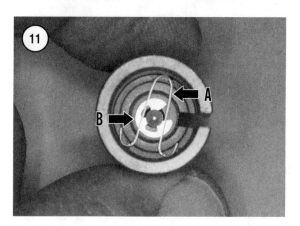
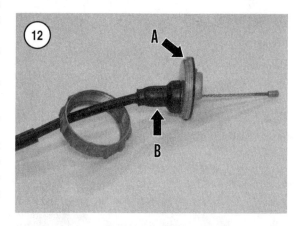

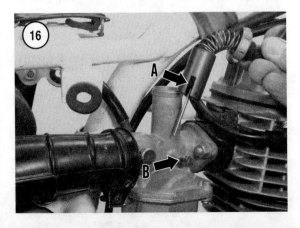

b. Drop the jet needle into the throttle valve (B, **Figure 11**) and secure with the retainer (A). Make sure the retainer (A, **Figure 11**) is sitting flush against the throttle valve and positioned so it cannot interfere with throttle cable installation.

c. Install the spring over the throttle cable and compress it against the top cap. Install the end of the throttle cable into the retaining hole in the bottom of the throttle valve while routing the cable through the slot in the side of the throttle valve (B, **Figure 10**). Release the spring.

7. Install the throttle valve by aligning its wide slot (A, **Figure 16**) with the throttle valve screw (B). At the same time, the throttle valve's groove (B, **Figure 10**) will align with a pin in the carburetor bore.

8. Tighten the top cap (C, **Figure 7**) securely.

9. Reconnect the fuel hose at the fuel tank and secure with the clamp.

10. Operate the throttle a few times to make sure the throttle valve moves through the carburetor bore with no binding or roughness. If there is any binding or roughness, note the following:

a. If the throttle valve does not move or moves roughly, check the groove and pin alignment as described in Step 7. If the alignment is okay, check the throttle valve assembly at the handlebar and the throttle cable for incorrect assembly, routing or adjustment.

b. If necessary, adjust the throttle cable as described in Chapter Three.

WARNING
Do not ride the motorcycle if the throttle valve does not operate correctly. Remove the top cap and pull the throttle valve back out. Check parts before starting the engine.

11. Turn the fuel valve on and check the hose and carburetor for leaks.

12. If the carburetor was overhauled or the air screw (80 cc models) or pilot screw (100 cc models) was removed or replaced, perform the *Idle Drop Adjustment* as described in *Carburetor Adjustments* in this chapter.

Intake Tube Removal/Installation

1. Remove the carburetor as described in this section.

2. Remove the bolts and the intake tube. Refer to **Figure 17** (80 cc models) or **Figure 18** (100 cc models). Remove and discard the gasket.

3. Inspect the intake tube for damage, especially where the aluminum end pieces attach to the rubber tube.

4. On 100 cc models, replace the O-ring if flattened or otherwise damaged.

5. Installation is the reverse of removal. Note the following:

   a. Install a new gasket.

   b. Tighten the intake tube mounting bolts securely.

CARBURETOR SERVICE

Disassembly (80 cc Models)

Refer to **Figure 19**.

1. Remove the carburetor as described in this chapter.

2. Remove the hoses (A, **Figure 20**) connected to the carburetor and float bowl nozzles (B).

3. Remove the float bowl screws and float bowl (C, **Figure 20**). Be careful of any gas that spills out of the float bowl. Remove the O-ring installed in the float bowl groove. Discard the O-ring.

4. Remove the float pin (A, **Figure 21**), float (B) and fuel valve. Unhook the fuel valve (**Figure 22**) from the float.

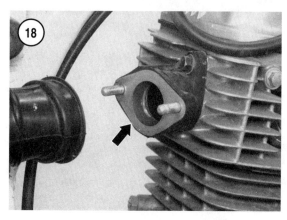

> *NOTE*
> *The fuel valve seat is permanently attached to the carburetor body. Do not attempt to remove it.*

5. Remove the pilot jet (A, **Figure 23**).

6. Hold the needle jet holder and remove the main jet (B, **Figure 23**) and the main jet holder (C).

7. Remove the needle jet holder (D, **Figure 23**).

8. Use a small round wooden stick and push the needle jet (E, **Figure 23**) out through the bottom of the carburetor.

> *NOTE*
> *A D-shaped pilot screw wrench is required to remove the air screw on 2006 and later models. Refer to* ***Carburetor Adjustment*** *in this chapter for the tool part numbers.*

9. Lightly seat the air screw (A, **Figure 24**), counting the number of turns for reassembly reference. Remove the screw (A, **Figure 25**) and spring (B) from the carburetor.

10. Remove the throttle stop screw (B, **Figure 24** and C, **Figure 25**) and spring (D, **Figure 24**).

11. Separate the carburetor body and float bowl.

12. Remove the float bowl drain screw and O-ring from the float bowl. Discard the O-ring

> *NOTE*
> *Do not remove the choke valve mechanism. Instead, check its operation as described in* ***Inspection*** *in this section.*

13. Clean and inspect all parts as described in *Inspection* in this section.

Reassembly (80 cc Models)

Refer to **Figure 19**.

1. Install the float bowl drain screw and a new O-ring. Tighten securely.

2. Install the throttle stop screw (C, **Figure 25**) and spring (D).

> *NOTE*
> *Because the throttle stop screw sets the engine idle speed, do not turn it too far into the carburetor or it will position the throttle valve too high in the carburetor. This condition will make the engine hard to start, especially when cold. Position the throttle stop screw so it just raises the throttle valve in the carburetor bore. Final adjustment will take place after installing the carburetor and starting the engine.*

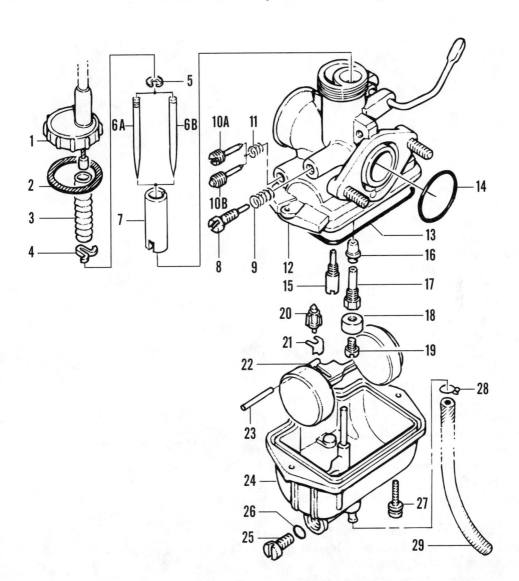

CARBURETOR (80 CC MODELS)

1. Top cap/throttle cable assembly
2. Seal
3. Spring
4. Retainer
5. E-clip
6A. Jet needle (1993-2005 models)
6B. Jet needle (2006-on models)
7. Throttle valve
8. Throttle stop screw
9. Spring
10A. Air screw (1993-2005 models)
10B. Air screw (2006-on models)
11. Spring
12. Carburetor body
13. O-ring
14. O-ring
15. Pilot jet
16. Needle jet
17. Needle jet holder
18. Main jet holder
19. Main jet
20. Fuel valve
21. Fuel valve clip
22. Float
23. Float pin
24. Float bowl
25. Drain screw
26. O-ring
27. Screw
28. Clamp
29. Hose

8

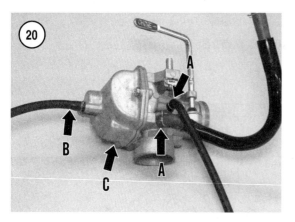

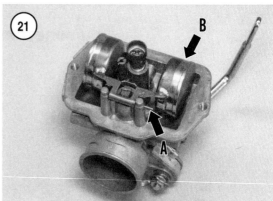

3. Install the air screw (A, **Figure 25**) and spring (B) assembly and lightly seat it. Then back the screw out the number of turns recorded during removal, or set it to the number of turns listed in **Table 2**.

4. Install the needle jet so its larger diameter end (A, **Figure 26**) faces toward the needle jet holder (B). From the bottom side of the carburetor, drop the need jet (E, **Figure 23**) into the carburetor bore.

5. Install and securely tighten the needle jet holder (D, **Figure 23**).

6. Install the main jet holder (C, **Figure 23**) and main jet (B). Hold the needle jet holder and tighten the main jet (A, **Figure 27**) securely.

7. Install and securely tighten the pilot jet (A, **Figure 23**). Refer to B, **Figure 27**.

8. Hook the fuel valve (**Figure 22**) onto the float and then install the fuel valve into its seat. Install the float pin (A, **Figure 21**) through the carburetor pedestal arms and float (B).

9. Measure the float level as described in this chapter.

10. Install a new O-ring into the float bowl groove.

11. Install the float bowl (C, **Figure 20**) and its mounting screws and tighten securely.

12. Install the hoses onto the carburetor (A, **Figure 20**) and float bowl nozzles (B).

13. Install the carburetor body O-ring, if removed.

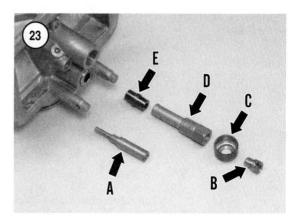

Disassembly (100 cc Models)

Refer to **Figure 28**.

1. Remove the carburetor as described in this chapter.

2. Remove the hoses connected to the carburetor and float bowl nozzles.

3. Remove the float bowl screws (A, **Figure 29**) and float bowl. Be careful of any gas that spills out of the float bowl. Note the O-ring installed in the float bowl groove. Discard the O-ring.

4. Remove the main jet holder (A, **Figure 30**).

NOTE
The fuel valve seat is permanently attached to the carburetor body. Do not attempt to remove it.

5. Remove the float pin (B, **Figure 30**), float (C) and fuel valve. Unhook the fuel valve (**Figure 31**) from the float.

CAUTION
Seat the pilot screw lightly or the screw tip can break off into the pilot screw bore.

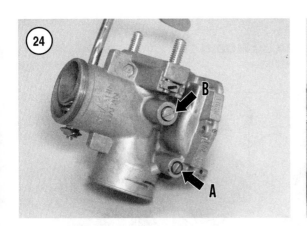

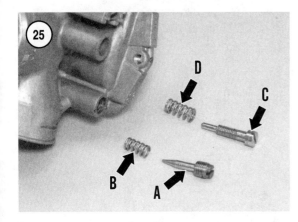

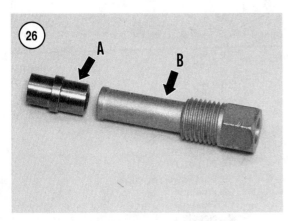

8. Hold the needle jet holder and remove the main jet (F, **Figure 32**).

9. Remove the needle jet holder (G, **Figure 32**).

10. Use a small round wooden stick and push the needle jet (H, **Figure 32**) out through the bottom of the carburetor.

11. Remove the throttle adjust screw and spring (A, **Figure 33**). On 2006-on models, note the X-ring seal installed on the screw.

12. Remove the carburetor body and float bowl O-rings. Discard the O-ring.

13. Remove the float bowl drain screw and O-ring from the float bowl. Discard the O-ring.

14. Refer to *Choke Assembly (100 cc Models)* in this section to service the choke.

15. Clean and inspect all parts as described in *Inspection* in this section.

Reassembly (100 cc Models)

Refer to **Figure 28**.

1. Install the float bowl drain screw and a new O-ring. Tighten securely.

2. Install the throttle adjust screw and spring (A, **Figure 33**). On 2006-on models, install the X-ring seal onto the screw.

NOTE

Because the throttle stop screw sets the engine idle speed, do not turn it too far into the carburetor or it will position the throttle valve too high in the carburetor. This condition will make the engine hard to start, especially when cold. Position the throttle stop screw so it just raises the throttle valve in the carburetor bore. Final adjustment will take place after installing the carburetor starting the engine.

3. Install the needle jet so its larger diameter end (A, **Figure 34**) faces toward the needle jet holder (B).

NOTE

*A D-shaped pilot screw wrench is required to remove the pilot screw on 2006-on models. Refer to **Carburetor Adjustment** in this chapter for the tool part numbers.*

6. Lightly seat the pilot screw (B, **Figure 29**), counting the number of turns for reassembly reference. Remove the screw (A, **Figure 32**) and its spring (B), washer (C) and O-ring (D) from the carburetor.

7. Remove the pilot jet (E, **Figure 32**).

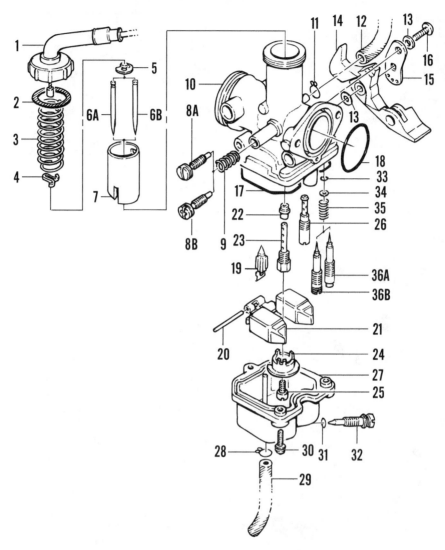

CARBURETOR (100 CC MODELS)

1. Top cap/throttle cable assembly
2. Seal
3. Spring
4. Retainer
5. E-clip
6A. Jet needle (1992-2005 models)
6B. Jet needle (2006-on models)
7. Throttle valve
8A. Throttle adjust screw (1992-2005 models)
8B. Throttle adjust screw and X-ring seal
    (2006-on models)
9. Spring
10. Carburetor body
11. Clamp
12. Hose
13. Washer
14. Choke lever and ball
15. Set plate
16. Screw
17. O-ring
18. O-ring
19. Fuel valve and clip
20. Float pin
21. Float
22. Needle jet
23. Needle jet holder
24. Main jet holder
25. Main jet
26. Pilot jet
27. Float bowl
28. Clamp
29. Hose
30. Screw
31. O-ring
32. Drain screw
33. O-ring
34. Washer
35. Spring
36A. Pilot screw (1992-2005 models)
36B. Pilot screw (2006-on models)

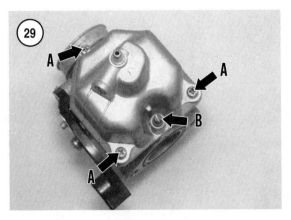

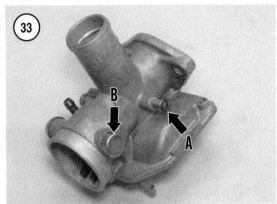

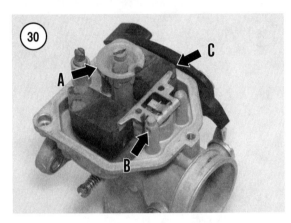

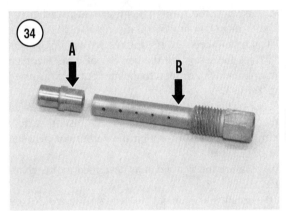

8

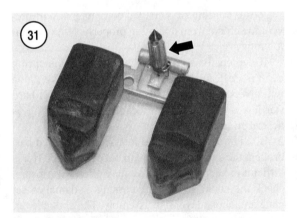

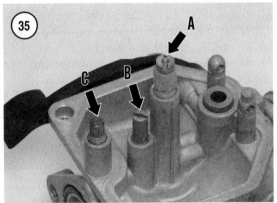

From the bottom side of the carburetor, drop the need jet (H, **Figure 32**) into the carburetor bore.

4. Install and tighten the needle jet holder (G, **Figure 32**).

5. Hold the needle jet holder and install and tighten the main jet (A, **Figure 35**).

6. Install and tighten the pilot jet (B, **Figure 35**).

CAUTION
Seat the pilot screw lightly or the screw tip can break off into the pilot screw bore.

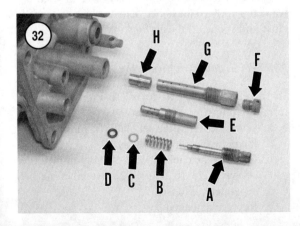

7. Assemble the spring (B, **Figure 32**), washer (C) and O-ring (D) onto the pilot screw (A, **Figure 32**). Then install the screw (C, **Figure 35**) and lightly seat it. Back the screw out the number of turns recorded during removal, or set it to the number of turns listed in **Table 3**.

8. Hook the fuel valve onto the float (**Figure 31**) and then install the fuel valve into its seat. Install the float pin (B, **Figure 30**) through the carburetor pedestal arms and float.

9. Measure the float level as described in this chapter.

10. Install the main jet holder (A, **Figure 36**) by aligning its slot with the raised projection on the carburetor (B).

11. Install a new O-ring into the float bowl groove.

12. Install the float bowl and its mounting screws (A, **Figure 29**) and tighten securely.

13. Install the hoses onto the carburetor and float bowl nozzles.

14. Install the carburetor body O-ring, if removed.

Choke Assembly (100 cc Models)

Operation

The choke plate (A, **Figure 37**) is controlled by the choke lever (B) mounted on the left side of the carburetor and a tension spring mounted on the right side of the choke shaft. When the choke lever is moved up, its control against the choke shaft is released. This automatically allows pressure from the tension spring to move the choke plate down and close off the carburetor bore and choke off the air flow into the carburetor. When the choke lever is moved up, it contacts the end of the choke shaft and opens the choke plate (overriding the tension spring) to allow more air flow into the carburetor. To lock the choke lever in position, an index ball on the choke lever sets into one of three holes on a set plate—full on choke position, partial choke position and full off choke position.

Loose, missing or damaged components will prevent the choke from operating properly. Note the following:

1. If the tension spring breaks, or the tension spring cap falls off and the spring is lost, the choke valve will always be open and cause hard starting. If hard starting is a problem, inspect the tension spring as described in this section.

2. If the choke lever ball is missing or a related part broken, the choke lever can slip out of position. If it is difficult to keep the engine running after it warms up, check the choke lever for a missing or damaged set plate and choke lever ball assembly. The choke lever, if unable to lock in position, may have pivoted upward and allowed the choke plate to close or partially close and choke off the air flow into the engine.

Removal/installation/inspection

1. To service the choke lever (A, **Figure 38**), perform the following:

   a. Mark the top of the set plate (B, **Figure 38**) so it can be installed correctly.

   b. Remove the choke lever assembly in the order shown in 13-16, **Figure 28**. Remove the ball separately, if loose.

   c. Replace damaged parts.

d. Reverse to install the choke lever assembly. Make sure the choke lever (A, **Figure 39**) is positioned under the arm on the end of the choke shaft (B). Operate the choke lever (B, **Figure 37**) to check that it sets and locks into each of the three set plate positions. If the choke lever ball easily skips past the set plate holes, the set plate may be installed upside down. The set plate is bowed slightly and should be installed with the curved part of the plate facing down to provide tension against the ball.

2. To inspect and service the tension spring assembly, perform the following:

a. Move the choke lever (B, **Figure 37**) all the way up. The choke plate should be in its fully closed position (A, **Figure 37**). If the choke plate is open, the tension spring is broken or has been incorrectly installed. If the choke plate failed to operate correctly, continue with substep B.

b. Pry the tension spring cap (B, **Figure 33**) off the carburetor so that it does not disturb the tension spring installed underneath it.

c. If the tension spring is missing or broken, it will be necessary to replace it with a spring from a discarded carburetor. Replacement springs are not available from the manufacturer.

d. Note the position of the tension spring in relation to the choke plate position. **Figure 40** shows the choke shaft/tension spring position when the choke plate is closed (on position). **Figure 41** shows the choke shaft/tension spring position when the choke plate is open (off position).

e. If the tension spring position is incorrect or if it fell out when the cap was removed, install the spring according to the directions in substep D.

f. Tap the tension spring cap (B, **Figure 33**) into position on the carburetor. Make sure it is locked in place. If the cap is loose, peen it in place with an angled tip punch and hammer or secure it in place with a piece of duct tape.

Inspection (All Models)

1. Clean all parts in a petroleum-based solvent, then clean in hot soapy water. Rinse parts with cold water and blow dry with compressed air. If a special carburetor cleaning solution is used, the float, fuel valve and all gaskets and O-rings should be omitted from the bath and cleaned separately.

2. Make sure all passages and openings in the carburetor body and float bowl are clear. Clean with compressed air.

3. Check the pilot jet as follows:

a. Replace the pilot jet if the screwdriver slot at the top of the jet is cracked or damaged.

b. Check the pilot jet for clogging and clean with compressed air. If compressed air will not clean the jet, soak the jet in solvent and then try to pass a small diameter wire or drill bit through the jet. Work carefully to avoid scratching or enlarging the jet opening. If the jet passage cannot be opened, replace it.

4. Clean the hoses with compressed air.

5. Replace any O-ring that is flattened or damaged. Float bowl O-rings will often tear when removed.

Check the O-ring groove in the float bowl for bits of rubber.

NOTE
On 80 cc models, the O-rings are only available in a gasket set. On 100 cc models, the O-ring can be purchased separately or as a complete gasket set.

6. Inspect the fuel valve assembly as follows:

NOTE
The fuel valve and seat controls the flow of fuel from the fuel tank to the float bowl. The fuel valve is closed by the float system when there is a sufficient amount of fuel in the float bowl. A worn or damaged fuel valve and/or seat, or dirt in the fuel valve seat, can prevent the fuel valve from closing. If this happens, the engine will operate with a too rich fuel mixture at all throttle openings. If the condition is severe, fuel will leak from the float bowl overflow tube when the engine is turned off and the fuel valve is left on. When the engine is experiencing these types of conditions, and the fuel level measurement is correct, inspect the fuel valve and seat for damage.

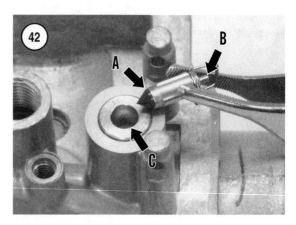

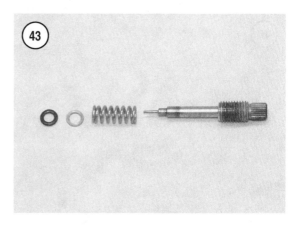

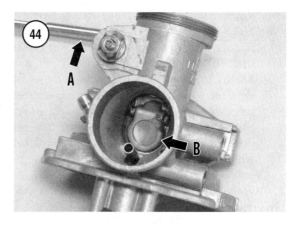

a. Check the end of the fuel valve (A, **Figure 42**) and replace if grooved, severely worn or otherwise damaged.

b. Push the small plunger (B, **Figure 42**) in the middle of the fuel valve. It should compress and return smoothly. Replace the fuel valve if the plunger sticks or moves roughly.

c. Inspect the fuel valve seat (C, **Figure 42**) for steps, uneven wear or other damage. Because the fuel valve seat is an integral part of the carburetor body, the carburetor body must be replaced if the seat is severely worn or damaged. However, before replacing the carburetor body, install a new fuel valve (A, **Figure 42**) to see whether the condition improves or remains the same.

7. Inspect the float for deterioration or other damage. Check the float by submersing it in a container of water. If the float takes on water, replace it.

8A. On 80 cc models, inspect the air screw assembly for wear or damage.

8B. On 100 cc models, refer to **Figure 43** and inspect the pilot screw assembly for wear or damaged parts. A damaged screw tip will prevent smooth low-speed engine operation. Replace the O-ring if worn or damaged.

9A. On 80 cc models, operate the choke lever (A, **Figure 44**) and inspect the choke valve assembly (B) for proper operation.

9B. On 100 cc models, refer to *Choke Assembly (100 cc Models)* in this section to inspect and service the choke assembly.

10. Check the throttle valve for scoring, cracks and other damage. Check the throttle valve bore inside the carburetor for the same conditions.

11. Inspect the jet needle for damage and excessive wear. Jet needles will eventually wear and allow more fuel to pass through the needle jet, causing a rich mid-range condition.

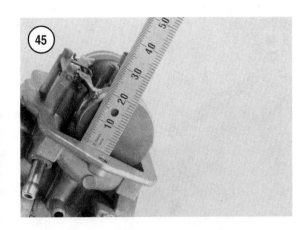

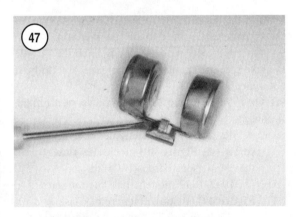

3. Position the carburetor so that the fuel valve is resting in its seat. At the same time make sure the float arm is resting on the fuel valve without compressing the small plunger in the top of the fuel valve. Then measure the float level distance from the carburetor body gasket surface to the top of the float using a ruler; refer to **Figure 45** (80 cc models) or **Figure 46** (100 cc models). Refer to **Table 2** (80 cc models) or **Table 3** (100 cc models) for the correct float level specifications. Note the following:

   a. If the fuel level is correct, go to Step 5.

   b. If the fuel level is incorrect, inspect the fuel valve and seat for wear or damage.

   c. If the fuel valve and seat are okay and the float level is incorrect, adjust the float level as described in Step 4.

4. To adjust the fuel level, note the following:

   a. Remove the float pin and float as described in *Carburetor Service* in this chapter.

   b. Remove the fuel valve (**Figure 31**, typical) from the tang on the float.

   c. Bend the float tang with a screwdriver (**Figure 47**) to move the float up or down. Make each adjustment in small increments to avoid breaking off the center float tang.

   d. Hook the fuel valve onto the float tang (**Figure 31**, typical), then install the fuel valve and float as described in this chapter.

   e. Remeasure the fuel level. Repeat these steps until the fuel level is correct.

5. On 100 cc models, install the main jet holder (A, **Figure 36**) by aligning its slot with the raised projection on the carburetor (B).

6. Reinstall the float bowl and install the carburetor as described in this chapter.

CARBURETOR ADJUSTMENTS

Idle Speed Adjustment

Refer to *Carburetor* in Chapter Three.

Idle Drop Adjustment

The air screw (80 cc models) and pilot screw (100 cc models) are preset. Adjustment is not necessary except under the following conditions:

1. The carburetor has been overhauled.
2. The air screw or pilot screw was replaced.
3. The carburetor is being adjusted for high altitude.
4. The carburetor was adjusted incorrectly.

FLOAT LEVEL ADJUSTMENT

The fuel valve and float maintain a constant fuel level in the carburetor float bowl. Because the float level affects the fuel mixture throughout the engine's operating range, this level must be maintained within specifications. The specified float level is the position where the float arm tang just closes the fuel valve.

The carburetor must be removed and partially disassembled for this adjustment.

1. Remove the carburetor as described in this chapter.
2. Remove the float bowl screws, float bowl and gasket. On 100 cc models, remove the main jet holder (A, **Figure 36**).

Tools

On 2006-on models, the air screw (80 cc models) and pilot screw (100 cc models) use D-shaped heads and require a D-shaped driver head tool to turn them. Note the following options:

1. Mounting a D-shaped 1/4-inch hex drive bit (A, **Figure 48** [Motion Pro part No. 08-0242]) on any standard driver (B) that accepts 1/4-inch hex-shaped bits.

2. D-shaped pilot screw wrench (C, **Figure 48** [Honda part No. 07KMA-MS60101]) and a pilot screw wrench guide (part No. 07PMA-MZ20110). The pilot screw wrench guide is only required on 100 cc models.

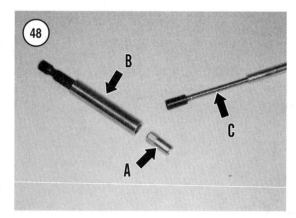

80 cc models

This carburetor uses an air screw (A, **Figure 49**) for adjustment. Turning the air screw clockwise richens the mixture while counterclockwise leans the mixture.

Refer to **Table 2** for specifications.

> *WARNING*
> *Do not run the engine in an enclosed area when performing this adjustment. Doing so will cause carbon monoxide gas to build up in the garage. Dangerous levels of carbon monoxide gas causes loss of consciousness and death in a short time.*

1. Clean the air filter (Chapter Three).
2. Connect a shop tachometer to the engine following the manufacturer's instructions.

> *NOTE*
> *To accurately detect speed changes during this adjustment, use a tachometer with graduations of 50 rpm or smaller.*

3. Turn the air screw clockwise until it lightly seats, then back out the number of turns specified under initial opening in **Table 2**.
4. Start the engine and warm to normal operating temperature.
5. Open and release the throttle a few times, making sure it returns to its closed position. If necessary, turn the engine off and adjust the throttle cable as described in Chapter Three.
6. With the engine idling, turn the throttle stop screw (B, **Figure 49**) to set the engine idle speed to the rpm specified in **Table 2**.
7. Turn the air screw (A, **Figure 49**) in or out to obtain the highest engine idle speed.

8. Turn the throttle stop screw (B, **Figure 49**) to reset the engine idle speed to the specified rpm.
9A. On 1998-1999 models, slowly open the throttle to make sure the engine speed increases smoothly. If not, repeat Steps 6-8.
9B. On 1993-1997 and 2000-on models, perform the following:

   a. While reading the tachometer, turn the air screw (A, **Figure 49**) clockwise slowly until the engine speed drops 100 rpm.
   b. On 1993-1997 models, turn the air screw (A, **Figure 49**) one turn counterclockwise.
   c. On 2000-on models, turn the air screw (A, **Figure 49**) counterclockwise the number of turns specified under final opening in **Table 2**.
   d. Turn the throttle stop screw to reset the engine idle speed to the specified rpm.
   e. Open the throttle slowly to make sure the engine speed increases smoothly. If not, repeat this procedure.
10. Turn the engine off and remove the tachometer.

100 cc models

This carburetor uses a pilot screw (**Figure 50**) for adjustment. Turning the pilot screw clockwise leans

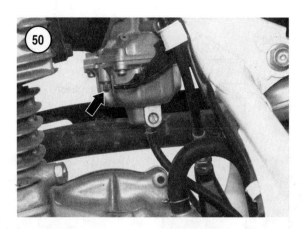

the mixture while counterclockwise richens the mixture.

Refer to **Table 3** for specifications.

> *WARNING*
> *Do not run the engine in an enclosed area when performing this adjustment. Doing so will cause carbon monoxide gas to build up in the garage. Dangerous levels of carbon monoxide gas causes loss of consciousness and death in a short time.*

1. Clean the air filter (Chapter Three).
2. Connect a shop tachometer to the engine following the manufacturer's instructions.

> *NOTE*
> *To accurately detect speed changes during this adjustment, use a tachometer with graduations of 50 rpm or smaller.*

> *CAUTION*
> *Seat the pilot screw lightly or the screw tip can break off into the pilot screw bore.*

3. Turn the pilot screw clockwise until it lightly seats, then back out the number of turns specified under initial opening in **Table 3**.
4. Start the engine and warm to normal operating temperature.
5. Open and release the throttle a few times, making sure it returns to its closed position. If necessary, turn the engine off and adjust the throttle cable as described in Chapter Three.
6. With the engine idling, turn the throttle stop screw (**Figure 51**) to set the engine idle speed to the specified rpm.
7A. On 1992-1997 models, turn the pilot screw (**Figure 50**) clockwise until the engine cuts out and stops, then turn the screw one turn counterclockwise. Restart the engine and if necessary, turn the throttle stop screw to readjust the idle speed to the specified rpm.
7B. On 1998-on models, perform the following:
   a. Turn the pilot screw (**Figure 50**) in or out to obtain the highest engine idle speed.
   b. Turn the throttle stop screw (**Figure 51**) to reset the engine idle speed to the specified rpm.
   c. While reading the tachometer, turn the pilot screw clockwise slowly until the engine speed drops 100 rpm.
   d. Turn the pilot screw (**Figure 50**) counterclockwise the number of turns specified under final opening in **Table 3**.
   e. Turn the throttle stop screw to reset the engine idle speed to the specified rpm.
8. Turn the engine off and remove the tachometer.

High Elevation Adjustment

If the motorcycle is ridden for a sustained period at high elevation above 2000 m (6500 ft.), readjust the carburetor to improve engine performance and decrease emissions. Otherwise, the standard jetting will be too rich. This will cause hard starting and spark plug fouling, reduce engine performance and increase fuel consumption.

1. Remove the carburetor and float bowl as described in this chapter.
2. Replace the main jet with the high altitude main jet specified in **Table 2** or **Table 3**.
3. Reassemble and install the carburetor as described in this chapter.

> *NOTE*
> *A D-shaped pilot screw wrench is required to move the pilot screw on 2006-on models. Refer to **Tools** in this section.*

8

4A. On 80 cc models, turn the air screw (A, **Figure 49**) counterclockwise the number of turns specified in **Table 2** for high altitude.

4B. On 100 cc models, turn the pilot screw (**Figure 50**) clockwise the number of turns specified in **Table 3** for high altitude.

5. Start the engine and warm to normal operating temperature. Adjust the idle speed to the specifications in **Table 2** or **Table 3**.

6. When the motorcycle is returned to elevations below 2000 m (6500 ft.), replace the main jet with the one previously removed and adjust the air screw (80 cc models) or pilot screw (100 cc models) to their standard settings. Then reset the engine idle speed. Make sure to make these adjustments with the motorcycle at a lower altitude and with the engine at normal operating temperature.

> *CAUTION*
> *Always adjust the carburetor for the elevation that it is operated in. Operating the motorcycle at altitudes lower than 1500 m (5000 ft.) with the carburetor adjusted for high altitude may cause the engine to idle roughly and stall. Overheating may also cause engine damage.*

Jet Needle Adjustment

1992-2005 models

The jet needle controls the mixture at medium speeds, from approximately 1/8 to 3/4 throttle. The top of the needle has 5 evenly spaced clip grooves (**Figure 52**). The bottom half of the needle is tapered; this portion extends into the needle jet. While the jet needle is fixed into position by the clip, fuel cannot flow through the space between the needle jet and jet needle until the throttle valve is raised approximately 1/8 open. As the throttle valve is raised, the jet needles tapered portion moves out of the needle jet. The grooves permit adjustment of the mixture ratio. If the clip is raised (thus dropping the needle deeper into the jet), the mixture will be leaner; lowering the clip (raising the needle) will result in a richer mixture.

1. Remove the throttle valve and jet needle as described in *Carburetor* in this chapter.

2. Note the position of the clip and raise or lower the clip (**Figure 52**) as required. Refer to **Table 2** or **Table 3** for the standard jet needle clip position.

3. Reverse these steps to install the jet needle.

2006-on models

The jet needle is not adjustable on these models.

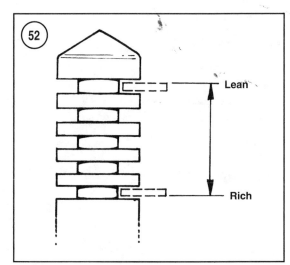

CRANKCASE BREATHER SYSTEM (1999-ON XR80R, 1998-2000 XR100R CALIFORNIA MODELS AND ALL 2001-ON XR100R MODELS)

These models are equipped with a closed crankcase breather system. Refer to **Figure 53** for typical components of the crankcase breather system. The system draws blow by gasses from the crankcase and recirculates them into the air/fuel mixture to be burned.

Inspection

Make sure the breather separator (A, **Figure 53**) is mounted securely. Also check that the hose clamps are tight and check both hoses (B, **Figure 53**) for deterioration. Replace as necessary. Check that hoses are not clogged or crimped.

THROTTLE CABLE

Removal/Installation

1. Remove the fuel tank as described in this chapter.

2. Before disconnecting or removing the throttle cable, make a drawing of the cable routing from the handlebar to where it is attached at the carburetor. Replace the cable exactly as it was, avoiding any sharp turns.

3. Remove the throttle valve and disconnect the throttle cable from the throttle valve as described in *Carburetor and Intake Tube* in this chapter.

4. Disconnect the throttle cable at the throttle housing as described in *Handlebar* in Chapter Eleven.

5. Compare the new and old throttle cables to make sure the new cable is correct.

6. Lubricate the new throttle cable before reconnecting it as described in Chapter Three.

7. Install the new throttle cable by reversing these removal steps. Make sure it is correctly routed with no sharp turns. Adjust the throttle cable as described in Chapter Three.

Table 1 FUEL TANK CAPACITY

	Full Liters (gal.)	Reserve Liters (gal.)
1992-1997 models	6.5 (1.71)	0.9 (0.24)
1998-2000 models	6.2 (1.64)	2.1 (0.55)
2001-2003 models	5.6 (1.48)	1.1 (0.29)
2004-2007 models	5.5 (1.45)	1.1 (0.29)
2008-on models	5.0 (1.32)	0.7 (0.18)

Table 2 CARBURETOR SPECIFICATIONS (XR80R AND CRF80F)

Air screw adjustment*	
Initial opening	
1993-1999 models	1 3/4 turns out
2000-on models	2 1/8 turns out
Final opening	
1993-1999 models	–
2000-on models	1/2 turns out
High altitude	
1993-1999 models	1 turn out from standard position
2000-on models	1/2 turn out from standard position
Float level	21.5 mm (0.85 in.)
Identification number	
XR80R	
1993-1999 models	PC20B
2000 models	PC20F
2001-2003 models	PC20J
CRF80F	
2004-2005 models	PC20M
2006-2007 models	PC20P
2008-on models	PC20Q
Idle speed	1400-1600 rpm
Jet needle clip position	
1993-1999 models	Second groove from top
2000-2005 models	Third groove from top
2006-on models	Not adjustable
Main jet	
Standard	95
High altitude	90
Pilot jet	35
Type	Keihin

*Refer to text for adjustment procedure.

8

Table 3 CARBURETOR SPECIFICATIONS (XR100R AND CRF100F)

Float level	12.5 mm (0.49 in.)
Identification number	
1992-1997 models	PD80C
1998-2000 models	
49-state and Canada	PD80C
California	PDC3D
2001-2005 models	PDC3L
2006-2007 models	PDCBF
2008-on models	PDCBL
Idle speed	1300-1500 rpm
Jet needle clip position	
1992-2005 models	Third groove from top
2006-on models	Not adjustable
Main jet	
Stock	
1992-1999 models	95
2000-on models	98
High altitude	
1992-1999 models	90
2000-on models	92
Pilot screw adjustment*	
Initial opening	
1992-2000 models	1 3/4 turns out
2001-on models	2 3/8 turns out
Final opening	
1992-1997 models	–
1998-on models	1/2 turns out
High altitude position	
1992-1997 models	1 3/4 turns in from standard position
1998-2000 models	
California models	1 turn in from standard position
49-state models	1/2 turns in from standard position
2001-on models	3/4 turns in from standard position
Pilot jet	
1992-2000 models	
49-state and Canada	38
California	35
2001-on models	35
Type	Keihin

*Refer to text for adjustment procedure.

Table 4 FUEL SYSTEM TORQUE SPECIFICATIONS

	N•m	in.-lb.
Fuel tank mounting bolts	12	106

CHAPTER NINE

ELECTRICAL SYSTEM

This chapter describes service procedures for the capacitor discharge ignition (CDI) system.

Refer to Chapter Three for spark plug recommendations and gapping. Refer to Chapter Two for troubleshooting information.

Table 1 and **Table 2 are** at the end of this chapter.

ELECTRICAL COMPONENT REPLACEMENT

Most motorcycle dealerships and parts suppliers will not accept the return of any electrical part. If you cannot determine the exact cause of an electrical system malfunction, have a dealership retest that specific system to verify your test results. If you purchase a new electrical component(s), install it, and then find that the system still does not work properly, you will probably not be able to return the unit for refund.

Consider and test result carefully before replacing a component that tests only slightly out of specification, especially for resistance. A number of variables can affect test results dramatically. These include the testing meter's internal circuitry, as well as the ambient temperatures and conditions under which the motorcycle has been operated. All instructions and specifications have been checked for accuracy;

however, successful test results depend largely upon individual precision.

ELECTRICAL CONNECTORS

Refer to the wiring diagrams at the end of this manual to identify the connectors and wire terminal color codes called out in this chapter. Note that the position of the connectors may have been changed during previous repairs. Always confirm the wire colors to and from the connector and follow the wiring harness to the various components when performing tests.

> *CAUTION*
> *Connector internal pins are easily damaged and dislodged, which may cause a malfunction. Use care when handling or testing the connectors.*

Under normal operating conditions, the connectors are weather-tight. However, the connectors and their locking mechanisms become worn from general service, abuse, age and heat deterioration. To help prevent contamination from water and other contaminants, pack the connectors with dielectric grease. Do not use a substitute that may interfere with current flow. Dielectric grease is specifically formulated to seal the connector and not increase current resistance. For best results, the compound should fill the entire inner area of the connector. It is recommended that each time a connector is unplugged, that it be cleaned and sealed with dielectric grease.

The ground connections are often overlooked when troubleshooting. Make sure they are tight and corrosion free. Apply dielectric grease to the terminals before reconnecting them.

CDI PRECAUTIONS

When servicing the CDI system, note the following:

1. Keep all electrical connections clean and secure.
2. Never disconnect any of the electrical connections while the engine is running, or excessive voltage may damage the ignition control module (ICM).
3. When kicking the engine over with the spark plug removed, make sure the spark plug or a spark checker is installed in the plug cap and grounded against the cylinder head. If not, excessive resistance may damage the ICM. Refer to *Spark Test* in *Engine Will Not Start* in Chapter Two.
4. The ICM is mounted inside a thick rubber case to protect it from vibration. Make sure the ICM is mounted correctly. Handle the ICM carefully when removing and installing it in the frame. The ICM is a sealed unit. Do not attempt to open it as this will cause permanent damage.

LEFT CRANKCASE COVER

The area behind the left crankcase cover is a dry operating area. Contamination can occur from water and dirt (leaking cover gasket) or engine oil (damaged crankshaft oil seal). Dirt and water that does leak into this area will cause rust to build on the flywheel and onto the metal parts of the stator assembly. Dirt will also damage the crankshaft oil seal.

Removal/Installation

1. Support the motorcycle on its sidestand or workstand.
2. Remove the bolts and the left crankcase cover (A, **Figure 1**).
3. Remove the gasket and clean the cover and crankcase gasket surfaces.

> *NOTE*
> *The paper gasket used on these models will usually tear when the cover is removed. Any gasket residue that remains stuck on the cover and crankcase mating surfaces can be difficult to remove. To avoid damaging these surfaces,*

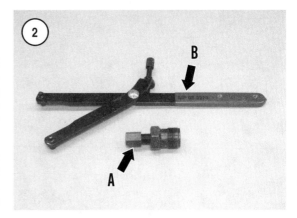

> *spray the gasket with gasket remover, making sure to follow the manufacturer's directions. Then carefully remove with a gasket scraper. Refer to **Gasket Remover** in **Shop Supplies** in Chapter One for additional information.*

> *NOTE*
> *If there is engine oil behind the cover, the left crankcase oil seal is leaking. On 80 cc models, refer to Chapter Five to replace this seal. On 100 cc models, replace this seal as described in **Exciter Coil and Ignition Pulse Generator** in this chapter.*

4. Install the cover together with a new gasket. Tighten the mounting bolts securely in a crossing pattern. Note the bolt identified in B, **Figure 1** is longer than the other bolts.

FLYWHEEL

The flywheel fits over the crankshaft with a taper fit. A Woodruff key aligns the flywheel with the crankshaft for proper ignition timing. When the fly-

wheel nut is tightened, it forces the tapers together, locking the flywheel to the crankshaft.

Tools

The following is required to remove the flywheel from the crankshaft:

1. A 27 mm × 1.0 left-hand thread flywheel puller.
   a. Motion Pro flywheel puller (A, **Figure 2**): part No. 08-0026.
   b. Honda flywheel puller: part No. 07733-0010000.
2. Flywheel holding tool used when loosening and tightening the flywheel nut.
   a. Motion Pro rotor and sprocket holder (B, **Figure 2**): part No. 08-0270.
   b. Honda universal holder: part No. 07725-0030000.

Removal

1. Place the bike on a workstand.
2. Remove the left crankcase cover as described in this chapter.

NOTE
*If troubleshooting an ignition problem, check the tightness of the flywheel and flywheel nut **before** loosening the nut. If these parts are loose, check the flywheel and crankshaft Woodruff key alignment.*

3. Hold the flywheel by inserting the holding tool pins into the holes in the flywheel (A, **Figure 3**), then loosen and remove the flywheel nut (B).

CAUTION
Do not attempt to remove the flywheel without an appropriate flywheel puller. Do not pry or hammer on the flywheel to remove it. Damage to the flywheel and crankshaft will likely occur.

CAUTION
Do not use excessive force to remove the flywheel. Forcing the puller may strip the threads in the flywheel. If the flywheel cannot be removed, take the engine to a dealership and have them remove the flywheel.

4. Apply grease onto the end of the flywheel pressure bolt where it contacts the flywheel.
5. Thread the flywheel puller (**Figure 4**) onto the flywheel by turning it counterclockwise until it bottoms, then back out 1/4 turn. Turn the pressure bolt by hand until it contacts the flywheel. Then check that the flywheel puller is positioned squarely in the flywheel.

NOTE
If it appears the flywheel puller is installed at an angle, either the flywheel or flywheel puller threads are damaged.

6. Hold the puller body (A, **Figure 4**) with a wrench, then turn the center bolt (B) until the flywheel pops free from the crankshaft taper.
7. Remove the flywheel, then remove the puller from the flywheel.

CAUTION
If the Woodruff key is a tight fit, remove it carefully to prevent the removing tool from jumping and possibly damaging the exciter coil assembly.

8. If necessary, remove the Woodruff key (**Figure 5**) from the crankshaft groove.

9

NOTE
On 80 cc models, the stator plate can be removed with the Woodruff key in place. On 100 cc models, the Woodruff key must be removed before the stator plate can be removed.

9. Inspect the parts as described in this section.

Inspection

The flywheel is permanently magnetized and cannot be tested. Installing a flywheel that is known to be good is the only way of determining if the flywheel is faulty. A flywheel can lose magnetism from sharp blows. A defective flywheel must be replaced; it cannot be re-magnetized.

1. Clean and dry the flywheel.

WARNING
Always replace a cracked or chipped flywheel. A damaged flywheel can fly apart at high rpm, throwing metal fragments and damaging the stator coils. Do not repair a damaged flywheel.

2. Check the flywheel (**Figure 6**) for cracks or breaks and replace if damaged. Do not attempt to repair a cracked or damaged flywheel.
3. Inspect the bore taper and keyway for damage.
4. Check the flywheel for rust or other contamination, and clean with sandpaper and solvent.
5. Check the flywheel for abrasions from contact with the stator coils. If abrasions are evident, inspect the crankshaft bearing.
6. Inspect the flywheel nut and replace if damaged.
7. Check the flywheel tapered bore, keyway and the crankshaft taper for cracks and other damage.
8. Inspect the Woodruff key for damage. Replace the key if the edges are not square.

Installation

1. Before installing the flywheel (**Figure 6**), inspect its magnets for metal shavings and parts that may be attached to the magnets.

CAUTION
Installing a flywheel with a washer or other metal part magnetized inside of it will damage the stator coil when the engine is turned over.

2. Rotate the crankshaft so the keyway points up.

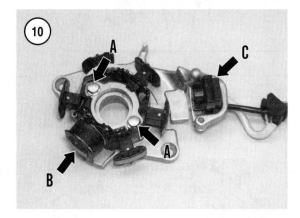

3. If removed, align and lightly tap the Woodruff key (**Figure 5**) into the crankshaft keyway. The Woodruff key must fit snugly in the keyway. Position the straight edge of the key parallel with the crankshaft to allow easy installation of the flywheel.

4. Clean the crankshaft and flywheel tapers with contact cleaner and allow to dry before installing the flywheel. These surfaces must be dry and free of oil.

5. Lubricate the flywheel nut threads and its seating surface with engine oil.

6. Align the flywheel keyway with the Woodruff key and install the flywheel onto the crankshaft. Make sure the Woodruff key remains in place.

7. Hold the flywheel in place and install the flywheel nut.

8. Secure the flywheel with a holding tool (A, **Figure 3**) and tighten the flywheel nut (B) to 64 N•m (47 ft.-lb.). Remove the holding tool.

NOTE
If the flywheel, stator plate or ICM unit were replaced, check the ignition timing as described in this chapter.

9. Install the left crankcase cover as described in this chapter.

EXCITER COIL AND IGNITION PULSE GENERATOR (STATOR PLATE ASSEMBLY)

The exciter coil (A, **Figure 7**) is mounted on the stator plate, inside the flywheel. The ignition pulse generator (B, **Figure 7**) is mounted on the stator plate, outside of the flywheel. The exciter coil and ignition pulse generator are permanently wired into the same harness and cannot be replaced separately.

On 80 cc models, the exciter coil, ignition pulse generator and stator plate must be removed at the same time. On 100 cc models, the exciter coil and ignition pulse generator can be removed without having to remove the stator plate (C, **Figure 7**, typical). This method is suggested because the crankshaft oil seal is mounted inside the stator plate and the coils can be removed without disturbing the seal.

Exciter Coil, Ignition Pulse Generator and Stator Plate Removal/Installation

80 cc models

1. Remove the fuel tank (Chapter Eight).
2. Remove the flywheel as described in this chapter.
3. Disconnect the exciter coil and ignition pulse generator electrical connectors (A, **Figure 8**). Note the routing of the wiring along the frame and then remove the wiring harness. If necessary, remove the fuel tank pad (B, **Figure 8**) to access the connectors.
4. Pull the wiring grommet (D, **Figure 7**) out of the crankcase.
5. Remove the stator plate mounting screws (A, **Figure 9**) and the stator plate (B) with both coils attached.
6. To replace the exciter coil and ignition pulse generator:
   a. Remove the exciter coil screws (A, **Figure 10**).
   b. Turn the stator plate over and remove the ignition pulse generator screws (**Figure 11**).

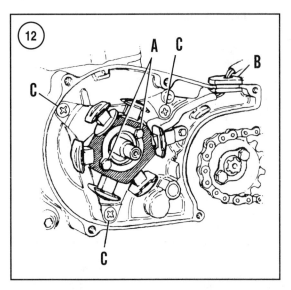

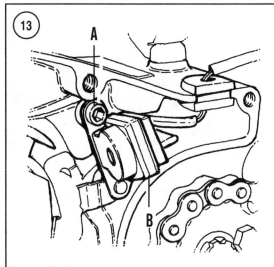

c. Remove the exciter coil (B, **Figure 10**) and ignition pulse generator (C) assembly.

7. Installation is the reverse or removal. Tighten the ignition pulse generator screws (**Figure 11**) to 6 N•m (53 in.-lb.). Tighten the remaining screws securely.

100 cc models

This section services the exciter coil, ignition pulse generator, stator plate and the crankshaft oil seal and O-ring installed in the stator plate.

1. Remove the fuel tank (Chapter Eight).

2. Remove the flywheel as described in this chapter.

3. Disconnect the exciter coil and ignition pulse generator electrical connectors (A, **Figure 8**). Note the routing of the wiring along the frame and then remove the wiring harness. If necessary, remove the fuel tank pad (B, **Figure 8**) to access the connectors.

4A. To remove the coils separately from the stator plate:

    a. Remove the screws (A, **Figure 12**) securing the exciter coil to the stator plate.

    b. Remove the bolt (A, **Figure 13**) securing the ignition pulse generator (B) to the stator plate.

    c. Remove the wiring grommet (B, **Figure 12**) from the crankcase and remove the coil assembly.

4B. To remove the coils with the stator plate:

    a. Remove the Woodruff key (**Figure 5**) from the crankshaft keyway.

    b. Remove the wiring grommet (B, **Figure 12**) from the crankcase.

    c. Remove the stator plate mounting screws (C, **Figure 12**) and stator plate with the two coils attached.

5. To service the crankshaft oil seal and stator plate O-ring, refer to **Figure 14** and perform the following:

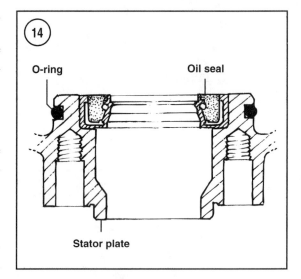

    a. Remove the coils from the stator plate as described in Step 4A.

    b. Pry the oil seal from the stator plate.

    c. Remove and discard the O-ring.

    d. Clean and dry the oil seal bore and O-ring groove.

    e. Install a new oil seal by driving it into the stator plate bore with its closed side facing down. Lubricate the seal lips with grease.

    f. Lubricate a new O-ring with grease and install it in the stator plate groove.

6. Installation is the reverse or removal. Tighten the ignition pulse generator screw (A, **Figure 13**) to 6 N•m (53 in.-lb.). Tighten the remaining screws securely.

Testing

Refer to *Ignition System Testing* in this chapter.

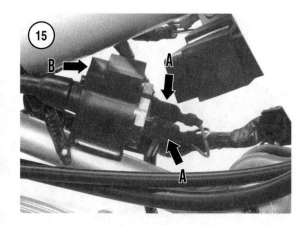

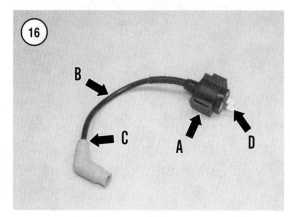

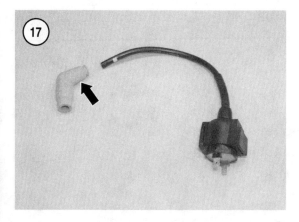

IGNITION COIL

Removal/Installation

1. Remove the fuel tank (Chapter Eight).
2. Disconnect the spark plug cap at the spark plug.
3. Disconnect the primary wires (A, **Figure 15**) at the ignition coil (B).
4. Remove the ignition coil (B, **Figure 15**) and its rubber grommet from the frame.
5. Remove the rubber grommet from the ignition coil and inspect the ignition coil body (A, **Figure 16**) for cracks and other damage.

6. Check the secondary wire (B, **Figure 16**) for brittleness, cracks and worn insulation. The secondary wire is permanently attached to the ignition coil. Do not attempt to remove this wire as it will damage the ignition coil.
7. Check both ends of the spark plug cap (C, **Figure 16**) for tears and other damage.
8. Check the primary terminals (D, **Figure 16**) and wiring harness connectors for dirty or loose connections. Check for a broken wire, brittleness or frayed insulation.
9. Installation is the reverse of removal. Note the following:
   a. Remove any corrosion from the coil primary terminals before reconnecting the connectors.
   b. Pack the electrical connectors with dielectric grease.

Spark Plug Cap Replacement

The spark plug cap can be replaced with the ignition coil mounted on the motorcycle. Hold the secondary wire and unscrew the plug cap (**Figure 17**) to remove it. Do not pull the plug cap off the secondary wire as this will damage the end of the secondary wire. Clean the cap terminal and secondary wire ends. To install the cap, thread it tightly onto the secondary coil wire, making sure it seals tightly against the wire.

> *NOTE*
> *Water leaking into a damaged or loose-fitting spark plug cap is a common cause of ignition misfire.*

Testing

Refer to *Ignition System Testing* in this chapter.

IGNITION CONTROL MODULE (ICM)

Removal/Installation

1. Remove the fuel tank (Chapter Eight).
2. Pry the ICM wire harness clamp open with a screwdriver (A, **Figure 18**). Do not use a pick or similar tool that could puncture the wires.
3. Remove the ICM (B, **Figure 18**) and its rubber grommet from the frame.
4. Each ICM connector is equipped with a locking tab (**Figure 19**). Disconnect the locking tab and then pull the connector from the ICM. Repeat for the other connector.
5. Check each connector for dirty or loose connections. Check for broken wires or frayed insulation.
6. Install by reversing these removal steps. Note the following:

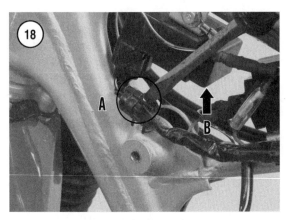

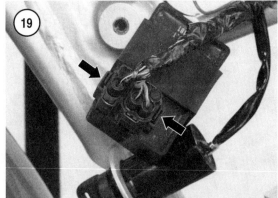

a. Clean the ICM connectors with contact cleaner and pack them with dielectric grease.
b. Reconnect each ICM connector, making sure its locking tab clicks to indicate it is locked in place.
c. If a new ICM was installed, check the ignition timing as described in this chapter.

IGNITION SWITCH
(2001-ON MODELS)

Testing/Installation/Removal

1. Remove the fuel tank (Chapter Eight).
2. Disconnect the two ignition switch electrical connectors.
3. To test the ignition switch, connect an ohmmeter between the two ignition switch side connectors (**Figure 20**). There should be continuity when the ignition switch is turned off and no continuity when the ignition switch is turned on. Replace the ignition switch if faulty.
4. Squeeze the two tabs (located 180° apart [A, **Figure 21**]) securing the ignition switch to its mounting bracket and push the switch forward to remove it.
5. Install the ignition switch by aligning the guide on the ignition switch with the groove in the switch mounting bracket (B, **Figure 21**). Then push the ignition switch through its mounting bracket until the two locking tabs snap behind the mounting bracket and lock the switch in place.
6. Reverse Steps 1 and 2 to complete installation.

ENGINE STOP SWITCH

The engine stop switch (A, **Figure 22**) is mounted on the left side of the handlebar. The engine stop switch is equipped with two wires—one wire connects to the ICM and the other is a separate ground wire that grounds the switch assembly to the frame.

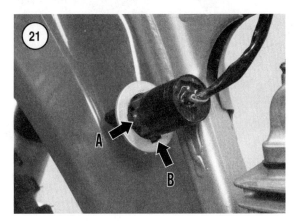

Testing/Removal/Installation

1. Remove the fuel tank (Chapter Eight).
2. Test the engine stop switch as follows:
a. Connect an ohmmeter between the upper (B, **Figure 22**) and lower (A, **Figure 23**) ground wire connections—test the lower ground wire connection at the bolt head and not at the wire terminal. There should continuity at all times. If not, test the lower ground wire connection at the wire terminal. If there is still no continuity, the ground wire is damaged and the engine stop switch should be replaced. However,

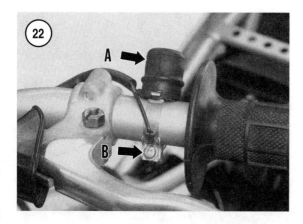

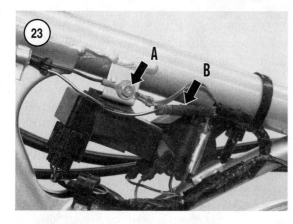

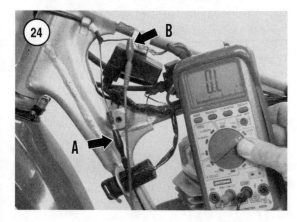

NOTE
Another way to test the engine stop switch is to perform a spark test with the engine stop switch connected and then disconnected from the main wire harness. If there is no spark when the switch is connected but spark when disconnected, the switch is faulty. Refer to **Spark Test** *in* **Engine Will Not Start** *in Chapter Two.*

c. Replace the engine stop switch if faulty.

3. Note the switch wire harness routing from the switch to the connectors underneath the fuel tank.

4. Remove the screw, clamp and switch assembly.

5. Installation is the reverse of removal. Make sure the upper ground wire connection (B, **Figure 22**) is secured to the switch housing.

6. Start the engine and operate the engine stop switch to make sure it stops the engine. If not, turn the ignition switch (2001-on models) off and retest the engine stop switch.

IGNITION SYSTEM TESTING

All models are equipped with a solid state capacitor discharge ignition (CDI) system.

Alternating current from the magneto is rectified and used to charge the capacitor. As the piston approaches the firing position, a pulse from the ignition pulse generator triggers the silicon controlled rectifier. This causes the capacitor to discharge into the primary side of the high-voltage ignition coil where the charge is amplified to a high enough voltage to jump the spark plug gap.

Refer to *Electrical Component Replacement, Electrical Connectors* and *CDI Precautions* in this chapter for additional information.

Resistance Testing

Resistance specifications are provided for 1992-1997 XR100R models. The manufacturer does not provide resistance specifications for XR80R and CRF80F models. However, the ignition coil and stator plate (pulse generator and exciter coil) part numbers for the later XR100R and CRF100F models are the same as for the 1997 and earlier XR100R models, so the resistance specifications and test procedures can be used.

When using an ohmmeter, follow the manufacturer's instruction manual, while keeping the following guidelines in mind:

1. Make sure the test leads are connected properly.

2. Take all ohmmeter readings when the engine is cold (ambient temperature of 20° C [68° F]).

if there is now continuity, check for corrosion between the lower ground wire terminal and where it mounts against the frame. Clean all contact surfaces with sandpaper and electrical contact cleaner and retest. If the ground wire connection is good, continue with substep b.

b. Disconnect the engine stop switch electrical connector (B, **Figure 23**). Connect an ohmmeter between the switch side connector (A, **Figure 24**) and the ground bolt (B). There should be continuity when the switch (A, **Figure 22**) is pressed and no continuity when the switch is released.

Readings taken on a hot engine will show increased resistance caused by engine heat and may lead to unnecessary parts replacement.

> *NOTE*
> *With the exception of certain semiconductors, the resistance of a conductor increases as its temperature increases. In general, the resistance of a conductor rises 10 ohms per each degree of temperature change. The opposite is true if the temperature drops. To ensure accurate testing, The manufacturer performs its tests at a controlled temperature of 20° C (68° F) and bases its specifications on tests performed at this temperature.*

3. When using an analog ohmmeter and switching between ohmmeter scales, always cross the test leads and zero the needle to assure a correct reading.
4. If a test is made and the resistance reading is incorrect, take the component to a dealership and have them confirm the test result. Most dealerships will not accept the return of any electrical component.

Exciter coil

The exciter coil can be tested while mounted on the engine.
1. Disconnect the ICM connector with the black/red wire as described in *Removal/Installation* in *Ignition Control Model (ICM)* in this chapter.
2. Connect the ohmmeter between the black/red connector and ground.
3. Refer to **Table 1** for the resistance specification.
4. If the resistance is not within specifications, disconnect the black/red connector closest to the exciter coil and repeat the resistance test at the exciter coil connector. If the resistance is still out of specification, the exciter coil is faulty. If the resistance is now correct, the wiring harness and/or connectors installed between the exciter coil and the ICM unit are contaminated or damaged. Clean/repair the wiring harness and connectors and repeat the test. If the exciter coil is damaged, replace the stator coil assembly as described in this chapter. The exciter coil cannot be replaced separately.
5. Reverse these steps to reconnect the connector(s).

Ignition pulse generator

The ignition pulse generator can be tested while mounted on the engine.

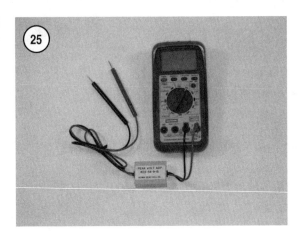

1. Disconnect the ICM connector with the blue/yellow wire as described in *Removal/Installation* in *Ignition Control Model (ICM)* in this chapter.
2. Connect the ohmmeter between the blue/yellow connector and ground.
3. Refer to **Table 1** for the resistance specification.
4. If the resistance is not within specifications, disconnect the blue/yellow connector closest to the ignition pulse generator and repeat the resistance test at the ignition pulse generator connector. If the resistance is still out of specification, the ignition pulse generator is faulty. If the resistance is now correct, the wiring harness and/or connectors installed between the ignition pulse generator and the ICM unit are contaminated or damaged. Clean/repair the wiring harness and connectors and repeat the test. If the ignition pulse generator is damaged, replace the stator coil assembly as described in this chapter. The ignition pulse generator cannot be replaced separately.
5. Reverse these steps to reconnect the connector(s).

Ignition coil

The ignition coil can be tested while mounted on the frame.

> *NOTE*
> *A defective coil may pass a resistance test. If the ignition coil fails one or all of the following tests, take the coil to a dealership and have them make an operational spark test to see if the coil is producing an adequate spark under operating conditions.*

1. Remove the fuel tank (Chapter Eight).
2. Disconnect the primary electrical connectors and the spark plug cap at the spark plug as described in *Ignition Coil* in this chapter.
3. Check the primary coil resistance as follows:

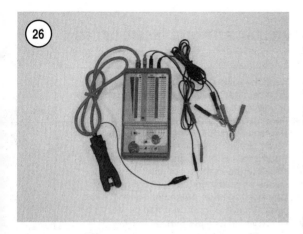

a. Set the ohmmeter to R × 1.
b. Connect the ohmmeter leads across the two primary coil terminals.
c. Refer to **Table 1** for the primary winding resistance specification.
d. Replace the ignition coil if the resistance is out of specification.
4. Check the secondary coil resistance with the plug cap as follows:
a. Set the ohmmeter to R × 1000.
b. Connect one ohmmeter lead to the ignition coil/s green primary terminal and the other lead to the spark plug cap terminal.
c. Refer to **Table 1** for the secondary winding resistance (with plug cap) specification.
d. Replace the ignition coil if the resistance is out of specification.
5. Check the secondary coil resistance without the plug cap as follows:
a. Set the ohmmeter to R × 1000.
b. Unscrew the spark plug cap from the secondary wire as described in *Ignition Coil* in this chapter.
c. Connect one ohmmeter lead to the ignition coil's green primary terminal and the other lead to the secondary wire terminal.
d. Refer to **Table 1** for the secondary winding resistance (without plug cap) specification.
e. Replace the ignition coil if the resistance is out of specification.

NOTE
If the test result without the plug cap is correct, but incorrect with the plug cap, the plug cap is probably faulty. Replace the plug cap and retest.

f. Before installing the spark plug cap, clean the cap terminal and secondary wire ends.
6. Reconnect the primary coil electrical connectors and the spark plug cap at the spark plug.

7. Perform a spark test as described in *Engine Will Not Start* in Chapter Two to make sure the plug cap is correctly installed onto the secondary wire.

Peak Voltage Testing and Equipment

WARNING
High voltage is present during ignition system operation. Do not touch ignition system components, wires or test leads while starting or running the engine.

The following tests describe ignition system troubleshooting using a peak voltage tester. Peak voltage tests are designed to check the voltage output of the ignition coil, exciter coil and ignition pulse generator at normal cranking speed. These tests make it possible to accurately test the voltage output under operating conditions.

The peak voltage specifications listed in the text and in **Table 1** are minimum values. If the measured voltage meets or exceeds the specification, the test results are satisfactory. In some cases, the voltage may greatly exceed the minimum specification.

To check peak voltage, a peak voltage tester is required. One of the following testers or an equivalent can be used to perform peak voltage tests described in this chapter. Refer to the manufacturer's instructions when using these tools.
1. Kowa Seiki Peak Voltage Adapter (part No. KEK-54-9B). This tool must be used in combination with a digital multimeter with a minimum impedance of 10M ohms/DCV (10-megaohm). The Kowa Seiki peak voltage adapter plugs into the digital multimeter and displays the peak voltage readings directly off the multimeter. A meter with a lower impedance does not display accurate measurements. Refer to **Figure 25**.
2. IgnitionMate Peak Voltage Ignition Tester (**Figure 26** [Motion Pro part No. 08-0193 or Honda part No. MTP-07-0286]). This tester reads and displays the test results without the need of a multimeter.

Preliminary Checks

Before testing the ignition system, perform the *Spark Test* as described in *Engine Will Not Start* in Chapter Two. If a crisp, blue spark is noted, the ignition system is working correctly. If there is no spark, check for a disconnected or contaminated connector or a damaged engine stop switch or ignition switch (2001-on models). Also check for a fouled or damaged spark plug, loose or damaged spark plug cap, or water in the spark plug cap. If the problem was not found and the inspected parts are in good working

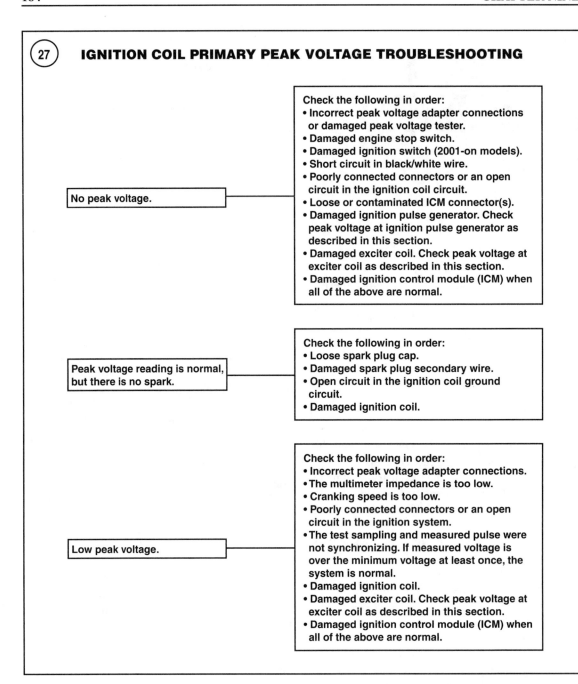

(27) **IGNITION COIL PRIMARY PEAK VOLTAGE TROUBLESHOOTING**

No peak voltage.

Check the following in order:
• Incorrect peak voltage adapter connections or damaged peak voltage tester.
• Damaged engine stop switch.
• Damaged ignition switch (2001-on models).
• Short circuit in black/white wire.
• Poorly connected connectors or an open circuit in the ignition coil circuit.
• Loose or contaminated ICM connector(s).
• Damaged ignition pulse generator. Check peak voltage at ignition pulse generator as described in this section.
• Damaged exciter coil. Check peak voltage at exciter coil as described in this section.
• Damaged ignition control module (ICM) when all of the above are normal.

Peak voltage reading is normal, but there is no spark.

Check the following in order:
• Loose spark plug cap.
• Damaged spark plug secondary wire.
• Open circuit in the ignition coil ground circuit.
• Damaged ignition coil.

Low peak voltage.

Check the following in order:
• Incorrect peak voltage adapter connections.
• The multimeter impedance is too low.
• Cranking speed is too low.
• Poorly connected connectors or an open circuit in the ignition system.
• The test sampling and measured pulse were not synchronizing. If measured voltage is over the minimum voltage at least once, the system is normal.
• Damaged ignition coil.
• Damaged exciter coil. Check peak voltage at exciter coil as described in this section.
• Damaged ignition control module (ICM) when all of the above are normal.

order, perform the peak voltage tests in this section to locate the damaged component.

Ignition Coil Peak Voltage Test

Refer to **Figure 27** for test results.

1. Remove the fuel tank (Chapter Eight).

2. Check engine compression as described in Chapter Three. If the compression is low, the following test results will be inaccurate.

3. Check all of the ignition component electrical connectors and wiring harnesses. Make sure the connectors are clean and properly connected. Use the

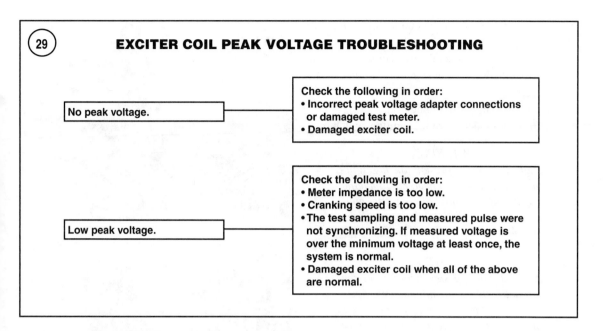

EXCITER COIL PEAK VOLTAGE TROUBLESHOOTING

No peak voltage.

Check the following in order:
- Incorrect peak voltage adapter connections or damaged test meter.
- Damaged exciter coil.

Low peak voltage.

Check the following in order:
- Meter impedance is too low.
- Cranking speed is too low.
- The test sampling and measured pulse were not synchronizing. If measured voltage is over the minimum voltage at least once, the system is normal.
- Damaged exciter coil when all of the above are normal.

correct wiring diagram at the end of this manual to identify the different connectors.

4. Shift the transmission into neutral.

5. Disconnect the spark plug cap. Then connect a new spark plug to the plug cap and ground the plug against the cylinder head (A, **Figure 28**). Do not remove the spark plug installed in the cylinder head.

6. On 2001-on models, turn the ignition switch on.

NOTE
Do not disconnect the primary wire from the ignition coil. This wire must remain connected to the ignition coil during the test.

7. Connect the tester's positive test lead to the ignition coil black/yellow primary coil terminal (B, **Figure 28**) and the negative test lead to ground.

WARNING
High voltage is present during ignition system operation. Do not touch the spark plug, ignition components, connectors or test leads while cranking the engine.

NOTE
*B, **Figure 28** shows a small jumper cable used to connect the positive peak voltage test lead (C, **Figure 28**) to the ignition coil.*

8. Kick the engine over with the kickstarter while reading the meter and note the following:
   a. The meter should read a minimum of 100 volts (**Table 1**).

NOTE
*All peak voltage specifications in **Table 1** are minimum voltages. As long as the measured voltage meets or exceeds the specification, consider the test results satisfactory. On some components, the voltage may greatly exceed the minimum specification.*

   b. If there is no peak voltage reading, check for an open circuit in the black/yellow and green wires between the ignition coil and the ICM. Check the connectors and wire terminals for corrosion and bent or damaged terminals. If the wires and connectors are good, follow the troubleshooting procedure in **Figure 27**.
   c. If the peak voltage reading is below 100 volts, follow the troubleshooting procedures in **Figure 27**.
   d. If the peak voltage reading is correct, continue with Step 9.

9. Disconnect the test leads and remove the spark plug from the spark plug cap.

10. Reverse the disassembly steps.

Exciter Coil Peak Voltage Test

Refer to **Figure 29** for test results.

1. Remove the fuel tank (Chapter Eight).

2. Check engine compression as described in Chapter Three. If the compression is low, the following test results will be inaccurate.

3. Check all of the ignition component electrical connectors and wiring harnesses. Make sure the connectors are clean and properly connected. Use the

9

correct wiring diagram at the end of this manual to identify the different connectors.

4. Remove and disconnect the two connectors at the ICM as described in *Ignition Control Module (ICM)* in this chapter.

5. Shift the transmission into neutral.

6. On 2001-on models, turn the ignition switch on.

> *WARNING*
> *High voltage is present during ignition system operation. Do not touch the spark plug, ignition components, connectors or test leads while cranking the engine.*

> *NOTE*
> *All peak voltage specifications in the text and **Table 1** are minimum voltages. As long as the measured voltage meets or exceeds the specification, consider the test results satisfactory. On some components, the voltage may greatly exceed the minimum specification.*

7. Check the peak voltage by performing the following:

a. Connect the tester's positive test lead to the black/red terminal in the ICM wire harness 2-pin connector (A, **Figure 30**) and the negative test lead to ground.

b Kick the engine over with the kickstarter while reading the tester. Record the highest meter reading. The minimum peak voltage is 100 volts.

8. If the peak voltage reading is less than specified, disconnect the exciter coil black/red 1-pin connector (**Figure 31**) and perform the following:

a. Connect the tester's positive test lead to the black/red 1-pin connector (on the exciter coil side) and the negative test to ground.

b. Operate the kickstarter and crank the engine while reading the meter. Record the highest meter reading. The minimum peak voltage is 100 volts.

9. If the meter reading in Step 8 was less than the specified voltage, then the exciter coil is faulty. If the meter reading in Step 8 was correct, but the meter reading in Step 7 was incorrect, check for faulty wiring or connections in the black/red wire between the exciter coil and ICM connector. If further testing is required, follow the troubleshooting procedures in **Figure 29**.

10. Disconnect the test leads.

11. Reverse the disassembly steps.

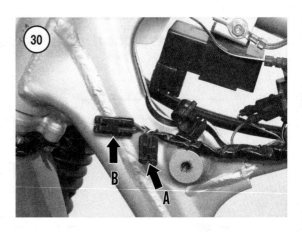

Ignition Pulse Generator Peak Voltage Test

Refer to **Figure 32** for test results.

1. Remove the fuel tank (Chapter Eight).

2. Check engine compression as described in Chapter Three. If the compression is low, the following test results will be inaccurate.

3. Check all of the ignition component electrical connectors and wiring harnesses. Make sure the connectors are clean and properly connected. Use the correct wiring diagram at the end of this manual to identify the different connectors.

4. Remove and disconnect the two connectors at the ICM as described under *Ignition Control Module* in this chapter.

5. Shift the transmission into neutral.

6. On 2001-on models, turn the ignition switch on.

> *WARNING*
> *High voltage is present during ignition system operation. Do not touch the spark plug, ignition components, connectors or test leads while cranking the engine.*

> *NOTE*
> *All peak voltage specifications in the text and **Table 1** are **minimum** voltages.*

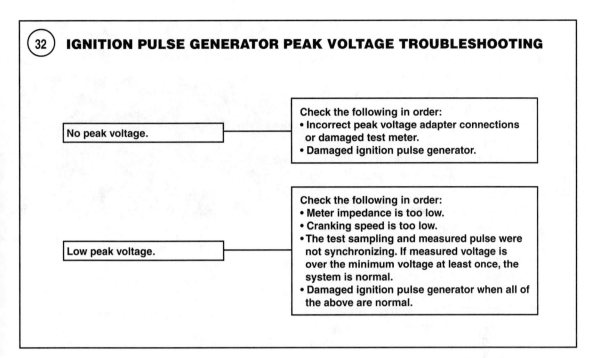

32 **IGNITION PULSE GENERATOR PEAK VOLTAGE TROUBLESHOOTING**

| No peak voltage. | Check the following in order:
• Incorrect peak voltage adapter connections or damaged test meter.
• Damaged ignition pulse generator. |

| Low peak voltage. | Check the following in order:
• Meter impedance is too low.
• Cranking speed is too low.
• The test sampling and measured pulse were not synchronizing. If measured voltage is over the minimum voltage at least once, the system is normal.
• Damaged ignition pulse generator when all of the above are normal. |

As long as the measured voltage meets or exceeds the specification, consider the test results satisfactory. On some components, the voltage may greatly exceed the minimum specification.

7. Check the peak voltage by performing the following:

   a. Connect the tester's positive test lead to the blue/yellow terminal in the ICM wire harness 4-pin connector (B, **Figure 30**) and the negative test lead to ground.

   b. Kick the engine over with the kickstarter while reading the tester. Record the highest meter reading. The minimum peak voltage is 0.7 volts.

8. If the peak voltage reading is less than specified, disconnect the ignition pulse generator blue/yellow 1-pin connector (**Figure 31**) and perform the following:

   a. Connect the tester's positive test lead to the black/yellow 1-pin connector (on the ignition pulse generator side) and the negative test to ground.

   b. Operate the kickstarter and crank the engine while reading the meter. Record the highest meter reading. The minimum peak voltage is 0.7 volts.

9. If the meter reading in Step 8 was less than the specified voltage, then the ignition pulse generator is faulty. If the meter reading in Step 8 was correct, but the meter reading in Step 7 was incorrect, check for faulty wiring or connections in the blue/yellow wire between the ignition pulse generator and ICM

connector. If further testing is required, follow the troubleshooting procedures in **Figure 32**.

10. Disconnect the test leads.

11. Reverse the disassembly steps.

IGNITION TIMING

All models are equipped with a capacitor discharge ignition (CDI), which has no moving parts or provision for adjusting the timing. However, checking the ignition timing can be used as a troubleshooting aid. If the ignition timing is incorrect, there is a defective component in the ignition system.

WARNING
Never start and run the motorcycle in a closed area. The exhaust gases contain carbon monoxide, a colorless, odorless, poisonous gas. Carbon monoxide levels build quickly in enclosed areas and can cause unconsciousness and death in a short time. When running the engine, always do so in a well-ventilated area.

NOTE
A 12-volt battery will be required to operate the timing light.

1. Start the engine and warm to normal operating temperature. Turn the engine off.

2. Place the bike on a workstand.

3. Remove the left crankcase cover as described in this chapter.

9

4. Connect a shop tachometer to the engine following the manufacturer's directions.

5. Connect the timing light battery leads to a separate 12-volt battery. Connect the timing light inductive lead to the spark plug wire. Route the wires so they do not contact the exhaust pipe.

6. Start and run the engine at 1400 rpm. Point the timing light at the top of the flywheel. The ignition timing is correct when the F mark on the flywheel (A, **Figure 33**) aligns with the index notch on the left crankcase (B).

7. Now increase the engine speed with the throttle. The F mark on the flywheel should begin to move clockwise.

8. Turn the engine off.

9. If the ignition timing is correct as described in Steps 6 and 7, the ignition system is working correctly. If the ignition timing is incorrect, one or more components in the ignition system are defective. To find the defective component(s), refer to *Engine Will Not Start* in Chapter Two.

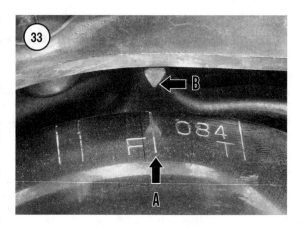

10. Disconnect the timing light leads from the spark plug and battery.

11. Reinstall the left crankcase cover.

WIRING DIAGRAMS

Wiring diagrams for all models are located at the end of this manual.

Table 1 ELECTRICAL SYSTEM TEST SPECIFICATIONS

Peak voltage	
Exciter coil	100 volts minimum
Ignition coil	100 volts minimum
Ignition pulse generator	0.7 volts minimum
Resistance specifications (XR100R and CRF100F)	
Alternator exciter coil	400-800 ohms*
Ignition coil	
Primary resistance	0.1-0.3 ohms*
Secondary resistance	
With spark plug cap	6.4-10.1 k ohms*
Without spark plug cap	2.7-3.5 k ohms*
Ignition pulse generator	50-200 ohms*

*Tests must be made at an ambient temperature of 20° C (68° F). Do not test when the engine or component is hot.

Table 2 ELECTRICAL SYSTEM TORQUE SPECIFICATIONS

	N•m	in.-lb.	ft.-lb.
Flywheel nut	64	–	47
Ignition pulse generator mounting screw	6	53	–

CHAPTER TEN

WHEELS, TIRES AND DRIVE CHAIN

This chapter describes repair and maintenance for the front and rear wheels, hubs, drive chain, sprockets and tires. Routine maintenance procedures for these components are found in Chapter Three.

Tables 1-4 are at the end of this chapter.

FRONT WHEEL

Removal

1. Support the motorcycle with the front wheel off the ground.
2. Remove the bolt (**Figure 1**) and the front brake cable clamp at the left slider.
3. Remove the axle nut (**Figure 2**) and remove the front axle (**Figure 3**) from the right side. Lower the wheel to disconnect the brake panel groove from the guide on the left slider.

> *NOTE*
> *If the axle is stuck, spray a penetrating fluid (WD-40, or equivalent) along both sides of the wheel at the most accessible axle points. Allow time for the fluid to penetrate along the axle, then reinstall the axle nut and drive the axle with a hammer to break it loose. If the axle is still tight, try to drive it far enough where a knock puller can be installed on its right shoulder. Then remove the*

axle nut and operate the puller to remove the axle. When an axle must be removed this way, the wheel bearings are probably damaged. In addition, the axle surfaces that originally aligned with the wheel bearings may be severely corroded and damaged. Inspect the wheel as described in this section.

4. Remove the right side collar (**Figure 4**).
5. Pull the brake panel out of the brake drum and remove the front wheel. If the brake drum is tight, loosen the front brake cable adjuster at the handlebar. Turn the wheel over and pour any accumulated brake dust into a garbage bag. Tie the bag closed and discard it.
6. Inspect the wheel as described in this section.
7. If necessary, service the brake linings and brake drum as described in Chapter Thirteen.

Installation

1. Clean the axle bearing surfaces on the fork tube.
2. Lubricate the right hub seal lips with grease and install the collar (**Figure 4**).
3. Lubricate the axle shoulder with grease. Do not lubricate the axle or axle nut threads. These threads must be free of oil and grease when the nut is tightened.

4. Install the brake panel into the brake drum and position the front wheel between the slider so the groove in the brake panel aligns with the guide on the left slider (**Figure 5**).

5. Install the front axle nut (**Figure 2**) and tighten finger-tight.

6. Adjust the front brake (Chapter Three).

7. Remove the motorcycle from the stand so the front wheel is on the ground. Apply the front brake, then compress and release the front suspension several times to reposition and seat the front axle and align the brake shoes with the brake drum.

8. Hold the axle and tighten the axle nut (**Figure 2**) to 62 N•m (46 ft.-lb.).

9. Secure the front brake cable with the clamp and tighten the mounting bolt (**Figure 1**) securely.

10. Recheck the front brake as described in Step 7.

Inspection

1. Inspect the seal (A, **Figure 6**) for wear, hardness, cracks or other damage. If necessary, replace the seal as described in *Front and Rear Hubs* in this chapter.

2. Inspect the bearings on both sides of the wheel for:

a. Smooth bearing operation. Turn each bearing inner race (B, **Figure 6**) by hand to check for any catching or roughness.

b. Radial and lateral play (**Figure 7**). Try to push the bearing in and out to check for lateral play. Slight play is normal. Try to push the bearing up and down to check for radial play. Any radial play should be difficult to feel. If play is easily felt, the bearing is worn out. If necessary, replace both bearings as a set as described in *Front and Rear Hubs* in this chapter.

3. Clean the axle and collar in solvent to remove all grease and dirt. Make sure the axle contact surfaces are clean.

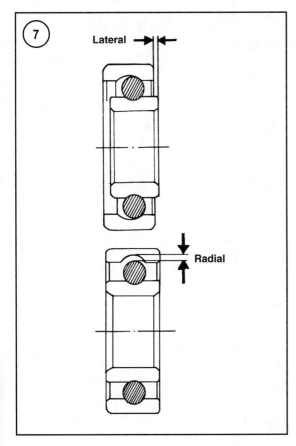

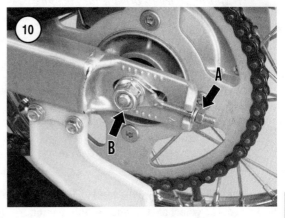

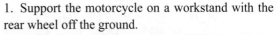

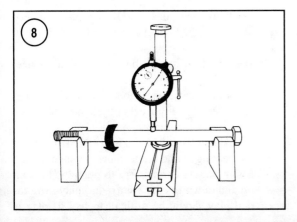

4. Check the axle for straightness with a set of V-blocks and dial indicator (**Figure 8**). Refer to **Table 1** for maximum axle runout. Actual runout will be one-half of the gauge reading. Do not attempt to straighten a bent axle.

5. Clean and inspect the brake drum and brake shoes (Chapter Thirteen).

6. Refer to *Wheel Service* in this chapter to inspect the spokes and true the rim.

REAR WHEEL

Removal

1. Support the motorcycle on a workstand with the rear wheel off the ground.

2. Unscrew the adjust nut from the brake rod (A, **Figure 9**). Depress the brake pedal and withdraw the brake rod (B, **Figure 9**) from the brake arm. Remove the collar and spring.

3. Loosen the chain adjuster nuts (A, **Figure 10**) on both side of the swing arm.

4. Hold the axle and remove the axle nut (B, **Figure 10**) and the chain adjuster.

5. Push the rear wheel forward and slip the drive chain off the driven sprocket.

6. Remove the rear axle (C, **Figure 9**), chain adjuster (D) and the rear wheel. Pull the brake panel out of the brake drum. Turn the wheel over and pour any accumulated brake dust into a garbage bag. Tie the bag closed and discard it.

NOTE
If the axle is stuck, spray a penetrating fluid (WD-40 or equivalent) along both sides of the wheel at the most accessible axle points. Allow time for the fluid to penetrate along the axle, then reinstall the axle nut and drive the axle with a hammer to break it loose. If the axle is still tight, try to drive it far enough where a knock puller can be installed on its right side shoulder. Then remove the axle nut and operate the puller to remove the axle. When an axle must be removed this way, the wheel bearings are probably damaged and should be inspected as described in this section. In addition, the axle surfaces that originally aligned with the wheel bearings may be severely corroded and damaged.

7. Remove the collar from the left side (**Figure 11**).
8. Inspect the wheel as described in this section.
9. If necessary, service the brake linings and brake drum as described in Chapter Thirteen.

Installation

1. Clean the axle, nut, chain adjusters and swing arm axle surfaces.
2. Lubricate the left hub seal lips with grease and install the collar (**Figure 11**).
3. Lubricate the axle shoulder with grease. Do not lubricate the threads on the axle and axle nut. These threads must be free of oil and grease when the nut is tightened.
4. Lift the drive chain and place it on the left side of the swing arm.
5. Install the brake panel into the brake drum and position the rear wheel into the swing arm. Center the brake panel groove over the swing arm pin (**Figure 12**).
6. Lift the wheel and install the axle (C, **Figure 9**) with the chain adjuster (D) from the right side. Make sure the collar did not fall off the left side.
7. Push the wheel forward and slip the drive chain over the driven sprocket. If the drive chain was disconnected, install the master link so its closed end (**Figure 13**) is toward the direction of chain travel.
8. Remove any grease from the axle threads.

9. Install the axle adjuster (A, **Figure 10**) and the axle nut (B).
10. Install the spring onto the brake rod the collar through the brake arm. Install the brake rod through the collar and secure with the adjust nut (A, **Figure 9**).
11. Adjust the drive chain (Chapter Three). Then hold the rear axle and tighten the axle nut (B, **Figure 10**) to 62 N•m (46 ft.-lb.).
12. Adjust the rear brake (Chapter Three).

Inspection

1. Inspect the seal (A, **Figure 14**) for wear, hardness, cracks or other damage. If necessary, replace the seal as described under *Front and Rear Hubs* in this chapter.
2. Inspect the bearings on both sides of the wheel for:
   a. Smooth bearing operation. Turn each bearing inner race (B, **Figure 14**) by hand and check for any catching or roughness.
   b. Radial and lateral play (**Figure 7**). Try to push the bearing in and out to check for lateral play. Slight play is normal. Try to push the bearing up and down to check for radial play. Any radial play should be difficult to feel. If play is

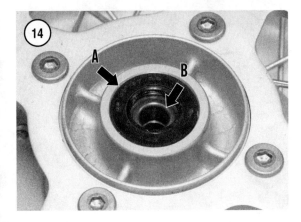

Inspection

The bearings can be inspected with the wheels installed on the motorcycle. With the wheels installed, leverage can be applied to the bearings to detect wear. In addition, the wheels can be spun to listen for roughness in the bearings. Use the following procedure to check the bearings while the wheels are installed. If the wheels must be removed, perform the checks in the wheel removal procedures described in this chapter.

1. Support the motorcycle with the wheel off the ground. The axle nut must be tight.

2. Grasp the wheel with both hands, 180 degrees apart. Have an assistant apply the brake, then rock the wheel up and down, and side to side, to check for radial and lateral play. Play will be detected in severely worn bearings.

3. Loosen the front or rear brake adjuster for the wheel being checked.

4. Spin the wheel and listen for bearing noise. A grinding or catching noise indicates worn bearings.

NOTE
If the brake shoes are dragging and the bearing cannot be heard, remove the wheel and support it on a truing stand.

5. If damage is evident, replace the bearings as a set and install a new seal.

CAUTION
Do not remove the wheel bearings to check their condition. If the bearings are removed, they must be replaced.

6. If the brake adjuster was loosened, readjust the brake as described in Chapter Three.

Seal Removal/Installation

The hub seal protects the adjacent bearing from dirt and moisture contamination. The opposite bearing is protected by the brake drum. Always install a new seal when replacing bearings.

1. Pry the seal out of the hub with a seal puller, tire iron (**Figure 15**) or wide-blade screwdriver. Place a shop cloth under the tool to protect the hub from damage.

NOTE
If new bearings will be fitted, replace the bearings before installing the seals.

2. Clean the seal bore.

easily felt, the bearing is worn out. If necessary, replace both bearings as a set as described in *Front and Rear Hubs* in this chapter.

3. Clean the axle and collar in solvent to remove all grease and dirt. Make sure the axle contact surfaces are clean.

4. Check the axle for straightness with a set of V-blocks and dial indicator (**Figure 8**). Refer to **Table 1** for maximum axle runout. Actual runout will be one-half of the gauge reading. Do not attempt to straighten a bent axle.

5. Check the driven sprocket nuts for tightness. If loose, hold the Allen bolts and tighten the driven sprocket nuts to 32 N•m (24 ft.-lb.).

6. Clean and inspect the brake drum and brake shoes (Chapter Thirteen).

7. Refer to *Wheel Service* in this chapter to inspect the spokes and true the rim.

FRONT AND REAR HUBS

The front and rear hubs each contain a seal, wheel bearings and distance collar.

Procedures for servicing the front and rear hubs are essentially the same. Where differences occur, they will be described in the procedure.

10

3. Inspect unshielded bearings for proper lubrication. If necessary, clean and repack the bearings while installed in the hub.

NOTE
Unshielded bearings were not originally installed the hubs. If so equipped, a previous owner installed them.

4. Pack grease into the lip of the new seal.
5. Place the seal in the bore with the closed side of the seal facing out. The seal must be square in the bore.
6. Press the seal into the hub bore by hand (**Figure 16**) or use a seal driver or socket. Install the seal so it is flush with the top of the hub bore surface. Refer to A, **Figure 6** (front) or A, **Figure 14** (rear).

CAUTION
When driving a seal, the edge of the driver must fit at the perimeter of the seal. If the driver outside diameter is appreciably smaller than that of the seal, the driver will press against the center of the seal and damage it.

Wheel Bearing Removal/Installation

Wheel bearings are installed with a slight press fit. Work carefully to avoid damaging the hub when replacing the bearings. Discard the bearings after removing them.

Tools

Tools used in this section to remove the front and rear wheel bearings are as follows:
1. A 12 mm expanding collet (A, **Figure 17**) and driver rod (B) are required.
2. Wheel bearings can also be removed with a propane torch, drift and hammer.

Removal

Two methods for removing the front and rear wheel bearings are provided. To remove a bearing where the inner race assembly has fallen out, refer to *Damaged Bearings* in this section.
1. Remove the seal as described in this section.
2. Examine the wheel bearings for excessive damage, especially the inner race. If the inner race of one bearing is damaged, remove the opposite bearing first. If both bearings are damaged, select the bearing with the least amount of damage and remove it first. On rusted and damaged bearings, applying pressure against the inner race can cause the inner race to pop out, leaving the outer race pressed in the hub.

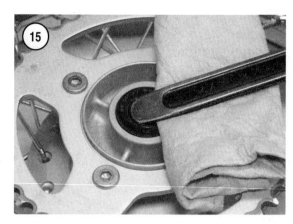

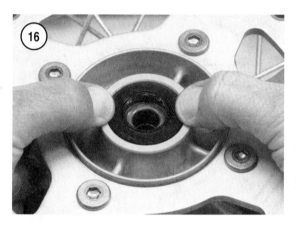

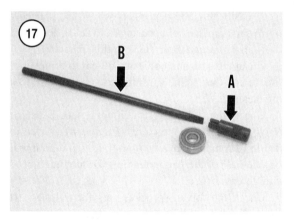

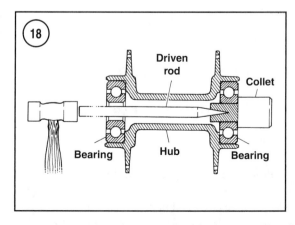

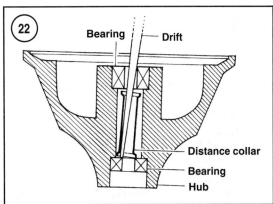

c. Position the wheel upright so the driver rod is parallel with the floor. Strike the end of the driver rod (**Figure 20**) and repeat as necessary to force the bearing out of the hub (A, **Figure 21**). Remove the bearing and tool. Release the remover head from the bearing. Discard the bearing.

d. Remove the distance collar (B, **Figure 21**) from the hub.

e. Repeat the procedure to remove the opposite bearing.

4. To remove the wheel bearings with a hammer, drift and propane torch perform the following:

WARNING
*When using a propane torch to heat the hub, work in a well-ventilated area away from combustible materials. Wear protective clothing, including eye protection and insulated gloves. For additional information, refer to **Interference Fit** in **Service Methods** in Chapter One. Observe all safety and handling procedures when the hub is heated.*

a. Clean all lubricants from the wheel.

b. Heat the hub around the bearing to be removed. Work the torch in a circular motion around the hub, taking care not to hold the torch in one area. Turn the wheel over and support it on wooden blocks, then remove the bearing as described in the following steps.

c. Tilt the distance collar away from one side of the bearing with a long drift (**Figure 22**). This will be difficult to do if the bearings are pressed tightly against the distance collar.

CAUTION
Do not allow a bearing to bind in its mounting bore during removal. This can gouge the bore and cause permanent hub damage.

WARNING
Wear safety glasses when removing the bearings in the following steps.

3. To remove the wheel bearings with an expanding collet (**Figure 18**) perform the following:

a. Select the correct size collet (**Figure 19**) and insert it into one of the hub bearings.

b. From the opposite side of the hub, insert the driver rod into the slot in the backside of the collet (**Figure 18**). Position the hub with the collet resting against a solid surface and strike the driver rod to expand the collet against the bearing.

NOTE
Do not damage the distance collar when removing the bearing. If necessary, grind a clearance groove in the drift to enable it to contact the bearing while clearing the distance collar.

d. Place the drift on the bearing's inner race and drive it with a hammer. Make several passes around the bearing to remove it evenly from the hub.

e. Remove the distance collar from the hub.

f. Turn the hub over and heat the opposite side.

g. Drive out the opposite bearing using a large socket or bearing driver inserted through the hub.

h. Inspect the distance collar for burrs created during removal. Remove burrs with a file.

5. Clean and dry the hub and distance collar.

6. Check the hub mounting bore for cracks or other damage. If the bearings were a loose fit in the hub, the hub mounting bore and hub may be damaged.

7. Inspect the distance collar for flared ends. Check the ends for cracks or other damage. Do not try to repair the distance collar by cutting or grinding its end surfaces as this will shorten the distance collar. Replace the distance collar if one or both ends are damaged.

NOTE
The distance collar operates against the wheel bearing inner races to prevent them from moving inward when the axle is tightened. If a distance collar is too short, or if it is not installed, the inner bearing races will move inward and bind on the axle, causing bearing damage and seizure.

Installation

1. Before installing the new bearings and seal, note the following:

a. Install bearings with their closed side facing out. If a bearing is sealed on both sides, install the bearing with its manufacturer's marks facing out.

b. Apply grease (NLGI No. 2) to bearings that are open on one or both sides (**Figure 23**). Work the grease thoroughly into the cavities between the balls and races.

c. Support the bottom side of the hub, near the bore, when installing bearings.

d. Install the right bearing first, then the left bearing.

e. The two rear wheel bearings are different. The left wheel bearing is marked 6301U and the

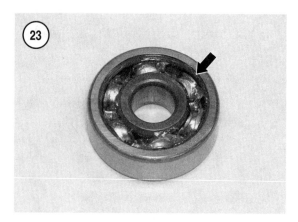

right bearing marked 6201U. The 6301U bearing is wider than the 6201U.

2. Heat the hub evenly around the bearing bore.

3. Place the first bearing squarely against the bore opening with its closed side facing out. Select a driver with an outside diameter slightly smaller than the bearing's outside diameter. Then drive the bearing into the bore until it bottoms (**Figure 24**).

4. Turn the hub over. Install the distance collar and center it against the center race.

5. Position the opposite bearing squarely against the bore opening with its closed side facing out. Drive the bearing partway into the bearing bore. Make sure the distance collar is centered in the hub. If not, install the axle through the hub to align the distance collar with the bearing. Then remove the axle and continue installing the bearing until it bottoms.

6. Insert the axle though the hub and turn it by hand. Check for any roughness or binding, indicating bearing damage.

NOTE
If the axle will not go in, the distance collar is not aligned correctly with one of the bearings.

7. Install the seal as described in this section.

Damaged bearings

If damaged wheel bearings remain in use, the inner race can break apart, leaving the outer race pressed in the hub. Removal is difficult because only a small part of the race is accessible above the hub's shoulder, leaving little material to drive against. To remove a bearing's outer race under these conditions, first heat the hub evenly with a propane torch. Drive out the outer race with a drift and hammer. It may be necessary to grind a clearance tip on the end of the drift, to avoid damaging the hub bore. Remove the race evenly by applying force at different points around the race. Do not allow the race to bind in its bore. After removing the race, inspect the hub mounting bore for cracks or other damage.

WHEEL SERVICE

To prevent wheel failure, inspect the wheels, bearings and tires at the intervals specified in Chapter Three.

Component Condition

Wheels used on off-road motorcycles receive a lot of abuse. It is important to inspect the wheel regularly for lateral (side-to-side) and radial (up-and-down) runout, spoke tension, and rim damage. When a wheel has a noticeable wobble, it is out of true. This is usually caused by loose spokes, but it can be caused by a damaged hub or rim.

Truing a wheel corrects the lateral and radial runout to bring the wheel back into specification.

The condition of the individual wheel components will affect the ability to successfully true the wheel. Note the following:
1. Spoke condition: Do not attempt to true a wheel with bent or damaged spokes. Doing so places an excessive amount of tension on the spoke, hub and rim. Overtightening the spoke may damage the spoke

nipple hole in the hub or rim. Inspect for and replace damaged spokes.

> *NOTE*
> *When a properly trued wheel hits a sharp object, all of the torque or wheel impact is equally divided or transferred among all of the wheel's spokes. The spokes are able to bend or bow slightly, thus absorbing the shock and preventing the rim and hub from damage. When the spokes are overtightened, they are unable to flex, causing all of the impact to be absorbed by the hub or rim. When the spokes are too loose, the torque or wheel impact is divided unequally between the spokes, with the tighter spokes receiving most of the torque and isolating the impact in one area along the rim and hub. This eventually causes a cracked or broken hub or rim.*

2. Nipple condition: When truing the wheels the nipples must turn freely on the spokes. However, corroded and rusted spoke threads are common and difficult to adjust. Spray a penetrating liquid (WD-40 or equivalent) onto the nipples and allow sufficient time for it to penetrate before trying to turn the nipples. Turn the spoke wrench in both directions and continue to apply penetrating liquid. If the spoke wrench rounds off the nipple, it will be necessary to remove the tire from the rim, cut the spokes out of the wheel and install new spokes.
3. Rim condition: Minor rim runout can be corrected by truing the wheel; however, overtightening the spokes to correct a damaged rim may damage the hub and rim. Inspect the rims for cracks, flat spots or dents (**Figure 25**). Check the spoke holes for cracks or enlargement. Replace damaged rims.

Wheel Truing Preliminaries

Before checking the runout and truing the wheel, note the following:
1. Clean the rim and spoke nipples.
2. Make sure the wheel bearings are in good condition. Refer to the front and rear wheel inspection procedures in this chapter.
3. Inspect the spoke holes in the rim for cracks, hole elongation and other damage. Replace the rim if damaged.
4. Check the head of the spokes for proper seating in the hub. Improperly seated spokes may indicate loose spokes and can cause hub damage. Note the following:

10

a. On the front wheel, all of the spokes are installed from the outside and the spoke heads are recessed into holes in the hub. Check for spoke heads that are positioned closer to the upper edge of the spoke hole. When in doubt, tap the spoke head with a punch to see if the spoke head moves.

b. On the rear wheel, inner and outer spokes are used. The outer spoke heads seat into recess holes in the hub. The inner spoke heads seat against a flat surface on an inner part of the hub. Compare the installed spokes to locate unseated spoke heads.

5. A small amount of wheel runout is acceptable. Attempting to true the wheel to a zero reading may damage the rim and hub from overtightened spokes. Also, considering the environment dirt bikes operate in, minor rim and spoke damage make it more difficult to accurately true the wheel.

6. Check runout by mounting a pointer against the fork or swing arm and slowly rotating the wheel. When checking the rear wheel, it will be easier if the chain is first removed from the driven sprocket. If the wheel needs major tuning, remove the tire and mount the wheel on a truing stand (**Figure 26**). An adjustable pointer or dial indicator can then be mounted next to the rim to measure runout in both directions (**Figure 27**).

NOTE
A solid pointer works better than a dial indicator when truing rims with deep scratches, dents and other contact wear.

7. Use the correct size spoke wrench (**Figure 28**) to avoid damaging the spoke nipples. Do not use an adjustable wrench or locking pliers as these tools will round or crush the spoke nipples.

Tightening Loose Spokes

This section describes steps for checking and tightening loose spokes without effecting the wheel runout. When many spokes are loose and the wheel is running out of true, refer to *Wheel Truing Procedure* in this section.

1. Support the wheel so that it can turn freely. If the rear wheel is being checked while on the motorcycle, remove the chain from the driven sprocket.

2. Spokes can be checked for looseness by one of three ways:

a. Spoke torque wrench: When using a spoke torque wrench, the correct torque specification is 3 N•m (26.5 in.-lb.). Spoke wrenches work better on wheels that are properly main-

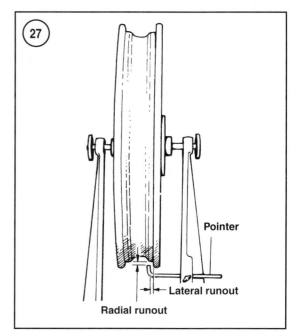

Pointer

Lateral runout

Radial runout

tained (no rust or corrosion on spoke threads or rounded spoke nipples).

b. Hand check: Grasp and squeeze two spokes where they cross. Loose spokes can be flexed by hand. Tight spokes feel stiff with little noticeable movement. Tighten the spokes until the tension between the different spoke groups feels the same.

c. Spoke tone: Tapping a spoke causes it to vibrate and produce sound waves. Loose and tight spokes produce different sounds or tones. A tight spoke will ring. A loose spoke has a soft or dull ring and sounds flat. Tap each spoke with a spoke wrench or screwdriver to identify loose spokes.

3. Check the spokes using one of the methods described in Step 2. If there are loose spokes, spin the wheel and note the following:

a. If the wheel is running true, continue with Step 4 to tighten the loose spokes.

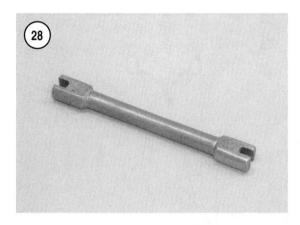

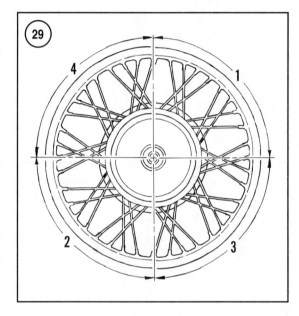

b. If the wheel is running out of true, refer to *Wheel Truing Procedure* in this section to measure runout and true the wheel.

4. Use tape and divide the rim into four equally spaced sections. Number the sections as shown in **Figure 29**.

5. Start by tightening the loose spokes in Section 1, then in sections 2, 3 and 4. Do not turn each spoke more than 1/4 to 1/2 turn at a time as this will overtighten the spokes and bring the wheel out of true. Work slowly while checking spoke tightness. Continue until all of the spokes are tightened evenly.

NOTE
If the spokes are hard to turn, spray penetrating liquid (WD-40 or equivalent) into the top of the nipple. Wipe excess penetrating liquid from the rim.

6. When all of the spokes are tightened evenly, spin the wheel. If there is any noticeable runout, true the wheel as described in this section.

Wheel Truing Procedure

Table 1 lists lateral (side-to-side) and radial (up-and-down) runout specifications.

1. Clean the wheel assembly.

2. Position a pointer against the rim as shown in **Figure 27**. If the tire is mounted on the rim, position the pointer as shown in **Figure 26**.

3. Spin the wheel slowly and check the lateral and radial runout. If the rim is out of adjustment, continue with Step 4.

NOTE
It is normal for the rim to jump at the point where the rim is welded together. Also small cuts and dings in the rim will affect the runout reading, especially when using a dial indicator. It is more effective to use a solid pointer when checking runout on used and scratched rims.

4. Spray penetrating liquid (WD-40 or equivalent) into the top of each nipple. Wipe excess penetrating liquid from the rim.

NOTE
If the runout is minimal, the tire can be left on the rim. However, if the runout is excessive, or if the rim offset must be adjusted with the hub (Step 5), remove the tire from the rim as described in this chapter.

5. If there are a large number of loose spokes, or if some or all of the spokes were replaced, measure the hub to rim offset as shown in **Figure 30** (front) or **Figure 31** (rear) and compare to the specifications in **Table 1**. If necessary, reposition the hub before truing the wheel.

6. Lateral runout adjustment: If the side-to-side runout is out of specification, adjust the wheel. For example, to pull the rim to the left side (**Figure 32**), tighten the spokes on the left side of the hub (at the runout point) and loosen the adjacent spokes on the right side of the hub. Always loosen and tighten the spokes in equal number of turns.

NOTE
Determining the number of spokes to loosen and tighten will depend on how far the runout is out of adjustment. Loosen two or three spokes, then tighten the opposite two or three spokes. If the runout is excessive and affects a greater area along the rim, loosen and tighten a greater number of spokes.

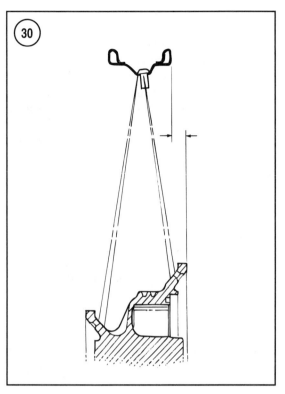

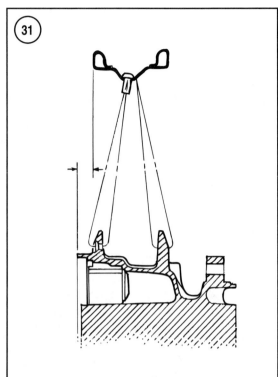

7. Radial runout adjustment: If the up and down runout is out of specification, the hub is not centered in the rim. Draw the high point of the rim toward the centerline of the wheel by tightening the spokes in the area of the high point, and loosening the spokes on the side opposite the high point (**Figure 33**). Tighten the spokes in equal amounts to prevent distortion.

NOTE
Alternate between checking and adjusting lateral and radial runout. Remember, changing spoke tension on one side of the rim will affect the tension on the other side of the rim.

8. After truing the wheel, seat each spoke in the hub by tapping it with a flat nose punch and hammer. Then recheck the spoke tension and wheel runout. Readjust if necessary as described in *Tightening Loose Spokes* in this section.
9. With the tire off the rim, check the ends of the spokes where they are threaded in the nipples. Grind off any ends that protrude through the nipples to prevent them from puncturing the tube.

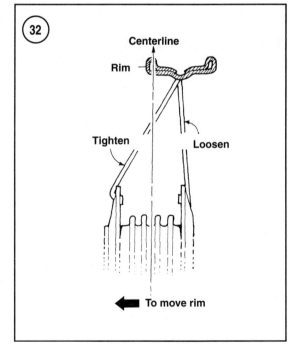

DRIVE CHAIN

Refer to **Table 2** for drive chain specifications. Refer to *Drive Chain and Sprockets* in Chapter Three for routine drive chain inspection, adjustment and lubrication procedures.

When checking the condition of the chain, also check the condition of the sprockets, as described in Chapter Three. If either the chain or sprockets are worn, replace all drive components at the same time. Using new sprockets with a worn chain, or a new chain on worn sprockets will shorten the life of the new part.

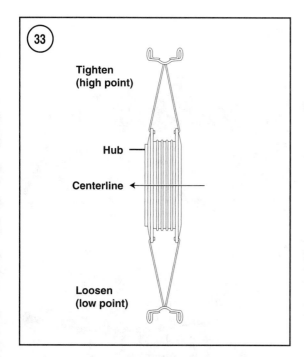

(33)

Tighten
(high point)

Hub

Centerline

Loosen
(low point)

(34)

Removal/Installation

1. Support the motorcycle on a workstand with its rear wheel off the ground. Shift the transmission into neutral.

2. Find the master link on the chain. Remove the spring clip (**Figure 34**) with a pair of pliers, then remove the side plate and connecting link from the chain (**Figure 35**).

3. Remove the drive chain.

4. Clean and inspect the chain (Chapter Three).

5. Clean the drive and driven sprockets.

6. Check the drive chain rollers, slider and guide for worn or damaged parts (Chapter Three).

7. Reverse this procedure to install the chain. Note the following:

   a. Install the chain and reassemble a new master link (**Figure 35**).

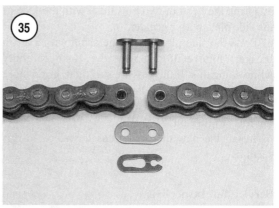

(35)

(36)

   b. Install the spring clip on the master link with the closed end of the clip pointing toward the direction of travel (**Figure 36**).

   c. Adjust the chain (Chapter Three).

Cutting a Drive Chain To Length

Table 2 lists the correct number of chain links required for original equipment gearing. If the replacement drive chain is too long, cut it to length as follows:

1. Stretch the new chain on a workbench.

2. If installing a new chain over stock gearing, refer to **Table 2** for the correct number of links for the new chain. If sprocket sizes were changed, install the new chain over both sprockets, with the rear wheel moved forward, to determine the correct number of links to remove (**Figure 37**). Make a chalk mark on the two chain pins to cut. Count the chain links one more time or check the chain length before cutting. Include the master link when counting the drive chain links.

WARNING
Using a hand or bench grinder will cause flying particles. Do not operate a grinding tool without proper eye protection.

3. Grind the head of two pins flush with the face of the side plate with a grinder.

4. Press the side plate out of the chain with a chain breaker (**Figure 38**); support the chain carefully while doing this. If the pins are still tight, grind more material from the end of the pins and then try again.

5. Remove the side plate and push out the connecting link (**Figure 39**).

6. Install the new drive chain as described in this section.

Service and Inspection

For routine service and inspection of the drive chain, refer to *Drive Chain and Sprockets* in Chapter Three.

SPROCKET

This section describes service procedures for replacing the drive (front) and driven (rear) sprockets. Refer to **Table 2** for sprocket sizes.

Inspection

Check drive chain and sprocket wear as described under *Drive Chain and Sprockets* in Chapter Three.

Drive Sprocket Removal/Installation

1. Remove the left crankcase cover (Chapter Nine).

2. Shift the transmission into fifth gear and have an assistant apply the rear brake. If the drive chain is not installed on the motorcycle, hold the sprocket with a holding tool.

3. Remove the sprocket retaining bolts (A, **Figure 40**) and retainer plate (B). Turn the retainer plate and align its slots with the slots in the countershaft. Slide the drive sprocket (C, **Figure 40**) off the countershaft and disconnect it from the drive chain.

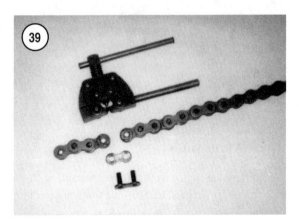

NOTE
If the drive sprocket cannot be removed because the drive chain is too tight, loosen the rear axle nut and loosen the chain adjusters, or if necessary, disconnect the drive chain as described in this chapter.

4. Inspect the sprocket as described in *Drive Chain and Sprockets* in Chapter Three.

5. Install the drive sprocket (C, **Figure 40**) with its marked or stamped side facing out.

6. Install the retainer plate (B, **Figure 40**) with its flat side facing toward the sprocket. Install the sprocket

retaining bolts (A, **Figure 40**). Use the same method to prevent the sprocket from turning and tighten the sprocket retaining bolts securely.

7. Check the drive chain adjustment (Chapter Three).

8. Install the left crankcase cover (Chapter Nine).

Driven Sprocket Removal/Installation

NOTE
The driven sprocket is attached to the rear hub with Allen bolts and nuts. Do not loosen these fasteners by turning

the Allen bolt. Instead, hold the Allen bolt and loosen the nut to avoid damaging the hex recess in the Allen bolt heads.

1. Support the motorcycle on a workstand with the rear wheel off the ground.

2. Have an assistant apply the rear brake, then hold the Allen bolts and loosen the nuts.

3. Remove the rear wheel as described in this chapter.

4. Remove the nuts, Allen bolts and driven sprocket (**Figure 41**) from the rear hub.

5. Check the sprocket mounting tabs for cracks or other damage. Replace the hub if damaged.

6. Clean and dry the sprocket fasteners. Replace damaged fasteners.

7. Install the new sprocket onto the rear hub with its tapered hole side facing out (**Figure 42**).

8. Install the Allen bolts and nuts and finger-tighten.

9. Install the rear wheel as described in this chapter.

10. Hold the Allen bolts and tighten the nuts in two or three steps and in a crossing pattern to 32 N•m (24 ft.-lb.).

NOTE
*The Motion Pro Torque Adapter (part No. 08-0134) can be used with a torque wrench to access and torque the nuts (**Figure 43**). Refer to **Torque Adapters** in **Tools** in Chapter One for additional information.*

11. Adjust the drive chain and tighten the rear axle nut as described in Chapter Three.

TIRE CHANGING

The following items are required for changing tires:

1. Tire irons. Note that most tire irons are designed with one spoon (A, **Figure 44**) end and one flat (B) end. The spoon end is used during tire removal and the flat end is used for tire installation.

2. 12 mm wrench to turn the rim lock nut on the rear wheel.

3. Squirt bottle filled with soapy water.

4. Valve core tool.

5. Duct tape to replace rubber rim band.

The following sections shows the tire change procedure performed with the wheel placed on a metal drum. A length of water hose has been split and placed around the rim of the drum to protect the wheel and spokes. The wheel can also be supported on a small metal bucket, wooden blocks or placed on a piece of carpet.

10

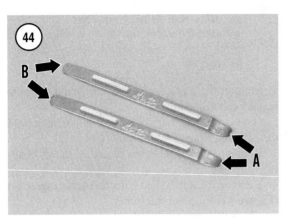

Removal

1. If the tire is flat, make an alignment mark across the tire and rim in line with the valve stem.

2. Remove the valve core and deflate the tire.

3. If so equipped, loosen the rim lock nut by threading it to the end of the rim lock. Then push the rim lock down with a tire iron (**Figure 45**) to break the rim lock loose from the tire.

4. Break the bead on the side of the tire facing up. Place a knee on the tire and then push the upper part of the tire toward the rim by hand (**Figure 46**). When this section of the of the bead pops free, turn the wheel and repeat until the upper bead is free. After the upper bead is free, the lower bead can usually be broken by squeezing both sides of the tire by hand. Note the following:

 a. On front wheels, place the brake drum side down.

 b. On rear wheels, place the sprocket side down.

5. Lubricate the upper bead with soapy water.

> *NOTE*
> *When removing the tire in the following steps, make sure to keep the tire bead centered with the rim (**Figure 47**). Otherwise, the tire bead will tighten because it has to move farther and require more force for removal, especially when prying the last part of the bead over the rim, which can split and damage the edge of the tire.*

> *NOTE*
> *Use tire irons without sharp edges. If necessary, file the ends of the tire irons to remove any rough edges.*

6. Insert the tire iron under the bead next to the rim lock (if used) (**Figure 48**). At the same time, kneel on the opposite side of the tire to force the bead into the center of the rim, then pry the bead over the rim with the tire iron.

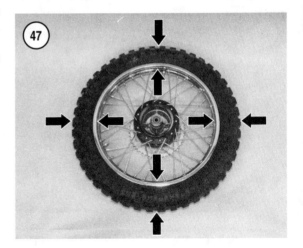

7. Release pressure on the first tire iron and insert a second tire iron on the opposite side of the rim lock to hold the bead over the rim (**Figure 49**). Apply more pressure with the first tire and hold it in position, then work around the tire with the second tire iron, prying the tire over the rim. If the tire bead is tight and hard to move, check that the tire is still centered with the rim. Take small bites, being careful not to pinch the inner tube with the tire irons.

8. Push the valve stem into the tire and carefully remove the inner tube from the tire (**Figure 50**).

NOTE
For the models covered in this manual, a single rim lock is used only on the rear wheel. If this procedure is being followed with a wheel that uses two rim locks, remove one of the rim locks before removing the tire from the rim.

9. Stand the tire upright and while keeping the tire centered with the rim, use a tire iron and pry the second tire bead (**Figure 51**) over the rim
10. Remove and discard the rim band.

11. If the tire was originally flat, reinstall the valve core and inflate the tube with air. Locate the hole or damaged area in the tube and then inspect the same area on the tire so see if a foreign object is projecting through the tire, and remove if found.

Inspection

1. Inspect the tire for any damage, especially on the inside of the tire that could cause a flat.
2A. If the tire was not flat, fill the tube with air to check for damage that may have occurred during tire removal. If the tube holds air, check the area around the valve stem for cracks that could cause a leak later on.
2B. If the tire was originally flat, locate the hole in the tube and then check the tire and rim at the same locations for problems that may have caused the flat.
3. Check the rim lock for wear where it seats against the tire. Check the bolt for tightness and thread damage. Replace the rim lock if necessary.
4. Make sure the spoke ends do not protrude above the nipple heads and into the center of the rim. Grind or file off any protruding spoke ends.
5. Wrap the center of the rim with two separate revolutions of duct tape. Punch holes through the tape at the rim lock and valve stem hole positions.

Installation

NOTE
Installation will be easier if the tire is pliable. This can be achieved by warming the tire in the sun or in an enclosed vehicle.

1. Sprinkle talcum powder around the interior of the tire casing. Distribute the powder so it is on all surfaces that will touch the inner tube. The powder minimizes chafing and helps the tube distribute itself when inflated.

NOTE
Depending on the make and type of tire installed, check the sidewall and determine if it must be installed in a specific direction. A direction arrow is often embossed in the sidewall.

2. Install the rim lock (A, **Figure 52**), lockwasher and nut. Thread the nut just enough to hold it onto the rim lock. Do not tighten at this time. The rim lock must be over the edge of both tire beads when installation is completed.

NOTE
For the models covered in this manual, a single rim lock is used only on the rear wheel. If this procedure is being followed with a wheel that uses two rim locks, install the second rim lock after the tire is installed on the rim.

3. If a rubber rim band is used, be sure the band is in place with the rough side toward the rim. Align the holes in the band with the holes in the rim or place it over the rim lock (B, **Figure 52**).

4. Lubricate one bead and push it onto the rim by hand (**Figure 53**), starting in the area over the rim lock (if used). If necessary, use a tire iron.

5. Turn the wheel over and squeeze the tire to check that the rim lock edge is positioned inside the tire (**Figure 54**). If necessary, use the tire irons to pry the tire outward slightly while pushing the rim lock into place (**Figure 55**). If working on a rear tire, work around the driven sprocket.

6. Install the core into the valve stem and apply a little air into the tube. A flat tube is harder to install and position inside the tire. Align the valve stem with the hole in the rim, then pull the tire back and install the tube into the tire (**Figure 56**). Check that the tube is not twisted as it is tucked into the tire. Pull the tire back and install the valve stem through the hole in the rim. Install the locknut on the upper end of the valve stem to prevent the stem from falling out of the hole.

7. If the valve stem is positioned at an angle, hold the spokes and turn the tire slightly to move the tube and align the valve stem with the rim.

8. Check that the tube is positioned behind the rim lock and not pinched between the sides of the rim lock and tire casing.

9. Check the tube to make sure it is rounded and not wrinkled. If necessary, add more air to the tube to straighten it, then release some of the air. Too much air will make tire installation difficult and too little air will increase the chance of pinching the tube.

10. Lubricate the second tire bead, then start installation a few inches to the right of the rim lock (**Figure**

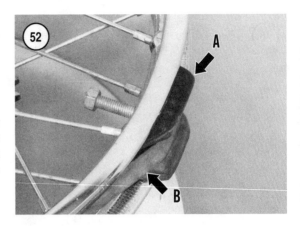

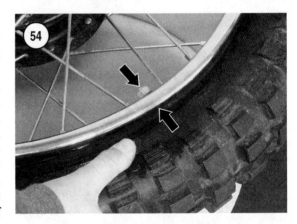

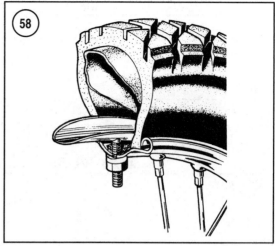

lock is positioned inside the tire (**Figure 58**) and the tube is not pinched between the tire and rim.

WARNING
If the tire does not seat at the recommended pressure, do not continue to overinflate the tire. Deflate the tire and reinflate to the recommended seating pressure. Relubricate the beads, if necessary.

11. Lubricate both beads and inflate the tire to seat the beads onto the rim. Inflate the tire to 25-30 psi (172-207 kPa). Check the bead for uniform fit, on both sides of the tire.

12. Tighten the rim lock nut to 12 N•m (106 in.-lb.).

13. Bleed the tire pressure to the specification in **Table 3**.

14. Install the air valve cap and finger-tighten the valve stem locknut against the cap.

57). Work around the rim, hand-fitting as much of the tire as possible while keeping the tire centered with the rim. If necessary, relubricate the bead. When approaching the rim lock, stop and push the rim lock into the tire, then install the last part of the bead. If it is necessary to use a tire iron the last few inches, work carefully to avoid forcing the tire iron into the tire and pinching the tube. Release the rim lock and then check both sides of the tire to make sure the rim

10

Table 1 TIRE AND WHEEL SPECIFICATIONS

Axle runout	0.2 mm (0.008 in.)
Front tire size	
XR80R	2.50-16
CRF80F	70/100-16 M/C 39M
XR100R	2.50-19
CRF100F	70/100-19 M/C 42M
Rear tire size	
XR80R	3.60-14
CRF80F	80/100-14 M/C 43M
XR100R	3.00-16
CRF100F	90/100-16 M/C 51M
Front and rear tire manufacturer	
XR80R	IRC
CRF80F	Cheng Shin
XR100R	Bridgestone
CRF100F	Cheng Shin
	(continued)

Table 1 TIRE AND WHEEL SPECIFICATIONS (continued)

Tire tread depth limit	3.0 mm (0.12 in)
Wheel rim runout (lateral and radial maximum)	
Front and rear	2.0 mm (0.08 in.)
Wheel rim-to-hub offset*	
Front wheel	11-13 mm (0.43-0.51 in.)
Rear wheel	10-12 mm (0.39-0.47 in.)
*Refer to text for measurement procedure.	

Table 2 DRIVE CHAIN AND SPROCKET SPECIFICATIONS

Drive chain	
Type	
XR80R	DID 420M or RK 420MZ
CRF80F	DID 420MBK1 or RK 420MSZ1
XR100R	DID 428HGI or RK 428FD
CRF100F	RK 420FDZ
Number of links	
80 cc models	110
100 cc models	118
Drive chain wear limit (41 pins)	511 mm (20.1 in.)
Stock sprocket sizes (front/rear)	
80 cc models	14/46
100 cc models	14/50

Table 3 TIRE INFLATION PRESSURE

	kPa	psi
Front	100	15
Rear		
XR80R and XR100R	125	18
CRF80F and CRF100F	100	15

Table 4 FRONT AND REAR WHEEL TORQUE SPECIFICATIONS

	N•m	in.-lb.	ft.-lb.
Axle nut	62	–	46
Driven sprocket nut	32	–	24
Rim lock	12	106	–
Spoke nipple	3	26.5	–

CHAPTER ELEVEN

FRONT SUSPENSION AND STEERING

This chapter describes service procedures for the handlebar, steering stem and front fork.

Tables 1-5 are at the end of the chapter.

HANDLEBAR

NOTE
This section describes service to the original equipment handlebar. When installing an aftermarket handlebar, refer to the manufacturer's instructions for additional information.

Removal

1. Support the motorcycle on a workstand.
2. Remove the number plate (**Figure 1**).
3. Remove the handlebar crossbar pad if used.
4. Remove the clamps (A, **Figure 2**) securing the engine stop switch wiring harness to the handlebar.
5. Remove the screw, ground cable and the engine stop switch (B, **Figure 2**).
6. Remove the screws, holder and the clutch lever bracket (C, **Figure 2**). Do not disconnect the clutch cable unless necessary.

NOTE
The handlebar can be removed without having to disassemble the throttle housing.

7A. If the throttle housing will not be disassembled, loosen, but do not remove, the throttle housing screws (A, **Figure 3**). Slide the housing off when removing the handlebar.
7B. If the throttle housing will be disassembled, perform the following:
   a. Remove the throttle housing screws (A, **Figure 3**) and separate the housing.
   b. Disconnect the throttle cable from the throttle tube (**Figure 4**).
   c. Remove the throttle tube and grip from the handlebar.
8. Remove the screws, holder and brake lever (B, **Figure 3**).
9. Remove the upper handlebar holder bolts (A, **Figure 5**) and the upper holders (B). Remove the handlebar while sliding the throttle housing off the handlebar (if still assembled).
10. Perform the *Inspection* in this section.

Replacement Handlebar

Before installing an aftermarket handlebar, refer to the manufacturer's instructions, while noting the following:
1. Remove the stickers from the handlebar with solvent. Do not nick or damage the handlebar.
2. When installing aluminum bars, radius the handlebar holder and both clutch and brake clamp edges with a file. Remove the sharp edges from each hole opening. Do not remove a lot of material.

11

3. The handlebar width can be adjusted by cutting the ends off with a hacksaw. When doing so, cut small, equal amounts from both ends until the desired width is achieved. To ensure a straight cut, wrap a strip of electrical tape around the handlebar and use one edge as a cutting guide. Chamfer the edges to remove any burrs or roughness that could damage the left grip or interfere with throttle operation.

Installation

1. Lightly lubricate the right side of the handlebar where the throttle tube operates with a light-weight oil. Do not lubricate the area under the throttle housing clamp.

2. If the throttle housing was not disassembled, slide the throttle housing over the handlebar and place the handlebar into the lower clamps. Install the upper holders (A, **Figure 6**) with their punch mark facing forward and install the mounting bolts finger-tight. To set the handlebar to its stock mounting position, align its punch mark with the lower clamp surface on the upper fork bridge (B, **Figure 6**).

3. Tighten the front mounting bolts to hold the handlebar in place, then check the handlebar position while sitting and standing on the pegs. The handlebar should be comfortable in both positions. These positions can be confirmed when test riding the motorcycle.

4. Tighten the front handlebar bolts first, then tighten the rear bolts. Check that the gap between the upper holders is at the back (C, **Figure 6**).

> *WARNING*
> *Do not ride the motorcycle until the handlebar clamps are mounted and tightened correctly. Improper mounting may cause the bars to slip, resulting in loss of control.*

5. If the throttle housing was disassembled, perform the following:
   a. Lightly grease the throttle cable end.
   b. Reconnect the throttle cable onto the throttle tube as shown in **Figure 4**.
   c. Install the throttle cover (A, **Figure 3**) and tighten the screws finger-tight.

6. Align the clamp mating surface on the throttle housing with the punch mark (A, **Figure 7**) on the handlebar. Tighten the upper screw first, then tighten the lower screw. Tighten both screws securely. Open and release the throttle grip, making sure it returns smoothly. Then turn the handlebar and check the throttle operation in both lock positions.

7. Install the front brake lever bracket (B, **Figure 3**). Install the clamp with its punch mark (B, **Figure 7**) facing up. Align bracket and clamp mating surface

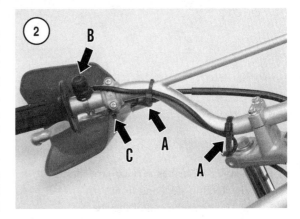

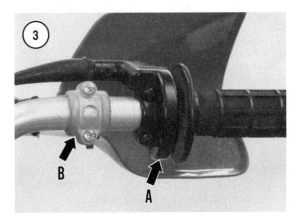

with the punch mark on the handlebar (C, **Figure 7**). Tighten the upper screw first, then the lower screw.

8. Install the clutch lever bracket (C, **Figure 2**). Install the clamp with its punch mark facing up. Align the bracket and clamp surface with the punch mark on the handlebar. Tighten the upper screw first, then the lower screw.

9. Install the engine stop switch (B, **Figure 2**) and its ground cable. Align the clamp mating surfaces with the punch mark on the handlebar. Tighten the screw securely.

10. Secure the engine stop switch wiring harness to the handlebar with the clamps (A, **Figure 2**).

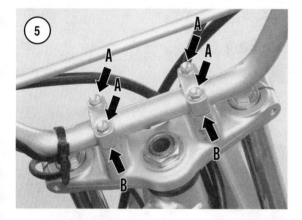

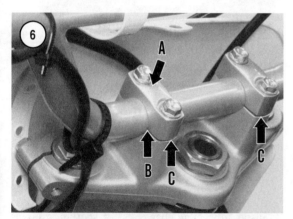

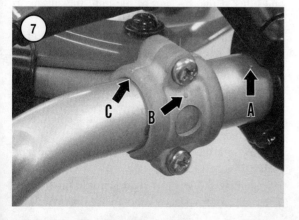

11. Install the number plate (**Figure 1**).

12. Sit on the motorcycle and recheck the riding position. Adjust the handlebar and controls, if necessary. Note the following:

    a. Position the control levers and engine stop switch so they can be operated when seated and standing.

    b. Turn the handlebar from side-to-side to check both cables for binding.

Inspection

1. Do not clean the handlebars with any cleaner that will leave an oil residue. When cleaning the clamp area and holders, use solvent or an electrical contact cleaner.

2. Inspect the handlebar for scores or cracks, especially at the handlebar, throttle and operating lever clamp mounting areas on aluminum handlebars. If *any* damage is found, replace the handlebar. Cracks and scoring of the metal in these areas may cause the handlebar to break.

> *WARNING*
> *Never attempt to repair a damaged handlebar. These attempts can weaken the handlebar and may cause it to break while under stress or during a crash.*

3. Inspect the handlebar mounting bolts for bending and damaged threads. Check the threaded holes in the upper fork bridge for the same conditions. Clean the threads to remove all dirt and grease residue. Replace rounded or damaged bolts.

4. Clean the upper and lower handlebar holders with a stiff brush and solvent or electrical contact cleaner. Clean the clamp area on aluminum handlebars with solvent or contact cleaner and a soft brush. Clean the knurled clamp area on steel handlebars with a brush and solvent or contact cleaner.

11

HANDLEBAR GRIP

Removal/Installation

Different methods are available to remove handlebar grips, depending on the condition of the grips and whether they will be reused. Use contact cleaner and compressed air to remove the grips if they are to be reused. If the grips are torn and damaged, it may be possible to push them off by hand. This section lists some different ways on removing grips. While some riders cut the grips off, the tool can score the throttle tube or the aluminum handlebar (if used), so use caution if this method is used. Replace the grips with the handlebar installed on the motorcycle.

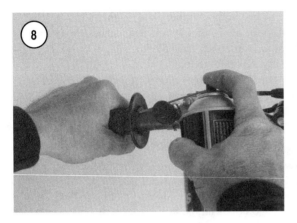

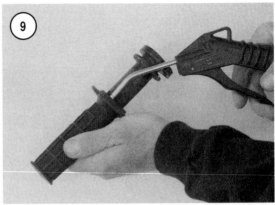

NOTE
When removing handlebar grips that are in good condition, it is best to use a technique that pushes or slides them off the handlebar. Trying to pull a grip off the handlebar stretches the grip and tightens it against the handlebar.

1. If the grips are to be reused, note any alignment marks on the grips or make your own.

2. If the grips are torn and damaged, grab the inner grip flange and pull it off the handlebar or throttle tube, inside out.

3. If cutting the grips, carefully cut through the grip flange and pull it back to expose the handlebar or throttle pipe. Continue to pull the grip away from the handlebar or throttle pipe while cutting it lengthwise. Pulling the grip will help to prevent the blade from contacting the handlebar or throttle pipe. After cutting the grip, spread it and pull it off, inside out.

4. To remove the left grip so it can be reused, insert a thin screwdriver between the grip and handlebar. Work carefully to prevent tearing the grip or gouging the handlebar. Then squirt contact cleaner into the open area under the grip (**Figure 8**). Immediately remove the screwdriver and turn the grip by hand to break the adhesive bond between the grip and handlebar, then push or slide the grip off. If necessary, repeat this step at different points around the grip until it slides off.

5. To remove the right grip from the throttle tube so it can be reused:
   a. Make sure the grip is in good condition. This technique will not work on cut or damaged grips.
   b. Disconnect the throttle cable and remove the throttle tube as described in *Removal* in *Handlebar* in this chapter.
   c. Insert the nozzle from an air gun between the grip and throttle tube and carefully blow the grip slowly off the throttle pipe (**Figure 9**).

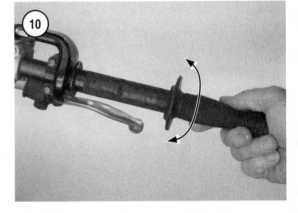

6. Remove grip adhesive from the handlebar and throttle tube with solvent or WD-40. Then clean with contact cleaner to remove any oil residue.

7. Inspect the throttle tube for any cracks and damage and replace if necessary.

CAUTION
Do not install a new grip over a damaged or broken throttle tube. The glue will leak through and stick to the handlebar and the inner throttle tube surfaces.

8. Inspect the handlebar ends for scoring, grooves and other damage. Sand or file until the surface is smooth.

9. Reinstall the throttle pipe (without the new grip) and the throttle cable as described in *Installation* in *Handlebar* in this chapter.

10. Some aftermarket grips are directional as to how they mount on the handlebar and throttle tube. Check the grips and manufacturer's instructions before installing them.

11. Recheck the riding position and adjust the handlebar, if necessary.

12. Identify the left and right (throttle tube) grips. The right side grip has a larger inside diameter.

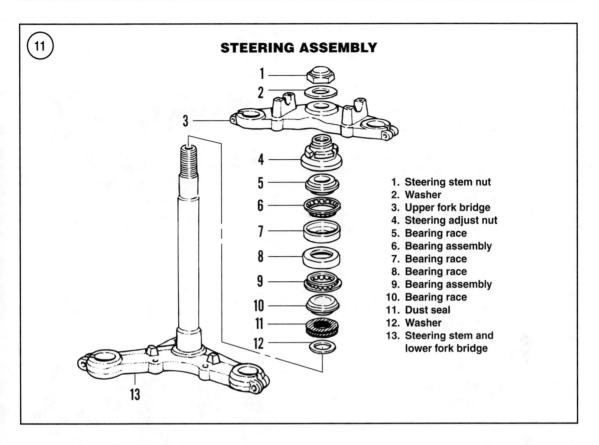

STEERING ASSEMBLY

1. Steering stem nut
2. Washer
3. Upper fork bridge
4. Steering adjust nut
5. Bearing race
6. Bearing assembly
7. Bearing race
8. Bearing race
9. Bearing assembly
10. Bearing race
11. Dust seal
12. Washer
13. Steering stem and lower fork bridge

NOTE
Make sure the grip cement is applicable for the grips being installed. ThreeBond GRIPLOCK (1501C) and Honda Hand Grip Cement can be used on most grips. However, a specific grip cement may be required when installing Gel grips and other soft compound grips. Use Renthal Grip Glue when installing soft or medium-compound Renthal grips. Always refer to the manufacturer's instructions for application and drying time.

13. Install the grips as follows:
   a. Cover the hole in the end of the throttle tube with duct tape to prevent the cement from contacting the handlebar and inner throttle tube surface.
   b. If hidden end caps are to be used, install them into the handlebar ends before installing the grips.
   c. Apply grip cement to the inside surface of the grip and to the grip contact surface on the left side of the handlebar or on the throttle tube.
   d. Install the grip with a twisting motion (**Figure 10**) to spread the cement evenly. Then quickly align the grip with the handlebar or throttle tube. Squeeze the outer end of the left grip to make sure it contacts the end of the handlebar.

For the right grip, make sure there is small gap between the grip and the throttle housing, and the grip contacts the end of the throttle pipe.
14. Observe the grip cement manufacturer's drying time recommendations before riding the motorcycle.

STEERING HEAD

The steering head (**Figure 11**) pivots on either loose or caged ball bearings. The inner bearing races (mounted in the frame) and the outer bearing race (mounted on the steering stem) should not be removed unless they require replacement.

Remove the steering stem and lubricate the bearings at the intervals specified in Chapter Three.

Tools

A number of different tools can be used to loosen and tighten the steering adjust nut (4, **Figure 11**):
1. Steering stem socket wrench (A, **Figure 12** [Honda part No. 07916-3710100 or 07916-3710101] or equivalent).
2. Spanner wrenches (B and C, **Figure 12**). Note that the spanner wrench with the square hole (B, **Figure 12**) can be used with a torque wrench to tighten the steering adjust nut during assembly.

3. When used carefully, a punch and hammer can be used to turn the steering adjust nut during disassembly and adjustment.

Disassembly

NOTE
When troubleshooting a steering complaint, check the steering adjustment before removing the front forks and steering assembly.

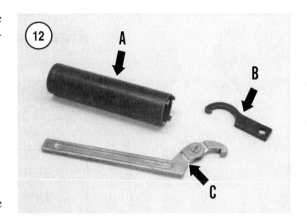

1. Note the cable and wiring harness routing before removing them in the following steps.
2. Remove the front wheel (Chapter Ten).
3. Remove the front fender (Chapter Fourteen).
4. Remove the handlebar as described in this chapter.
5. Loosen the steering stem nut (A, **Figure 13**).
6. Remove the front forks as described in this chapter.
7. Remove the steering stem nut (A, **Figure 13**) and washer.
8. Remove the upper fork bridge (B, **Figure 13**).

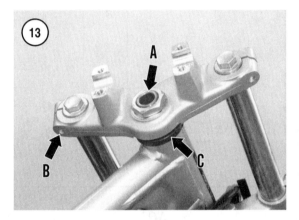

NOTE
If a spanner wrench is not available when performing Step 9, loosen the nut by tapping against its notches with a punch and hammer.

9. Loosen the steering adjust nut (**Figure 14**).

CAUTION
Hold the up the steering stem so it cannot drop out while performing the following steps.

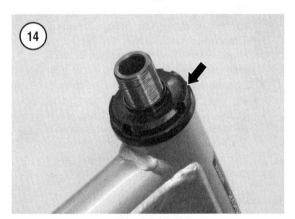

10. Remove the steering adjust nut (**Figure 14**), then lower and remove the steering stem (**Figure 15**).
11. Remove the upper bearing race (5, **Figure 11**) and individual ball bearings or the caged bearing (6).
12. Remove the bearings (A, **Figure 16**) or the caged bearing assembly (B) from the steering stem.
13. Perform the *Inspection* in this section.

Assembly and Steering Adjustment

Refer to **Figure 11**.
1. Make sure the upper and lower bearing races are properly seated in the frame.
2. Make sure the lower bearing race is properly seated on the steering stem.
3. Lubricate the bearing races with a waterproof bearing grease.
4A. If using individual ball bearings, install the bearings around the upper and lower bearing races. Each

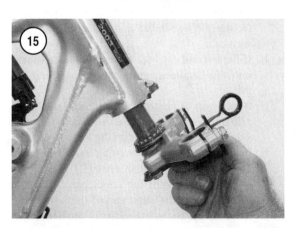

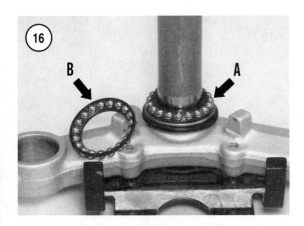

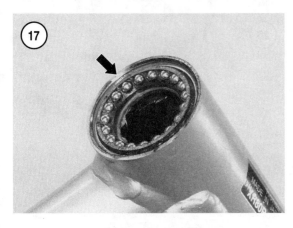

race uses 21 ball bearings. Apply additional water-proof bearing grease over the bearings with a brush.

4B. If using caged bearings, perform the following:

a. Lubricate the caged bearing assemblies with waterproof bearing grease.

b. Install the lower bearing over the steering stem and seat it against its race as shown in A, **Figure 16**.

c. Install the upper bearing (B, **Figure 16**) and seat it into its race as shown in **Figure 17**.

5. Install the steering stem (**Figure 15**) through the bottom of the frame and hold it in place.

6. Install the upper bearing race and seat it against the bearing (**Figure 18**).

7. Spray electrical contact cleaner on a rag and use it to wipe grease off the steering stem threads. Allow the threads to dry.

8. Install the steering adjust nut (**Figure 14**) and tighten finger-tight.

NOTE
Two methods are provided for adjust-ing the steering stem bearings when assembling the steering assembly. Step 9A requires special tools and Step 9B does not.

NOTE
In Step 9A and Step 9B, the steering ad-just nut must be tight enough to remove play, both horizontal and vertical, yet loose enough so the steering assembly can turn to both lock positions without any excessive play.

9A. To seat the bearings using the steering stem sock-et wrench (A, **Figure 12**), perform the following:

a. Initially tighten the steering adjust nut (**Figure 14**) to 25 N•m (18 ft.-lb.).

b. Turn the steering stem from lock-to-lock five times to seat the bearings. The steering stem must pivot smoothly with no binding or rough-ness

c. Loosen the steering adjust nut completely.

d. Retighten the steering adjust nut to 2 N•m (18 in.-lb.) on 1992-2003 models or 2.5 N•m (22 in.-lb.) on 2004-on models.

e. Repeat substep b to check steering play.

NOTE
It is difficult to adjust steering play to a specific torque specification as there are many variables that come into play. If the steering stem is still too loose or tight after performing Step 9A, readjust it as described in Step 9B.

9B. If the tools described in Step 9A are not avail-able, tighten the steering adjust nut as follows:

a. Tighten the steering adjust nut (**Figure 14**) to seat the bearings. Turn the steering stem five times to seat the bearings, then loosen the nut completely.

b. Tighten the steering adjust nut while checking bearing play.

10. Install the upper fork bridge (B, **Figure 13**).

11. Install the washer and the steering stem nut (A, **Figure 13**). Tighten the nut finger-tight.

12. Slide both fork tubes into position and tighten the upper and lower fork tube pinch bolts so the forks cannot slide out. Do not overtighten these bolts.

11

13. Tighten the steering stem nut (A, **Figure 13**) to 74 N•m (55 ft.-lb.).

> *NOTE*
> *Because tightening the steering stem nut affects the steering bearing preload, it may be necessary to repeat these steps several times until the steering adjustment is correct.*

14. Check bearing play by turning the steering stem from side to side. The steering stem must pivot smoothly. If the steering stem adjustment is incorrect, readjust the bearing play as follows:

   a. Loosen the steering stem nut (A, **Figure 13**).

   b. Using a punch and hammer, loosen or tighten the steering adjust nut (C, **Figure 13**) as required to adjust the steering play.

   c. Retighten the steering stem nut (A, **Figure 13**) to 74 N•m (55 ft.-lb.).

   d. Recheck bearing play by turning the steering stem from side-to-side. If the play feels correct, turn the steering stem so the front forks are facing straight ahead. While an assistant steadies the motorcycle, grasp the fork tubes, and try to move them front to back. If there is play and the bearing adjustment feels correct, the bearings and races are probably worn and require replacement.

15. Position the fork tubes and tighten the fork tube pinch bolts as described in this chapter.

16. Install the handlebar as described in this chapter.

17. Install the front fender (Chapter Fourteen).

18. Install the front wheel (Chapter Ten).

19. After 30 minutes to 1 hour of riding time, check the steering adjustment. If necessary, adjust as described in *Steering Play Check and Adjustment* in this chapter.

Inspection

Replace worn or damaged parts as described in this chapter. If sufficient damage is noted with any steering component, have a dealership check the frame and steering assembly.

> *NOTE*
> *Steering bearings are usually damaged from a lack of lubrication and incorrect adjustment. A loose steering adjustment increases clearance between bearings and races. High shock loads received from off-road use pounds the bearings into the races and damages them. Over-tightening the bearing adjustment will also damage the bearings and races.*

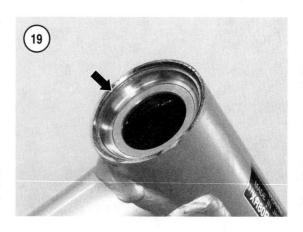

1. Clean the bearings and races in solvent.

2. Clean the steering stem, steering adjust nut and steering stem nut threads thoroughly to ensure accurate torque readings and steering adjustment during reassembly.

3. Check the steering head frame welds for cracks and fractures. Refer repair to a qualified frame shop or welding service.

4. Check the steering stem nut and steering adjust nut for damage.

5. Check the steering stem and upper fork bridge for cracks and damage. Check the steering stem for straightness.

6. Check the bearing races (**Figure 19**) in the frame for dimples, pitting, galling and impact damage. If a race is worn or damaged, replace both races and bearings as described in this chapter.

7. Check the individual ball bearings (B, **Figure 16**) and the caged bearings (A) for flat spots, pitting, wear and other damage. Check the bearing cage for cracks. Replace bearings and races as a set if damage is noted as described in this chapter.

8. When reusing bearings, clean them thoroughly with a degreaser. Pack the caged bearings with waterproof bearing grease.

9. Check the front fender mounting bracket mounting bolts (**Figure 20**) for looseness. Tighten the bolts securely.

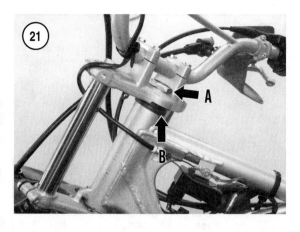

10. If so equipped, check the number plate mounting bracket on the upper fork bridge for tightness. Tighten the mounting bolts securely.

STEERING PLAY CHECK AND ADJUSTMENT

Steering adjustment takes up any slack in the steering stem and bearings and allows the steering stem to operate with free rotation. Any excessive play or roughness in the steering stem will make the steering imprecise and difficult and cause bearing damage. Improper bearing lubrication or an incorrect steering adjustment usually causes these conditions. Incorrect clutch and throttle cable routing can also effect steering operation.

1. Support the motorcycle with the front wheel off the ground.
2. Turn the handlebar from side to side. The steering stem should move freely and without any binding or roughness. If it feels like the bearings are catching, the bearings and races are probably damaged.
3. Turn the handlebar so the front wheel points straight ahead. Alternately push slightly one end of the handlebar and then the other. The front end must turn to each side from center under its own weight. Note the following:
   a. If the steering stem moved roughly or stopped before hitting the frame stop, check the clutch and throttle cable routing. Reroute the cable(s) if necessary.
   b. If the cable routing is correct and the steering is tight, the steering adjustment is too tight or the bearings require lubrication or replacement.
   c. If the steering stem moved from side to side correctly, perform Step 4 to check for excessive looseness.

NOTE
When checking for excessive steering play, have an assistant steady the motorcycle.

4. Grasp the fork tubes firmly near the axle and attempt to move the wheel front to back. Note the following:
   a. If movement can be felt at the steering stem, the steering adjustment is probably loose. Go to Step 5 to adjust the steering.
   b. If there is no movement and the front end turns correctly as described in Steps 2-4, the steering adjustment is correct.
5. Loosen the steering stem nut (A, **Figure 21**).
6. Use a punch and hammer to adjust the steering adjust nut (B, **Figure 21**) as follows:
   a. If the steering is too loose, tighten the steering adjust nut.
   b. If the steering is too tight, loosen the steering adjust nut.
7. Tighten the steering stem nut (A, **Figure 21**) to 74 N•m (55 ft.-lb.).
8. Recheck the steering adjustment as described in this procedure.

NOTE
Because tightening the steering stem nut affects the steering bearing pre-load, it may be necessary to repeat Steps 5-8 a few times until the steering adjustment is correct. If the steering adjustment cannot be corrected, the steering bearings may require lubrication or are damaged. Remove the steering stem and inspect the bearings as described in this chapter.

STEERING HEAD BEARING RACES

The steering head bearing races (**Figure 19**, typical) are pressed into the frame's steering neck and on the steering stem. Do not remove the bearing races unless they require replacement.

Steering Neck Bearing Race Removal/Installation

Replace both bearing races and bearings at the same time.

CAUTION
If binding occurs when removing or installing a bearing race, stop and release tension from the race. Check the tool alignment to make sure the bearing race is moving evenly in its mounting bore. Otherwise, the race may gouge the frame mounting bore and cause permanent damage.

11

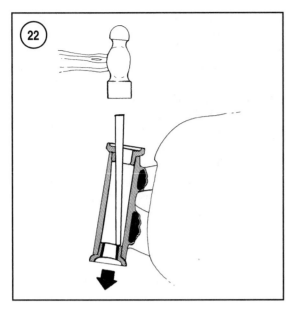

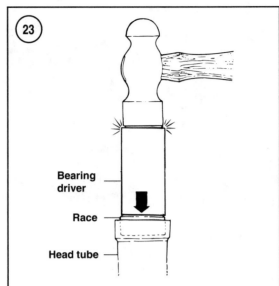

1. Insert a punch into the frame neck (**Figure 22**) and tap the race out from the inside. After it is started, tap around the race so that neither the race nor the steering neck is damaged.

2. Repeat for the other bearing race.

3. Clean the steering neck and check the race bore for corrosion, cracks and other damage.

4. Place the race squarely in the bore with its tapered side facing out.

NOTE
The bearing driver used must have an outside diameter slightly smaller than the bearing so it can install the bearing without contacting the frame's steering neck.

NOTE
When installing the bearing race, start slowly and check the progress often to make sure the race enters and moves squarely into the bore.

5. Install the race by tapping it squarely with a bearing driver (**Figure 23**) or use a threaded rod tool as shown in **Figure 24**. The race (**Figure 19**) must seat fully and squarely in the steering neck.

6. Repeat for the other bearing race.

Steering Stem Lower Bearing Race Removal/Installation

Perform the following steps to replace the lower steering stem bearing race, dust seal and washer (**Figure 25**).

1. Unbolt and remove the front fender mounting bracket (**Figure 20**).

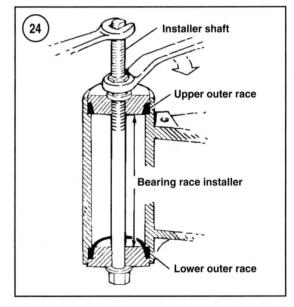

2. Thread the steering stem nut onto the steering stem (**Figure 26**).

WARNING
Wear safety glasses when removing the bearing race.

3. Remove the bearing race with a hammer and chisel as shown in **Figure 26**. Strike the race at different points to prevent it from binding on the steering stem. When the bearing race is free, remove the steering stem nut, race, dust seal and washer.

4. Clean the steering stem with solvent and dry thoroughly.

5. Inspect the steering stem and bearing race mounting surface for damage.

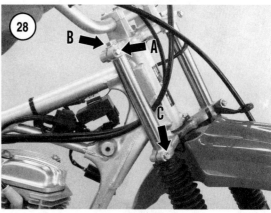

26 Steering stem nut

Steering stem

Chisel

Dust seal and bottom race

27

C

A

B

FRONT FORK

Removal

1. Remove the number plate.
2. Remove the front wheel (Chapter Ten).
3. If the fork tube is going to be disassembled, perform the following:

> *NOTE*
> *The Allen bolt installed inside the bottom of the slider may be difficult to remove because the damper rod will turn inside the slider. The difficulty increases if a threadlocking compound was used on the bolt during its installation. It is easier to loosen the Allen bolt while the fork is assembled and mounted on the motorcycle. However, care should be taken to avoid stripping or rounding the hex recess inside the Allen bolt. When this happens, the only recourse is to drill the bolt head off the bolt.*

a. Clean the Allen bolt's recess in the bottom of the slider so the hex socket can grip the bolt fully. If it appears the bolt's recess is rounded or otherwise damaged, apply valve lapping compound inside the recess to increase the hex socket's grip against the bolt.
b. Install the front axle through both sliders (A, **Figure 27**) to prevent them from turning.
c. Loosen, but do not remove, the fork tube Allen bolt with a 6 mm hex socket and breaker bar (B, **Figure 27**).

4. Loosen the upper fork tube pinch bolt (A, **Figure 28**).
5. If the fork will be serviced, loosen, but do not remove, the fork cap (B, **Figure 28**) while the fork tube is mounted on the motorcycle.
6. Loosen the lower fork tube pinch bolt (C, **Figure 28**) and remove the fork tube. If necessary, rotate the fork tube while pulling it down and out.

6. Install the washer (12, **Figure 11**).
7. Lubricate the new dust seal lip (11, **Figure 11**) with grease and slide it over the steering stem.
8. Slide the new bearing race onto the steering stem with the tapered side facing up until it stops.
9. Slide a bearing driver over the steering stem until it seats against the bearing race inner shoulder. Make sure the driver does not contact the bearing surface. Drive the bearing race onto the steering stem until it bottoms (**Figure 25**).
10. Reinstall the front fender mounting bracket (**Figure 20**) and tighten the bolts securely.

11

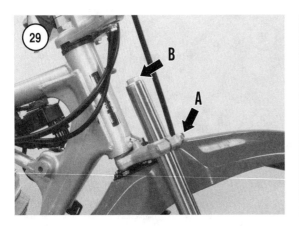

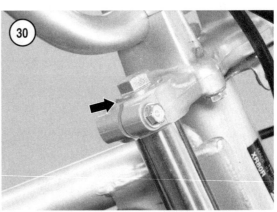

7. Remove, clean and inspect the fork tube pinch bolts. Replace damaged bolts.

Installation

> *CAUTION*
> *Do not overtighten the fork tube pinch bolts in the following steps. Excessive tightening can permanently deform the fork tube.*

> *NOTE*
> *Install the fork tube with the brake anchor boss (C, Figure 27) on the left side.*

1. Loosen the fork boot hose clamp and slide the boot down slightly so it does not interfere with fork installation.
2. If the fork cap is loose, install the fork tube partway and tighten the lower pinch bolt (A, **Figure 29**). Then tighten the fork cap (B, **Figure 29**) to 23 N•m models (17 ft.-lb.). Loosen the pinch bolt and continue with Step 3.
3. Install and position the fork tube so the top of the fork tube is flush with the upper fork bridge (**Figure 30**). Tighten the lower fork tube pinch bolt (C, **Figure 28**) to 26 N•m (19 ft.-lb.).
4. Tighten the upper fork tube pinch bolt (A, **Figure 28**) to 11 N•m (97 in.-lb.) on 1992-2003 models and 18 N•m (13 ft.-lb.) on 2004-on models.
5. Slide the fork boot up until it just contacts the lower fork bridge and tighten its hose clamp securely.
6. Repeat for the other fork tube.
7. If the Allen bolts in the bottom of the sliders are loose, reinstall the front axle through both sliders (A, **Figure 27**) and tighten as follows:
   a. 1992-1997 models: Tighten the Allen bolts securely.
   b. 1998-on models: Tighten the Allen bolts to 20 N•m (15 ft.-lb.).
8. Install the front wheel (Chapter Ten).

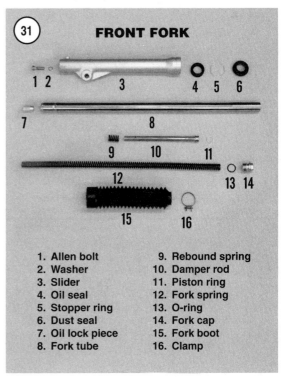

FRONT FORK

1. Allen bolt
2. Washer
3. Slider
4. Oil seal
5. Stopper ring
6. Dust seal
7. Oil lock piece
8. Fork tube
9. Rebound spring
10. Damper rod
11. Piston ring
12. Fork spring
13. O-ring
14. Fork cap
15. Fork boot
16. Clamp

9. Install the number plate.

FORK SERVICE

Disassembly

This section describes complete disassembly of the fork tubes. If only changing the fork oil and/or setting the oil level, begin at Step 1 and follow the required steps listed in the text.

Refer to **Figure 31**.

1. Remove the fork tube as described in *Removal* in *Front Fork* in this chapter.
2. Remove the fork boot from the fork tube. If necessary, spray a small amount of WD-40 or equivalent near the end of boot to help slide it off the fork tube.

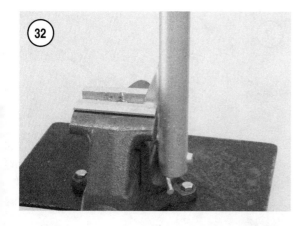

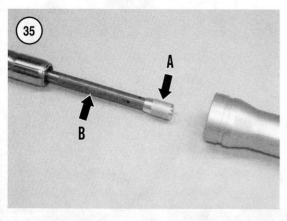

NOTE
When necessary to hold or support the fork assembly in this procedure, clamp the slider across its axle boss in a vise with soft jaws **(Figure 32).** *Do not clamp the fork tube or the slider body.*

3. If not loosened in Step 3 of *Removal* in *Front Fork* in this chapter, and the fork tube will be disassembled, loosen the Allen bolt in the bottom of the slider. Disregard this step if only changing the fork oil or setting the oil level.

WARNING
Be careful when removing the fork cap as the fork cap and spring is under pressure. If the fork tube is bent and compressed, the pressure on these parts will be greater.

NOTE
The fork cap was loosened during fork removal.

4. With the slider mounted in a vise, pull the fork tube up with one hand and slowly unscrew and remove the fork cap (**Figure 33**) and its O-ring.
5. Lower the fork tube and place a plastic tie (**Figure 34**) on the top of the fork spring to identity its upper end and remove the spring.
6. Turn the fork tube over a drain pan and pour out the fork oil by operating the fork tube several times.

NOTE
If only changing the fork oil and/or setting the oil level, refer to **Fork Oil Adjustment** *in this section. If disassembling the fork, continue with Step 7.*

7. Remove the Allen bolt, previously loosened, and washer from the base of the slider. Discard the washer.
8. Hold the fork tube and remove the slider from the bottom side. Remove the oil lock piece (A, **Figure 35**) from the end of the damper rod or retrieve it from inside the slider.
9. Turn the fork tube over and slide out the damper rod (A, **Figure 36**) and rebound spring (B).
10. Support the slider vertically in a vise with soft jaws (**Figure 32**).
11. Remove the dust seal (**Figure 37**) from the top of the slider.
12. Remove the stopper ring (**Figure 38**) from the groove in the slider.
13. If the oil seal is leaking oil or otherwise damaged, remove it as follows:

11

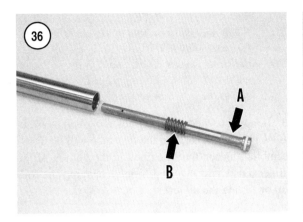

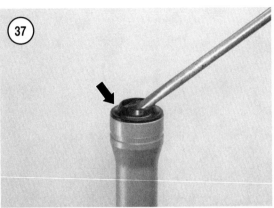

CAUTION
Remove the oil seal carefully to avoid
damaging the slider. Depending on the
condition of the seal, it may be difficult
to remove.

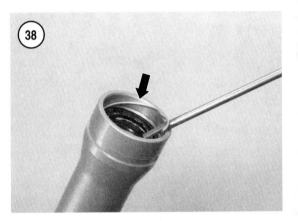

a. If available, use a seal removal tool as shown in **Figure 39**. Pad the area underneath the tool to avoid damaging the slider.

b. If a seal removal tool is unavailable, remove the seal by prying it out with a wide-blade screwdriver (**Figure 40**). Pad the area underneath the tool to avoid damaging the slider. Loosen the seal by working the screwdriver around the seal. Do not use excessive force when prying the seal out or allow the tip of the screwdriver to contact and gouge the slider bore.

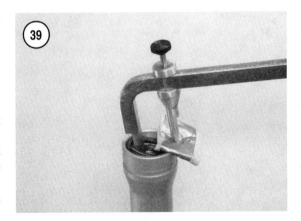

14. Inspect as described in this section.

Assembly

1. Before assembly, make sure there is no solvent left in the slider or on any part.

2. Pour some fork oil on a small cloth and run it through the inside of the fork tube to lubricate the inside wall. Make sure to remove the cloth.

3. Lubricate the piston ring on the damper rod with fork oil.

4. Install the rebound spring (B, **Figure 36**) onto the damper rod (A). Slide the damper rod assembly (B, **Figure 35**) through the fork tube.

5. Install the oil lock piece (A, **Figure 35**) onto the end of the damper rod (B).

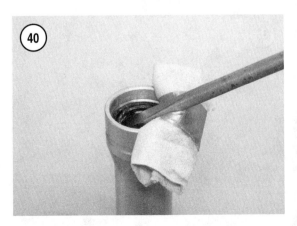

6. Install the fork tube into the slider until the oil lock piece bottoms against the bottom of the slider.

7. Mount the slider horizontally in a vise with soft jaws (**Figure 32**).

8. Install a new washer on the Allen bolt.

9. Make sure all old threadlocking compound is cleaned from the Allen bolt and the damper rod. Then apply a medium strength threadlocking compound onto the fork tube Allen bolt threads and thread the

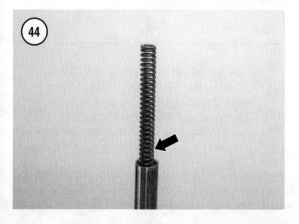

Allen bolt into the bottom of the damper rod and tighten until the damper rod starts to turn.

10. Temporarily install the fork spring and fork cap to apply tension against the damper rod.

11A. On 1992-1997 models, securely tighten the fork tube Allen bolt.

11B. On 1998-on models, tighten the fork tube Allen bolt to 20 N•m (15 ft.-lb.)

12. Remove the fork cap and fork spring.

13. If the oil seal was removed, install a new seal as follows:

   a. Lubricate the seal lip with fork oil and slide it down the fork tube with its closed side facing up (**Figure 41**). Center the seal in the top of the slider.

   b. Drive the seal into the slider using a suitable fork seal driver tool (**Figure 42**) until the stopper ring groove can be seen above the top surface of the oil seal.

14. Slide the stopper ring over the fork tube and install it into the groove in the slider (**Figure 43**). Make sure the stopper ring is completely seated in the slider groove.

NOTE
If the stopper ring cannot seat completely into the slider groove, the seal may not be installed far enough into the slider.

15. Slide the dust seal down the fork tube and seat it into the slider.

16. Fill the fork with fork oil and set the oil level as described in *Fork Oil Adjustment* in this section.

17. Slowly install the fork spring with either its tapered spring end (1992-1997 models) or closer wound spring end (1998-on models [**Figure 44**]) facing down. If an aftermarket spring is installed, install it facing in its original position. If a plastic tie (**Figure 34**) was used to identify the spring, install the spring with the plastic tie end facing up. Cut and remove the plastic tie from the fork spring.

18. Install a new O-ring onto the fork cap.

19. Lubricate the fork cap O-ring with fork oil. Install the fork cap (**Figure 33**) hand tight.

NOTE
The fork cap will be tightened completely after the fork tube is installed onto the motorcycle.

20. Install the fork boot. Seat the bottom part of the boot into the groove in the top of the slider. Do not tighten the hose clamp at the top of the boot until the fork tube is installed on the motorcycle.

11

Inspection

When measuring the fork components, compare the actual measurements to the specifications in **Table 2**. Replace worn or damaged parts as described in this section.

1. Thoroughly clean all parts in solvent and dry them. Remove all threadlocking compound residue from the fork damper and Allen bolt threads.

2. Check the fork tube for severe wear or scratches. Check the chrome for flaking or other damage that could damage the oil seal.

3. Check the fork tube for straightness with a set of V-blocks and dial indicator. Refer to **Table 2** for maximum fork tube runout. Actual runout will be one-half of the gauge reading.

4. Check the slider for dents or exterior damage. Check the stopper ring groove for cracks or damage. Check the oil seal mounting bore for dents, grooves or other damage.

5. Inspect the damper rod (A, **Figure 45**) for straightness, damage or roughness. Check the threads for damage. Make sure the oil passage holes in the bottom of the rod are clear.

6. Inspect the piston ring (**Figure 46**) on the end of the damper rod for wear or damage. Replace if necessary.

7. Inspect the rebound spring (B, **Figure 45**) on the damper rod for stretched coils, cracks or other damage.

8. Inspect the oil lock assembly (C, **Figure 45**) for wear or damage.

9. Measure the free length of the fork spring (**Figure 47**). Replace the spring if it is too short (**Table 2**). Replace the springs as a set if they are unequal in length.

10. Replace the fork cap O-ring if damaged or leaking.

Fork Oil Adjustment

This section describes steps on filling the fork with oil and setting the oil level.

Refer to **Table 1** for the recommended type of fork oil.

1. Remove the fork spring and drain the fork tube as described in *Disassembly* in this section.

2. Push the fork tube down and bottom out against the slider. Support the slider so it cannot tip over.

3. Slowly pour the recommended fork oil type (**Table 1**) and quantity (**Table 3**) into the fork.

> *NOTE*
> *As oil replaces air during the bleeding procedure, the oil level in the fork drops. Continue to add oil to main-*

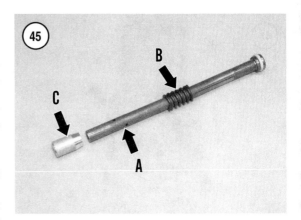

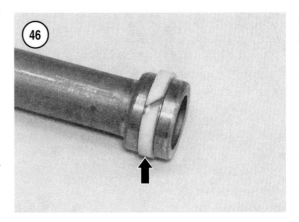

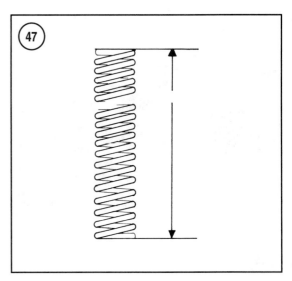

tain a high oil level in the fork. When bleeding the fork tube, do not be concerned with maintaining or achieving the proper oil capacity. Setting the oil level determines the actual amount of oil used in each fork tube.

4. Hold the slider with one hand and slowly extend the fork tube. Repeat until the fork tube moves smoothly with the same amount of tension through

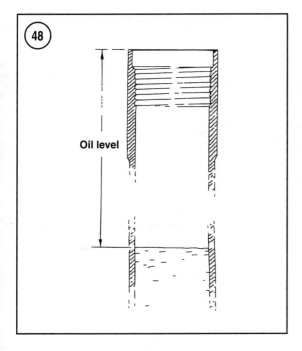

Oil level

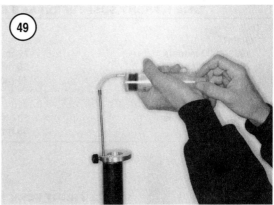

a. Make sure the fork tube is bottomed against the slider and placed in a vertical position.
b. Use an oil level gauge (**Figure 49**) and set the oil level to the specification listed in **Table 4**.

NOTE
If an oil level gauge is not available, measure down from the top of the fork tube with a ruler, using a flashlight. Either add or siphon oil from the fork until the level is correct.

the compression and rebound travel strokes. Then stop with the fork tube bottomed out.

5. Set the fork tube aside for approximately five minutes to allow any suspended air bubbles in the oil to surface.

6. Set the oil level (**Figure 48**) as follows:

c. Remove the oil level gauge.

7. Complete fork assembly as described in *Assembly* in this section.

11

Table 1 FRONT SUSPENSION AND STEERING SPECIFICATIONS

Caster angle	
XR80R	
1993-2000 models	28° 30'
2001-2003 models	27° 34'
CRF80F	28° 02'
XR100R	
1992-2000 models	28° 30'
2001-2003 models	29° 52'
CRF100F	28° 50'
Fork oil	
1992-1997 models	Automatic transmission fluid (ATF)
1998-on models	Pro Honda Suspension Fluid SS-8 or equivalent 10 wt fork oil
Front wheel travel	
XR80R	
1993-1997 models	140 mm (5.5 in.)
1998-1993 models	126 mm (5.0 in.)
CRF80R	123 mm (4.8 in.)
XR100R	
1992-2000 models	120 mm (4.7 in.)
2001-2003 models	140 mm (5.5 in.)
CRF100F	148 mm (5.83 in.)
	(continued)

Table 1 FRONT SUSPENSION AND STEERING SPECIFICATIONS (continued)

Trail	
XR80R	
1993-2000 models	75 mm (3.0 in.)
2001-2003 models	68 mm (2.7 in.)
CRF80F	74 mm (2.9 in.)
XR100R	
1992-2000 models	110 mm (4.3 in.)
2001-2003 models	103 mm (4.1 in.)
CRF100F	99 mm (3.9 in.)

Table 2 FRONT FORK SERVICE SPECIFICATIONS

	New mm (in.)	Service limit mm (in.)
Fork spring free length		
XR80R	525.2 (20.68)	514.7 (20.26)
CRF80F	531.2 (20.91)	520.7 (20.50)
XR100R		
1992-2000 models	566.0 (22.28)	554.7 (21.84)
2001-2003 models	548.0 (21.57)	537.0 (21.14)
CRF100F	546.0 (21.50)	535.0 (21.06)
Fork tube runout	–	0.20 (0.008)

Table 3   FRONT FORK OIL CAPACITY

	ml	oz.
XR80R		
1993-1997 models	83.0	2.8
1998-2003 models	80.5-85.5	2.72-2.90
CRF80F	82.5-87.5	2.80-2.96
XR100R		
1992-1997 models	88.0	3.0
1998-2000 models	85.5-90.5	2.90-3.06
2001-2003 models	83.5-88.5	2.82-3.00
CRF100F	81.5-86.5	2.76-2.92

Table 4 FRONT FORK OIL LEVEL

	mm	in.
XR80R	184	7.24
CRF80F	177	6.97
XR100R		
1992-2000 models	205	8.07
2001-2003 models	200	7.87
CRF100F	207	8.15

Table 5 FRONT FORK AND STEERING TORQUE SPECIFICATIONS

	N•m	in.-lb.	ft.-lb.
Fork Allen bolt[1]			
1998-on models	20	–	15

(continued)

Table 5 FRONT FORK AND STEERING TORQUE SPECIFICATIONS (continued)

	N•m	in.-lb.	ft.-lb.
Fork cap	23	–	17
Front fork pinch bolts			
Upper			
1992-2003 models	11	97	–
2004-on models	18	–	13
Lower	26	–	19
Handlebar clamp bolts	12	106	–
Steering adjust nut[2]			
Initial torque to seat bearings	25	–	18
Final torque			
1992-2003 models	2	18	–
2004-on models	2.5	22	–
Steering stem nut	74	–	55

1. If removed, apply medium-strength threadlocking compound.
2. Refer to text.

11

CHAPTER TWELVE

REAR SUSPENSION

This chapter describes service procedures for the rear shock absorber, shock linkage assembly and swing arm.

Tables 1-3 are at the end of the chapter.

SHOCK ABSORBER

Removal/Installation

1. Support the motorcycle with the rear wheel off the ground. Then block the rear wheel so the wheel and swing arm cannot fall down when the lower shock absorber mounting bolt is removed.
2. On 1992-1997 models, remove the left side cover (Chapter Fourteen).

NOTE
Note the side the mounting bolts are installed from so they can be reinstalled facing in their original direction.

3. Remove the nut (A, **Figure 1**) and bolt securing the connecting rod to the frame. When removing the bolt, the wheel will drop to the ground.
4. Remove the lower shock absorber nut (B, **Figure 1**) and bolt. Swing the connecting rod assembly down and away from the shock absorber.

5. Remove the upper shock absorber nut (**Figure 2**) and bolt. Lower the shock absorber until it is between the swing arm. Raise the rear wheel/swing arm assembly and remove the shock absorber (**Figure 3**).
6. Service the shock spring as described in this section.
7. Installation is the reverse of removal. Note the following:
   a. Clean and dry the shock fasteners. Inspect and replace damaged fasteners.
   b. Lubricate the upper and lower mounting bolt shoulders with grease. Do not lubricate the bolt or nut threads. Clean the fastener threads with brake or contact cleaner.

NOTE
The bolt and nut threads must be clean and dry when tightened; otherwise, the threads may strip if the nuts are tightened with a torque wrench.

   c. Install the upper and lower shock mounting bolts and the connecting rod bolt from their original mounting side as noted during removal.
   d. Tighten the upper shock absorber mounting nut (**Figure 2**) to 34 N•m (25 ft.-lb.) on 1992-2000

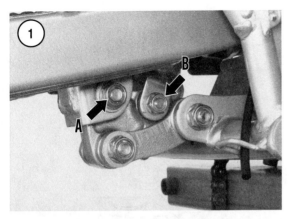

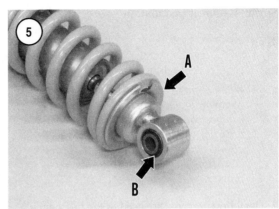

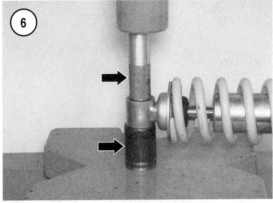

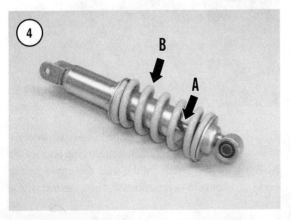

models and to 44 N•m (32 ft.-lb.) on 2001-on models.

e. Tighten the lower shock absorber mounting nut (B, **Figure 1**) to 34 N•m (25 ft.-lb.).

f. Tighten the connecting rod nut (A, **Figure 1**) to 44 N•m (32 ft.-lb.).

Shock Inspection

1. Replace the shock absorber if oil is leaking around the damper housing and rod (A, **Figure 4**). The shock cannot be rebuilt.

2. Check the damper rod (A, **Figure 4**) for bending, rust or other damage. If parts of the damper rod have turned blue, the rod is overheating, probably due to a lack of oil in the shock.

3. Inspect the shock spring (B, **Figure 4**) for cracks and other damage. The spring seat (A, **Figure 5**) at the top of the spring must seat flush against the spring.

4. Inspect the bushing (B, **Figure 5**) installed in the upper shock mount for looseness, damage and rubber deterioration. If necessary, replace the bushing with a press and suitable adapters (**Figure 6**).

5. Remove and inspect the spring as described in this section.

12

Spring Removal/Installation

Tools

> **WARNING**
> *When using an aftermarket spring removal tool, make sure the spring compressor is capable of safely compressing the spring. On these shock absorbers the spring coils are spaced close together and most spring compressors will be too large.*

The following tools are used in the procedure:
1. Holder base (Honda part No. 07967-KC10100).
2. Press attachment (Honda part No. 07LME-GE20100).

Procedure

> **WARNING**
> *Do not attempt to remove the shock spring without a shock spring compressor. The spring seat (A, **Figure 5**) is under high spring tension and can fly off and cause injury.*

1. Using two blocks, support the shock's lower spring seat in a press (**Figure 7**).
2. Mount the holder base across the spring and center the press attachment across the top of the shock and place onto the holder base (**Figure 7**). Operate the press to compress the shock spring and remove the spring seat. Then slowly release the press to release spring tension and remove the shock assembly from the press.
3. Remove the spring.
4. Measure the spring free length (**Figure 8**) and compare to the specification in **Table 2**. Note the following:
    a. On 1992-2003 models, replace the spring if it is too short.
    b. On 2004-on models, replacement springs are not available from the manufacturer. Ask a dealership if aftermarket springs are available.
5. Inspect the upper and lower spring seats for damage. The upper spring seat can be replaced separately on 1992-2003 models. The lower spring seat is permanently attached to the shock damper. If damaged, replace the shock damper assembly.
6. Hold the shock body and then compress and return the shock damper by hand. There should be more resistance on the compression stroke than on the rebound stroke. If the shock damper compression and rebound resistance is the same, replace the shock absorber.

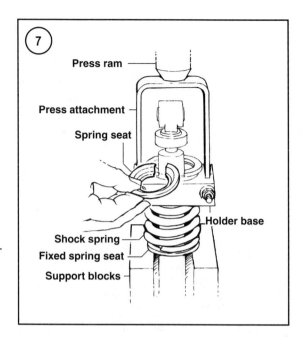

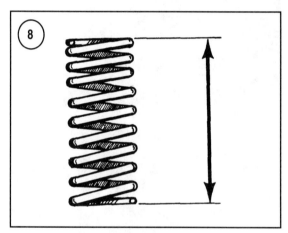

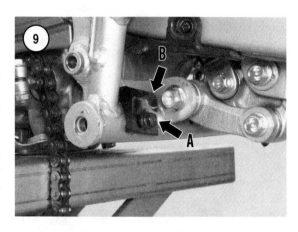

7. Using the same tools described in Step 2 to compress the shock spring, reinstall the spring and secure it with the spring seat. Make sure the upper spring seat (A, **Figure 5**) seats flush against the top of the spring.

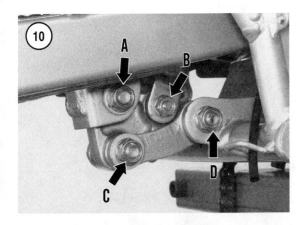

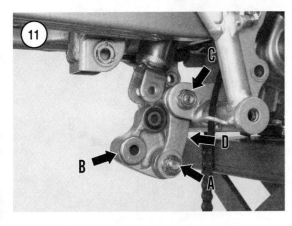

SHOCK LINKAGE

The shock linkage consists of the shock arm, connecting rod, pivot bolts, seals and bushings. Perform maintenance procedures at the intervals specified in Chapter Three.

Removal

1. Clean the shock linkage assembly.
2. Support the motorcycle with the rear wheel off the ground. Then block the rear wheel so the wheel and swing arm can not fall down when the pivot bolts are removed.
3. Remove the left footpeg/sidestand assembly (Chapter Fourteen).
4. Remove the bolt (A, **Figure 9**) and the lower chain slider (B).
5. Remove the following:

NOTE
Note the side the mounting bolts are installed from so they can be reinstalled facing in their original direction.

a. Connecting rod nut and pivot bolt (A, **Figure 10**).

b. Shock absorber nut and pivot bolt (B, **Figure 10**).
c. Shock arm nut and pivot bolt (A, **Figure 11**) securing the shock arm (B).
d. Connecting rod nut and pivot bolt (C, **Figure 11**) securing the connecting rod (D).
6. Clean and inspect the shock linkage components as described in this section.

Installation

1. Lubricate and assemble the shock linkage components as described in this section.
2. Clean and dry the pivot bolts and nuts. Lubricate the pivot bolt shafts with a waterproof grease and set aside for installation. Do not lubricate the pivot bolt and mounting nut threads. These threads must be clean and dry when tightened.

NOTE
Install the pivot bolts from the original mounting side as recorded during removal.

3. Install the connecting rod (D, **Figure 11**) with the pivot bolt and nut (C).
4. Install the shock arm (B, **Figure 11**) with the pivot bolt and nut (A).
5. Raise the shock arm and center it between the lower shock mount. Install the pivot bolt and nut (B, **Figure 10**).
6. Raise the swing arm and align its mounting hole with the shock arm and install the pivot bolt and nut (A, **Figure 10**).
7. Tighten the shock arm (A, **Figure 10**) and connecting rod (B and D) nuts to 44 N•m (33 ft.-lb.).
8. Tighten the shock arm to shock absorber mounting nut (C, **Figure 10**) to 34 N•m (25 ft.-lb.).
9. Install the lower chain slider (B, **Figure 9**) and tighten its mounting bolt (A) securely.
10. Install the left footpeg/sidestand assembly (Chapter Fourteen).

Disassembly/Cleaning /Inspection/Assembly

1. Remove the dust seal caps and collars from the shock arm (A, **Figure 12**) and connecting rod (B). Remove the seals (**Figure 13**) from both sides of the shock arm.
2. Clean and dry all parts. Remove any rust and corrosion from the pivot bolt surfaces.
3. Check the seal in each dust seal cap. If damaged, replace the dust seal cap. The seals cannot be replaced separately.
4. Inspect the bushings for cracks, scoring and excessive wear.

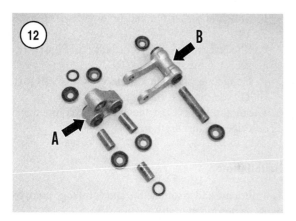

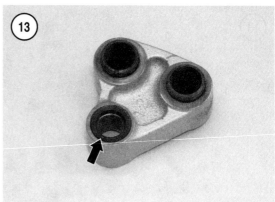

5. Perform the following:

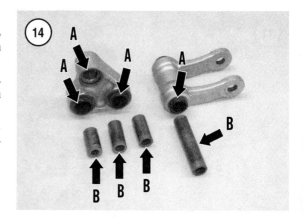

a. Measure each bushing inside diameter (A, **Figure 14**) and compare to the dimensions in **Table 2**.

b. Measure each collar outside diameter (B, **Figure 14**) and compare to the dimensions in **Table 2**.

c. Replace any part that is out of specification. Replace the bushings as described in this section.

NOTE
Use a waterproof bearing grease during assembly.

6. Lubricate the bushings and collars with grease.

7. Install new seals (**Figure 13**) into the shock arm with their closed side facing out.

8. Install the collars into the shock arm (A, **Figure 12**) and connecting rod (B).

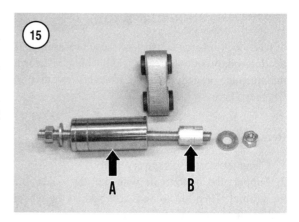

9. Lubricate the seal in each dust seal cap and install them onto the ends of the shock arm and connecting rod. The shock arm bore with the seals (**Figure 13**) does not use the dust seal caps.

10. Install the shock arm and connecting rod as described in this section.

Bushing Removal/Installation

This section describes removal and installation of the bushings installed inside the shock arm and connecting rod.

1. Measure the distance the bushings extend from the end of connecting rod bore (B, **Figure 12**). Install the new bushings to the same dimension. The shock arm bushings (A, **Figure 12**) are centered in each bore.

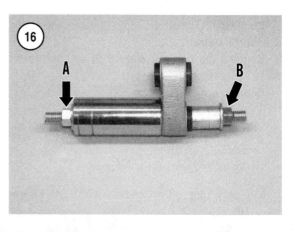

2. Assemble a threaded rod tool consisting of a length of threaded rod, two nuts, two washers, deep socket (A, **Figure 15**) that can accept the bushing and a small socket or piece of metal (B) that can be used as a bushing driver. The bushing driver must be able to pass through the bore with the bushing.

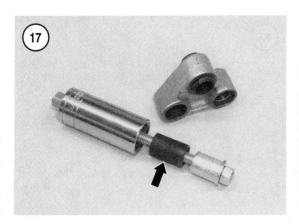

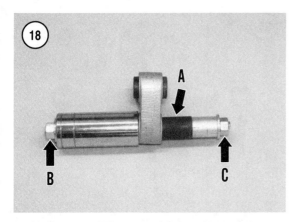

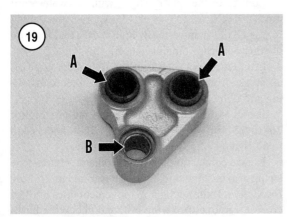

3. Assemble the threaded rod tool through the bushing (**Figure 16**) to be removed.

4. Hold the nut (A, **Figure 16**) next to the large socket and turn the opposite nut (B) to remove the bushing. Refer to **Figure 17**.

5. Clean the bushing bore and check for cracks and other damage.

6. Repeat for each bushing to be replaced.

7. Assemble the threaded rod tool along with the new bushing (A, **Figure 18**). Then hold one nut (B, **Figure 18**) and turn the other nut (C) to install the bushing. Note the following:

   a. Install the connecting rod bushings with their exposed shoulders extending the same distance recorded in Step 1.

   b. Center the nylon shock arm bushings into their bores so the exposed shoulders are equal on both sides (A, **Figure 19**). Center the bronze shock bushing (B, **Figure 19**) in its bore so there is no exposed shoulder.

12

SWING ARM

Bushing Inspection

Periodically inspect the swing arm bushings with the swing arm mounted on the motorcycle for excessive play, roughness or damage.

1. Remove the rear wheel (Chapter Ten).

2. Remove the shock arm nut and bolt (A, **Figure 10**) at the swing arm and separate the linkage from the swing arm.

3. Loosen the swing arm pivot shaft nut (A, **Figure 20**), then retighten to the specification in **Table 3**.

4. Check the swing arm bushings as follows:

   a. Have an assistant steady the motorcycle.

   b. Grasp the rear end of the swing arm (**Figure 21**) and try to move it from side to side in a horizontal arc. There should be no detectable play in the bearings.

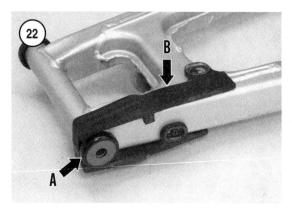

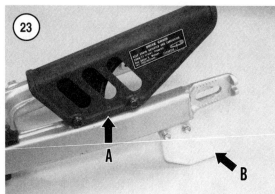

c. Pivot the rear of the swing arm up and down through its full travel. The swing arm must pivot smoothly.

d. If there is play or roughness in the bushings, remove the swing arm and inspect the bushings and pivot shaft for wear as described in this section. Inspect the swing arm bushing bores for damage.

5. Install and tighten the shock arm bolt and nut as follows:

a. Clean and dry the pivot bolt and nut. Lubricate the pivot bolt shaft with a waterproof grease. Do not lubricate the threads on the pivot bolt or the mounting nut threads. These threads must be clean and dry when tightened.

b. Install the shock arm bolt from the left side. Install the nut (A, **Figure 10**) and tighten to 44 N•m (32 ft.-lb.).

Removal

The swing arm can be removed without having to remove the shock linkage assembly.

1. Remove the rear wheel (Chapter Twelve).

2. Remove the right footpeg/rear brake pedal assembly (Chapter Fourteen).

3. Remove the master link (Chapter Ten) and remove the drive chain from the drive chain case.

4. Remove the shock arm nut and bolt (A, **Figure 10**) at the swing arm and separate the linkage from the swing arm.

5. Remove the swing arm pivot shaft nut (A, **Figure 20**), pivot shaft and swing arm (B). Locate the dust seal caps (A, **Figure 22**) if they fell off the swing arm.

6. Clean, inspect and lubricate the swing arm bushings as described in this section.

Installation

1. Lubricate and install the pivot collar and dust seal caps (A, **Figure 22**) as described in this section.

2. Lubricate the pivot shaft with a waterproof grease.

3. Install the swing arm (B, **Figure 20**), making sure the dust seal caps did not fall off.

4. Install the pivot shaft from the right side. Wipe off all grease from the pivot shaft threads before installing and tightening the nut.

5. Install and tighten the pivot shaft nut (A, **Figure 20**) to 62 N•m (46 ft.-lb.) on 1992-2000 models and to 64 N•m (47 ft.-lb.) on 2001-on models.

6. Before connecting the shock linkage, recheck the swing arm bushing operation as described in *Bushing Inspection*. If the swing arm movement does not feel correct, remove the swing arm and check the bushings and pivot collar for damage as described in this section.

7. Install and tighten the shock arm bolt and nut as follows:

a. Clean and dry the pivot bolt and nut. Lubricate the pivot bolt shaft with a waterproof grease. Do not lubricate the threads on the pivot bolt or the mounting nut threads. These threads must be clean and dry when tightened.

b. Install the shock arm bolt from the left side. Install the nut (A, **Figure 10**) and tighten to 44 N•m (32 ft.-lb.).

8. Reinstall the right footpeg/rear brake pedal assembly (Chapter Fourteen).

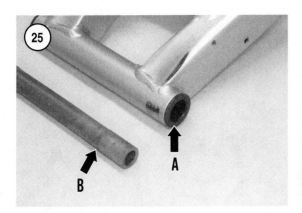

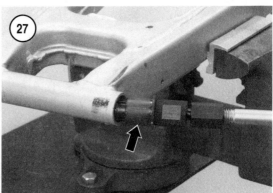

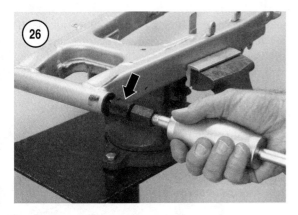

1. Clean and dry the swing arm and its components.
2. Check the seal in each dust seal cap (A, **Figure 24**). If damaged, replace the dust seal cap. The seals cannot be replaced separately.
3. Inspect the swing arm bushings (A, **Figure 25**) for cracks, scoring and excessive wear.
4. Inspect the pivot collar (B, **Figure 25**) for scoring, severe wear, rust or other damage.
5. Perform the following:
    a. Measure each swing arm bushing inside diameter (A, **Figure 25**) and compare to the dimensions in **Table 2**.
    b. Measure the pivot collar outside diameter at both bushing operating positions (B, **Figure 25**) and compare to the dimensions in **Table 2**.
    c. Replace any part that is out of specification. Replace the bushings as described in this section.
6. Check the swing arm for cracks and other damage.
7. Inspect the chain slider for damage. The slider prevents the drive chain from contacting the swing arm. Refer to Chapter Three for information on measuring the chain slider to check for excessive wear.
8. Inspect the swing arm pivot shaft for scoring, rust, bending and other damage. Install the pivot collar onto the pivot shaft and slide back and forth by hand. There must be no binding or roughness.

9. Reconnect the drive chain using a new master link (Chapter Ten).
10. Reinstall the rear wheel (Chapter Ten) and adjust the drive chain (Chapter Three).
11. Make sure the rear brake pedal and rear brake work properly.

Disassembly/Reassembly

1. Remove the drive chain case (A, **Figure 23**) and guard (B).
2. Remove the drive chain slider (B, **Figure 22**).
3. Remove the dust seal caps (A, **Figure 24**) and pivot collar (B).
4. Perform the *Inspection* in this section.
5. Lubricate the pivot collar and bushings with waterproof grease.
6. Install the pivot collar (B, **Figure 24**) and both dust seal caps (A).
7. Install the drive chain slider (B, **Figure 22**) and tighten the screws securely.
8. Install the drive chain case (A, **Figure 23**) and guard (B). Tighten the bolts securely.

Inspection

Replace parts that show excessive wear or damage as described in this section.

Bushing Replacement

This section describes replacement of the swing arm bushings. Always replace both bushings as a set.

1A. Support the swing arm in a vise with soft jaws. Assemble a blind bearing removal tool (**Figure 26**) so it locks against the inner edge of one bushing. Operate the puller and remove the bushing (**Figure 27**).

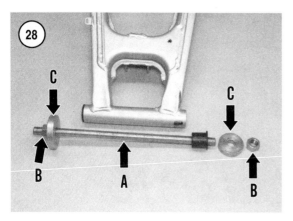

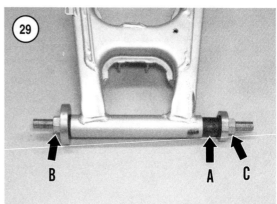

1B. If a puller is not available, drive the bushing out from each side with a long drift. Work the drift around the bushing to drive it squarely out of the bore.
2. Repeat to remove the opposite bushing.
3. Clean and inspect the bushing bore in each side of the swing arm.
4. Assemble a threaded rod tool consisting of a length of threaded rod (A, **Figure 28**), two nuts (B)

and two spacers (C) or washers with an outside diameter larger than the swing arm bearing bore.
5. Assemble the threaded rod tool through the swing arm along with the new bushing (A, **Figure 29**). Then hold one nut (B, **Figure 29**) and turn the other nut (C, **Figure 29**) to install the bushing until its shoulder seats against the swing arm (A, **Figure 25**).
6. Repeat to install the opposite bushing.

Table 1 REAR SUSPENSION SPECIFICATIONS

Rear wheel travel	
XR80R and CRF80F	110 mm (4.3 in.)
XR100R	
1992-2000 models	120 mm (4.7 in.)
2001-2003 models	140 mm (5.5 in.)
CRF100F	148 mm (5.8 in.)

Table 2 REAR SUSPENSION SERVICE SPECIFICATIONS

	New mm (in.)	Service limit mm (in.)
Shock absorber spring free length		
XR80R	136.0 (5.35)	133.3 (5.25)
CRF80F	137.0 (5.39)	134.3 (5.29)
XR100R		
1992-2000 models	136.5 (5.37)	133.8 (5.27)
2001-2003 models	140.4 (5.53)	137.6 (5.42)
CRF100F	123.5 (4.86)	121.0 (4.76)
Shock linkage bushing inside diameter	18.000-18.052 (0.7087-0.7107)	18.25 (0.719)
Shock linkage collar outside diameter	17.941-17.968 (0.7063-0.7074)	17.91 (0.705)
Swing arm bushing inside diameter	14.990-15.030 (0.5902-0.5917)	15.30 (0.602)
Swing arm pivot collar outside diameter	14.966-14.984 (0.5892-0.5899)	14.94 (0.588)

Table 3 REAR SUSPENSION TORQUE SPECIFICATIONS

	N•m	ft.-lb.
Connecting rod and shock arm nuts	44	32

(continued)

Table 3 REAR SUSPENSION TORQUE SPECIFICATIONS (continued)

	N•m	ft.-lb.
Shock absorber mounting nuts		
Upper		
1992-2000 models	34	25
2001-on models	44	32
Lower	34	25
Swing arm pivot shaft nut		
1992-2000 models	62	46
2001-on models	64	47

12

CHAPTER THIRTEEN

BRAKES

Drum brakes are used at the front and rear wheels. **Figure 1** illustrates the major components of the brake assembly. Activating the brake lever or pedal pulls the cable or rod which in turn rotates the brake cam. This forces the brake shoes out into contact with the brake drum.

Brake lever and pedal free play must be maintained on both brakes to minimize brake drag and premature wear and maximize braking effectiveness. Refer to *Brakes* in Chapter Three for complete adjustment procedures.

Glaze buildup on the brake shoes reduces brake effectiveness. The brake shoes should be removed and cleaned regularly to ensure maximum brake shoe contact.

The brake cable must be inspected and replaced periodically, as it will stretch with use until it can no longer be properly adjusted.

Table 1 and **Table 2** are at the end of this chapter.

> *WARNING*
> *When working on the brake system, do **not** inhale brake dust. It may contain asbestos, which can cause lung injury and cancer. Wear a disposable face mask and wash your hands thoroughly after completing the work. Wet down the brake dust on brake components before working on them. Secure and dispose of all brake dust and cleaning materials properly. Do **not** use compressed air to blow off brake parts.*

FRONT AND REAR BRAKES

The front (**Figure 2**) and rear (**Figure 3**) brake assemblies are almost identical and both are covered in the same procedure. Where differences occur, they are identified.

Brake Lining Wear

Brake lining wear can be determined by the wear indicator plate mounted on the brake cam on the outside of the brake panel. Refer to *Brakes* in Chapter Three.

Disassembly

1A. To remove the front brake panel:
  a. Loosen the brake cable adjuster at the handlebar.
  b. Then loosen the two locknuts (A, **Figure 4**) at the brake panel and disconnect the brake cable at the brake arm (B). If it is difficult to disconnect the cable from the brake arm, disconnect it from the brake lever first.

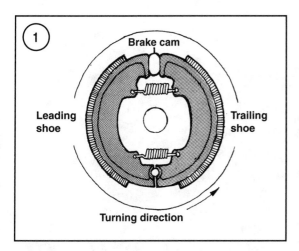

Brake cam

Leading shoe

Trailing shoe

Turning direction

2 FRONT BRAKE ASSEMBLY

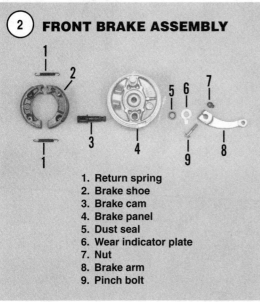

1. Return spring
2. Brake shoe
3. Brake cam
4. Brake panel
5. Dust seal
6. Wear indicator plate
7. Nut
8. Brake arm
9. Pinch bolt

3 REAR BRAKE ASSEMBLY

1. Return spring
2. Brake shoe
3. Brake cam
4. Brake panel
5. Dust seal
6. Wear indicator plate
7. Nut
8. Brake arm
9. Pinch bolt

c. Remove the front wheel (Chapter Ten) and remove the brake panel from the brake drum.

1B. To remove the rear brake panel:

a. Unscrew the adjust nut from the brake rod (A, **Figure 5**). Depress the brake pedal and withdraw the brake rod (B, **Figure 5**) from the brake arm. Remove the collar and spring.

b. Remove the rear wheel (Chapter Ten) and remove the brake panel from the brake drum.

2. Spread some old newspapers over the ground and then place the brake panel plate on top of them with the brake shoes facing up. Spray the brake shoes and brake panel with an aerosol type brake cleaner to remove brake dust and dirt from the brake assembly. Wait until the brake cleaner evaporates from the brake assembly to service the brakes. Fold the newspapers over and store them in a sealed plastic bag. Dispose of the bag.

NOTE
Place a clean shop rag on the linings
to protect them from oil and grease
during removal.

3. Measure and inspect the brake linings as described under *Inspection* in this section.

13

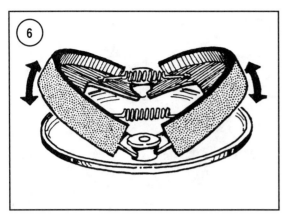

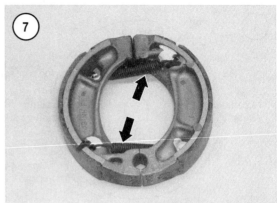

4. Place a paint mark on the web of each brake shoe so the shoes can be reinstalled facing in their original direction.

5. Spread the brake shoes apart (**Figure 6**) and pull them off the anchor pin and brake cam.

6. Remove the return springs (**Figure 7**) and separate the brake shoes.

7. Note the alignment marks on the brake arm and brake cam (**Figure 8**, typical).

> *NOTE*
> *The alignment marks must align as shown in **Figure 8**. If the marks do not align, someone probably installed the brake arm in a different position to compensate for worn brake shoes.*

8A. On the front brake, remove the brake arm and brake cam assembly as follows:

   a. Remove the pinch bolt, nut and brake arm (**Figure 9**).

   b. Remove the wear indicator plate (A, **Figure 10**).

   c. Remove the brake cam.

8B. On the rear brake, remove the brake arm and brake cam assembly as follows:

   a. On 2004-on models, remove the brake arm cover.

   b. Remove the pinch bolt, nut and brake arm (**Figure 11**).

   c. Remove the wear indicator plate (A, **Figure 12**).

   d. Remove the brake cam.

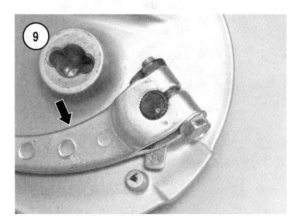

9. Inspect the brake components as described under *Inspection* in this chapter.

Reassembly

> *NOTE*
> *Use a high temperature waterproof wheel bearing grease when grease is called for in the following steps. Apply*

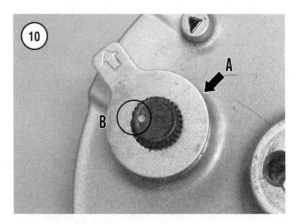

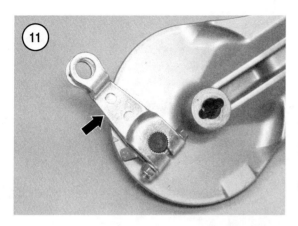

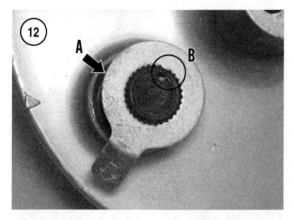

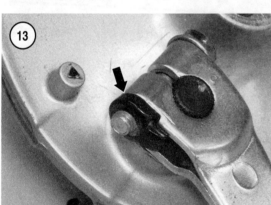

the grease sparingly to keep it from getting on the brake linings or drum.

1. Lubricate the brake cam pivot surface with grease.

2. Install the brake cam into the brake panel from the backside.

3. From the outside, install the wear indicator plate by aligning its wide spline with the wide spline on the brake cam. Refer to B, **Figure 10** (front) or B, **Figure 12** (rear). Push the plate all the way down to the brake panel.

4. Install the brake arm by aligning the punch marks on the two parts (**Figure 8**, typical). Refer to **Figure 9** (front) or **Figure 11** (rear).

5. Install the pinch bolt and nut as shown in **Figure 9** (front) or **Figure 11** (rear). On the front brake, install the nut with its flat side and shoulder facing against the brake arm as shown in **Figure 13**. On the front brake, tighten the pinch bolt securely. On the rear brake, hold the pinch bolt and tighten the nut securely.

6. On 2004-on models, install the brake arm cover on the rear brake arm.

7. Lubricate the brake shoe contact surfaces on the anchor pin and brake cam with grease (**Figure 14**).

8. Install the return springs onto the brake shoes as shown in **Figure 7**. Make sure the spring ends hook onto the brake shoes completely.

9. Hold the brake shoes in a V formation with the return springs attached and snap them in place across the anchor pin and brake cam. Make sure the shoes are firmly seated in place and that the return springs are properly attached to both brake shoes. Refer to **Figure 15** (front) or **Figure 16** (rear).

10. Install the brake panel into the brake drum.

11. Install the front or rear wheel as described in Chapter Ten.

12. Reconnect the front brake cable or rear brake rod onto the brake arm.

13. Adjust the front or rear brake as described in Chapter Three.

13

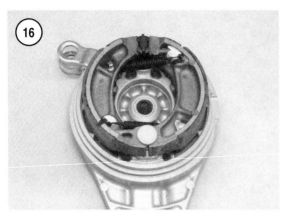

Inspection

When measuring the brake components in this section, compare the actual measurements to the specifications in **Table 1**. Replace parts that are out of specification or show damage as described in this section. Replace brake shoes or return springs in sets.

1. Read the *Warning* in the introduction of this chapter.

2. Thoroughly clean and dry all parts except the brake linings.

NOTE
In Step 3, measure the lining thickness only. Do not include the shoe thickness.

3. Measure the brake shoe lining thickness at both ends and in the center (**Figure 17**). Replace the brake shoes if out of specification.

4. Inspect the brake linings for imbedded foreign material and remove with a stiff wire brush. If the linings are severely worn or grooved, the brake drum may be damaged or out-of-round. Replace brake shoes where oil or grease has penetrated the lining material.

5. If the lining thickness and material is okay, check for a hard glaze formation on the surface of each lining. Some glaze will be normal, but if the glaze is hard or heavy, the brake linings may have been dragging on the drum. To remove glaze from the linings:

WARNING
Perform this procedure outside and not in a garage or any other enclosed area.

a. Remove glaze by sanding the lining surface (**Figure 18**). Do not over-sand one spot as this will create a depression in the lining and reduce the lining-to-drum contact area. Sand just enough to remove the glaze.

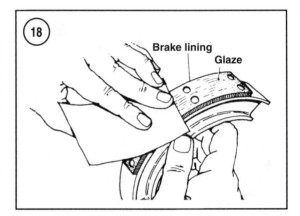

b. Spray the brake linings and shoes with an aerosol type brake cleaner and allow to air dry.

c. Discard the sandpaper and wash thoroughly.

6. To clean the brake drum, perform the following:

a. Turn the wheel over and pour any accumulated brake dust into a garbage bag. Tie the bag closed and discard it.

b. Cover the wheel bearing with a piece of tape. Then spray the brake drum with an aerosol type brake cleaner and allow to air dry.

c. Remove any rust on the brake drum surface with a fine-to-medium grade sandpaper and then reclean with brake cleaner.

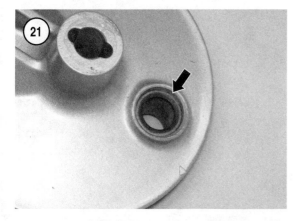

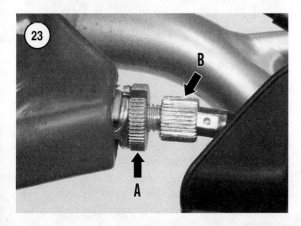

7. Inspect the brake drum (**Figure 19**) surface. Light scratches on the drum's surface are normal. Roughness, scoring, cracks or distortion are caused by dirt and water contamination, rust and brake drag. Service the brake drum as follows:

    a. Remove light roughness, rust, and glaze with a fine-to-medium grade sandpaper.

    b. Drums that are cracked or damaged require replacement. This service requires, wheel disassembly, relacing and truing.

8. Measure the brake drum inside diameter lining surface (**Figure 20**). Because the brake drum can wear unevenly, take a minimum of three measurements. Replace the brake drum if the inside diameter is out of specification. The maximum brake drum diameter dimension is cast into each brake drum.

9. Inspect the returns springs for stretched coils, rust contamination or damaged ends. Stretched or severely worn return springs will not fully retract the brake shoes from the drum, resulting in brake drag on the drum and premature brake lining wear.

10. Inspect the brake panel dust seal (**Figure 21**) and replace if damaged:

    a. Carefully pry the dust seal out of the brake panel.

    b. Clean and inspect the bore for damage.

    c. Place the seal in the bore with its closed side facing out. Install the seal (**Figure 21**) with a seal driver or socket until it bottoms in its bore.

11. Inspect the brake cam and brake arm splines for damage.

12. Inspect the brake panel and anchor pin for damage.

FRONT BRAKE CABLE

Removal/Installation

Check the front brake cable periodically. The cable stretches with use and increases brake lever free play. If the correct brake lever free play can no longer be achieved due to cable stretch, replace the cable.

1. Before disconnecting or removing the brake cable, note how the cable is routed through the cable stays (**Figure 22**).

2. If used, remove the right hand guard (Chapter Fourteen).

3. Loosen the locknut (A, **Figure 23**) and turn the adjuster (B) to loosen the cable. Align the slots in the locknut, adjuster and brake lever.

4. Loosen the cable locknuts (A, **Figure 24**) at the brake panel.

5. Disconnect the brake cable from brake lever at the handlebar.

13

6. Remove the bolt and the front brake cable clamp (**Figure 25**) and remove the cable through the cable guide on the lower fork bridge.

7. Disconnect the brake cable and remove the tension spring at the brake arm (B, **Figure 24**), then remove the cable.

8. Compare both brake cables to make sure the new cable is correct.

9. Lubricate the new brake cable before reconnecting it as described in Chapter Three.

10. Install the new brake cable by reversing these removal steps. Make sure to route the cable through the cable guides (**Figure 22**).

11. Adjust the front brake as described in Chapter Three.

REAR BRAKE PEDAL AND ROD

Removal/Installation

1. Disconnect the return spring (A, **Figure 26**).

2. Unscrew the adjust nut from the brake rod (A, **Figure 27**). Depress the brake pedal and withdraw the brake rod (B, **Figure 27**) from the brake arm. Remove the collar and spring.

3. Remove the two bolts (B, **Figure 26**) and the right footpeg (C).

4. Remove the brake pedal (A, **Figure 28**) and pivot collar (B).

5. If necessary, remove the cotter pin (C, **Figure 28**) and joint pin and separate the brake rod (D) from the brake pedal.

6. Perform the *Inspection* in this section.

7. If removed, secure the brake rod to the brake pedal with the joint pin and a new cotter pin (C, **Figure 28**). Bend the cotter pins arms over to lock it.

8. Lubricate the brake pedal bore (E, **Figure 28**) and pivot collar (B) with waterproof bearing grease. Then install the pivot collar into the brake pedal.

9. Lubricate the long footpeg mounting bolt shoulder with grease as this bolt is also used as a pivot

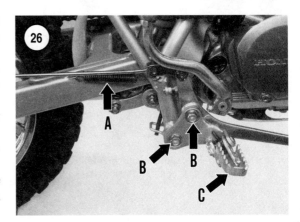

shaft for the brake pedal. Do not lubricate the bolt threads.

10. Hold the brake pedal against the frame and install the footpeg with the two mounting bolts (B, **Figure 26**). Tighten the bolts to 39 N•m (29 ft.-lb.) on 1992-2003 models or 55 N•m (41 ft.-lb.) on 2004-on models.

11. Install the spring onto the brake rod and install the brake rod into the collar. Install the adjustment nut onto the end of the brake rod (A, **Figure 27**).

12. Connect the return spring (A, **Figure 26**) between the swing arm and rear brake pedal.

13. Adjust the rear brake (Chapter Three).

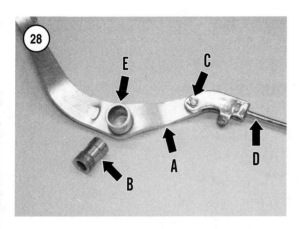

Inspection

1. Clean and dry the brake pedal and footpeg assembly parts.
2. Inspect the brake pedal bore, pivot collar and pivot bolt for excessive wear, cracks and other damage.
3. Measure the brake pedal bore inside diameter (E, **Figure 28**) and the pivot collar outside diameter (B) and compare to the dimensions in **Table 2**. Replace parts out of specification.
4. Check the brake rod spring and return spring and replace if the spring coils are stretched, cracked or the spring ends damaged.

Table 1 BRAKE SPECIFICATIONS

	New mm (in.)	Service limit mm (in.)
Brake drum inside diameter		
Front and rear	95.0 (3.74)	96.0 (3.78)
Brake lining thickness		
Front and rear	4.0 (0.16)	2.0 (0.08)
Brake pedal pivot collar outside diameter	17.294-17.298 (0.6809-0.6810)	17.27 (0.680)
Brake pedal bore inside diameter	17.300-17.327 (0.6811-0.6822)	17.34 (0.683)

Table 2 BRAKE TORQUE SPECIFICATIONS

	N•m	in.-lb.	ft.-lb.
Footpeg bracket mounting bolts			
1992-2003 models	39	–	29
2004-on models	55	–	41
Rear brake arm nut	10	89	–

13

CHAPTER FOURTEEN

BODY

Table 1 is at the end of the chapter.

SEAT

Removal/Installation

1A. On 1993-2000 models:
   a. Remove both side covers as described in this chapter.
   b. Remove the bolt from each side of the seat and remove the seat.
1B. On 2001-on models, remove the two nuts and collars (**Figure 1**) from underneath the seat and remove the seat.
2. Install the seat by aligning the front seat hook (A, **Figure 2**) with the mounting boss on the fuel tank (B) and the rear seat hook (C) with the frame (D).
3. Installation is the reverse of removal. Tighten the fasteners securely. Pull the seat to make sure it is locked in place.

SIDE COVERS

Removal/Installation

1. Remove the nut and collar (A, **Figure 3**), then pull the side cover (B) to disconnect its two pins from the frame grommets.

2. Installation is the reverse of removal. Tighten the nut securely.

FUEL TANK SHROUDS
(2001-ON MODELS)

Removal/Installation

1. Remove the bolt (**Figure 4**) from the outside of the shroud and the retaining clip from the front inside of the shroud. **Figure 5** shows how to remove and install the retaining clip.
2. Pull the shroud rearward to disconnect its pin from the boss (**Figure 6**) on the fuel tank and remove it.
3. Installation is the reverse of removal.

NUMBER PLATE

Removal/Installation

1. Remove the fuel tank vent hose from the guide on the number plate.
2. Remove the number plate strap (A, **Figure 7**) from around the handlebar.
3. Remove the bolt (B, **Figure 7**) from the middle of the number plate and remove the number plate.
4. Install the number plate by inserting its two mounting tabs into the holes in the mounting bracket.

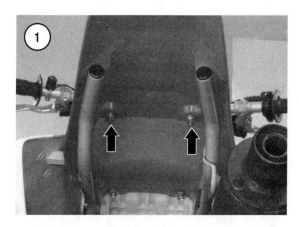

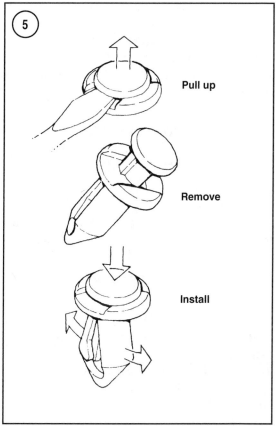

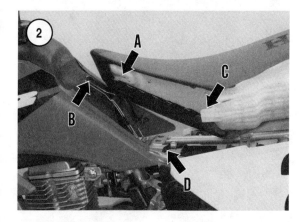

14

Make sure the front brake cable is routed on the outside of the number plate.

5. Install the bolt (B, **Figure 7**) and tighten securely.

6. Secure the number plate strap (A, **Figure 7**)
around the handlebar and install the fuel tank vent
hose into the guide.

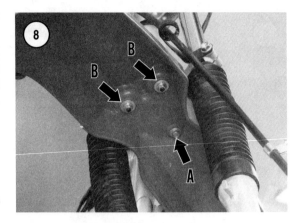

FRONT FENDER

Removal/Installation

1. Remove the bolt (A, **Figure 8**), nuts (B), collars
and front fender.

2. Installation is the reverse of removal. Tighten the
front fender mounting bolt to 12 N•m (106 in.-lb.).

REAR FENDER

Removal/Installation

1. Remove the seat and both side covers as described
in this chapter.

2. Remove the bolts and the rear fender.

3. Installation is the reverse of removal. Tighten the
bolts securely.

SKID PLATE

Removal/Installation

1. Remove the front lower engine mount nut and
bolt (**Figure 9**).

2. Remove the skid plate mounting bolts (A, **Figure
10**) and skid plate (B).

3. Replace the rubber damper mounted on the skid
plate if damaged.

4. Installation is the reverse of removal. Note the
following:

    a. Clean and dry all of the fastener threads.

    b. Install the engine mounting bolt from the left
    side. Tighten the front lower engine mount nut
    (A, **Figure 9**) to 34 N•m (25 ft.-lb.).

    c. Tighten the two rear skid plate mounting bolts
    (A, **Figure 10**) securely.

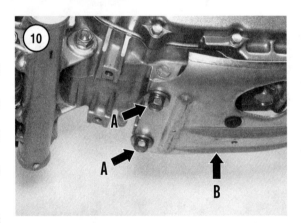

SIDESTAND

WARNING
A sidestand that will not stay retracted
when the motorcycle is being ridden is
hazardous and can cause an accident.
Do not ride the motorcycle until the sid-
estand assembly is working correctly.

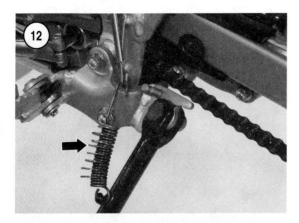

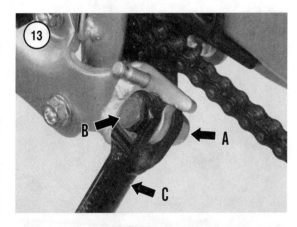

Spring Removal/Installation

Replace the spring immediately when it appears weak or damaged or whenever it fails to hold the sidestand in its full upright position.

1. Support the motorcycle on a work stand.
2. Insert pennies between the sidestand spring coils with locking pliers as shown in **Figure 11**.
3. Lower the sidestand to its down position, then disconnect the spring from the post on the sidestand (**Figure 12**).
4. To install the new spring, fit pennies between the spring coils, then install the spring (**Figure 12**) be-

tween the two posts. Remove the pennies from the spring to tighten the spring, making sure the spring ends engage the posts fully.
5. Raise and lower the sidestand by hand while checking the spring position. Make sure the return spring has sufficient tension to lock the sidestand in its up and down positions.

Sidestand Removal/Installation

1. Remove the spring as described in this section.
2. Remove the locknut (A, **Figure 13**), pivot bolt (B) and sidestand (C).
3. Inspect the sidestand. Replace if damaged.
4. Clean the pivot bolt and locknut. Replace if damaged.
5. Install the sidestand and tighten the pivot bolt and locknut as follows:
   a. Lubricate the pivot bolt with a waterproof grease and install the sidestand and pivot bolt (B, **Figure 13**).
   b. Tighten the pivot bolt (B, **Figure 13**) to 10 N•m (88 in.-lb.).
   c. Loosen the pivot bolt 1/8 to 1/4 turn. Then hold the pivot bolt and tighten the locknut (A, **Figure 13**) to 39 N•m (29 ft.-lb).
6. Install the spring as described in this section.
7. Raise and lower the sidestand by hand. Make sure the return spring has sufficient tension to lock the sidestand in its upper and lower positions.

FOOTPEGS AND MOUNTING BRACKETS

Left Footpeg Mounting Bracket Removal/Installation

1. Support the motorcycle on a work stand.
2. If necessary, remove the sidestand as described in this chapter.
3. Remove the bolts and the left footpeg assembly (**Figure 14**).
4. Installation is the reverse of removal. Tighten the footpeg mounting bolts to 39 N•m (29 ft.-lb.) on 1992-2003 models or 55 N•m (41 ft.-lb.) on 2004-on models.

Right Footpeg Mounting Bracket Removal/Installation

The upper footpeg mounting bolt (A, **Figure 15**) is also used as the rear brake pedal pivot shaft. To service the brake pedal assembly, refer to *Rear Brake Pedal and Rod* in Chapter Thirteen. The right footpeg can be removed, leaving the brake pedal in place.
1. Support the motorcycle on its sidestand.

14

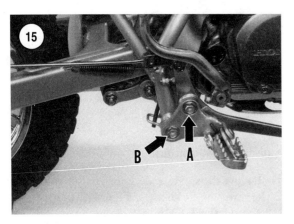

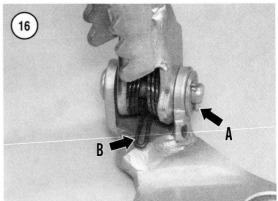

2. Remove the two bolts (A and B, **Figure 15**) and the right footpeg. Temporarily install the upper bolt (A, **Figure 15**) to hold the brake pedal in place.

3. Clean and dry the mounting bolts.

4. Installation is the reverse of removal. Note the following:

   a. Lubricate the long footpeg mounting bolt shoulder with grease. Do not lubricate the bolt threads.

   b. Hold the brake pedal against the frame and install the footpeg with the two mounting bolts (A and B, **Figure 15**). Install the longer bolt (A, **Figure 15**) through the brake pedal. Tighten the bolts to 39 N•m (29 ft.-lb.) on 1992-2003 models or 55 N•m (41 ft.-lb.) on 2004-on models.

Footpeg Removal/Installation

Refer to **Figure 16**.

1. Remove the cotter pin (A, **Figure 16**) and washer from the joint pin. Discard the cotter pin.

2. Hold the footpeg and push the joint pin out of the footpeg assembly. Remove footpeg and the return spring (B, **Figure 16**).

3. Check the footpeg assembly for:

   a. Worn, bent or damaged joint pin.

   b. Weak or damaged return spring. Check the spring coils for cracks.

   c. Elongation of the joint pin holes in the footpeg and footpeg mounting bracket.

   d. Replace parts as required.

4. Installation is the reverse of removal. Note the following:

   a. Position the return spring as shown in B, **Figure 16**.

   b. Secure the joint pin with a new cotter pin (A, **Figure 16**) and bend the arms over to lock it in place.

   c. Pivot the footpeg by hand, making sure it returns under spring pressure.

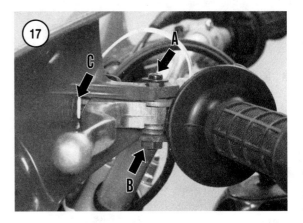

HAND GUARDS

Removal/Installation

1. Remove the screw and washer (A, **Figure 17**) from the top of the pivot bolt.

2. Insert a screwdriver into the notch in the top of the pivot bolt to prevent it from turning and remove the nut (B, **Figure 17**) from the bottom side.

3. Spread the hand guard and lift it over the pivot bolt while disconnecting the guard plate from the notch (C, **Figure 17**) on the hand guard.

4. Replace the hand guard if damaged.

5. Spread the hand guard and install it over the pivot bolt while at the same time inserting the guard plate into the notch (C, **Figure 17**) in the hand guard.

6. Hold the pivot bolt to prevent it from turning and install the nut (B, **Figure 17**) so that its shoulder enters the hole in the hand guard. Tighten the nut securely.

7. Install the screw and washer (B, **Figure 17**) and tighten securely.

8. Operate the brake or clutch control lever to make sure it pivots smoothly and does not contact the hand guard.

Table 1 BODY TORQUE SPECIFICATIONS

	N•m	in.-lb.	ft.-lb.
Footpeg bracket mounting bolts			
1992-2003 models	39	–	29
2004-on models	55	–	41
Front fender mounting bolt	12	106	–
Front lower engine mount nut	34	–	25
Sidestand pivot nut*	39	–	29
*Refer to text.			

INDEX

15

15

15

1993-2000 XR80R AND 1992-2000 XR100R

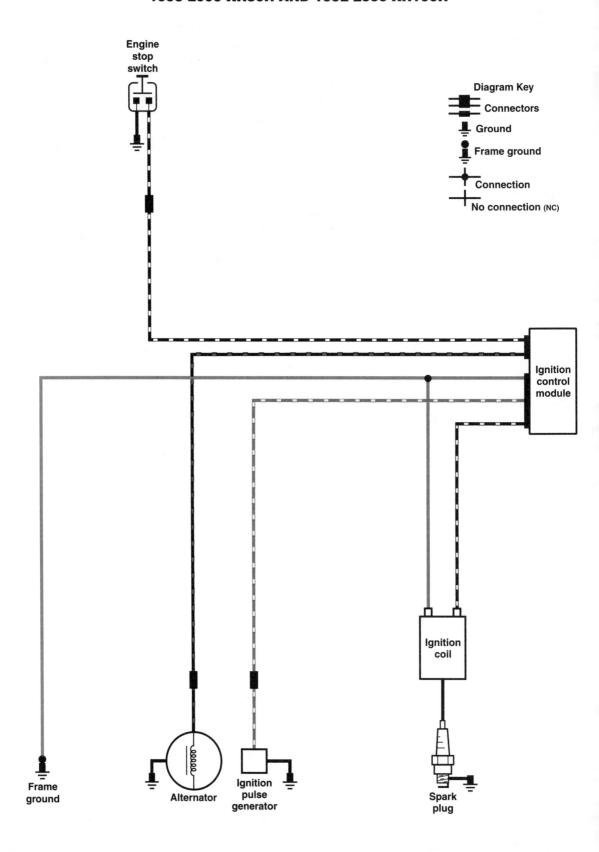

2001-2003 XR80R, 2004-ON CRF80F, 2001-2003 XR100R, AND 2004-ON CRF100F

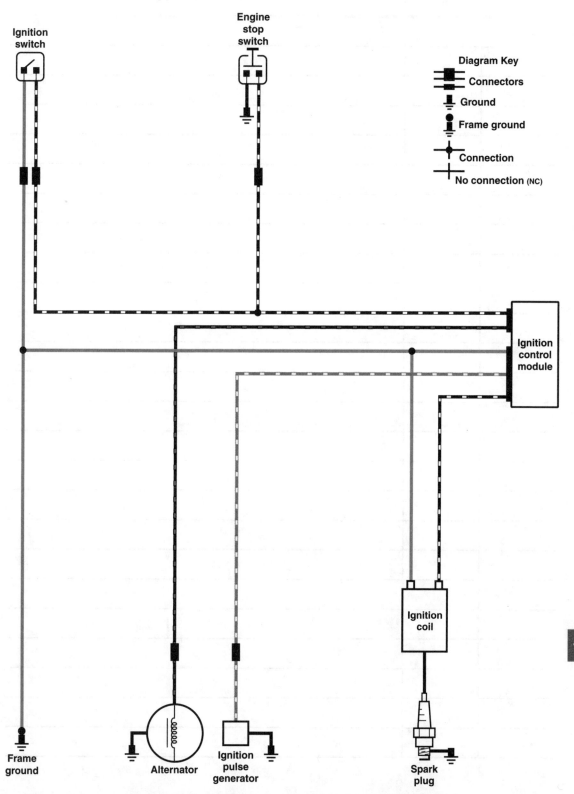

MAINTENANCE LOG

Date	Miles/ Hours	Type of Service